OBJECTIVE MEASUREMENT:

THEORY INTO PRACTICE

VOLUME 3

OBJECTIVE MEASUREMENT:
THEORY INTO PRACTICE
VOLUME 3

GEORGE ENGELHARD, JR.
MARK WILSON

EDITORS

 Ablex Publishing Company
Norwood, New Jersey

Library of Congress Cataloging-in-Publication Data

(Revised for vol. 3)

Objective measurement.

"Papers presented at successive International Objective Measurement Work   shop (IOMW)"—Pref.
    Includes bibliographical references and indexes.
    ISBN 0-89391-727-3 (v. 1) — ISBN 0-89391-814-8 (v. 1 : pbk.)
    1. Psychometrics—Congresses. 2. Psychometrics—Data   processing—
    Congresses. 3. Educational tests and measurements—Congresses.
I. Wilson, Mark. II. International Objective Measurement Workshop.
BF39.024   1991
150'.1'5195   91-16210
                                                          CIP

Ablex Publishing Corporation
355 Chestnut St.
Norwood, NJ 07648

Table of Contents

Preface

This is the third volume in a series of papers that brings together recent work on objective measurement conducted by researchers from around the world. Most, but not all, of the chapters presented in this volume were presented at the Seventh International Objective Measurement Workshop (IOMW7) held at Emory University in Atlanta, Georgia (see the appendix for the program for IOMW7). These Workshops are typically held every two years, and measurement researchers and practitioners come together to discuss recent advances in social science measurement with a general focus on the measurement work of Georg Rasch. Volume 1 (Wilson, 1992a) and Volume 2 (Wilson, 1994) of this series should be consulted regarding earlier work presented at the Fifth and Sixth International Objective Measurement Workshops respectively. Wright (1992) provides an historical perspective on the earlier workshops and their purposes.

The term "objective measurement" may have a variety of connotations for different people. Given the recent proliferation of performance-based assessments in educational settings, the adjective "objective" has come to be associated primarily with assessments composed of multiple-choice items. As used in this volume, the conditions of objective measurement can apply to any mode of assessment including performance-based assessments. Objective measurement denotes a special set of conditions related to the concept of "specific objectivity" as developed within the measurement theory of Rasch. These conditions relate to the idea of invariant measurement (Engelhard, 1992); a brief discussion of the concept of "specific objectivity" is presented in Wilson (1992b). Chapters in this book illustrate how Rasch measurement can be productively applied to a full range of assessment procedures ranging from traditional multiple-choice items to performance-based assessments in a variety of applied settings. Other chapters advance various aspects of measurement theory, both within the Rasch framework and beyond; others apply new mathematical and statistical methods to measurement problems.

Given the strong commitment to furthering sound measurement practices that motivates our approach, it seems appropriate to start this volume with a set of four chapters that exemplify this commitment. Larry Ludlow and Stephen Haley present a variety of graphical tools that can be used to display change in pediatric functional performance that go beyond the simple presentation of difference scores typically used in these types of assessments. The next two chapters address measurement problems that arise within the context of higher education: Barry Sheridan and Les Puhl use Rasch measurement to examine an indirect measure of literacy that is commonly used for high stakes decisions in Australia, whereas Carol Morrison provides a comparative analysis of the graded response and partial credit models for scaling course grades in order to improve the predictability of academic performance in college. One of the perennial issues in measurement is how to examine item bias or differential item functioning. The last chapter in this section by Matthew Schulz, Carole Perlman, William Rice, and Ben Wright presents an empirical comparison of Rasch and Mantel-Haenszel procedures for examining differential item functioning, and discuss the strengths and weaknesses of each procedure.

In the second and third sections, recent advances related to the Rasch measurement model are described and illustrated. The four chapters presented within the section entitled "The Many-Facet Rasch (FACETS) Model" illustrate how the Rasch model can be extended and applied to measurement situations that depend on judgements. Mike Linacre compares the use of Generalizability Theory and the FACETS model for assessment situations that involve raters rating examinees on test items. The next two chapters in this section by Mary Lunz and John Stahl illustrate the use of the FACETS model to increase our understanding and control of judge behavior in performance assessments. Finally, Judy Monsaas and George Engelhard describe and illustrate how the FACETS model can be used to perform both measurement and statistical analyses of changes in home environments within the context of program evaluation. In the third section of the volume, a very general approach based on the "Random Coefficients Multinomial Logits (RCML) Model" is described and illustrated. Ray Adams and Mark Wilson provide an overview of the RCML model in the first chapter of this section, and the next three chapters describe applications. Wen-chung Wang and Wilson describe how the RCML model can be used to compare the information obtained from multiple-choice and performance-based items; Karen Draney, Mark Wilson, and Peter Pirolli demonstrate how the RCML model can be used to develop a better understanding of the complexities of student learning and performance; Stephen Moore examines the use of the RCML model for the detection of differential item functioning within the context of the partial credit and rating scale models for polytomous data. The RCML model provides a very general framework for estimating a variety of measurement models, including Rasch models, and provides a great deal of flexibility for examining the utility of these models.

The seven chapters in section four present a variety of recent theoretical advances in measurement theory. Ben Wright describes an innovative approach called "composition analysis" for examining group functioning. Continuing his measurement work on rating scales, David Andrich describes the theoretical and empirical problems that are encountered when graded responses are dichotomized. One of the persistent problems in educational testing is how to equate scores obtained from different test forms that may consist of items that vary in difficulty; Richard Smith proposes an approach to test equating that deals with assessment situations that do not have common items or common persons. In order to realize the advantages of Rasch measurement it is important to meet several conditions. One of the conditions is that the instrument should be measuring one underlying latent variable; Tsuey-Hwa Chen and Mark Davison propose a new approach based on paired comparisons for assessing unidimensionality in the Rasch model. Computerized adaptive tests (CAT) are becoming more prevalent in all areas of assessment; Randal Carlson and Hoi K. Suen investigate the efficacy and efficiency of four different item selection strategies that can be used for CAT. Eddy Roskam and Nick Broers present an innovative approach to the construction of measuring instruments that brings together Guttman's Facet design with recent advances in item response theory reflected in the Linear Logistic Test Model. Finally, Robert Jannarone proposes several new models that include the measurement of response time and correctness concurrently.

Section five includes three chapters on recent mathematical and statistical applications to measurement that arise within the context of test construction. In some measurement situations, practitioners need to control the shape of observed-score distributions; using item response theory and linear programming, Wim van der Linden and Richard Luecht illustrate how to accomplish this task. Linear programming also offers an approach for constructing tests by computer based on a set of test requirements specified by the test constructor; Ellen Timminga and Jos Adema describe how to deal with problems that arise when infeasible conditions have been proposed by the test constructor. Finally, Martijn Berger and Wim Veerkamp review selection methods that have been used for optimal test design including fixed-form tests, adaptive tests, and testlets. The depth and breadth of the ideas presented in the chapters within these last two sections will challenge and stimulate our thinking during the coming years.

The authors of the chapters in this volume have our warmest thanks. Many of the authors spent a considerable amount of time responding to our comments and revising their chapters; the high quality of their final chapters is clearly evident. Several authors have contributed to earlier volumes, and continue to stimulate and challenge our thinking about Rasch measurement. Hopefully, these authors and others will join us in forthcoming workshops. The Eighth International Objective Measurement Workshop was held at the University of California, Berkeley in April 1995; volume 4 of this series will be forthcoming after this next workshop.

—George Engelhard, Jr. and Mark Wilson

REFERENCES

Engelhard, G. (1992). Historical views of invariance: Evidence from the measurement theories of Thorndike, Thurstone and Rasch. *Educational and Psychological Measurement, 52*(2) 275–292.

Wilson, M. (1992a) (Ed.). *Objective measurement: Theory into practice, Volume 1.* Norwood, New Jersey: Ablex Publishing Corporation.

Wilson, M. (1992b). Objective Measurement: The state of the art. In M. Wilson (Ed.), *Objective measurement: Theory into practice, Volume 1.* Norwood, New Jersey: Ablex Publishing Corporation.

Wilson, M. (1994) (Ed.). *Objective measurement: Theory into practice, Volume 2.* Norwood, New Jersey: Ablex Publishing Corporation.

Wright, B. D. (1992). The International Objective Measurement Workshops: Past and future. In M. Wilson (Ed.), *Objective measurement: Theory into practice, Volume 1.* Norwood, New Jersey: Ablex Publishing Corporation.

Acknowledgments

Many of the chapters included in this volume were originally presented at the Seventh International Objective Measurement Workshop (IOMW7) held at Emory University in Atlanta, Georgia (April 10–11, 1993). We would like to sincerely thank Judy Monsaas for co-chairing IOMW7 with George Engelhard. We would also like to thank Professor Robert Jensen, who was the acting chair of the Division of Educational Studies at Emory University, for providing financial support for the conference. Two graduate students, Molly Weinburgh (now on the faculty of Georgia State University) and David Tallant, deserve special praise for their contributions to IOMW7. The subject index for this book was compiled by George Engelhard, Jr. with the assistance of Mary Garner, who is currently a graduate student at Emory University.

Dedication

To Judy Monsaas, David Monsaas Engelhard, and Emily Monsaas Engelhard, Janet Williams, Alistair Wilson and Penelope Wilson.

part one

Practice

chapter **1**

Displaying Change in Functional Performance

Larry H. Ludlow
Boston College
Chestnut Hill, MA

Stephen M. Haley
New England Rehabilitation Hospital
Woburn, MA

In 1988, the National Institute on Disability and Rehabilitation Research (NIDRR) funded a three-year project to develop a state-of-the-art functional assessment instrument for pediatric rehabilitation. The requirements of the project included the development of a child-oriented functional assessment instrument, demonstration of its reliability and validity, and standardization of the instrument on a normative sample.

The Pediatric Evaluation of Disability Inventory (PEDI) resulted from this effort (Haley, Coster, Ludlow, Haltiwanger & Andrellos, 1992). The PEDI is a comprehensive clinical assessment that samples key functional abilities of children from the ages of six months to 7.5 years. The PEDI is primarily designed for the functional evaluation of young children, but it can be used for the evaluation of older children if their functional abilities fall below that expected of a non-disabled seven-year-old child. The intended uses of the PEDI include serving as:

(a) a discriminative device to determine if functional deficits exist and, if so, the extent and content area of those deficits, (b) an evaluative instrument to monitor individual or group progress in pediatric rehabilitation programs, and (c) an outcome measure for program evaluation of pediatric rehabilitation services or for therapeutic programs in an educational setting.

The purpose of this chapter is to present the methodology employed in our assessment of change in functional performance using the PEDI. Accomplishing this task entails the utilization of a variety of graphical tools. Specifically, we form composite pictures for the purposes of understanding: a) the items a child is originally evaluated as capable of accomplishing, b) the items describing level of functioning at the time of two or more testing situations, c) the items accomplished as a direct result of change, and d) the items which, from a developmental perspective, are next in line to work on.

METHOD

Sample

Normative data for the PEDI were gathered from 412 children and families distributed throughout Massachusetts, Connecticut and New York. To achieve a stratified quota representation, the following goals (in priority order) were established in the sampling plan:

1. relatively equal age distribution across the age span of 6 months through 7½ years in 6 month intervals,
2. equal representation of males and females,
3. distribution of race approximating the region and U.S. population,
4. proportional representation of parent educational levels, and
5. appropriate distribution of type of community and size (urban/rural).

In general, these goals were met.

Pediatric Nurse Practitioners in general pediatric practices and schools within Massachusetts, Connecticut and New York were recruited to participate in the data collection process. Each nurse practitioner was given extensive training on administration of the PEDI in their own setting by one of the PEDI Research Group project staff. As data collection sites were recruited and nurse practitioners were submitting data, the demographic characteristics for each site and for the entire sample were monitored, and attempts were made to compensate for over- or under-represented variables both within and across sites. This was accomplished by the selection of appropriate new sites and by limiting active sites to collection of data on children with under-represented demographic variables. The basic demographic characteristics of the normative sample are presented in Table 1.1. A fuller description of the data is provided in Haley et al., 1992.

Instrument

The PEDI was created from formal and informal consultations with content-specific experts in the fields of pediatrics, pediatric rehabilitation, physical therapy, and occupational therapy. The development of the PEDI was originally based on concepts derived from developmental adaptive tests and models of functional tests used in rehabilitation medicine. Based on a formal content-validity study, pilot reliability results, and extensive field testing of the PEDI at New England Medical Center Hospitals, the current edition of the instrument was developed (Haley et al., 1992).

The PEDI assesses three major content domains: self-care, mobility, and social function. The self-care domain includes activities such as eating, grooming and bathing skills, dressing, and toilet skills (73

Table 1.1. Distribution of the Normative Sample by Age Level and Gender (n = 412)

Age (yrs)	Females		Males		Total Number
	n	%	n	%	
0.5-0.9	15	41.7	21	58.3	36
1.0-1.4	22	56.4	17	43.6	39
1.5-1.9	14	46.7	16	53.3	30
2.0-2.4	14	43.8	18	56.2	32
2.5-2.9	14	35.9	25	64.1	39
3.0-3.4	16	64.0	9	36.0	25
3.5-3.9	14	41.2	20	58.8	34
4.0-4.4	14	56.0	11	44.0	25
4.5-4.9	16	61.5	10	38.5	26
5.0-5.4	16	45.7	19	54.3	35
5.5-5.9	13	46.7	15	53.3	28
6.0-6.4	14	56.0	11	44.0	25
6.5-6.9	15	68.2	7	31.8	22
7.0+	12	75.0	4	25.0	16
Totals	209	50.7	203	49.3	412

items). The mobility domain samples key functional items in the area of transfer and locomotion (59 items). Four transfers are sampled: chair, car, toilet, and tub. Indoor and outdoor mobility are considered separate mobility skills, and use of stairs is also sampled in the mobility domain. Three areas of social function are sampled in the PEDI: communication skills, social interaction, and the management of home/community daily routines (65 items).

Each content domain is assessed by two separate, but complementary dimensions: functional skills/behaviors, and caregiver assistance. The Functional Skills Scales were designed to sample meaningful subtasks of a series of complex functional activities. In non-disabled children, various aspects of a functional activity may be integrated over a relatively short period of time. In contrast, children with disabilities may have impairments that selectively affect one aspect of a functional activity. In this situation, they may be unduly penalized by an assessment that requires mastery of all components to receive a passing score. Attempts were made to identify meaningful functional units within a given activity. The Caregiver Assistance Scales document the levels of caregiver assistance and the amount of help that the child needs to complete the functional activity. These scales have six scoring levels. Most of the increments are designed to reflect changes in caregiver assistance at the lesser end of the amount of caregiver assistance. This concentration of scale points toward the "no caregiver assistance" end of the spectrum is not only more functionally meaningful, but also is more concrete and easier to operationalize.

The PEDI consists of a total of six measurement scales comprised of 197 functional skill/behavior items and 20 caregiver assistance items.

Scoring

The Functional Skills items are scored as either 0 for unable to perform the item or 1 for being capable of performing it. The Caregiver Assistance Scales, however, are more exhaustive in their representation of performance capability. During the scoring of items, the first issue to address is whether the child is independent (Score = 5) in the activity. If no physical help is required during the activity, but supervision, monitoring or equipment setup is necessary, then Score = 4 is chosen as the most appropriate score. If only occasional help is provided, then Minimal Assistance (Score = 3) is chosen. If consistent help is required, yet not exceeding half of the effort, then the scale point of Moderate Assistance (Score = 2) is indicated. If more than half of the activity is performed by the caregiver, then two choices are available. If the child provides some meaningful assistance, then the level of Maximal Assistance (Score = 1) is chosen. Finally, if the child is unable to provide any meaningful assistance during the activity, then Total Assistance (Score = 0) is indicated.

Administration

The PEDI can be administered by clinicians and educators who are familiar with the child, or by structured interview and parent report. It is designed for use by physical therapists, occupational therapists, rehabilitation nurses, nurse practitioners, speech pathologists, special educators, psychologists, and other professionals who are interested in measuring the functional abilities of young children with disabilities.

MEASUREMENT MODELS

True-Score Theory

A variety of traditional reliability analyses have been performed. These include test–retest, internal consistency, inter-rater, and intra-rater reliability. Validity studies have addressed issues of content, construct, concurrent, and discriminative validity. Correlational studies have addressed between-scale, and item-total score relationships both over the entire sample and by selected subsets. In summary, the PEDI was found to be reliable under a variety of definitions, valid in terms of what was intended to be measured, and generalizable across different sub-groups of children. The complete results are reported in Haley et al., 1992.

Item Response Theory

Of the multitude of item response theory (IRT) models that have been proposed, the statistical models generally referred to as Rasch models (Rasch, 1960; Wright & Masters, 1982) have consistently drawn the attention of measurement specialists. The specific IRT model employed in this project is referred to as the Rasch rating scale model (Andrich, 1978; Ludlow, 1992). With this model, a child functional-capability parameter, a set of scoring category threshold parameters, and an item difficulty parameter are estimated.

In conducting analyses of change in functional capability, we have found it useful to convert the logit estimates to two different forms of transformed scores. We obtain and report "Normative Standard Scores" and "Scaled Scores". The Normative Standard Scores take into account the child's age. The Scaled Scores provide a measure of the child's performance without taking age into account. The PEDI does not provide a composite summary score for the total instrument since such a score would average across different domains of function and thus would obscure meaningful differences in performance.

For each of the content domains of the Functional Skills and Caregiver Assistance Scales, normative standard scores and scaled scores are calculated. In order to develop the normative measures, the logit estimates of ability for all the children were obtained for each of the six separate scales. Means and standard deviations (in logits) for each of 14 age groups (0.5 years through 7.5; 0.5-year intervals) were calculated. Normative measures were then obtained by converting individual ability estimates to a T-scale measure with a mean of 50 and standard deviation of 10 (Wright & Stone, 1979). A standard error, transformed to the new normative measure metric, is also calculated.

Scaled scores, in contrast to the normative standard scores, provide an indication of the actual performance of the child along the continuum of relatively easy to relatively difficult items. These scores are not adjusted for age and therefore can be used to describe the functional status of children of all ages, including children above the chronological age of 7.5 years. These scores are obtained by transforming the original logit estimates to a zero-to-100 distribution (item logits are also transformed to this scale). Zero represents no ability and 100 represents a perfect score. A scaled score of 50 roughly corresponds to a logit estimate of (0.0). As with the normative measures, each scaled measure has an accompanying standard error of measurement.

RESULTS

One of the major assumptions of the PEDI is that the development of functional behaviors is age-related, and thus a strong developmental function should emerge across ages. Figure 1.1 represents a "Normative Profile" for the 20 items of the Social Function Self-Care and Mobility domains of the Caregiver Assistance Scale. The horizontal bars in this figure indicate the interquartile range within which "independence" was achieved on specific items (e.g. at what age do 25% of the children achieve independence on the item, then 50%, and then 75%). A brief inspection of this figure quickly reveals that items we might expect to be easy are indeed mastered at the younger ages (like "indoor locomotion") while items we might expect to be difficult are

Percent of Children
Achieving Independence

Test Items

25%   50%   75%

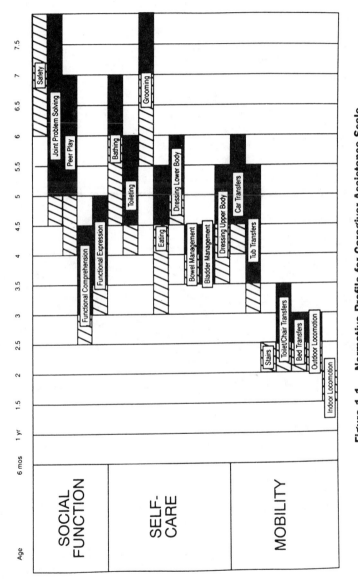

Figure 1.1.   Normative Profile for Caregiver Assistance Scale

only mastered at the older age levels (like "is cautious in routine daily safety situations"). This graphical representation clearly displays the age-range within which children of six months to 7.5 years of age may be expected to achieve independence on specific items and it shows where change is most likely to occur next across a set of domains.

Furthermore, means of the scaled scores for age-groupings were computed. Figure 1.2 contains the mean scores obtained at each .5 increment in age on each of the three content domains of the Functional Skills Scales. The shape of the developmental functions (a rapid rate of increase at young ages and a slower progression at older ages) describes the developmental attainment of functional competencies through the age of 7.5 years. Where Figure 1.1 displayed the item-level changes to be expected over time, Figure 1.2 summarizes across the items within the domains to portray overall developmental expectation of change. Like typical developmental functions, standard error bands could be drawn around the curves.

In fact, the developmental growth curves of Figure 1.2 can be con-

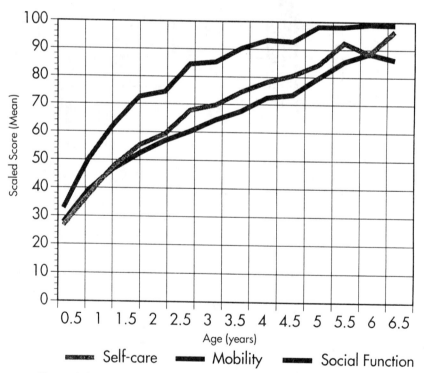

Figure 1.2. Developmental Function for Functional Skills Scales

structed not only for cross-sectional age groups but also at the individual level. Figure 1.3 represents the Functional Skills rehabilitation pattern for a child who was hospitalized for four months. The child was evaluated five times while in the recovery unit and three weeks after discharge. As can clearly be seen, self-care and social function showed a modest rapid improvement, followed by a steady-state period, and then an important large improvement in social function after the child had been home for three weeks. In contrast, because of the nature of the major injuries, mobility showed only a modest (but steady) improvement over the course of this period.

An example of the complementary utility of the two types of scores (age-relative normative standard scores and scaled scores) is illustrated in Figure 1.4. The self-care and mobility summary scores were computed at four time points for a child with a severe brain injury. These summary scores were converted to logit estimates of functioning. These logits were then transformed to the age-relative standard score and scaled score measures.

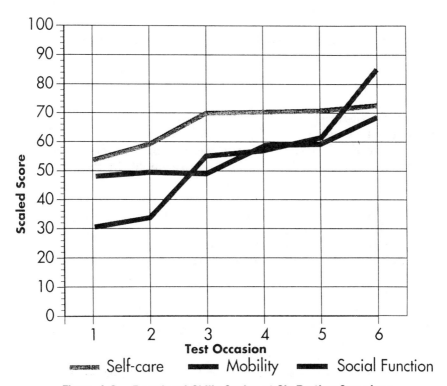

Figure 1.3.   Functional Skills Scales at Six Testing Occasions

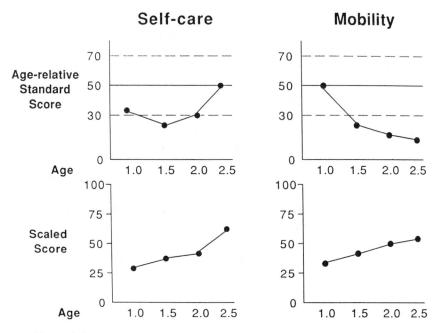

Figure 1.4.   Age-related and Scaled Score Performance for One Child

On the self-care scale, the child demonstrates significant improvement in scaled score change (the lower left chart). In fact, this improvement represents a full recovery to age appropriate levels (note the return to an age-relative standard score near 50 in the left upper chart).

In the case of performance on the mobility scale, considerable progress was made in terms of scaled score ability (the lower right chart), but the child was still not able to recover to age-appropriate functioning and actually fell further behind in capability (upper right chart). This type of clinical description of progress both in terms of age-relative standard scores and scaled performance scores provides a comprehensive analysis of change, particularly for the young child who is still in the process of developing functional capabilities.

A primary purpose of Rasch models is to facilitate the construction of measurement scales that fit a *hypothesized,* hierarchical, unidimensional structure (Ludlow, Haley & Gans, 1992). A hierarchical scale defines a set of sequential items that represent increasingly complicated cumulative functions along a single dimension. Each independent dimension is then defined in terms of a continuum of less difficult to more difficult items. If the clinical data fit this intended structure, then the scale is unidimensional in the sense that mastery of lower level items is requisite for success on higher level items.

The scales of the PEDI were specifically constructed to meet the objective of forming hierarchical dimensions. The construct validity for each scale was assessed by comparing the resulting scale structure with the structure hypothesized for each scale prior to item selection and analysis. An example illustrating scale structure is presented in Figure 1.5. The three subsets of items comprising the Social Function, Functional Skills Scales are identified and graphed separately. The item difficulty logits have been transformed to the scaled score distribution. Proceeding from the left (easier) to the right (harder), the black boxes indicate the difficulty level of each item in the three components of Social Function.

These solutions were consistent with the expectations of the scale developers. For example, on the Communication Scale item 1 is "orients to sound," item 3 is "understands 10 words," and item 20 is "connects two or more thoughts to tell a simple story." On the Social Function Scale, item 26 is "shows awareness and interest in others," item 28 is "takes turn in simple play when cued for turn," and item 40 is "makes up elaborate pretend sequences from imagination." On the Home and Community Scale, item 61 is "child may play safely at home without being watched constantly," item 54 is "occasionally initiates simple household chores," and item 60 is "crosses busy street safely without an adult."

Important clinical information may be derived from the hierarchical nature of the items within any given scale such as that represented in Figure 1.5. On one hand, it is useful to identify which items are relatively easy or more difficult for a child to achieve. On the other hand, such a structure requires the researcher/clinician to understand the specific performance requirements of items as they proceed from low to high difficulty. With the sequence of item difficulty defined and presented in a form like Figure 1.5 rehabilitation clinicians can identify the next expected achievement in a performance domain and can plan incremental treatment programs with greater precision. This refinement in how a patient's observed clinical behavior may be interpreted provides an opportunity to tailor rehabilitation components most appropriate for a given child.

Figure 1.5 also illustrates two other points to bear in mind when trying to understand whether or not change has occurred. The first point concerns quantity of change—is the difference between two PEDI evaluations qualitatively significant or is it likely due to

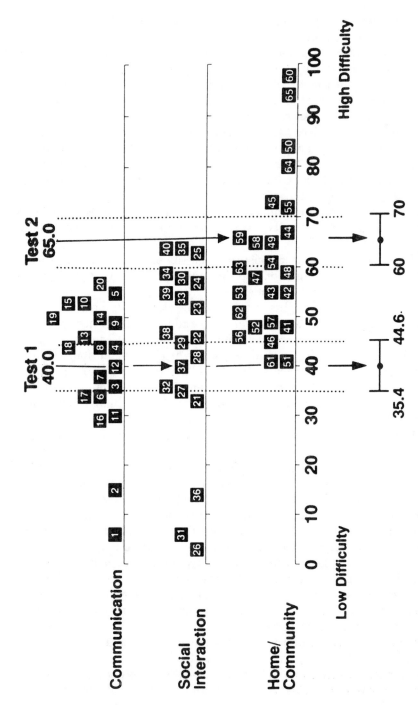

Figure 1.5.   Item Calibrations for Functional Skills Scales: Social Function

chance? In order to address this question, we employ confidence intervals to take into account the standard error of measurement for a particular score. The confidence interval provides a region within which a child's "true" level of functional performance most likely lies. These confidence intervals are constructed by determining the plus- or minus- two standard error region around the estimated functional performance level. This region is important when examining change from one test occasion to another because unless the amount of change exceeds two standard errors, there is a relatively high degree of uncertainty over whether the change in PEDI scores is due to random factors (reflected in the width of the confidence interval) or due to real change in the child's functional performance.

This point is highlighted in Figure 1.5 by the two test scores of 40.0 and 65.0, designated "TEST 1" and TEST 2," respectively. A confidence interval, based on plus or minus two standard errors, is shown around each test score. Note that there is no overlap in the confidence intervals between the two test occasions, indicating that the change in scores represents a magnitude of change decidedly larger than estimated measurement error (or, there is less than a 5% probability that this difference could have occurred by chance if there were truly no difference in functional capability on these two occasions).

The second point alluded to earlier is also critical for this type of analysis. It is now possible to chart quality of progress in a meaningful manner as performance status undergoes change. No longer does the clinician simply have to accept change as a difference score. Now change can be explicitly represented in terms of what additional items a child has accomplished from pre- to post-rehabilitation. For example, a score of 40 on Social Interaction corresponds to a 50% chance of success on Item 28 ("takes turn in simple play when cued for play"). A score of 65 on the same scale corresponds to a 50% chance of success on Item 40 ("makes up elaborate pretend sequences from imagination"). That degree and type of change is obviously significant from a rehabilitation perspective. The above type of analysis is available for any two scores on any of the scales and could just as easily have been constructed for the children discussed in Figure 1.3 and Figure 1.4.

In contrast to the "item map" represented in Figure 1.5 for dichotomously scored items, we seek to represent status and change on the Caregiver Assistance scales using a different graphical format. Although it would be possible to take the item difficulty for each item and add to it the category threshold estimate for the difficulty of making the transition from a score of 4 to a score of 5 for complete independence, such a map would only reveal whether or not a child was likely to achieve complete independence on each of the items. This map would not reveal what the actual functional capability of the child was while taking into account all the scoring options.

Figure 1.6 is our map of what it means to obtain any score on the Social Function, Caregiver Assistance scale. Each of the numerals 1 through 5 marks the category scoring transition points representing where a child is likely to perform on any particular item. For example, the vertical line corresponds to a scaled score of 50. In terms of performance this translates into the following expected performance pattern: for the Safety and Problem Solving items the child is expected to have obtained a score of "1"; for the Peer Play and Expression items the child is expected to have obtained a score of "2"; and, finally, on Comprehension the child is expected to have scored "3". Confidence intervals can be drawn around the score of 50 and multiple scores can be drawn on a single figure to represent multiple test scores.

This type of map not only shows relative item difficulty (item difficulty increases as one moves up the figure) but it also explicitly reveals the level of functioning expected on a particular item. Now instead of representing items only in terms of success or failure, as seen in Figure 1.5, the specifics of what needs to be addressed next can be portrayed for specific items. Change is now understood in terms of advancement up the scoring categories, not just moving from one item to the next. In contrast to Figure 1.1, showing the interquartile ranges for all the scales of Caregiver Assistance, this figure can be used to understand not only just at what age a particular skill is likely to be

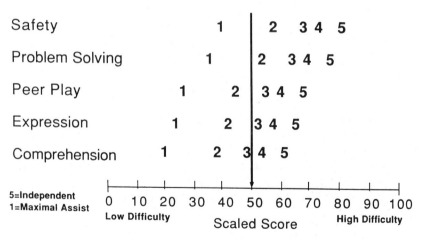

Figure 1.6. PEDI Caregiver Assistance Scales: Social Function

mastered but also what it means in terms of the actual expected performance for different age levels.

DISCUSSION

The purpose of this chapter was to present some graphical representations of functional capability status and change in status. The figures we discussed have proven useful in clinical settings when trying to understand what levels of functional capability are most likely to appear at different age levels and what specific areas of functioning appear most likely as goals to address in planning subsequent rehabilitation efforts. Our goal has been to represent functional change not simply in terms of difference scores. Rather we have tried to explicitly represent change in terms of what the actual components of capability were that did change.

The current PEDI represents the efforts of over three years of work by the authors and a number of other collaborators. Based on comments from clinicians and teachers, and based on our experience with the PEDI project, we are committed to improve continually the current assessment in subsequent versions. Our goal is to develop ecologically valid functional assessments for three settings: a) hospital, b) home, and c) educational setting. We have found that for many children with disabilities, function is highly dependent upon the setting and social expectations. Relevant functional items also vary somewhat across settings. Our eventual plan is to provide a series of assessments that can stand independently, or can be combined. Thus, for any given child, an assessment of function at the hospital could be combined with specific functional assessments in the home or educational setting.

REFERENCES

Andrich, D. (1978). A rating formulation for ordered response categories. *Psychometrika, 43,* 561–573.

Haley, S.M., Coster, W.J., Ludlow, L.H., Haltiwanger, J.T. & Andrellos, P.J. (1992). *Pediatric Evaluation of Disability Inventory (PEDI): Development, Standardization and Administration Manual.* Boston: New England Medical Center and PEDI Research Group.

Ludlow, L.H., Haley, S.M. & Gans, B.M. (1992). A hierarchical model of functional performance in rehabilitation medicine: The Tufts Assessment of Motor Performance. *Evaluation & The Health Profession, 15,* 59–74.

Ludlow, L.H. (1992). SCALE: A Rasch Program for Rating Scale Data.

(computer program). Chestnut Hill, MA: Educational Research, Measurement and Evaluation Program, Boston College.

Rasch, G. (1960). *Probabilistic Models for Some Intelligence and Attainment Tests.* Copenhagen, Denmark: Danmarks Paedogogiske Institut, (Chicago: University of Chicago Press, 1980).

Wright, B.D. & Masters, G.N. (1982). *Rating Scale Analysis.* Chicago: MESA Press.

Wright, B.D. & Stone, M.H. (1979). *Best Test Design.* Chicago: MESA Press.

chapter **2**

Evaluating an Indirect Measure of Student Literacy Competencies in Higher Education using Rasch Measurement

Barry Sheridan
Edith Cowan University
Western Australia

Les Puhl
Edith Cowan University
Western Australia

The study reported in this chapter investigates the psychometric properties of an instrument for producing an indirect measure of literacy for students in higher education in Australia. This particular instrument, the English Skills Assessment (ESA) test, is employed for two reasons. Firstly, there is a perception among higher education staff that the standards of written literacy for many students are inadequate. Secondly, as there are large numbers of students involved, a quick, easily marked, and theoretically consistent measure of literacy is required. Until recently, the ESA test was favored because it seemed to have these characteristics. However, while its multiple-choice format makes it easy to administer and mark, the theoretical construct underlying this test has never been assessed satisfactorily, especially in terms of literacy theory.

The limited scope of a multiple-choice test to assess many of the underlying knowledge structures contributing to literacy is seen by many higher education staff to be a shortcoming of the ESA test. Concerns about the validity of the ESA test as a measure of literacy are supported by the literature which indicates that the task of writing is more complex than is suggested by the writing-related skills measured by tools such as the ESA test. A synthesis of recent literature dealing with cognitive process models for writing (Bereiter & Scardamalia, 1983, 1985; Flower, 1989a, 1989b; Flower & Hayes, 1981; Hayes & Flower, 1980, 1983; Stein, 1985; Stotsky 1990) indicates a need to go beyond a conceptualization which views writing as simply a product which can be assessed by examining the *surface features* such as spelling, punctuation, and grammar. Nightingale (1988), Parry (1989), and Taylor and Nightingale (1990) identified the lack of understanding of the underlying content, and the structures and organizational formats needed to express that understanding (that is, the *deep structures* of writing), as being the problem rather than the mechanics of students' writing. Lack of purpose and poor organization result in incoherent writing (McCulley, 1985). In contrast, technical errors such as spelling and punctuation, rarely cause entire essays to be incoherent.

An Australian study by Holbrook and Bourke (1989) found that the ESA test did not assess the structural and organizational aspects of students' narrative writing. They also found the type of errors made by students in the categories measured by the ESA test did not necessarily equate to the kinds of errors made by students in the same categories when writing a narrative. For example, students who performed poorly in the spelling component of the ESA test did not necessarily manifest poor spelling in their narrative writing. This study gives support to the notion that the ESA test may be limited as a measure of the *deep structures* of writing as well as not reflecting the kinds of surface feature errors made by students in their "real" or "authentic" writing. It should be noted here that the term "subtest" is preferred to that of "category" as employed by Holbrook and Bourke as the latter term has a specific meaning in item response theory through its association with the item scoring function.

PURPOSE OF STUDY

Of special interest to this study is the opportunity to provide an understanding of what the ESA test is measuring in terms of both *surface features* and *deep structures*. The former refers to aspects such as spelling, punctuation, and vocabulary, while the latter is more concerned with paragraph and sentence structures and the development of logical thought processes. An examination of the ESA Test Manual (ACER, 1982a) reveals that the conceptual framework guiding the test specifies 26 aspects that contribute to a measure of literacy as assessed by this test. More specifically, the 188 individual multiple-choice items comprising the test are conceived in terms of these 26 subgroups such that the set of items comprising each subgroup appears to be tapping an aspect of literacy associated with *surface features* and *deep structures*. However, previous studies reporting on the psychometric properties of the ESA test have concentrated on the individual multiple-choice items as the basis of analysis, despite the fact that the conceptual framework for this test identifies these items in terms of 26 subgroups of items sets.

The major focus for the study reported in this chapter is therefore directed to an understanding of the meaning of the measurement variable constructed for the ESA test in terms of the conceptual framework and how this relates to literacy theory. However, the very act of classifying sets of item groupings in accordance with this conceptual framework makes it highly probable that dependencies are created between items within subgroups. While "items in traditional multiple-choice tests are usually carefully designed to be independent of one another" (Yen, 1993, p 187), the construction of specific forms of multiple-choice tests are such that dependence between items is an inevitable consequence of the test design. This highlights a problem which, if left unchecked, leads to inflated parameter estimates for the test. The requirement that a test should possess what is usually referred to as conditional, or local, independence of items has been acknowledged for decades but investigations assessing this property in tests have been largely ignored until more recent times (Andrich, 1985b; Rosenbaum, 1988; Wilson & Adams, 1992). Besides assessing the variable of measurement, the present investigation analyzes the ESA test in terms of the 26-item subgroups, and thus also addresses the issue of the dependencies most likely present between items comprising each subgroup.

By concentrating on the property of conditional independence between items, it is possible to provide a resolution of the dependence issue while at the same time address the measurement implications associated with the conceptual framework of the ESA test. In a strategy proposed by Andrich (1985b), a resolution of these problems presents itself through the use of the Extended Logistic Model (ELM) of Rasch, a model developed as an extension of the SLM (Rasch, 1960/1980). The strategy concentrates on grouping individual multiple-choice items into a smaller number of polytomous type items variously referred to in the literature as subtests (Andrich 1985b), item bundles (Rosenbaum, 1988), or testlets (Wainer & Kiely, 1987). The attraction of this strategy over those proposed in recent years (for example, by Wainer & Kiely, 1987; Bell, Pattison & Withers, 1988; Thissen, Steinberg & Mooney, 1989; Wainer & Lewis, 1990) is that the particular model involved, the ELM, is capable of providing a more parsimonious solution for the issue of dependencies between items while at the same time providing a means of addressing the theoretical construct associated with the very test design that creates such dependencies.

Use of the ESA test directly in terms of its original multiple-choice, dichotomous-scored format would not be the best way to investigate the capabilities of this test as a measure of literacy for two main reasons. Firstly, this approach is unable to assess the conceptual framework as presented in the Test Manual. Secondly, the issue of conditional independence is not addressed, despite the fact that the conceptual framework for the ESA test generates a design that increases significantly the likelihood of item dependence between the individual multiple-choice items identified with each of the 26 subgroups defining the instrument. By examining the individual item responses collectively in terms of these item subgroups, conditional independence can be addressed and accounted for with the measurement model employed in this study.

The following section presents the measurement model and the strategy employed to address the two problem areas identified by this study.

MEASUREMENT MODEL

The measurement model employed in this study is the Extended Logistic Model (ELM) of Rasch (Andrich, 1985a, 1985b, 1988). Rasch (1960/80) models provide for "separable person and item parameters and hence sufficient statistics . . . which makes possible 'specifically objective' comparisons of persons and items and thus fundamental measurement" (Masters & Wright, 1984, p. 529). The ELM takes the general form where person n of ability β_n responds to item i of difficulty δ_i and where there are m ordered thresholds τ_{ki}, for k = 1, m, on the measurement continuum:

$$\Pr\{X = x; \beta_n, \delta_i, \tau_{ki}\} = \exp\left\{ x(\beta_n - \delta_i) - \sum_{k=1}^{x} \tau_{ki} \right\} \bigg/ \gamma_{ni} \qquad (1)$$

where the score $x \in \{0, 1, \ldots, m\}$ and the normalizing factor is

$$\gamma_{ni} = 1 + \sum_{k=1}^{m} \left\{ \exp k(\beta_n - \delta_i) - \sum_{j}^{K} \tau_{ji} \right\}$$

The constraints $\sum_i \hat{\delta}_i = 0.0$ and $\sum_k \hat{\tau}_{ki} = 0.0$ are imposed, without loss of generality, for each item i in estimating these parameters.

Thresholds are conceptualized as a set of boundaries between the response categories of an item and specify the change in probability of a response occurring in one or the other of two categories separated by each threshold. These thresholds can also be reparameterized, through the category coefficient, to form a hierarchy of item parameters that are directly related to the Guttman (1954) principal components, where the number of parameters is governed by the number of categories in the scoring function of the item. For example, with four categories, three-item parameters can be estimated. To date, four parameters have been identified and clarified, although it is possible to have more, provided the number of categories per item is greater than five. The reparameterized form of the general expression of the model expressed in (1) is:

$$\mathrm{PR}\{x; \beta_n, \delta_t, \theta_i, \eta_i, \psi_i\} = \frac{1}{\gamma_{ni}} \exp\{-x\delta_i + x(m - x)\theta_i \tag{2}$$
$$+ x(m - x)(2x - m)\eta_i$$
$$+ x(m - x)(5x^2 - 5xm + m^2 + 1)\psi_i$$
$$+ x\beta_n\}$$

The item parameters are labelled, in hierarchical order, as *location* (δ_ι), *scale* (θ_ι), *skewness* (η_ι) and *kurtosis* (ψ_ι). In a real sense, the higher order parameters (from *scale* onward) qualify the location of an item on the latent trait continuum, with the second parameter, *scale,* defining the unit of measurement for that item. If the threshold estimates τ_{ki} for a particular item do not appear in a sequential, ordered, manner then this is evidence of misfit to the construction of the model (Andrich, 1985a; Sheridan, 1993). Threshold disorder can often provide valuable insights into the nature of the variable under review.

The set of thresholds and their reparameterized form, as presented in (1) and (2) respectively, provide the basis of a model that is very versatile and capable of assessing a wide range of measurement situations. With the familiar Likert format, for example, where the number of categories per item is usually limited to about six, the scoring function has a sequence logic that is directly interpretable. Here, the threshold estimates relate directly to the boundaries between categories in which meaning is clear within a sequence such as "Strongly Agree—Strongly Disagree"; "Always—Never", and so on. Threshold order can be assessed by examining the threshold estimates directly and the alternative reparameterized estimates consulted for additional, more specific, information.

In other situations, however, attention must be focused on the second-order, or *scale,* parameter where the summary information it provides can be employed to better effect than by using the threshold estimates directly. One such situation involves the technique of combining sets of dichotomous items into item subgroups within a test. In this case, the total score obtained for a set of individual dichotomous items provides a multiple category scoring function for a particular item subgroup, where the scores range from 0 (no items correct) to a maximum value equal to the total number of items in the subgroup. As *different* combinations of items can produce the *same* total score for this situation, the association between the scoring sequences and thresholds across categories does not have a unique meaning. Therefore, threshold disorder is not directly interpretable as is the case with the normal Likert format.

Andrich (1985b) addressed this problem by focusing attention on the reparameterized formulation of the category function and on the *scale* parameter in particular. To account for dependencies, the item subgroups are made the focus of the analysis and the category scores for each subgroup obtained from the sum of scores on the individual dichotomous items comprising the subgroup. The analysis is conducted in a manner similar to that used with the Likert format. Andrich has demonstrated that the presence of dependence between items comprising a composite item subgroup can be detected if the *scale* parameter estimate for that subgroup falls below that of a prescribed upper-bound value which pertains to the general situation prescribing no dependence between items. This boundary value is constant for a particular category size, but decreases as the number of categories, and hence the number of individual dichotomous items, per subgroup increases.

To derive these upper-bound values, Andrich first invokes the situation in which the distance between successive categories for the item subgroup structure is equal; that is, the thresholds are equally spaced. Secondly, the component dichotomous-scored items of the subgroup involved are considered as both independent of each other and of equal difficulty. The response outcomes for items under these conditions would then constitute a series of Bernoulli trials with identical success probabilities that, in turn, leads to the notion of a binomial distribution. A series of threshold coefficients that correspond to binomial coefficients can be derived for each value of m, the number of items in the subgroup. Each item subgroup is now considered as a multiple category, polytomous type item scored in the usual Likert format and comprising $m + 1$ categories. The average half-threshold distance ($\bar{\theta}$) between categories derived for no dependence between the component dichotomous items of the subgroup, and for each value of m, provides an upper-bound value which becomes a "rule-of-thumb" estimate for the boundary below which the presence of dependencies become significant. By noting the probability response distribution when the difficulties of the dichotomous items comprising a subgroup are not equal and when dependencies are present, it is possible to place an interpretation on the size of the *scale* estimate (the observed average half-threshold distance, θ_i) relative to the upper-bound value (the prescribed average half-threshold distance under special conditions, $\bar{\theta}$) obtained for the subgroup.

Consider the sequence of steps involved in this process by commencing with the ideal situation of equal item difficulties and no dependencies between these items. If the constraint of equal difficulty of dichotomous items in a subgroup is now relaxed in the absence of dependencies between these items, the response distribution for that subgroup becomes more peaked, resulting in an increased value of the average half-threshold distance, θ_i, which will now be greater than the upper-bound value, $\bar{\theta}$. Conversely, if dependence between the dichotomous items is present but the item difficulties are equal, the effect is for increased responses in the extreme categories to the exclusion of the middle categories, resulting in a smaller value of the average half-threshold distance, θ_i, associated with a flatter response distribution. These two features of unequal-item difficulties and dependencies between items work against each other and thus provide the basis for detecting the presence of dependencies. Further, the threshold distance incorporates any differences in difficulties and the averaging effect of dependencies among items of a subgroup. By combining the dichotomous responses of the ESA test into the respective subgroups as specified in the Test Manual, it is possible to address the relevance of the individual subgroups as aspects of the measurement variable identified in terms of literacy theory while at the same time accounting for any dependencies that may be present between the dichotomous items comprising these subgroups.

As the analysis presented in this chapter relates to an assessment of the theoretical conceptualization of the ESA test, emphasis will be given to the test-of-fit to the model provided by the set of threshold parameters and in their reparameterized form. Attention will also be focused on the person separation reliability index (Andrich, 1982), which is the Rasch model equivalent of the Cronbach Alpha. This index specifies the degree to which a test can separate persons in a meaningful way along the latent trait continuum and thus provides a measure of the power of the other tests-of-fit employed in an analysis. It also provides an index for assessing the degree of inflation that can occur in the parameter estimates if dependencies between items are allowed to remain unchecked. This aspect of the analysis will be considered in more detail later in this chapter.

THE ENGLISH SKILLS ASSESSMENT (ESA) TEST

The ESA test was adapted for Australian conditions from two American tests: the Sequential Tests of Education Progress Series I, for grades 10 to 12, and the Descriptive Tests of Language Skills for College Freshman (ACER, 1982b). In presentation, the ESA test is a two-part battery of standardized tests intended for use with students in years 11 and 12 of high school and the first year beyond high school. Figure 2.1 provides a schematic arrangement of the structure of the ESA test and the inter-relationship between the 188 individual dichotomous scored items and the 26 subgroups constructed from these component items. By way of clarification, each of the eight standardized tests will be referred to as a subtest. Part 1 of the ESA test consists of three timed subtests: spelling (containing 40 items), punctuation and capitalization (40 items), and comprehension 1 (15 items relating to three extended text passages each of 400 to 500 words in length). Part 2 consists of a further five timed subtests: comprehension 2 (15 items relating to five separate single paragraph texts of 60 to 70 words each), usage (20 items), vocabulary (20 items), sentence structure (18 items), and logical relationships (20 items). The number of individual dichotomous items is therefore 95 in Part 1 and 93 in Part 2, making a total of 188 for the ESA test overall. These 188 items can also be considered in terms of the 26 subgroups of items arranged in accordance with the conceptual framework and as identified with different aspects of literacy. For example, the 40 multiple-choice spelling items are classified into four subgroups relating to type of spelling error: initial syllable or sound (comprising 3 items), medial syllable or sound (8 items), final syllable or sound (18 items), and consonants (10 items). Similarly, the 40 punctuation and capitalization multiple-choice items are classified into four subgroups defined as capitalization (10 items), apostrophe (8

PART	SUBTEST	ITEM SUBGROUP	

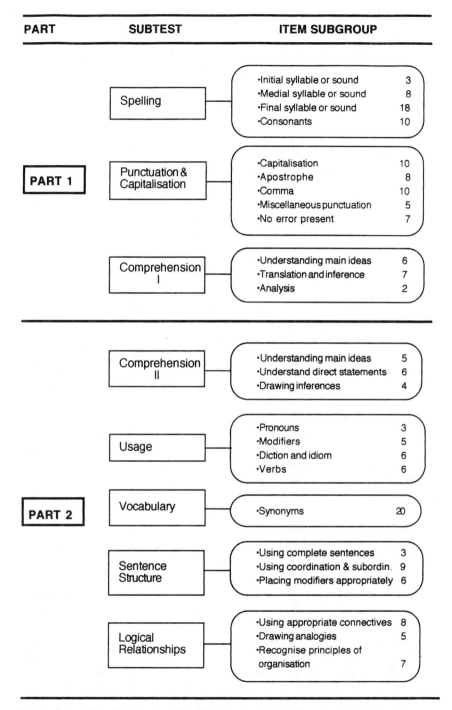

	Spelling	•Initial syllable or sound	3
		•Medial syllable or sound	8
		•Final syllable or sound	18
		•Consonants	10
PART 1	Punctuation & Capitalisation	•Capitalisation	10
		•Apostrophe	8
		•Comma	10
		•Miscellaneous punctuation	5
		•No error present	7
	Comprehension I	•Understanding main ideas	6
		•Translation and inference	7
		•Analysis	2
	Comprehension II	•Understanding main ideas	5
		•Understand direct statements	6
		•Drawing inferences	4
	Usage	•Pronouns	3
		•Modifiers	5
		•Diction and idiom	6
		•Verbs	6
PART 2	Vocabulary	•Synonyms	20
	Sentence Structure	•Using complete sentences	3
		•Using coordination & subordin.	9
		•Placing modifiers appropriately	6
	Logical Relationships	•Using appropriate connectives	8
		•Drawing analogies	5
		•Recognise principles of organisation	7

Figure 2.1. The Structure of the ESA Test, and the Number of Multiple-Choice Items in each Item Subgroup

items), comma (10 items), and miscellaneous punctuation (5 items), together with a fifth type containing no errors present (7 items).

The Sample and Data Collection

The ESA test was administered in 1992 during the first semester to all newly enrolled students in the education degree program offered at the Edith Cowan University, which is the largest provider of teacher trainees in Western Australia. Responses were collected from 495 students using special optical scoring sheets. All item analyses reported in this chapter were undertaken using the computer program RUMM (Andrich, Lyne & Sheridan, 1995), which incorporates the ELM.

The ESA as a Multiple-Choice Test

While the focus of this chapter is on the 26 subgroups of items as the unit of analysis for the ESA test, an initial analysis involving the 188 multiple-choice items on an individual basis is required for two reasons. Firstly, the analysis provides information on the difficulty estimates of each individual item within the subgroups. These estimates are required for a plot of the item and person parameter estimates to assess the degree to which the items target the persons. Secondly, the value of the person separation reliability index for the ESA test estimated in terms of the original dichotomous scored items, is required for highlighting the inflationary effect of dependence between these items. This form of analysis, which employs the simple logistic model of Rasch, is well known in the item response literature and is undertaken using the RUMM program.

The analysis involving all 188 dichotomous-scored items reveals that the majority of these items fit the requirements of the measurement model. Of the 16 items that show general misfit to the model, 4 are from the spelling subtest, 6 from the punctuation and capitalization subtest, 3 from the comprehension 2 subtest, and one each from three of the remaining subtests. In terms of a multiple-choice design, the ESA test appears to possess sound psychometric properties as all but 16 of its 188 items conform to the requirements of the measurement model. In addition, a person separation reliability index of 0.91 is a very satisfactory outcome in terms of the power of the tests-of-fit involved in this analysis. However, this value would most likely be inflated due to the inevitable presence of dependencies between the items involved as a result of the test design for the ESA test. This aspect will be addressed in more detail later in the chapter.

Before leaving this analysis of the ESA test, an examination of the distribution of person ability estimates relative to the multiple-choice item estimates is considered. As Figure 2.2 reveals, the test is on the easy side for the students involved and thus not as well-targeted to the

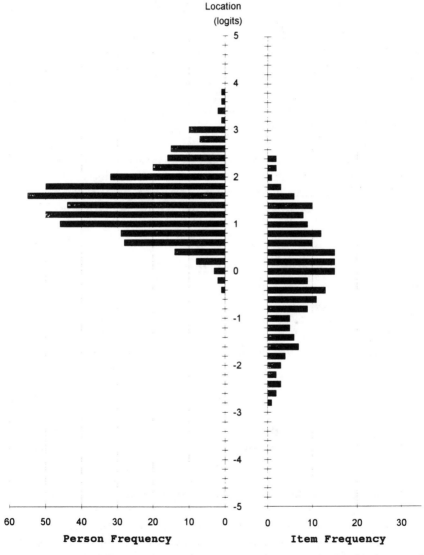

Figure 2.2.   Distribution of Ability Estimates for Higher Education Students and Item Location Estimates for the 188 item ESA test (N = 495)

student ability level as it might be when calibrating a test. This skewness is not totally unexpected, as the calibration sample is located toward the upper age group of the target population recommended in the test manual. The issue of target mismatch is very important in calibration analyses as it affects the precision of the parameter estimates and can increase the level of uncertainty with respect to knowledge and meaning of the variable under review. This important aspect of test construction will also be considered in more detail later in the chapter when assessing the threshold estimates for the item subgroups.

While the empirical evidence relating to the ESA test in terms of the multiple-choice design is very satisfactory, a difficulty arises when trying to interpret the meaning of the variable in terms of such a large number of items. The problem here is trying to make sense of the location of 172 separate items along a continuum while at the same time trying to account for the conceptual framework as posited. By combining this large number of individual items into a much smaller number of subgroups, 26 in all, and taking advantage of the special measurement features available with the ELM, a more parsimonious solution to the problem at hand is provided in association with desirable measurement outcomes.

Item Subgroups within the ESA test

As specified, the ESA test is based on a conceptual framework comprising 26 subgroups associated with the 188 multiple-choice items created for the test. The logic of the analysis which follows considers each subgroup as a multiple-category item scored in the familiar Likert format, where the number of categories is determined by the number of multiple-choice items comprising the subgroup. For ease of interpretation, the number of categories per item subgroup should be approximately equal when analyzing polytomous items. Apart from subgroups 3 and 20 in the ESA test, this goal is within reasonable limits, as the listing of the number of items per subgroup in Figure 2.1 reveals. Accordingly, 10 items were selected from the 18 comprising subgroup 3 ("final syllable or sound" in the spelling subtest) and 10 from the 20-item subgroup 20 (the vocabulary subtest); these reductions were achieved by selecting alternate items from both subgroups. The respective individual dichotomous scores were then summed across all items in each subgroup to produce an amended data file comprising 26 subgroups of items scores in place of the original 188 item scores for each student. These 26 scores then represented the category score obtained on each subgroup. An analysis involving the subgroups as 26 polytomous items was then undertaken using the same strategy employed for Likert-type rating scales.

The analysis involving all 26 subgroups of items resulted in threshold disorder for several subgroups as Table 2.1 reveals. Most of this disorder appears localized among those item subgroups associated with the subtests of spelling, punctuation and capitalization, and vocabulary, aspects most readily identified with the *surface features* of literacy. In addition, the three subgroups associated with the subtest Comprehension 2 also exhibit threshold disorder. Of interest here is that the Comprehension 2 subtest contains very short text paragraphs for assessing comprehension as compared to the subtest Comprehension 1 that contains much longer sets of text passages. In this situation, it is tempting to conclude that the substance of Comprehension 2 leans more towards *surface features* than is the case for Comprehension 1. As threshold disorder represents a fundamental problem for the construction of a variable (Andrich, de Jong & Sheridan, 1994), attention must now be focused on this aspect to ascertain a likely source of the misfit.

To proceed from here, one must be guided by the theoretical consequences arising from the conceptual framework and observe that for the ESA test, a distinction between the *surface features* and *deep structures* aspects of literacy appears to have emerged. The issue to be addressed now is how to interpret the meaning behind why thresholds for some subgroups are disordered and why those for other subgroups are not. Threshold disorder occurs when the proportion of responses across the item categories does not proceed in a logical pattern or sequence. This usually results from one of two reasons. Either the calibrating sample is mistargeted or respondents are unable to distinguish between categories on a consistent and logical basis. The former is easier to assess and should be addressed first.

For the ESA test, an examination of the pattern of responses across the different item subgroup categories is informative. As Table 2.2 reveals, the source of threshold disorder would appear to be more a result of target mismatch than the presence of illogical response patterns across categories. This is supported by the evidence that for most item subgroups, no responses appear in the first two categories at all, which is consistent with the threshold disorder occurring at the lower end of the sequence in all cases, as reference to Table 2.1 reveals. Of the two item subgroups (*sp02* and *co06*) with some responses in the second category, there is a low response count across the next few categories that is symptomatic of under-representation across the categories at the lower end of the scoring function. In addition, the number of responses across the categories are clearly unimodal, which suggests

Table 2.1. Threshold and Scale Estimates, and Scale Upper-Bound Vales for the 26 Subgroups of the ESA Test

Subgroup Label		Threshold Estimates										Scale Estimates		
		1	2	3	4	5	6	7	8	9	10	θ		θ̄
sp01		-1.23	0.31	0.92								0.54	#	0.55
sp02	*	-0.64	-0.97	-0.87	-0.48	0.07	0.62	1.05	1.22			0.17	#	0.22
sp03	*	0.33	-0.50	-0.87	-0.90	-0.67	-0.27	0.19	0.64	0.97	1.09	0.09	#	0.18
sp04	*	0.41	-0.14	-0.51	-0.72	-0.75	-0.61	-0.30	0.17	0.82	1.64	0.07	#	0.18
pc01	*	-0.02	-0.61	-0.88	-0.90	-0.70	-0.35	0.11	0.62	1.13	1.59	0.11	#	0.18
pc02		-1.06	-0.97	-0.76	-0.43	-0.01	0.49	1.06	1.69			0.20	#	0.22
pc03	*	-1.09	-1.29	-1.25	-1.01	-0.61	-0.10	0.48	1.07	1.65	2.16	0.20		0.18
pc04		-1.66	-0.85	-0.04	0.81	1.73						0.42		0.35
pc05		-2.81	-1.51	-0.57	0.16	0.81	1.51	2.40				0.41		0.26
co01		-1.55	-1.21	-0.61	0.19	1.11	2.07					0.37		0.29
co02		-2.09	-1.43	-0.77	-0.08	0.65	1.43	2.29				0.36		0.26
co03		-1.66	1.66									1.66		0.69

co04	*	-0.38	-0.93	-0.77	0.16	1.93						0.29	#	0.35
co05	*	-0.02	-1.41	-1.18	-0.09	1.09	1.60					0.24	#	0.29
co06	*	-0.68	-1.32	0.42	1.58							0.43		0.41
us01	*	-1.64	0.29	1.35	0.95	1.99						0.75		0.55
us02		-1.42	-1.24	-0.29	0.29	0.82	1.74					0.45		0.35
us03		-1.91	-0.79	-0.15	0.30	1.17	2.21					0.34		0.29
us04		-2.00	-1.21	-0.47								0.41		0.29
vo01		0.11	-0.84	-1.21	-1.14	-0.76	-0.20	0.42	0.97	1.32	1.34	0.13	#	0.18
ss01		-1.37	0.17	1.20	-0.75	-0.54	-0.17	0.40	1.19	2.22		0.64		0.55
ss02	*	-0.71	-0.81	-0.83	0.15	1.10	2.06					0.17	#	0.20
ss03		-1.42	-1.23	-0.66								0.36		0.29
lr01		-1.45	-1.14	-0.82	-0.45	-0.01	0.54	1.23	2.09			0.25		0.22
lr02	*	-1.12	-1.36	-0.35	1.01	1.83						0.41		0.35
lr03		-1.35	-0.72	-0.37	-0.11	0.20	0.72	1.63				0.22	#	0.26

Note: Subgroup labels refer to the code for subgroups in each subtest: sp01 to sp04 (spelling); pc01 to pc05 (punctuation & capitalization); co01 to co03 (comprehension 1); co04 to co06 (comprehension 2); us01 to us04 (usage); vo01 (vocabulary); ss01 to ss03 (sentence structure); lr01 to lr03 (logical relations). Asterisks (*) refer to item-subgroups exhibiting threshold disorder. Cross-thatch (#) indicates the likely presence of dependence between items comprising the subgroup.

Table 2.2.   Observed Proportion of Category Responses for the 26 Item-Subgroups in the ESA Test

Subgroup Label	Score										
	0	1	2	3	4	5	6	7	8	9	10
sp01	.06	.20	.33	.41							
sp02	.00	.01	.02	.08	.09	.18	.19	.20	.23		
sp03	.00	.00	.00	.02	.02	.07	.10	.17	.15	.22	.25
sp04	.00	.00	.00	.00	.02	.03	.07	.14	.20	.34	.20
pc01	.00	.00	.01	.02	.05	.07	.14	.21	.21	.17	.11
pc02	.00	.02	.02	.07	.09	.19	.25	.22	.15		
pc03	.00	.00	.02	.03	.07	.17	.18	.24	.14	.12	.04
pc04	.00	.04	.12	.26	.34	.23					
pc05	.02	.07	.15	.27	.24	.16	.07	.02			
co01	.00	.04	.08	.19	.32	.24	.12				
co02	.00	.02	.07	.13	.26	.26	.18	.07			
co03	.04	.28	.69								
co04	.00	.00	.03	.09	.36	.52					
co05	.00	.00	.00	.02	.11	.25	.60				
co06	.00	.02	.10	.31	.57						
us01	.02	.14	.33	.51							
us02	.00	.01	.10	.25	.37	.27					
us03	.01	.04	.08	.16	.22	.29	.20				
us04	.00	.02	.07	.17	.28	.30	.16				
vo01	.00	.00	.00	.01	.02	.06	.11	.19	.20	.17	.24
ss01	.06	.19	.37	.38							
ss02	.00	.00	.01	.01	.03	.08	.17	.26	.31	.14	
ss03	.00	.01	.02	.14	.21	.37	.25				
lr01	.00	.00	.01	.04	.10	.17	.26	.27	.14		
lr02	.00	.00	.03	.11	.29	.57					
lr03	.01	.01	.01	.06	.09	.14	.34	.34			

Note: Subgroup labels have same meaning as in Table 2.1.

that the source of misfit is unlikely to be a consequence of illogical category selections. An examination of Figure 2.2 supports the assertion that a target mismatch is present and that this skewness is biased away from the lower, or easier, categories of the item subgroup scoring mechanisms.

Before assessing the implications of these outcomes, it is instructive to examine the issue of item independence addressed earlier in the chapter. Table 2.1 provides the *scale* parameter estimates (θ_i) and the upper-bound value (θ) appropriate to each item subgroup, where the latter value is dependent on the number of categories present in the scoring function. As is evident from this listing, there is a very strong association between those item subgroups exhibiting threshold disorder (labelled *) and those exhibiting item dependence (labelled #). Recall that if the *scale* parameter for a polytomous item subgroup is less than the value for the upper-bound scale value for that subgroup, then dependencies are present between the component dichotomous items comprising the subgroup. Additional evidence for the presence of item dependencies is available from a comparison of the person separation reliability index obtained from the two analyses described so far. For the 26 subgroup design, the person separation reliability index is 0.88, compared to 0.91 for the original 188-item multiple-choice structure, which represent a drop of 3% in the variance accounted for between the two designs. This implies that the presence of dependencies as detected between the dichotomous items of the original test would lead to inflation in the precision of the parameter estimates if the original multiple-choice design is employed.

As a consequence of the uncertainty inherent in these analysis outcomes, any conclusions regarding the psychometric properties of the ESA test must be considered in terms of the target skewness in the calibrating sample. While the threshold disorder observed in the present analysis is most probably the result of target mismatch, a pattern is discernible regarding an association between the subtests identified and the degree of bias observed. This pattern relates to the item subgroups comprising the three subtests of spelling, punctuation and capitalization, and vocabulary, which are most easily identified as tapping *surface features,* together with the three subgroups comprising the comprehension 2 subtest.

In an attempt to assess the meaning of this apparent dichotomy between these four subtests and those remaining, a second analysis was conducted on the 13 subgroups of items comprising the four remaining subtests. As Table 2.3 reveals, the results are far from conclusive as threshold disorder is still present and no clear pattern discernible from these misfits which could suggest possible relationships between these aspects of the conceptual framework and *surface features* and *deep structures.*

From the evidence available, it appears likely that if the calibrating sample included students from years 11 and 12 at the high school level with those sampled for the present study, then the threshold estimates associated with the 26 subgroups of items would be ordered in accordance with the requirements of the measurement model. On the assumption that the thresholds would in fact fit the construction of the measurement model if the calibrating sample is properly targeted, a

Table 2.3 Threshold and Scale Estimates, and Scale Upper-Bound Vales for 13 Subgroups of the ESA Test

Subgroup Label		1	2	3	4	5	6	7	8	9		θ	$\bar{\theta}$
		Threshold Estimates										Scale Estimates	
co01	*	-1.19	-1.36	-0.84	0.10	1.18	2.10					0.36	0.29
co02		-1.76	-1.51	-0.97	-0.24	0.61	1.51	2.36				0.36	0.26
co03		-1.08	1.08									1.08	0.69
us01		-1.42	0.29	1.12								0.64	0.55
us02	*	-1.12	-1.19	-0.45	0.73	2.03						0.41	0.35
us03		-1.50	-0.97	-0.41	0.21	0.92	1.75					0.32	0.29
us04		-1.56	-1.38	-0.77	0.13	1.21	2.36					0.40	0.29
ss01		-1.47	0.19	1.29								0.69	0.55
ss02	*	-0.67	-0.72	-0.74	-0.69	-0.53	-0.21	0.31	1.09	2.16	#	0.16	0.20
ss03		-1.50	-0.89	-0.46	0.02	0.78	2.05					0.33	0.29
lr01	*	-0.86	-1.01	-0.95	-0.69	-0.25	0.39	1.19	2.17		#	0.22	0.22
lr02	*	-1.16	-1.25	-0.33	0.92	1.82						0.41	0.35
lr03		-1.52	-0.77	-0.33	-0.03	0.29	0.77	1.58			#	0.23	0.26

Note: Subgroup labels refer to the code for subgroups in each subtest: co01 to co03 (comprehension 1); us01 to us04 (usage); ss01 to ss03 (sentence structure); lr01 to lr03 (logical relations). Asterisks (*) refer to item-subgroups exhibiting threshold disorder. Cross-thatch (#) indicates the likely presence of dependence between items comprising the subgroup.

tentative assessment of the measurement variable associated with the ESA test could be considered.

To provide a structure for the measurement variable in terms of the item subgroups, knowledge is required of the fit of these subgroups to the model. The ASCORE program provides two statistics for assessing the fit of data to the model. First, an item-person interaction statistic examines the degree to which persons are responding to items of differing difficulty value in a logical and consistent manner and relates directly to the consistency of individual person and item response patterns. The fit statistic distribution approximates a t distribution when the data fit the model and have a mean of zero and a standard deviation of one (Andrich & Sheridan, 1980). Decreasing or negative values indicate a person or item pattern response that fits the model very closely, while increasing or positive values indicate poor fit to the model. The former case indicates that dependencies are present in the data while the latter informs that the data are largely "noise" and contributing nothing of significance to knowledge or to an understanding of the variable being constructed. The second statistic involves the item-trait interaction test-of-fit which examines the consistency of the item parameters over the range of person estimates. This statistic indicates the degree of consensus displayed collectively by all items of the instrument across persons located at differing ability levels.

An examination of the two fit statistics for the 26-item subgroups reveals strong fit to the model overall. The mean of the 26-item–person interaction statistics for these subgroups is −0.59 (the expected value is zero) which indicates a bias toward overfitting the model. This is interpreted as informing that some degree of dependency is present in the data, a situation already acknowledged due to the under representation of responses in the lower categories. One item subgroup, *lr02*, has a fit statistic of −2.7 that indicates a high level of dependency is present in this subgroup. As this subgroup is located at the easy extreme of the latent trait continuum as defined by the 26 subgroups, the lack of fit is almost certainly attributable to the target bias. With data available from high school students who presumably would exhibit, on average, lower ability relative to that of the present sample, it is probable that this item subgroup would fit the model, especially as the source of misfit indicates a lack of responses in the lower, or easier, region of the scoring function.

A second item subgroup, *pc05,* also exhibits misfit to the model but with a positive standardized residual value of 2.51. This subgroup comprises multiple-choice items designated as "no error present," so this aspect appears to be offering a feature that runs counter to the other, specifically designated, aspects of the conceptual framework defining the variable. Because this subgroup is located at the most difficult extreme of the latent trait continuum and therefore the least likely on which to achieve success, and because the target bias is not directed at this end of the continuum, it is difficult to justify the inclusion of this subgroup as part of the measurement variable. These same two-item subgroups also exhibit extreme values for the item–trait interaction fit statistic. The remaining 24 subgroups have a consistent pattern of fit to the model and can therefore be considered to contribute to a definition of the measurement variable for the ESA test.

To interpret the meaning of a variable constructed in this manner, the distribution along the latent trait continuum is required of the item statements comprising a test. The location of the items on this continuum are determined from the parameter estimates derived during the calibration process. With polytomous items, the *location* estimates δ_i are qualified by the higher order estimates, especially the *scale* values θ_i that determine the unit of measurement for each item. Ideally, the location estimates can only be compared, or placed on the one continuum, if the scale estimates for the items are equal. For the ESA test, the scale estimates θ_i vary considerably as the listing in Table 2.1 indicates. This means that any distribution of the item subgroups based on their location estimates is tenuous and caution must therefore be used in making any interpretations regarding the latent trait continuum defined in terms of such a distribution.

The distribution of the 26 subgroups of items used to define the measurement variable for the ESA test is presented in Figure 2.3. As noted earlier, the subgroups designated *pc05* (located at 1.2 logits) and *lr02* (located at −1.2 logits) are at the extremes of this distribution that covers a range of 2 logits if the misfitting subgroup *pc05* is excluded, as should be the case based on the fit statistics for this subgroup. Apart from subgroup *co03* for the subtest comprehension 1, and subgroup *lr02* for the logical relations subtest, the remaining item subgroups are clustered in close proximity according to the subtest with which they are associated. In terms of the subtests, the two aspects of comprehension are located at opposite extremes of the continuum, with comprehension 2 the easier of the subtests to master and comprehension 1 (less subgroup *co03*) the more difficult. Overall, the subtests of spelling, punctuation and capitalization, comprehension 1 and vocabulary are, in terms of the item subgroup clusters, about the same level of difficulty while the subgroups contributing to usage, sentence structure and logical relationships are a little more diverse and extend toward the easier end of the continuum. Apart from this disparity, there is little overall divergence between the subtests.

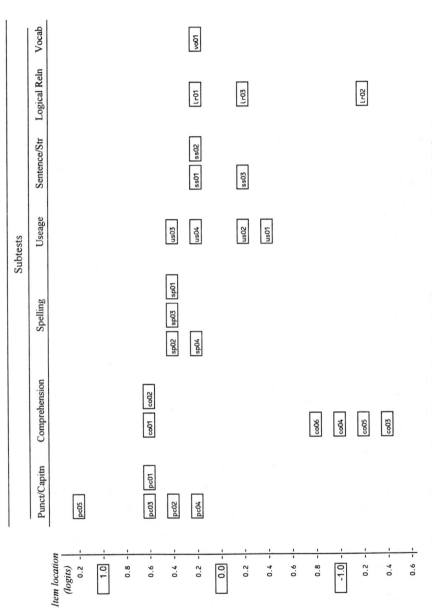

Figure 2.3. Location of the 26 ESA Item Subgroups along a Latent Trait Continuum

Again, the uncertainty associated with the use of location estimates for this type of assessment when the scale parameters are not uniform, together with the assumption of threshold order holding given improved targeting of the calibrating sample, makes any further interpretations of these data highly speculative.

DISCUSSION

The investigation reported in this chapter was motivated by three issues: (a) the perception of staff in higher education institutions of the specific limitations of a particular test commonly used to screen newly incoming students for literacy problems, (b) the research literature that pointed to the limitations of indirect multiple-choice tests as measures of performance, and (c) the fact that the adequacy of the conceptual framework underpinning the ESA test has never been properly assessed.

The perceived limitations of the ESA test as a measure of literacy arises as a consequence of the multiple-choice design employed. One limitation of multiple-choice tests is their emphasis on recall rather than on generation of answers (Wainer & Thissen, 1993). This has no doubt hastened the present growth in development of performance assessment procedures which, as Yen (1993) has observed, "require qualitatively different performance of students than do multiple-choice tests" (p 187). From a measurement perspective, the ESA test is seen as an indirect measure of literacy and the challenge for the present study was to determine how such measures relate to the *surface features* and *deep structures* inherent in student writing.

In approaching this problem, attention was focused on the conceptual framework provided for the ESA test as this formulation appeared to embrace aspects identified as *surface features* and *deep structures*. Further, previous research investigating the psychometric properties of this test has failed to relate in a convincing manner the outcome measures from the ESA test to the 26 aspects of literacy identified by the conceptual framework. The employment in the present study of the Extended Logistic Model of Rasch has demonstrated how such a relationship can be investigated. The analyses undertaken with this model revealed that the underlying construction of the ESA test is relatively coherent provided the separate 188 statements are not used as dichotomous items on an individual basis. Rather, 24 of the 26 subgroups of items identified for the test were found to fit the ELM. This situation was contingent, however, upon a resolution of the threshold disorder associated with a number of item subgroups, the solution of which appears to reside with the selection of a well-targeted calibrating sample.

The test manual specifies that the ESA test is suitable for students in their last two years at high school as well as for students in their first year beyond the high school level. It is clear from the evidence available in this study that the test is not properly targeted as it is too easy in general for the post high school students involved in the calibrating sample. While the presence of such skewness between student ability and item difficulty would not invalidate measures of student abilities per se, it will reduce the precision of the estimates obtained. In addition, this shift between item difficulty and person ability produced a disproportionate number of responses in the categories at the lower extreme of the scoring function for many of the item subgroups, which in turn affected the threshold order. As a consequence, it is not possible to investigate fully the threshold structure of the ESA test without recourse to students from the upper high school level and whose responses would presumably be such as to redress the imbalance in the lower scored categories. This means that the conclusions reached in this study regarding the coherency of the underlying construction of the ESA test as a measure must still be viewed with some caution.

These findings suggest that the way in which the ESA test is used by the Edith Cowan University and other higher education institutions, is not the best approach to adopt. The evidence provided by this study regarding the use of the ESA test as a measure of literacy indicates that this test should not be employed in the form prescribed by the test manual. At best, the procedures advocated are superficial, and it is difficult to see how the reporting of raw scores obtained from summing the respective dichotomous item responses for the eight subtests relates in a meaningful way to the 26 subgroup descriptions. Unless the variable constructed for an instrument is shown to relate in a meaningful way to some prescribed theoretical base that underpins the test, then it is unrealistic to claim that the test is a measure of any construct in which meaning can be established.

While this study has been able to improve on available knowledge concerning the construction of the ESA test and make recommendations about how the responses should be interpreted, the appropriateness of the test for the purpose for which it is being used is still not clearly understood. As stated, the ESA test is commonly used by higher education institutions throughout Australia to screen students with writing difficulties. However, there is some concern among staff, which is supported by the literature, that this test does not tap some of the important deficiencies in students' writing performance. These deficiencies relate to the underlying cohesion and coherence of the ideas contained in their text—that is, the *deep structures* of their writing. In order to assess the appropriateness of the ESA test as an indirect measure of students' writing performances, further investigation needs to be carried out that (a) identifies the range of areas in which students manifest difficulties in "authentic writing contexts" and compares these to the range of areas identified by the ESA test, and (b) compares the student performances in the areas identified by the ESA test with the same areas in their writing.

The current debate relating to the relative merits of the multiple-choice test format versus performance assessment procedures provides a focus for the findings of the present study. Wainer and Thissen (1993) highlight the issue by addressing the financial cost of one format against that of the other. Certainly, performance assessment procedures are more expensive to operate due to the high labor component involved. The use of procedures that account for grader, or marker harshness (Andrich & Hake, 1974; Engelhard, 1992; Hake & Andrich, 1974; Sheridan & Puhl, 1994) has demonstrated the effectiveness of assessing student written performance and opened the way for investigating the measurement of *surface features* and *deep structures* within the context of literacy theory. To satisfy the demands of large-scale requirements such as assessing the writing ability of students for course certification, the use of low-cost, easily scored procedures are sought. By taking advantage of the special features provided by measurement models such as the ELM, procedures could be established for including the multiple-choice format to complement performance assessment as part of the overall evaluation process. This is a challenge for research in the immediate future.

REFERENCES

ACER (1982a). *English Skills Assessment Interim Manual.* Melbourne: ACER.

ACER (1982b). *English Skills Assessment Parts I and II.* Melbourne: ACER.

Andrich, D. (1982). An Index of Person Separation in latent trait theory, the traditional KR.20 Index, and the Guttman Scale response pattern. *Educational research and perspectives, 9* (1), 95–104.

Andrich, D. (1985a). An elaboration of Guttman scaling with Rasch models for measurement. In N. Brandon-Tuma (Ed.). *Sociological Methodology,* (pp. 33–80). San Francisco: Jossey-Bass.

Andrich, D. (1985b). A latent-trait model for items with response dependencies: Implications for test construction and analysis. In S. E. Embretson (Ed.). *Test design: Developments in psychology and psychometrics,* (pp. 245–275). Orlando: Academic Press.

Andrich, D. (1988). A general form of Rasch's extended logistic model for partial credit scoring. *Applied Measurement in Education, 1* (4), 363–378.

Andrich, D., de Jong, J.H., & Sheridan, B. (1994). Diagnostic opportunities with the Rasch model for ordered response categories. Paper presented at the IPN Symposium on *Applications of latent trait and latent class models in the social sciences,* Akademie Sankelmark, Germany, May 16–19.

Andrich, D. & Hake, R. (1974). The application of a discourse theory and a Rasch Model for measuring in the evaluation of written expression. *Educational research and perspectives, 1* (2), 51–61.

Andrich, D., Lyne, A., & Sheridan, B. (1991). RUMM (Version 1.0): A Windows program for analysing the response data according to Rasch Unidimensional Measurement Models. Perth: School of Education, Murdoch University.

Andrich, D. & Sheridan, B. (1980). *RATE: A Fortran IV program for analysing rated data according to a Rasch model* (Research Report No. 5). Perth: University of Western Australia, Department of Education, Measurement and Statistics Laboratory.

Bell, R.C., Pattison, P.E. and Withers, G.P. (1988). Conditional independence in a clustered item test. *Applied Psychological Measurement, 12,* 15–26.

Bereiter, C., & Scardamalia, M. (1983). Levels of inquiry in writing research. In P. Mosenthal, L. Tamor, & S. Walmsley (Eds.), *Research on writing: Principles and Methods.* New York: Longman.

Bereiter, C., & Scardamalia, M. (1985). Levels of inquiry into the nature of expertise in writing. *Review of Research in Education, 13,* 259–282.

Engelhard, G. (1992). The measurement of writing ability with a many-faceted Rasch model. *Applied Measurement in Education, 5,* 171–191.

Flower, L. (1989a). Cognition, context, and theory building. *College Composition and Communication, 40,* 282–311.

Flower, L. (1989b). *Studying cognition in context: introduction to the study.* (Eric Document Reproduction Service No. ED 306593).

Flower, L., & Hayes, J. (1981). A cognitive process theory of writing. *College Composition and Communication, 32,* 365–387.

Guttman, L. (1954). The principal components of scalable attitudes. In P.F. Lazarsfeld (Ed.), *Mathematical Thinking in the Social Sciences.* New York: Free Press.

Hake, R. (1986). How do we judge what they write? In K.L. Greenburg, H.S. Wiener, & R.A. Donovan (Eds.), *Writing assessments: Issues and strategies* (pp. 153–167). New York: Longman.

Hake, R., & Andrich, D. (1974). *The Ubiquitous Essay: A discourse and psychometric theory to identify, measure, evaluate, and teach essay writing ability.* (Research Report). Perth: Faculty of Education, University of Western Australia.

Hayes, J., & Flower, L. (1980). Identifying the organisation of the writing process. In L. Gregg, & E. Steinberg (Eds), *Cognitive processes in writing.* Hillsdale: Erlbaum.

Hayes, J., & Flower, L. (1983). *A cognitive model of the writing process.* (ERIC Document Reproduction Service No. ED 240608)

Holbrook, A., & Bourke, S. (1989). Assessment of the English skills of tertiary students. *Higher Education Research and Development, 8* (2), 161–179.

Masters, G.N., & Wright, B.D. (1984). The essential process in a family of measurement models. *Psychometrika, 49*(4), 529–544.

McCulley, G. (1985). Writing quality, coherence and cohesion. *Research in the Teaching of English, 19*(3), 269–282.

Nightingale, P. (1988). Understanding processes and problems in student writing. *Studies in Higher Education, 13*(3), 263–283.

Parry, S. (1989). Achieving academic literacy: Disciplined discourse. *Higher Education Research and Development, 8*(2), 147–158.

Rasch, G. (1960/80). *Probabilistic Models for Some Intelligence and Attainment Tests.* (Expanded ed.) Chicago: University of Chicago Press.

Rosenbaum, P.R. (1988). Item bundles. *Psychometrika, 53,* 349–359.

Sheridan, B. (1993). Threshold location and Likert-style questionnaires. Paper presented at the Seventh International Objective Measurement Workshop, American Educational Research Association Annual Meeting, Atlanta, April 10–11.

Sheridan, B., & Puhl, L. (1994). An integrated approach for the assessment of essay writing performance using Rasch Measurement. Paper presented at the American Educational Research Association Annual Meeting, New Orleans, April 4–8.

Stein, N. (1985). Knowledge and process in the acquisition of writing skills. *Review of Research in Education, 13* (pp. 225–257).

Stotsky, S. (1990). On planning and writing plans—or beware of borrowed theories. *College Composition and Communication, 41,* 37–57.

Taylor, G., & Nightingale, P. (1990). Not mechanics but meaning: Error in tertiary students' writing. *Higher Education Research and Development, 9*(2), 161–175.

Thissen, D., Steinberg, L., & Mooney, J.A. (1989). Trace lines for testlets: A use of Multiple-Categorical-Response Models. *Journal of Educational Measurement, 26,* 247–260.

Wainer, H., & Kiely, G.L. (1987). Item clusters and Computerised Adative Testing: A case for Testlets. *Journal of Educational Measurement, 24,* 185–201.

Wainer, H., & Lewis, C. (1990). Towards a psychometics for testlets. *Journal of Educational Measurement, 27,* 1–14.

Wainer, H., & Thissen, D. (1993). Combining multiple-choice and constructed-response test scores: Towards a Marxist Theory of Test Construction. *Applied Measurement in Education, 6,* 103–118.

Wilson, M., & Adams, R. J. (1992). Rasch models for item bundles. Paper presented at the annual meeting of the American Education Research Association, San Francisco, April 20–24.

Yen, W. M. (1993). Scaling performance assessments: Strategies for managing local item dependence. *Journal of Educational Measurement, 30,* 187–213.

chapter 3

Predicting Academic Performance in College: An Investigation of the Utility of the Graded Response Model and the Partial Credit Model for Scaling First Year Course Grades

Carol A. Morrison
National Board of Medical Examiners

Each year, colleges and universities are faced with a difficult but important task: selecting a group of students who will be admitted to their institution from among a sometimes large pool of applicants. Standards for admission vary across institutions, but institutions typically rely on the same preadmissions measures to help them decide which students will be admitted and which students will not. The most commonly used preadmissions measures are high school rank (HSR) or high school grade point average (HSGPA) and scores from standardized admissions tests such as the Scholastic Aptitude Test (SAT) or the American College Testing Assessment (ACT).

Institutions may set a cut score on one or more of these preadmissions measures; those students who score at the cut score or above are eligible to attend the institution and those who score below the cut score are not eligible to attend the institution. Alternatively, institutions may compute and use a predicted grade point average or probability of academic success in making admissions decisions. Institutions may also use other criteria such as personal statements, interviews, and letters of recommendation to make admissions decisions. The cut scores on the preadmissions measures, the predicted grade point averages, or the probability of academic success are normally determined through a predictive validity study performed by the institution or by a validity study service provided by one of the major testing companies. A multiple regression model is developed with the preadmissions measures as the predictors and first-year college grade point average, in most cases, as the criterion. Based on the results of the validity study, cut scores, predicted grade point averages, or probabilities of academic success are identified and then used as part of the criteria to determine which students will be admitted to the institution.

The aforementioned description of the admissions process suggests the importance of accurate prediction of first-year college performance. Poor accuracy of prediction due to low predictor validity or low predictability of the criterion could result in incorrect admissions decisions, which could have profound implications for the students who are affected. Students could be denied admission to their preferred institution or, worse, could be denied admission to college completely. On the other hand, a prediction error in the opposite direction could result in failing grades and eventual withdrawal if a student cannot perform in accordance with the standards of the institution to which he or she is admitted. Because of the importance of accurate prediction of college performance, trends in the predictive validity of admissions measures such as the SAT, ACT, and HSR, and trends in college grading standards are followed closely by institutions and testing companies. Research suggests that there was a downward trend in the average multiple correlation of first-year grade point average (FGPA) with the SAT-Verbal score (SAT-V) and SAT-Mathematical score (SAT-M) from the mid 1970s to the mid 1980s (Willingham, 1990). Further, studies indicate that the downward trend is more likely attributable to the noncomparability of course grades than to characteristics of the SAT (Willingham, 1990).

Grading standards vary widely across instructors and departments within an institution. A grade from a course in one department is often not comparable to the same grade from a course in another department. Further, the disparity in grading standards may be increasing due to trends in higher education such as changing admissions stan-

dards and the availability of remedial courses for academically bor-
derline students. The noncomparability of course grades directly affects the FGPA criterion because FGPA is simply a weighted average
of a student's course grades from his or her first year of college. If
course grades are not comparable, then FGPAs are not comparable
across students who take different courses.

If course grades could be made more comparable in some way, the
predictability of FGPA would probably increase and the accuracy of
admissions decisions most likely would improve also. Young (1989,
1990a, 1990b, 1991a, 1991b) demonstrated that polytomous item response theory (IRT) models could be used to put course grades onto a
common scale of measurement with some success. He used Muraki's
(1990) rating scale model and Masters' (1982) partial credit model, but
no systematic comparison of the models was made. Thus, although the
results of Young's research suggest that IRT models may be used to
increase the predictability of college performance, it is not clear which
polytomous model works better in this measurement situation.

In this chapter, the relative merits of the graded response model and
the partial credit model for scaling course grades to improve the predictability of college performance were investigated. A systematic
comparison of the two polytomous models was conducted, as well as a
comparison of the merits of the IRT-based approach relative to the
classical test theory-based approach of using unadjusted FGPA. The
graded response model and the partial credit model are described below.

THE GRADED RESPONSE MODEL

The graded response model (GRM) was developed by Samejima (1969)
as an extension of the two-parameter logistic model to be used with
items whose responses may be classified into two or more ordered
categories. The categories are ordered in terms of degree of attainment
of the solution or degree of intensity of the latent trait. The graded
response model is appropriate for essay items and other items for
which partial credit can be awarded for partially correct responses.
The GRM may also be used to scale Likert-type attitude scale items.

In the graded response model, responses to item i are classified into
$(m_i + 1)$ ordered categories. Higher-numbered categories represent
more of the underlying latent trait or proficiency measured by the
item than do lower-numbered categories. The category scores (x_i) for
item i are successive integers that range from 0 to m_i $(0, 1, \ldots, m_i)$.

A two-stage process must be followed to calculate the probability that an examinee of a particular proficiency level (θ) will obtain a given category score (x_i) on item i. First, the probability that an examinee with a particular proficiency level (θ) will receive a given category score of x_i or *higher* on item i is calculated using the following equation:

$$P_{x_i}^*(\theta) = \frac{\exp[Da_i(\theta - b_{x_i})]}{1 + \exp[Da_i(\theta - b_{x_i})]}$$

The D parameter is the scaling constant 1.7 that makes the cumulative logistic function almost identical to the normal ogive function, the a_i term is the item discrimination parameter, θ is the proficiency level, and b_{x_i} is the difficulty (category boundary) parameter for a particular value of category score x_i for the values $1, \ldots, m_i$. The probability of responding in the lowest category or higher is equal to 1.0; the probability of responding above the highest category is equal to 0.0.

In Samejima's second stage, the probability that an examinee will respond in a given category, x_i, is obtained by subtracting adjacent category characteristic curves (except for the lowest or highest category). The probability that an examinee of proficiency level θ will respond in a given category is defined as:

$$P_{x_i}(\theta) = P_{x_i}^*(\theta) - P_{(x_i+1)}^*(\theta)$$

for $x_i = 0, \ldots, m_i - 1$.

THE PARTIAL CREDIT MODEL

The partial credit model (PCM) was developed by Masters (1982) as an extension of the Rasch model (one-parameter logistic model) to be used with items whose responses may be classified into two or more ordered categories. The partial credit model, like the graded response model, may be used with items for which partial credit may be awarded as well as with Likert-type attitude scale items. Unlike the graded response model, however, the partial credit model assumes that items do not differ in their ability to discriminate among examinees of different proficiency levels.

Again, responses to item i are classified into ($m_i + 1$) ordered categories. Higher-numbered categories represent more of the underlying latent trait or proficiency measured by the item than do lower-numbered categories. The category scores (x_i) for item i are successive integers that range from 0 to m_i (0, 1, . . . , m_i). Like the graded response model, the partial credit model allows response alternatives to vary in number and structure across items.

The probability that an examinee of proficiency level θ will respond in a particular category, x_i, on item i is expressed as:

$$Px_i(\theta) = \frac{\exp \sum_{j=0}^{x_i} (\theta - b_{x_j})}{\sum_{k=0}^{m_t} \exp \sum_{j=0}^{k} (\theta - b_{x_j})}$$

The θ term is the proficiency level and the b_{x_j} term is the step difficulty (category boundary) for category score x_i.

METHOD

Data Set

The data set that was used to investigate the relative merits of the graded response model and the partial credit model for scaling course grades came from The University of Texas at Austin (UT Austin). The data set consisted of information for 5,267 students (2,838 males and 2,429 females) who first entered UT Austin as freshmen in the fall semester of 1990. Provisionally admitted students who entered in the summer of 1990 and transfer students from other colleges and universities were not included.

The data set consisted of the following variables for each student: identification number, course grade for each course the student completed during the fall 1990 and spring 1991 semesters, credit-by-examination (CBE) grades for each course for which the student received a CBE grade during the fall 1990 and spring 1991 semesters, course abbreviation and course number corresponding to each course grade, SAT-V and SAT-M if the SAT was taken, ACT English Test score (ACT-E), ACT Mathematics Test score (ACT-M), ACT Reading Test score (ACT-R), ACT Science Reasoning Test score (ACT-S), and ACT Composite score if the ACT Assessment was taken, HSR, and university-assigned codes for school/college, gender, and ethnicity. Only students who had course grades from both the fall and spring semesters were included.

A stratified proportionate random sample of 3,000 students was drawn from the population of students in the data set to serve as the calibration sample. Three mutually exclusive groups served as the strata: students who had taken the SAT but had not taken the ACT (82% of the population), students who had taken the ACT but had not taken the SAT (2% of the population), and students who had taken both the SAT and the ACT (16% of the population). Observations from the three strata were sampled at random proportionate to the size of the strata in the population. The calibration sample was used for the principal components analyses and the IRT calibrations.

The remaining students (approximately 2,000) formed the validation sample. The validation sample was divided into three subsamples: SAT Sample 1, SAT Sample 2, and the ACT Sample. The students in the validation sample who had taken the SAT were randomly assigned to either SAT Sample 1 or SAT Sample 2. SAT Sample 1 and SAT Sample 2 were mutually exclusive, but these samples were not mutually exclusive with the ACT sample because some students had taken both the SAT and the ACT. Two separate SAT samples were used so that the results of the regression analyses could be cross-validated. This chapter will focus on the results for the SAT samples because most students took the SAT. The results for the ACT sample were very similar to those of the SAT samples.

Subsets of Courses

For the purposes of this study, grades from multiple sections of a course with the same department designation and course number were treated as though they came from the same course, even though the sections may have been taught by different instructors and in different semesters. Credit-by-examination grades were also treated the same as grades from courses that a student took in residence. The University of Texas at Austin allows students to earn credit-by-examination with letter grades for any undergraduate course at the university; therefore, it seemed appropriate to treat CBE grades the same as other course grades earned at UT Austin.

Treating multiple sections of a course as a course with one section does not address the problem of possible inequities in grading standards across instructors. If every section of a course were to be treated as a separate course, however, there would be hundreds of courses to scale and it is unlikely that there would be enough students in each grade category to obtain stable course parameter estimates. For the same reason, although students in the population took over 700 different courses, only those courses that were taken by 50 or more students from the population were considered for inclusion in the study.

Because the partial credit model and the graded response model assume that the data are unidimensional, courses were initially partitioned into unidimensional subsets based on their curriculum and on the subsets of courses used by Young (1991a) in previous research in this area. The three subsets used were:

1. natural science, engineering, and mathematics courses,
2. social sciences courses, and
3. humanities courses

Because MULTILOG (Thissen, 1991), the estimation program used in this study, has limits on the number of courses it can scale using the graded response model (49) and the partial credit model (34) when run on an IBM-compatible microcomputer, the 34 courses in each subset with the largest enrollments of students from the population were initially included in the subset. Only one subset, the natural science, engineering, and mathematics subset, consisted of more than 34 courses with an enrollment of 50 or more students from the population. It should be noted that other estimation programs such as BIG-STEPS (Linacre & Wright, 1992) do not have such severe limits on the number of items or courses that can be scaled.

Principal Components Analyses to Assess the Dimensionality of the Subsets

A principal components analysis was then used to assess the dimensionality of each subset of course grades. A factor analysis is frequently used to assess the dimensionality of tests or attitude scales before an IRT calibration is conducted. Principal components analysis was used in this study, however, because of the unusual nature of the input matrices that were used. An intercorrelation matrix of the course grades for a subset from the calibration sample served as the input to the principal components analysis for the particular subset. These matrices, however, had some empty cells because some pairs of courses lacked students who took both courses in the pair. For example, two courses may have fulfilled the same requirement, so students took one course or the other course, but not both courses.

A correlation matrix with missing correlation coefficients cannot be used in a principal components analysis, so a decision had to be made concerning the missing data. In this study, two imputation procedures were tried:

1. impute a value of zero for each of the missing correlation coefficients, and
2. impute an arbitrarily chosen moderately low correlation (.20) for each of the missing coefficients.

A principal components analysis was then conducted for each subset of courses. It should be stressed that the intercorrelation matrix of the course grades was not an optimal input matrix for a procedure like principal components for at least two reasons. First, the problem of missing correlation coefficients in the matrix required the use of the imputation procedures described previously. Second, each correlation coefficient in the input matrix was based on a different group of students with different sample sizes.

A subset of course grades was considered to be approximately unidimensional if the eigenvalue for the first factor was large relative to the eigenvalue for the second factor and the eigenvalue for the second factor was not considerably larger than the eigenvalues for the remaining factors (Lord, 1980). Scree plots were also examined to help assess the dimensionality of the subsets.

Item Response Theory Calibration Procedures

Once the course grades from the calibration sample were partitioned into approximately unidimensional subsets, the grades in each subset were scaled according to the graded response model and the partial credit model using the MULTILOG estimation program (Thissen, 1991) on an IBM-compatible microcomputer. MULTILOG can be used to obtain marginal maximum likelihood parameter estimates for several dichotomous and polytomous IRT models, including the two polytomous models used in this study. Course grades were scaled using a procedure known as a simultaneous calibration in which all course parameters are put onto the same scale of measurement automatically because they are calibrated together. A set of step value estimates was obtained for each course in each subset from the partial credit model. Similarly, a set of category boundary estimates and a course discrimination estimate were obtained for each course in each subset from the graded response model. If course parameter estimates had very high standard errors or did not converge for a particular course or group of courses in a subset for a given calibration, the course(s) was (were) dropped from the subset and the calibration for the particular IRT model was repeated until reasonable course parameter estimates were obtained for every course remaining in the subset.

Some courses had very few or no students who had received a grade of F in the course. Consequently, the D and F categories were collapsed together and the course was scaled using four categories rather than five categories so that course parameter estimates could be obtained for the course. Similarly, some courses had no students who had received a grade of F in the course and very few or no students who had received a grade of D in the course. In this case, the C and D categories were collapsed together and the course was scaled using three categories.

Once the final course parameter estimates were obtained, the course parameter estimates from the partial credit model based on the calibration sample were then used to obtain a proficiency estimate from the partial credit model for each student in the validation sample for each subset of courses using MULTILOG. Similarly, the course parameter estimates from the graded response model based on the calibration sample were used to obtain a proficiency estimate from the graded response model for each student in the validation sample for each subset of courses using MULTILOG. It should be noted that some students did not take any courses in one or more of the subsets and, therefore, did not receive a proficiency estimate for the subset(s).

An average proficiency estimate was also calculated for each student in the validation sample by simply adding the student's proficiency estimates from each of the three subsets of courses for which he or she had a proficiency estimate and dividing by the number of proficiency estimates included in this sum. The average proficiency estimate was calculated to serve as a total IRT-based criterion that could be compared with total first-year grade point average across the three subsets.

Calculation of Estimated True Score Averages

An estimated true score average was calculated for each student in the validation sample for each subset of course grades for both the graded response model and the partial credit model according to the procedure described in the Appendix. It was hoped that the estimated true score averages might provide a procedure to check whether or not Young's (1990a) results were simply an artifact of less range restriction in the IRT-based proficiency estimates relative to the FGPAs rather than a result of the superiority of the IRT-based procedure itself. Both the proficiency estimates and the estimated true score averages were used in all analyses.

A total estimated true score average was also calculated for each student by simply adding the student's estimated true score average from each of the three subsets of courses for which he or she had an estimated true score average and dividing by the number of estimated true score averages included in this sum. Like the average proficiency estimate, the total estimated true score average was calculated to serve as a total IRT-based criterion that could be compared with total first-year grade point average across the three subsets.

Calculation of First-Year Grade Point Averages

Unweighted and weighted first-year grade point averages were calculated for each student for each subset of course grades. The unweighted FGPA for each student for each subset was simply the sum of the grade points for the letter grades in each course for which a student had a grade divided by the total number of grades reported for the student within the subset. To calculate the weighted FGPA for each student for each subset, the grade points for the letter grades for each course for which a student had a grade were first multiplied by the number of credit hours for the corresponding course. These products were then summed across all courses the student had taken in the subset and divided by the total number of credit hours completed by the student in the subset to get the weighted FGPA. Unweighted and weighted total FGPAs based on the grades from all courses taken by a student across the various subsets were also calculated for each student, using the same procedures.

Young (1990a) used unweighted GPAs in all analyses because the course grades that were scaled using the IRT models did not reflect varying numbers of credit hours. However, validation studies that use FGPA as the criterion typically calculate FGPA based on course grades that have been weighted by the number of credit hours for the course. Therefore, the decision was made to calculate both an unweighted and a weighted FGPA to investigate the merits of the IRT-based approach relative to the classical test theory-based approach that is actually used in practice as well as the classical test theory-based approach that was used in previous research in this area.

The traditional first-year grade point average based on the grades from all courses for which a student received a letter grade (weighted by the number of credit hours) was also calculated for each student to compare the predictability of the actual criterion variable used by the university with the predictability of the various IRT-based composite variables that were based on a reduced set of courses that could be scaled using the two polytomous IRT models.

Intercorrelations of the Various Measures of Academic Performance in College

Pearson product-moment correlation coefficients were computed to assess the degree of linear relationship among the various measures of academic performance in college within each subset for SAT Sample 1 and SAT Sample 2.

Predictive Validation Studies

A series of validation studies was conducted for students in SAT Sample 1 and for students in SAT Sample 2 with SAT-V, SAT-M, and HSR as the predictors and several different criteria for each subset. Only those students who had data for each of these measures within a particular subset were included in the validation studies for the subset.

The criterion in each multiple linear regression model differed. Regression models were developed to predict the proficiency estimate and the estimated true score average from the partial credit model for each subset of courses. Models were also developed to predict the proficiency estimate and the estimated true score average from the graded response model for each subset of courses. Similarly, models were developed to predict the unweighted and weighted FGPAs for each subset of courses. Finally, multiple linear regression models were developed to predict the total unweighted and weighted FGPAs, the traditional FGPA, the average proficiency estimate from each polytomous IRT model, and the total estimated true score average from each polytomous IRT model.

The relative predictability of the various IRT-based criteria and classical test theory-based criteria was assessed through a comparison of the R^2 (coefficient of multiple determination) values from the various multiple regression models with the same predictor variables within a particular subset. Any conclusions drawn from the comparison of R^2 values obtained from different models are strictly descriptive in nature.

Cross-Validation Studies

A series of double cross-validation studies was conducted using SAT Sample 1 and SAT Sample 2 to assess the stability of the multiple regression equations developed on one sample when the same equations were applied to the other sample. Cross-validation studies were conducted for the same combinations of criteria and predictors as those used for the predictive validation studies to assess the change in R^2 values that occurred when the optimal regression equation from one sample was used to predict the criterion variable for the other sample.

RESULTS

Principal Components Analyses to Assess the Dimensionality of the Subsets

The principal components analyses confirmed that the three subsets that had been formed on the basis of curriculum were essentially unidimensional, regardless of which imputation method was used. For the natural science, engineering, and mathematics subset, the first eigenvalue accounted for 39% of the total variance when a value of zero was imputed for each of the missing correlation coefficients in the input matrix and 43% of the total variance when a value of .20 was imputed for each of the missing correlation coefficients in the input matrix. In both cases, the first eigenvalue (13.14 and 14.66, respectively) was considerably larger than the second eigenvalue (5.13 and 3.74, respectively), and an examination of the Scree plots from the two analyses again revealed pronounced "elbows" at the second component.

For the social sciences subset, the first eigenvalue accounted for 43% of the total variance when a value of zero was imputed for each of the missing correlation coefficients in the input matrix and 47% of the total variance when a value of .20 was imputed for each of the missing correlation coefficients in the input matrix. Again, in both cases, the first eigenvalue (9.86 and 10.86, respectively) was considerably larger than the second eigenvalue (4.32 and 4.25, respectively), and an examination of the Scree plots from the two analyses revealed pronounced "elbows" at the second component.

Finally, for the humanities subset, the first eigenvalue accounted for 35% of the total variance when a value of zero was imputed for each of the missing correlation coefficients in the input matrix and 38% of the total variance when a value of .20 was imputed for each of the missing correlation coefficients in the input matrix. Again, in both cases, the first eigenvalue (9.02 and 9.87, respectively) was considerably larger than the second eigenvalue (3.86 and 3.85, respectively), and an examination of the Scree plots from the two analyses revealed pronounced "elbows" at the second component.

Thus, the principal components analyses confirmed that the three subsets of courses were fairly unidimensional, although a considerable amount of total variance remained after the first component was extracted. However, this result was not surprising given the nature of the input matrix and the imputation methods that had to be used.

Item Response Theory Calibrations

Some courses were dropped from the graded response model calibration and/or the partial credit model calibration for a particular subset because of problems with nonconvergence of one or more course parameter estimates during earlier calibration runs. Therefore, the final subsets used for the calibrations were not necessarily the same as the initial subsets. Further, the particular courses from a subset that were included in the final graded response model calibration or partial credit model calibration sometimes differed because occasionally one of the polytomous models was able to scale a course with no problems, whereas the other model produced nonconvergent or very unstable course parameter estimates for one or more of the courses in the subset.

The decision was made to allow the specific courses in a particular subset to differ for the calibration runs for the two IRT models because the goal of this study was to compare the relative merits of the graded response model and the partial credit model for scaling course grades. The ability of one polytomous model to scale a particular distribution of grades in a course when the other model could not seemed to be an important advantage of the former model over the latter model.

All of the courses that were included in either polytomous IRT model calibration for a particular subset were used for the calculation of unweighted and weighted first-year grade point averages for the subset for all students in the validation sample. This decision was based on the fact that the FGPA approach does not have problems with nonconvergence of course parameter estimates, etc., because FGPAs are simply a linear composite of the grades that a student has earned in courses in the subset. In practice, a student's FGPA for a subset would be based on every course grade he or she received in a particular subset. However, it was decided to limit the courses that were used to calculate unweighted and weighted FGPAs to those that were included in one or both of the IRT calibrations to keep the particular subset as comparable as possible across the item response theory-based approach and the classical test theory-based approach of assessing academic performance in college.

The graded response model and the partial credit model both produced reasonable course parameter estimates for all of the original 34 courses in the natural science, engineering, and mathematics subset. There were no problems with nonconvergence of the course parameter estimates for either polytomous model for the natural science, engineering, and mathematics subset, in part, because most of the courses had fairly large enrollments and fairly symmetric distributions of students across the grade categories.

Some of the course discrimination parameter estimates for courses in this subset and for courses in the other subsets were considerably higher than the discrimination parameter estimates that are typically reported for test and attitude scale items that have been scaled using the graded response model (discrimination parameters usually range from 1.00 to 3.00). The unusually high discrimination parameter estimates were usually associated with courses that had fairly uniform grade distributions, suggesting that these courses provided more information than courses with more skewed grade distributions.

Reasonable course parameter estimates from the graded response model were obtained for 21 of the original 24 courses in the social sciences subset. Similarly, reasonable course parameter estimates from the partial credit model were obtained for 23 of the original 24 courses in the subset. Interestingly, the course that was dropped from the partial credit model calibration of the subset was not one of the same courses that was dropped from the graded response model calibration of the subset. The courses that were dropped from the graded response model and partial credit model calibrations of the social sciences subset had very skewed grade distributions or small enrollments. The two polytomous IRT models examined in this study had difficulty arriving at stable course parameter estimates when most of the students received As and Bs in a course.

Reasonable course parameter estimates from the graded response model were obtained for 25 of the original 34 courses in the humanities subset. Similarly, reasonable course parameter estimates from the partial credit model were obtained for 26 of the original 34 courses in the humanities subset. The same courses that were dropped from the graded response model calibration were also dropped from the partial credit model calibration except one course, which could be scaled using the partial credit model. The courses were dropped from the subset due to the nonconvergence of one or more of the course parameter estimates. An examination of the grade distributions for the courses revealed that six of the nine courses had very skewed grade distributions with most of the students receiving As and Bs in the course. Two other courses also had fairly skewed distributions with very few students in the lower grade categories. Finally, one of the courses had a fairly low enrollment (46 students).

Intercorrelations of the Various Measures of Academic Performance in College

The correlations among the different measures of academic performance within a subset were generally above .95 in SAT Sample 1 and SAT Sample 2. The one exception was the humanities subset, for which the correlations between the IRT-based measures and the weighted and unweighted grade point averages were around .90. The correlations of traditional FGPA with the other total measures of academic performance were also generally slightly lower (.88 to .92).

Predictive Validation Studies

A summary of the R^2 values obtained from the validation studies for the various criteria for the various subsets for SAT Sample 1 and SAT Sample 2 is presented in Table 3.1. A summary of the R^2 values obtained from the validation studies for the various total criteria for SAT Sample 1 and SAT Sample 2 is presented in Table 3.2.

The results of the predictive validation studies were very consistent

Table 3.1. Summary of R^2 Values Obtained From Validation Studies for Various Criteria for Various Subsets

Sample	Criterion	Nat. Sci,. Math, & Eng.	Social Sciences	Humanities
SAT 1	GRMθ	.2955	.2518	.1361
	PCMθ	.3079	.2539	.1454
	GRMETS	.2854	.2455	.1284
	PCMETS	.2951	.2524	.1302
	UFGPA	.2270	.2418	.1108
	WFGPA	.2227	.2418	.1083
SAT 2	GRMθ	.2947	.2270	.1751
	PCMθ	.3036	.2176	.1821
	GRMETS	.2883	.2237	.1633
	PCMETS	.2953	.2167	.1641
	UFGPA	.2458	.2048	.1330
	WFGPA	.2422	.2048	.1267

PCMθ: proficiency estimate from the partial credit model
PCMETS: estimated true score average from the partial credit model
GRMθ: proficiency estimate from the graded response model
GRMETS: estimated true score average from the graded response model
UFGPA: unweighted first-year grade point average
WFGPA: weighted first-year grade point average

Table 3.2. Summary R^2 Values Obtained From Validation Studies for Various Total Criteria

Criterion	SAT Sample 1	SAT Sample 2
GRMAVθ	.2833	.2886
PCMAVθ	.2927	.2895
GRMTETS	.2860	.2846
PCMTETS	.2824	.2831
TUFGPA	.2472	.2522
TWFGPA	.2451	.2497
TFGPA	.2053	.2243

PCMAVθ:	average proficiency estimate from the partial credit model
PCMTETS:	total estimated true score average from the partial credit model
GRMAVθ:	average proficiency estimate from the graded response model
GRMTETS:	total estimated true score average from the graded response model
TUFGPA:	total unweighted first-year grade point average
TWFGPA:	total weighted first-year grade point average
TFGPA:	traditional first-year grade point average

for the two samples. In all cases, the IRT-based measures of academic performance in college were more predictable than the classical test theory-based measures, when compared in terms of R^2 values. The largest differences in R^2 values occurred for the natural science, engineering, and mathematics subset. The differences between the R^2 values for the IRT-based criteria and the classical test theory-based criteria were smaller for the social sciences subset and for the humanities subset. Further, the total (averaged across the subsets) IRT-based criteria were also more predictable than the total classical test theory-based criteria. Finally, the total IRT-based criteria that were based on course grades from a very reduced subset of the courses taken by the students were more predictable than the traditional FGPA.

The estimated true score averages from the partial credit model and the graded response model were slightly less predictable than the proficiency estimates from the corresponding model across the subsets. However, differences in degree of restriction of range between the criteria from the IRT-based approach and the classical test theory-based approach do not appear to be the sole reason (or even a main reason) for the greater predictability of the proficiency estimates from the two polytomous models when compared to the predictability of unweighted and weighted first-year grade point averages.

Across each of the subsets, the criteria from the partial credit model were generally slightly more predictable than the corresponding criteria from the graded response model (usually in the third decimal place). This difference, however, is negligible and probably has little practical significance.

The results of the validation studies from this investigation, based on graded response model and partial credit model calibrations of first-year course grades from students at The University of Texas at Austin, also replicated the findings reported by Young (1990a) which were based on a Muraki's rating scale model (Muraki, 1990) calibration of four years of course grades from students at Stanford University.

Cross-Validation Studies

The results of the double-cross validation studies for SAT Sample 1 and SAT Sample 2 indicated that the R^2 values were very stable within each sample, regardless of which multiple linear regression equation was used to predict the criterion variable—the validation equation (the equation developed using the particular sample) or the cross-validation equation (the equation developed using the other sample). Overall, across the subsets, the difference between the R^2 values obtained from the two equations within a sample was generally less than .01.

DISCUSSION

The results of the predictive validation studies were extremely consistent for the two SAT samples. In both samples across all the subsets, the IRT-based criterion variables were more predictable than were the classical test theory-based unweighted and weighted first-year grade point averages, when compared in terms of R^2 values. In both of the samples, the largest difference between the R^2 values from the IRT-based approach and the classical test theory-based approach occurred for the natural science, engineering, and mathematics subset. The differences in the predictability of the IRT-based criteria and classical test theory-based criteria were slightly smaller for the social sciences subset and for the humanities subset. Finally, the total IRT-based criteria were more predictable than the total unweighted and weighted grade point averages, including the traditional first-year grade point average (the criterion actually used by the university).

The aforementioned results replicate the results reported by Young (1990a) that were obtained from a Muraki's rating scale model calibration of four years of course grades from students at Stanford University. Young, however, did not find any improvement in the predictability of first-year college academic performance for the social sciences subset and the humanities subset when the IRT-based criteria were used rather than FGPA. Thus, the slight improvement in predictability for the criteria from the partial credit and graded response models for the social sciences subset and the humanities subset that was found in this study suggests that these two polytomous models may be better suited for the scaling of course grades than Muraki's rating scale model. This possibility will need to be investigated in future research in this area through a direct comparison of the graded response model and the partial credit model with Muraki's rating scale model.

One of the primary purposes of this study was to compare the relative merits of the graded response model and the partial credit model when the models were used to scale course grades. Overall, there was very little difference in the predictability of the corresponding criteria from the two models within a subset. The partial credit model criteria were generally slightly more predictable than the corresponding criteria from the graded response model, but the differences were too small to be of any practical significance. The partial credit model also had fewer problems with nonconvergence of course parameter estimates. It was expected that the graded response model would be the preferred model because courses might differ greatly in their ability to discriminate among students of different proficiency levels; this was not found to be the case, however. Therefore, the partial credit model seems to be the preferred model because it had fewer problems with nonconvergence of course parameter estimates and it is a simpler model with fewer parameters to estimate.

The results of this study suggest that the use of polytomous item response theory models, such as the graded response model and the partial credit model, to improve the predictability of academic performance in college is a promising area of research. This finding concurs with previous research by Young (1991a). Further research in this area is needed, however. This study systematically compared two polytomous models, but the applicability of several other polytomous models to a measurement problem of this type has not yet been systematically investigated.

REFERENCES

Lord, F.M. (1980). *Applications of item response theory to practical testing problems*. Hillsdale, NJ: Erlbaum.

Linacre, J.M., & Wright, B.D. (1992). *BIGSTEPS* [Computer program]. Chicago: MESA Press.

Masters, G.N. (1982). A Rasch model for partial credit scoring. *Psychometrika,*
47, 149–174.

Muraki, E. (1990). Fitting a polytomous item response model to Likert-type
data. *Applied Psychological Measurement, 14*(1), 59–71.

Samejima, F. (1969). Estimation of latent ability using a response pattern of
graded scores. *Psychometrika Monograph Supplement,* No. 17.

Thissen, D. (1991). *MULTILOG* [Computer program]. Mooresville, IN: Scientific Software.

Willingham, W.W. (1990). Understanding yearly trends: A synthesis of re-
search findings. In W.W. Willingham, C. Lewis, R. Morgan, & L. Ramist,
Predicting College Grades: An Analysis of Institutional Trends Over Two
Decades (pp. 23–84). Princeton, NJ: Educational Testing Service.

Young, J.W. (1989). Developing a universal scale for grades: Investigating
predictive validity in college admissions (Doctoral dissertation, Stanford
University, 1988). *Dissertation Abstracts International, 50,* 1641A.

Young, J.W. (1990a). Adjusting the cumulative GPA using item response theory. *Journal of Educational Measurement, 27*(2), 175–186.

Young, J.W. (1990b). Are validity coefficients understated due to correctable
defects in the GPA? *Research in Higher Education, 31*(4), 319–325.

Young, J.W. (1991a). Gender bias in predicting college academic performance:
A new approach using item response theory. *Journal of Educational Mea-*
surement, 28(1), 37–47.

Young, J.W. (1991b). Improving the prediction of college performance of ethnic
minorities using the IRT-based GPA. *Applied Measurement in Education,*
4(3), 229–239.

APPENDIX

Calculation of Estimated True Score Averages

To calculate an estimated true score average for a student with a given
proficiency level, Θ, for a given subset of courses for the graded response model and the partial credit model, the following procedure was
used:

1. Calculate the probability that an individual with a given proficiency level, Θ, will earn a grade in each of the grade categories for
   a given course using one of the polytomous models.
2. Multiply the probability of earning a grade in a given grade category by the number of grade points for the category for the given
   course (i.e., A = 4, B = 3, C = 2, D = 1, F = 0) to get the estimated
   true score for the course.
3. Repeat steps 1 and 2 for each course that the student has taken in
   the given subset.
4. Calculate the sum of the estimated true scores for all of the

courses that the student has taken in the given subset and divide by the total number of courses the student has taken in the subset to get the student's estimated true score average for the subset.

Example:

The probability that a student with a given proficiency level, Θ, will earn a grade in each of the following grade categories for course 1 when the partial credit model is used is given below:

Probability of earning a grade in category 4 (A) = .24
Probability of earning a grade in category 3 (B) = .36
Probability of earning a grade in category 2 (C) = .20
Probability of earning a grade in category 1 (D) = .16
Probability of earning a grade in category 0 (F) = .04

The student's estimated true score for course 1 is calculated in the following manner:
Estimated true score

$$= (4 \times .24) + (3 \times .36) + (2 \times .20) + (1 \times .16) + (0 \times .04)$$
$$= .96 + 1.08 + .40 + .16 + 0$$
$$= 2.60$$

This procedure is repeated for each course that the student took in the subset, and the mean of the estimated true scores for all of the courses that the student took in the subset is calculated to obtain the student's estimated true score average for the subset.

chapter 4

An Empirical Comparison of Rasch and Mantel-Haenszel Procedures For Assessing Differential Item Functioning

E. Matthew Schulz
American College Testing

Carole Perlman, William K. Rice
Chicago Public Schools

Benjamin D. Wright
The University of Chicago

Although the Rasch model is not widely recognized as a method of choice for assessing differential item functioning (DIF) (Hills, 1989), a Rasch DIF analysis is fundamentally similar to the popular Mantel-Haenszel (MH) procedure for assessing item DIF. Both procedures fall into the one parameter, unidimensional, classification of item-analysis procedures. Linacre and Wright (1986) conclude that if one is not prepared to accept the validity of the Rasch model for the item under examination, the implicit assumptions of the MH procedure will not be satisfied either. Holland and Thayer (1988) show that the Rasch and

Mantel Haenszel procedures are equivalent when the Rasch model holds and:

1. all items except possibly the studied item exhibit no DIF,
2. the criterion for matching includes the studied item, and
3. the data are random samples from the focal and comparison groups.

Among the criteria investigators may consider when choosing a DIF-detection method, is the interpretability of DIF indices. Indices of DIF are more interpretable when they are expressed in the same scale units used to represent differences in item difficulty and differences in measures of examinees. The MH delta index of DIF, for example, is a rescaling of the MH log odds ratio that expresses DIF in units of the ETS (Educational Testing Service) scale of item difficulty. Testing programs that use Rasch measurement may prefer to use a procedure based on the Rasch model for detecting DIF if Rasch DIF indices are at least equivalent to MH DIF indices. The tendency of procedures based on the Rasch model to be more computationally intensive may not be a significant consideration in many computer environments.

A RASCH METHOD FOR DETECTING DIF

One Rasch method for assessing item DIF is described by Wright and Stone (1979), Wright and Masters (1982), and Wright, Mead, and Draba (1976). The method is to perform a Rasch analysis of comparison group data (group 1) and another of focal group data (group 2) to produce two estimates of item difficulty for each item and two standard errors of estimate, $\hat{\delta}_{i,1}$, $SE_{\hat{\delta}_{i,1}}$, and $\hat{\delta}_{i,2}$, $SE_{\hat{\delta}_{i,2}}$. (The focal group is the minority group.) The mean difference in achievement between groups is controlled by setting the average item difficulty to zero:

$$\sum_1^N \hat{\delta}_{i,1} = \sum_1^N \hat{\delta}_{i,2} = 0 \tag{1}$$

The logit difference between paired item difficulty estimates from comparison and focal groups:

$$\hat{\Delta}_R = \hat{\delta}_1 - \hat{\delta}_2, \tag{2}$$

is a Rasch measure of DIF. The standardized Rasch DIF index is:

$$Z_R = \frac{\hat{\Delta}_R}{\sqrt{(SE\delta_{i1})^2 + (SE\delta_{i2})^2}} \tag{3}$$

Under the hypothesis of no DIF, the expected value of $\hat{\Delta}_R$ is 0, and Z_R has mean zero and variance 1. Positive values of $\hat{\Delta}_R$ and Z_R indicate DIF favoring the focal group. Negative values indicate DIF against the focal group.

Although this particular Rasch model-based procedure is called "the" Rasch procedure in this paper, other procedures based on the Rasch model for detecting item DIF have been developed (Kelderman, 1989; Moore, this volume).

MANTEL-HAENSZEL METHOD FOR DETECTING DIF

The Mantel-Haenszel procedure tests the hypothesis that the comparison and focal groups perform equally on the studied item, conditional on ability. Ability is usually represented by the total test score including the studied item. "Thin matching" means that each total test score is a separate ability level within which focal and comparison group students are expected to have equal probability of correctly answering the item under study. "Fat matching" means that an ability level consists of two or more contiguous total test scores. Although thin matching is less arbitrary and more precisely matches groups on ability, incomplete 2×2 tables are more likely to occur within ability levels, particularly at extreme scores.

At each of the K ability levels a 2×2 table is formed containing the numbers of examinees in each group who answered the item correctly/incorrectly. If A_k and C_k are the numbers of focal and comparison group examinees at level k who answered the item correctly, B_k and D_k are the corresponding numbers who answered the item incorrectly, and N_k is the total number of examinees at score level k, the common (for all K ability levels) odds ratio estimator is:

$$\hat{\alpha}_{MH} = \frac{\Sigma_k A_k D_k / N_k}{\Sigma_k B_k C_k / N_k} . \tag{4}$$

The Mantel-Haenszel null hypothesis for the item under study is Ho: $\alpha_{MH} = 1$. Under the conditions of equivalence between Rasch and MH procedures, $\alpha_{MH} = \exp(\Delta_R)$ (Linacre and Wright, 1986; Holland and Thayer, 1988; Zwick, 1990), where Δ_R is the quantity estimated in equation 2. The transformation of the estimated odds ratio to the ETS delta scale is:

$$\hat{\Delta}_{MH} = -2.35 * \ln(\hat{\alpha}_{MH}). \tag{5}$$

It therefore stands to reason that when Rasch and MH procedures are equivalent we also have the equality: $\Delta_{MH} = -2.35 * \Delta_R$. The standard error estimate for $\hat{\Delta}_{MH}$ (Phillips and Holland, 1986) is the counterpart of the standard error of $\hat{\Delta}_R$ in the denominator in equation 3, though the statistical significance test for MH DIF does not rely on this estimate.

The MH significance test for DIF is a chi-square test statistic, denoted MH-CHISQ. This statistic is computed from the K 2×2 tables where performance on the item (correct/incorrect) is crossed with group membership within ability levels (see Holland and Thayer, 1988 for formulae). Under the null hypothesis, the MH chi-square test statistic has an approximate chi square distribution with 1 degree of freedom. By taking the square root of a 1 degree of freedom chi square variable and attaching + or − sign randomly, one obtains a standard normal variable under the null hypothesis. If the indicator variable, $I = 1$ if $\hat{\alpha}_{MH} > 1$, $I = -1$ if $\hat{\alpha}_{MH} < 1$ is uncorrelated with MH-CHISQR, then:

$$Z_{MH} = I * \sqrt{MH\text{--}CHISQR} . \tag{6}$$

is a standard normal variable under the null hypothesis. The variable, Z_{MH}, is comparable to Z_R in both sign and magnitude.

EMPIRICAL COMPARISONS OF MH AND RASCH DIF PROCEDURES

Empirical studies suggest that Rasch and MH indices of DIF are equivalent when comparison and focal groups (contrast groups) have approximately the same average score on the matching variable, but differ when their average scores differ substantially. In an empirical comparison of four DIF detection methods, Perlman, Berzruczko, Junker, Reynolds, Rice, and Schulz (1988), found that the correlation between Z_R and Z_{MH}, corrected for attenuation, was 1 when contrasts were based on gender, but was only about .8 in contrasts between race groups. This difference appeared to be related to how similar contrast groups were in average total test score. Engelhard, Anderson, and Gabrielson (1990) compared Rasch and MH procedures for contrasts (Black/White) having larger differences on the matching variable than those reported in Perlman et al. Although they were satisfied overall with the agreement between methods, they concluded that additional research was needed to determine why the correlations, which were generally lower than .8 at group sizes comparable to Perlman et al., were not even higher.

There is currently mixed evidence that MH DIF procedures tend to show items as favoring the higher scoring group. In the Perlman et al. and Engelhard et al. studies, the MH procedure, but not the Rasch procedure, has this systematic trend. Both studies, however, used fat matching and Perlman, et al., excluded the studied item from the total score used for matching. Holland and Thayer (1988) recommend thin matching and including the studied item in the matching criterion. Raju, Bode, and Larson (1989) show that the tendency of MH DIF to favor the higher scoring group decreases significantly when the studied item is included in the total score used for matching, and decreases also as the number of ability levels for fat matching increases. However, Raju, et al. did not use thin matching, and used a maximum of 10 ability levels in fat matching; with 10 ability levels, the average estimated α_{MH} was still greater than 1, favoring the higher scoring group.

Empirical comparisons of the sensitivity and/or reliability of Rasch and MH procedures are equivocal. On one hand, evidence suggests that the Rasch procedure is at least as reliable or more reliable than the MH procedure. Engelhard et al. (1990) reported that Rasch DIF indices are more sensitive and reliable than MH DIF indices in terms of internal Pearson correlations and number of items flagged. Perlman, et al., found that the Rasch procedure was as reliable as the MH procedure. On the other hand, the misfit of real data to Rasch model assumptions may invalidate these comparisons.

Conceptual Basis for Empirical Comparison

More careful research may be able to shed light on these issues. In this study, we attempted to assess the differences between Rasch and Mantel-Haenszel procedures through a comparison of the empirical distributions and values of Z_R and Z_{MH}, within and across items under various conditions of sample size, achievement difference between contrast groups, and variants of the MH procedure (fat versus thin matching). We chose to focus on Z_R and Z_{MH} rather than on indices of DIF magnitude because Z_R and Z_{MH} can be compared to a normal (0,1) distribution. This comparison is directly related to the practice of flagging items for DIF based on Z_R or MH-CHISQR. (We also performed analyses using $\hat{\Delta}_R$ and $\hat{\Delta}_{MH}$, and found that these indices gave results similar to those obtained using the standardized indices.)

When comparison and focal groups are randomly equivalent, we expect Z_R and Z_{MH} to have mean zero and variance 1 both within and across items. Within-item variance is the error variance of the statistic, which should be 1 for a statistic distributed as standard normal under the null hypothesis. Since the item characteristic curves should be randomly equivalent between randomly equivalent groups, the variance of Z_R and Z_{MH} across items should only reflect the error variance of these statistics within items. This expectation is not strictly based on the hypothesis of "No DIF" for a particular item, because real data cannot satisfy the conditions for evaluating and comparing Rasch and MH DIF indices with respect to this hypothesis. True DIF can only be simulated. Moreover, we already know that real data will not fit the Rasch model, as no data fit any useful model. Nevertheless, since these procedures are only used with real data in practice, the behavior of their indices when groups are randomly equivalent seems of legitimate interest to practitioners. Real data from randomly equivalent groups is as close to "No DIF" as will occur in practice.

Whether comparison and focal groups are or are not randomly equivalent, we expect the mean Z_R or Z_{MH} across items to be zero. With randomly equivalent groups, the mean DIF across items should equal the expected zero DIF within items. Since DIF is a zero-sum variable in both the Rasch and MH procedures (due to matching or centering item difficulties on zero in both groups), mean DIF should also equal zero when groups are not randomly equivalent. This expectation may apply strictly only to indices of DIF magnitude, but indices of statistical significance should conform to this expectation approximately.

When groups are not randomly equivalent we expect the across-item, empirical *variance* of Z_R and Z_{MH} to be greater than 1, and the *within*-item empirical variance to remain at 1. Item characteristic curves should differ for non-randomly equivalent groups, resulting in systemmatically nonzero Z_R and Z_{MH} for all items. Repeated computations of Z_R and Z_{MH} for a given item using independent sets of data for a given contrast should center around a nonzero mean, but may have an error variance of 1 around that mean. Pooled, within-item variance should therefore be 1. Across items, the variance should be greater than 1 due to Z_R or Z_{MH} being nonzero for some or all items and the fact that DIF has a zero sum across items. This expectation has a direct practical implication for flagging items on the basis of Z_R or MH-

CHISQR. The number of items flagged will be above the alpha-level set by the investigator to the extent the across-item variance of Z_R or Z_{MH} is greater than 1. A difference between methods in this respect may be called a difference in sensitivity.

Estimates of the reliability of the Rasch or MH method within conditions are based on the conceptualization:

$$Total\ Var = Across\text{-}Item\ Variance$$
$$Error\ Var = Within\text{-}Item\ Variance$$

$$Reliability = \frac{Total\ Var\text{-}Error\ Var}{Total\ Var}$$

We verified that this estimate equals the empirical root mean squared correlation among repeated estimates in this study. This conceptualization was used because it is more informative and shows how reliability and sensitivity are related, but differ.

METHOD

The data consisted of 60,000 records of examinees' responses to 46 items in the Minimum Proficiency Skills Test (MPST) Item Bank (Bezruczko and Reynolds, 1987), and is the same data that was used in Perlman, et al. These items were common to two, 63-item MPST test forms that were administered in 1984 and 1985 to approximately 30,000 eighth graders each. The MPST is structured into a three-subscale test (language arts, computation, and problem solving), has an alpha reliability of approximately .90, and a principal component that accounts for 30% of test score variance (Reynolds and Bezruczko, 1989). The items in this study had not previously been screened for statistical DIF, although bias review panels were used. All items on the test were dichotomously scored, multiple choice items. There were 30,000 males, 30,000 females, 19,980 Race 1 and 20,040 Race 2. Males and females performed similarly—the male mean score was 32.0, while the female mean score was 32.1. Race groups performed unequally—mean scores were 30.0 for Race 1, but 35.5 for Race 2. Because race groups differed significantly in achievement, and the identity of races is not germane to this study, we refer to the race groups simply as Race 1 and Race 2.

Thirty samples each of 100, 300, or 1,000 records were drawn from each gender group (males or females) without replacement. Thirty samples each of 200 or 666 records were drawn from each race group without replacement. Sixty samples each of 100, 300, or 1,000 records per sample were drawn from the population of 60,000 records. These samples provided focal and comparison groups for 30 male/female contrasts, 30 Race 1/Race 2 contrasts, and 30 randomly equivalent group contrasts at each of the corresponding sample sizes. Gender contrasts represented equal achievement contrasts. Race contrasts represented unequal achievement contrasts.

The DIF analyses were performed so that a positive value of Z_{MH} or Z_R means that the item favors females in the female/male contrast or Race 1 (the lower scoring race) in the Race 1/Race 2 contrast. The Rasch procedure for DIF detection was performed with the computer programs MSCALE (Wright, et al., 1987), and LINK (Schulz, 1984). MSCALE uses the UCON estimation algorithm (Wright and Panchapakesan, 1969). The MH procedures were performed with a computer program written by Raju (1988). For fat matching in the MH procedure, the population of 60,000 MPST total scores was divided into seven levels containing approximately equal numbers of students. The raw score boundaries for these levels were the same for all contrasts.

Each condition in this study produced a 46 row by 30 column matrix of Z_R or Z_{MH} estimates from 30 replications on 46 items. Within-item standardized DIF variance was the pooled variance of the statistic within items (rows of the matrix). Across-item standardized DIF variance was the variance of the statistic around the mean (mean of 1380, or 46×30 observations). The standard error of the mean Z_R or Z_{MH} was estimated by the square root of the across-item variance divided by 1,380.

In order to assess the relationship between standardized DIF indices and the fit of data to the Rasch model, three standardized, weighted item fit statistics (Wright and Masters, 1982) were estimated for each item using a) all 60,000 records, b) Race 1 records only, and c) Race 2 records only. Standardized item fit indices have a distribution of mean zero and variance 1 when data fits the model (Wright and Stone, 1979). Items with negative fit tend to favor higher scoring students, while items with positive fit tend to favor lower scoring students. Item fit statistics were compared at the item-level to a) the difference between Z_R and Z_{MH} in the gender contrast (1,000 per group), b) the difference between Z_R and Z_{MH} in the race contrast (666 per group), and c) Z_R and Z_{MH} in the race contrast (666 per group).

RESULTS

The top panel of Table 4.1 shows the empirical within-item variance of the standardized DIF indices, Z_R and Z_{MH}. Within-item variance was

Table 4.1. Variance and Reliability of Standardized DIF Indices Based on 30 Replications

	Contrast Groups	Group Size	Rasch	Mantel-Haenszel	
				Thin	Fat
	Randomly Equivalent	100	.88	.70	.72
		300	.90	.81	.82
		1000	.95	.90	.91
Within-item variance	Equal Achievement (gender)	100	.92	.74	.77
		300	.94	.91	.90
		1000	.67	1.00	1.00
	Unequal Achievement (race)	200	.89	.79	.80
		666	.94	.91	.91
	Randomly Equivalent	100	.88	.69	.72
		300	.90	.81	.82
		1000	.94	.90	.90
Across-item variance	Equal Achievement (gender)	100	1.37	1.00	1.10
		300	2.26	2.02	2.11
		1000	5.66	5.42	5.55
	Unequal Achievement (race)	200	1.41	1.24	1.28
		666	2.56	2.47	2.54
	Equal Achievement (gender)	100	.33	.26	.30
		300	.58	.55	.57
		1000	.83	.82	.82
Reliability	Unequal Achievement (race)	200	.37	.36	.37
		666	.63	.63	.64

Note: Expected within-item variance = 1. Expected across-item variance = 1 for randomly equivalent groups, greater than 1 for gender and race contrasts. Fat matching: seven ability levels. Thin matching: one ability level per raw total score.

less than expected (1) for both Rasch and MH procedures under most conditions. Within-item variance ranged from .70 to the expected value, 1.0, and tended to be lower for smaller sample sizes and randomly equivalent groups; under these conditions, both thin and fat matching variants of the MH procedure had slightly lower within-item variance than the Rasch procedure.

The middle panel of Table 4.1 shows the variance of standardized DIF across items. For randomly equivalent groups, across-item variance was equivalent to within-item variance as expected, though this meant across-item variance was substantially less than 1.

For non-randomly equivalent groups, across-item variance exceeded within-item variance. Across-item variance in the thin-matching MH procedure, however, was only 1 in the gender contrast at 100 per group, and tended to be less than in the Rasch procedure under all conditions. This means that the MH procedure of thin matching would flag fewer items than the Rasch procedure and would not flag items above the chance level when group sizes are small (100 per group) even though DIF exists.

The bottom panel of Table 3.1 contains the estimated reliabilities of the standardized DIF indices. Overall, the reliabilities are very similar. For the female/male contrast, reliabilities increase from approximately .3 with 100 per group, to .83 with 1,000 per group. For the race contrast, reliabilities increase from approximately .37 with 200 per group, to .63 with 666 per group. The MH procedure is slightly less reliable than the Rasch procedure with 100 females/males per group. Thin matching is also slightly less reliable than fat matching.

The top panel of Table 4.2 shows across-item mean standardized DIF for each condition, and the bottom panel shows the number of standard errors each mean is from zero. When contrast groups are randomly

Table 4.2. Average Standardized DIF Index Across Items

| | Contrast Groups | Group Size | Rasch | Mantel-Haenszel | |
				Thin	Fat
	Randomly Equivalent	100	−.01	.01	.02
		300	.01	.01	.02
		1000	.00	.00	.00
Mean	Equal Achievement (gender)	100	−.03	.02	.02
		300	−.06	.05	.09
		1000	−.11	.11	.17
	Unequal Achievement (race)	200	.02	.02	−.08
		666	.02	.05	−.20
	Randomly Equivalent	100	−.28	−.27	.68
		300	.28	.29	.66
		1000	.08	.09	−.01
Standard Errors from Zero	Equal Achievement (gender)	100	−1.10	.76	.67
		300	−1.40	1.26	2.19
		1000	−1.78	1.74	2.52
	Unequal Achievement (race)	200	.62	0.82	−2.75
		666	.40	1.15	−4.40

Note: Expected mean is zero. Fat matching: seven ability levels. Thin matching: one ability level per raw total score.

equivalent, both Rasch and MH procedures had mean standardized item DIF less than .5 standard errors from zero.

With equally achieving, gender contrast groups Rasch and MH indices trended in opposite directions, but neither mean was significantly different from zero at 1,000 per group. The MH trend favored females (mean = .11), while the Rasch trend favored males (mean = −.11).

For unequally achieving, race contrast groups, mean standardized DIF was not significantly different from zero in the thin matching MH procedure and the Rasch procedure. The fat matching MH procedure tended to favor the higher scoring race, with the across-item mean being over four standard errors from zero when there were 666 examinees per group.

Figure 4.1 shows that Rasch and thin-matching MH procedures are

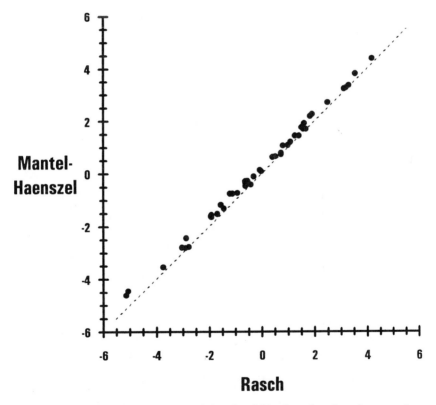

Figure 4.1. Standard normal statistics for DIF when focal and comparison groups have equal achievement (female/male, 1,000 per group). Dashed line is identity.

nearly equivalent for equally-achieving, gender group contrasts. The correlation of Z_R and Z_{MH} was .99, as reported in Perlman et al. (1988), and was as high as possible considering the error variance of these indices. The plotted points tended, however, to lie slightly above the identity line. This shift reflects the opposite trend in mean DIF these procedures have in the gender contrast as shown in Table 4.2. Figure 4.2 shows that the Z_R minus Z_{MH} difference in the gender contrast is uncorrelated with item fit to the Rasch model. The difference tends to be slightly negative, reflecting the mean differences in Table 4.2 ($-.11$ versus .11).

For unequally achieving, race contrast groups Z_{MH} and Z_R are not equivalent, as shown in Figure 4.3. The correlation of Z_R and Z_{MH} was .81, and was less than the maximum correlation possible. The Z_R mi-

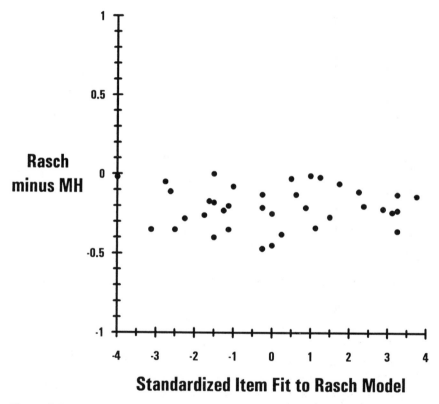

Figure 4.2. Difference between Rasch and MH standard normal statistics when focal and comparison groups have equal achievement (female/male, 1,000 per group) as a function of standardized item fit to the Rasch model.

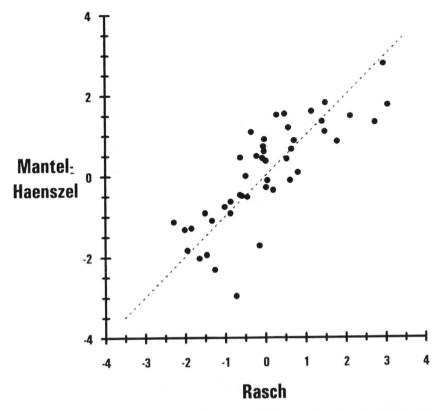

Figure 4.3.   Standard normal statistics for DIF when focal and comparison groups have unequal achievement (race 1/race 2, 666 per group). Dashed line is identity.

nus Z_{MH} difference is related to item fit to the Rasch model, as shown in Figure 4.4. The difference correlated .96 with the item fit statistic, and was smallest (in absolute value) for items that had fit statistics near zero.

The standardized item fit statistics plotted in Figures 4.2 and 4.4 were based on all 60,000 records, and ranged from approximately −6 to 7. This dispersion is not unusually high for such a large sample size. Fit statistics based on all 60,000 records correlated .92 and .96 with fit statistics based respectively on Race 1 and Race 2 exclusively.

The relationship between item fit statistics and the Z_R minus Z_{MH} difference in Figure 4.3 arises from the tendency of *both* Z_R and Z_{MH} to vary systematically, but differently, with item fit to the Rasch model. The Z_R index correlated $+.32$ ($p < .05$), while Z_{MH} correlated $-.26$ ($p <$

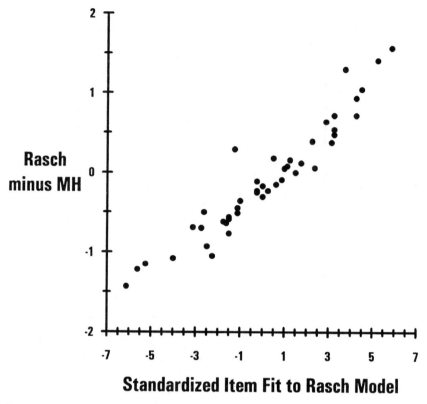

Figure 4.4. Difference between Rasch and MH standard normal statistics when focal and comparison groups have unequal achievement (race 1/race 2, 666 per group) as a function of standardized item fit to the Rasch model.

.05) with item fit statistics based on all 60,000 records. Correlations were similar with fit statistics based exclusively on Race 1 (.35 and −.22) or Race 2 (.16 and −.39) records.

DISCUSSION

The Rasch procedure was equivalent to the MH procedure using thin matching for the equally achieving gender contrast groups in this study. Corrected for attenuation, Rasch and MH indices of statistical significance (Z_R and Z_{MH}) correlated near 1. The Rasch procedure tended to favor males and the MH procedure females, but neither tendency reached statistical significance at 1,000 per group. It should be emphasized that this practical level of equivalence was found when data did not fit the Rasch model, as shown by the range of standardized item fit statistics (-6 to 7). (The level of standardized item misfit in these data is not unusual, given the large sample size used for estimation (60,000).) Further research is needed to generalize these findings to other tests and other demographic contrasts in which groups have similar levels of achievement.

Our results also suggest that the Rasch procedure may be a more sensitive and reliable DIF detection method for small sample sizes and equally achieving groups. When group size was 100 in the gender contrast Z_R (Rasch) had across-item variance of 1.37 and a reliability of .33, while Z_{MH} (Mantel-Haenszel) indices had across-item variance of 1.0 and a reliability of .26. The Z_{MH} indices in this condition would not have flagged items for DIF above the chance level if these indices were compared to a normal distribution (or equivalently, MH-CHISQR compared to a 1 df chi square distribution). Given the equivalence of Z_R and Z_{MH} at larger sizes of equally achieving gender-contrast groups, it does not seem plausible that at smaller sizes of these contrast groups, the more sensitive Z_R indices could be less valid than the Z_{MH} indices.

If the Rasch procedure is generally more sensitive and reliable for equally achieving groups and small sample size, it is probably because it uses more of the data than the thin-matching MH procedure. When all levels of the total score are to be used for matching, small samples lead to incomplete 2×2 tables for some levels of achievement. The MH procedure cannot use data from incomplete 2×2 tables. The resulting loss of data may reduce both the reliability and sensitivity of the MH procedure relative to the Rasch procedure, which uses all the available data.

Fat matching in the MH procedure may solve this inequity, but does not appear to match examinees adequately when contrast groups have unequal achievement. The tendency of MH DIF to favor the higher scoring group in both Perlman et al., and Engelhard et al. was probably due in whole or in part to using fat matching. In the present study, fat matching, but not thin matching, also produced net DIF favoring the higher scoring group. Evidently, the group with the higher average test score overall, also has a higher score within "fat" ability levels.

When contrast groups do not have the same level of achievement, Rasch and MH procedures do not agree as well ($r = .81$). This level of agreement nevertheless may be adequate in many practical applications of DIF detection methods (Engelhard, et al., 1990; Perlman, et al., 1988).

The correlation of Rasch and MH DIF indices with item fit statistics provides some insight into the nature of their difference when contrast groups differ in achievement. Items with positive fit are generally less discriminating, which in this context means they favor the lower-scoring group. Positive DIF in this study means the item favors the lower scoring group. The positive correlation between Rasch DIF and Rasch item fit means that in the Rasch DIF procedure an item which favors low-scorers by virtue of low discrimination, is more likely to be flagged as having DIF in favor of the lower scoring group. This makes sense because the Rasch DIF procedure estimates item difficulty separately using groups that differ in terms of their average performance on the test, as well as on the demographic variable used for grouping.

The mechanism for the negative correlation between Z_{MH} and indices of item misfit to the Rasch model is unclear. Zwick (1990) shows that when data conform to a 2-PL model and contrast groups have unequal achievement, the MH delta should indicate DIF favoring the higher scoring group for more discriminating items. This tendency should have produced a *positive* correlation between item fit and Z_{MH} (which was the situation for Z_R). While our results were consistent with Zwick's general conclusion that the MH result will favor the higher scoring group on some items and the lower scoring group on others when contrast groups differ in ability, the relationship to item fit was the opposite to what we expected. It should be noted that Zwick's predictions concerned data that fits the 2-PL model, whereas, in our study, the Rasch model and MH procedure were applied to real data.

Investigators interested in item-by-group interactions, per se, should be cautious in applying either the Rasch or the MH procedure to groups of unequal achievement on the matching variable. DIF indices from both procedures appear to be affected by item-by-ability interactions as well, as indicated by their correlation with Rasch item fit statistics. One solution to this problem is to use a comparison group that matches the ability distribution of the focal group. Because comparison groups are usually vastly larger than focal (i.e., minority) groups, it should be possible to use stratified random sampling to construct a comparison group that is large, and matches the achievement distribution of the focal group.

Another strategy is to make use of Rasch item fit statistics. It is important to realize that all forms of misfit to the Rasch model—item-by-achievement interactions as well as item-by-group interactions—are potential threats to the validity of certain test-based inferences. Masters (1988), shows how items with negative misfit, which tend to be highly discriminating, can reduce the validity of test-based inferences. Test developers who measure item DIF in order to improve the validity of their test-based inferences should not limit their concern to item-by-demographic group interactions, but consider other violations of their assumptions as well. These assumptions include equal item discrimination and unidimensionality whenever total scores based on number correct are used to represent performance. Highly discriminating items have the same effect as DIF against the focal group, when the focal group has lower achievement than the comparison group. Indices of item fit to the Rasch model may ultimately be more useful than traditional DIF indices.

REFERENCES

Bezruczko, N., & Reynolds, A.J. (1987). Minimum Proficiency Skills Test: 1987 item pilot report. *Citywide Report 87–1,* Chicago: Chicago Public Schools.

Engelhard, G. Jr., Anderson, D., & Gabrielson, S. (1990). An empirical comparison of Mantel-Haenszel and Rasch procedures for studying differential item functioning on teacher certification tests. *Journal of Research and Development in Education, 23*(3), 172–179.

Hills, J.R. (1989). Screening for potentially biased items in testing programs. *Educational Measurement, Issues and Practice, 8*(4), 5–11.

Holland, P.W. & Thayer, D.T. (1988). Differential item performance and the Mantel-Haenszel procedure. In H. Wainer & H. Braun (Eds.), *Test validity* (pp. 129–145). Hillsdale, New Jersey: Lawrence Erlbaum Associates, Inc.

Kelderman, H. (1988). Item bias detection using loglinear IRT. *Psychometrika, 54,* 223–245.

Linacre, J.M., & Wright, B.D. (1986). *Item bias: Mantel-Haenszel and the Rasch Model.* (Research Memorandom No. 39). Chicago, IL: University of Chicago, MESA Psychometric Laboratory.

Masters, G.N. (1988). Item discrimination: When more is worse. *Journal of Educational Measurement, 25*(1), 15–29.

Moore, S. (1996). Estimating differential item functioning in the polytomous case with the random coefficients multinomial logit model. In G. Engelhard, Jr. & M. Wilson (Eds.) *Objective Measurement: Theory Into Practice Volume 3,* Norwood, NJ: Ablex, (219–238).

Perlman, C.L., Bezruczko, N., Junker, L.K., Reynolds, A.J., Rice, W.K., & Schulz, E.M. (1988). *The stability of four methods for estimating item bias.* Paper presented at the annual meeting of the American Educational Research Association, New Orleans, LA.

Phillips, A., & Holland, P.W. (1986). *A new estimator for the variance of the Mantel-Haenszel log odds ratio estimator.* (Technical Report No. 86–67). Princeton, NJ: Educational Testing Service.

Raju, N.S. (1988). *MHDIF* [A FORTRAN program for assessing differential item functioning with the Mantel-Haenszel technique]. Chicago, IL: Department of Psychology, Illinois Institute of Technology.

Raju, N.S., Bode, R.K., & Larson, V.S. (1989). An empirical assessment of the Mantel-Haenszel statistic for studying differential item performance. *Applied Measurement in Education, 2,* 1–13.

Reynolds, A.J., & Bezruczko, N. (1989). Assessing the construct validity of a life skills competency test. *Educational and Psychological Measurement, 49,* 183–193.

Schulz, E.M. (1984). *LINK* [A FORTRAN program for comparing paired Rasch estimates and linking tests through common items or persons]. Chicago, IL: University of Chicago, MESA Psychometric Laboratory.

Wright, B.D., & Masters, G.N. (1982). *Rating scale analysis.* Chicago, IL: MESA Press.

Wright, B.D., Mead, R.J., & Draba, R. (1976). *Detecting and correcting test item bias with a logistic response model* (Research Memorandum No. 22). Chicago, IL: University of Chicago, MESA Psychometric Laboratory.

Wright, B.D., & Panchapakasan, N. (1969). A procedure for sample-free item analysis. *Educational and Psychological Measurement, 29,* 23–48.

Wright, B.D., Schulz, E.M., Congdon, R.T., & Rossner, M. (1987). *MSCALE* [A FORTRAN program for comparing paired Rasch estimates and linking tests through common items or persons]. Chicago, IL: University of Chicago, MESA Psychometric Laboratory.

Wright, B.D., & Stone, M.H. (1979). *Best test design.* Chicago: MESA Press.

Zwick, R. (1990). When do item response function and Mantel-Haenszel definitions of differential item functioning coincide? *Journal of Educational Statistics, 15*(3), 185–197.

part two
The Many-Facet Rasch (Facets) Model

chapter 5

Generalizability Theory and Many-Facet Rasch Measurement

John M. Linacre
University of Chicago

Performance assessment requires a rater to evaluate the quality of an examinee's performance on a task or performance item. The rater's evaluation is expressed as a qualitatively based rating on a rating scale. The numerical values assigned to the qualitative ratings obtained by each examinee are summed into a raw score. This raw score summarizes the examinee's performance level for decision-makers. But the raw score is obscured, to a greater or lesser extent, by variation in rater severity and item difficulty, and also examinee–rater–item interactions, rating scale non-linearity and random noise.

According to Cronbach, Gleser, Nanda & Rajaratnam (1972), "The score on which the decision is to be based is only one of many scores that might serve the same purpose . . . The ideal datum on which to base the decision would be something like the person's mean score over all acceptable observations, which we shall call his universe score. . . Knowing that observed score and universe score are not identical, the decision-maker will want to take the discrepancy into account. One way to do this is to accompany each (observed score) by an expression of uncertainty. Another possibility is to correct the observed score in some manner so that it better approximates the universe score; this corrected value will also have uncertainty." Thus, there are two approaches for managing the discrepancy between observed raw scores and universe scores.

Generalizability theory (G-Theory) follows Cronbach's first approach —"to take the discrepancy into account". G-Theory concerns itself with discovering how similar the observed raw scores might be to any other raw scores the examinees might obtain under identical circumstances. G-theory considers the examinees as a random group. Its aim is to estimate the error variance associated with examinee raw scores, but not to correct any examinee's raw score for the particular raters, tasks or items that the examinee encountered. The finalé of a G-Theory analysis is a reliability coefficient, "the generalizability coefficient", that summarizes the correlation between the sample of examinees' unobservable "universe" scores and the scores that happen to have been observed. This reliability is only generalizable to identical situations because all the variance components (main effects, interactions and random error) must maintain their sampled values. This is the "observation is a sample from a defined universe" requirement (Cronbach et al., p. 366).

From the decision-maker's viewpoint, the smaller the unwanted variances relative to the universe score variance, i.e., the higher the reliability, the fairer the test overall. No attempt is made to correct an individual examinee's raw score for difficulty of items encountered or for severity of raters performing the rating. Since a child's uncorrected raw score is reported as its measure, "conclusions about a child's [performance] would depend on the luck of the draw—a liberal rater rather than a stringent one" (Shavelson & Webb, 1991, p. 8).

Many-facet Rasch measurement (MFRM) follows Cronbach's second approach—"to correct the observed score in some manner." MFRM concerns itself with obtaining from each examinee's non-linear, rating-scale-dependent raw score a linear measure corrected for the particular raters, tasks or items encountered by that examinee. MFRM considers *each* examinee as an individual, and attempts to liberate, as far as statistically possible, each examinee's measure from the distributional details of the other examinees, items and raters that happen to be in the same analysis. The local error distribution for each examinee measure is used to ascertain the measure's precision and statistical validity. The finalé of a MFRM analysis is thus a linear measure of each examinee's performance level, qualified by its standard error and quality-control fit statistics. When the data approximately meet the "unidimensionality" and "invariance" requirements (Andrich, 1988), MFRM measures generalize to qualitatively similar, but quantitatively different, situations, such as adding harder items to a math test, or including lenient raters on a judging panel.

From the decision-maker's viewpoint, MFRM examinee measures are fairer than raw scores, provided that the locally relevant data fit the MFRM model. Discovery of local misfit, for example, an idiosyncratic rater or data entry errors, may disqualify some ratings, but do not invalidate the measurement process. Widespread, dramatic misfit of the data to the model suggests that the raw scores themselves have doubtful meaning, e.g., there are ambiguous rating scale category definitions.

A decision-maker's criteria for selection of an analytic approach are clear. If it is important to estimate the similarity between the observed raw scores of this group of examinees and the raw scores that similar groups of examinees might obtain under identical circumstances, then G-Theory may be helpful. But, if it is important to estimate for each examinee a measure as free as possible of the particularities of the components that generated the raw score, then MFRM is essential.

G-THEORY ANALYSIS

G-Theory proceeds in two stages. The generalizability study (G-Study) estimates variance components from a "pilot" data set. The decision study (D-Study) uses these estimates for decision-making directly from the pilot data, or for the design and analysis of further data collection on which decisions will be based.

Kenderski, reported in Shavelson and Webb (1991, p. 8), offers the pilot data set shown in Table 5.1, with fictitious identifying names added. Nine-year-old children were tape-recorded while solving mathematics problems in class, and again three weeks later. Two raters counted, independently, the number of times each child asked for help from other children. Children asked for help between 0 and 4 times.

The data is modelled as a sum of components in the raw-score metric:

$$X_{cro} = \mu_{gm} + \mu_c + \mu_r + \mu_o + \mu_{cr} + +\mu_{co} + +\mu_{ro} + \mu_{cro,e} \quad (1)$$

where

X_{cro} = the observed raw score count for child c by rater r on occasion o

μ_{gm} = the grand mean of the raw scores

μ_c = the effect for child c

μ_r = the effect for rater r

μ_o = the effect for occasion o

μ_{cr} = the interaction effect between child c and rater r

Table 5.1. How Many Times Does Each 9-Year-Old Child Ask for Help from Other Children to Solve Math Problems in Class[a]?

Occasion:	First		3 weeks later		Both
Child Rater:	Sue	Lucy	Sue	Lucy	Raw Score
Anne	4	4	3	4	15
Betty	3	4	1	2	10
Charles	1	2	2	1	6
David	2	2	1	0	5
Ethel	1	1	2	1	5
Fred	1	1	1	2	5
George	1	2	1	1	5
Harriet	1	2	1	1	5
Ida	2	1	1	1	5
Jenny	0	1	1	2	4
Kate	1	2	0	1	4
Luke	2	2	0	0	4
Mary	1	1	1	0	3

[a] Data from Kenderski, reported in Shavelson & Webb (1991, p.8)

μ_{co} = the interaction effect between child c and occasion o

μ_{ro} = the interaction effect between rater r and occasion o

$\mu_{cro,e}$ = the interaction effect between child c, rater r and occasion o, combined with, and indistinguishable from, random error, e.

In a G-Study, equation (1) is applied to the pilot data in Table 5.1, via ANOVA, to yield the raw score effect variances. Though the individual effect sizes, μ_c, would provide an estimate of each child's propensity to ask for help, it is not these individual effect values, but their distribution, summarized as variances, that is fundamental to G-Theory. The observed variances of the effects are shown in Table 5.2 as ANOVA mean-squares. The variance of the occasion effect, 3.77, appears much greater than that of the child–occasion (co) interaction, 0.85. But the ANOVA results are misleading. The mean-squares are themselves composites in which the variance of each effect has been inflated by other variances identified with interactions and error. Thus Table 5.2 identifies how the expected mean-squares, estimated by the observed ANOVA mean-squares, decompose into underlying variance components as though each child had been observed once on one occasion. The child–occasion mean-square, 0.85, is modelled to be compounded with random error, $\sigma^2_{cro,e} = 0.22$, and inflated by the number of raters, $n_r = 2$, observing each child–occasion. Thus, the child–occasion component, $\sigma^2_{co} = (0.85 - 0.22)/2 = 0.31$. Consequently, after decomposition,

Table 5.2. Generalizability Theory: Generalizability Study[a]

Raw Score	ANOVA		Variance Decomposition		G-Study
Source of Variation	df	Mean-square	Variance Component	Expected Mean Square	Estimated Variance Component
13 Children (c)	12	2.5769	σ^2_c	$\sigma^2_{cro,e} + n_c\sigma^2_{cr} + n_r\sigma^2_{co} + n_r n_o\sigma^2_c$	0.3974
2 Raters (r)	1	0.6923	σ^2_r	$\sigma^2_{cro,e} + n_c\sigma^2_{ro} + n_o\sigma^2_{cr} + n_c n_o\sigma^2_r$	0.0096
2 Occasions (o)	1	3.7692	σ^2_o	$\sigma^2_{cro,e} + n_c\sigma^2_{ro} + n_r\sigma^2_{co} + n_c n_r\sigma^2_o$	0.1090
cr	12	0.3590	σ^2_{cr}	$\sigma^2_{cro,e} + n_o\sigma^2_{cr}$	0.0673
co	12	0.8526	σ^2_{ro}	$\sigma^2_{cro,e} + n_r\sigma^2_{co}$	0.3141
ro	1	0.3077	σ^2_{ro}	$\sigma^2_{cro,e} + n_c\sigma^2_{ro}$	0.0064
cro,e	12	0.2244	$\sigma^2_{cro,e}$	$\sigma^2_{cro,e}$	0.2244

[a] described in Shavelson & Webb (1991)

the variance of the occasion effect, $\sigma^2_o = 0.11$, is less than that of the child–occasion interaction, $\sigma^2_{co} = 0.31$.

It is the variance components, now separated from other sources of variance, that are hypothesized to be generalizable. Since decomposing observed variances into their variance components requires detailed knowledge of the experimental design, the data analyzed must be in exact accordance with that design. Missing data would mean that each child–occasion (co) interaction in Table 5.1 was no longer observed by the same number of raters, n_r, and so would make variance decomposition more awkward or even impossible.

In the second stage, the D-Study, the variance components from the G-Study are applied to new (or the same) data to make decisions. In principle, the G-Study data were only those required to estimate variance components. The D-Study collects much more data in order to provide a firm basis for whatever decision making the entire study is intended to support. The experimental design of the D-Study can be different from the G-Study, but its variance components must be estimable from G-Study variance components. Thus the G-Study may have two raters for each of its few examinee's performances, but the D-Study may have only one rater for its many more examinee performances. The D-Study commences with consideration of alternative data collection strategies, as depicted in Table 5.3. In this Table, the G-Study results are the estimated variance components from Table

Table 5.3.   Generalizability Theory: Decision Study[a]

		G-Study	Alternative D-Studies		
Raters =		1	2	2	4
Occasions =		1	2	4	2
Source of Variation	$\hat{\sigma}^2$	Estimated Variance Component			
Children (c)	$\hat{\sigma}_p^2$	0.3974	0.3974	0.3974	0.3974
Raters (r)	$\hat{\sigma}_r^2$	0.0096	0.0048	0.0048	0.0024
Occasions (o)	$\hat{\sigma}_o^2$	0.1090	0.0545	0.0273	0.0545
cr	$\hat{\sigma}_{pr}^2$	0.0673	0.0337	0.0337	0.0168
co	$\hat{\sigma}_{po}^2$	0.3141	0.1571	0.0785	0.1571
ro	$\hat{\sigma}_{ro}^2$	0.0064	0.0016	0.0008	0.0008
cro,e	$\hat{\sigma}_{pro,e}^2$	0.2244	0.0561	0.0281	0.0281
Relative (Child Score) Error Variance (cr+co+cro,e)	$\hat{\sigma}_{Rel}^2$	0.6058	0.2469	0.1403	0.2020
Generalizability Coefficient	$\hat{\rho}^2$	0.40	0.62	0.74	0.66
Absolute (Child Score) Error Variance (r+o+cr+co+ro+cro,e)	$\hat{\sigma}_{Abs}^2$	0.7308	0.3078	0.1732	0.2597
Index of Dependability	$\hat{\phi}$	0.35	0.56	0.70	0.60

[a] described in Shavelson & Webb (1991)

5.2. The D-Study columns are the predicted sizes of the variance components for different rater–occasion combinations. If it were decided to observe each child eight times, this could be done by two raters on four occasions or by four raters on two occasions. These contrasting designs lead to the different variances predicted in the right-hand two columns.

Table 5.3 captures the relationship between data collection effort for each projected D-Study and raw score reliability. The "relative (child score) error variance", σ_{Rel}^2, contains all unwanted sources of variance that differentially affect child raw scores. The "generalizability coefficient" is the ratio of the "true" child raw-score variance, σ_c^2, to between-child raw-score variance, $\sigma_c^2 + \sigma_{Rel}^2$. It is seen that using two raters on four occasions, 0.74, is more "generalizable" than using four raters on two occasions, 0.66. The generalizability of the original G-Study data, two raters on two occasions, is seen to be 0.62. The generalizability coefficient is analogous to the Cronbach alpha coefficient, and is the reliability of relative decisions among child raw scores. The "index of dependability" is the reliability of absolute decisions relative to fixed raw score criteria. All unwanted sources of variance are included in its computation.

G-Theory is concerned with the precision of the observed raw scores. Variance components estimated from the G-Study imply an optimal data collection design for the D-Study. Data for decision-making may then be collected according to this design. These new data, or those analyzed for the G-Study, will then be reported in their observed raw score form. These reported scores will be assumed to have the same reliability as that estimated for this design from the G-Study. These scores are not corrected for the different samples of raters or different task difficulties encountered by examinees in less than fully crossed designs.

MFRM ANALYSIS

Kenderski's data in Table 5.1 is modelled to be the stochastic outcome of the logit-linear probability model:

$$\log \left(\frac{P_{cerox}}{P_{cerox-1}} \right) = B_c + C_r + D_o - F_x \tag{2}$$

where

P_{crox} = the probability of child c being given by rater r on occasion o a rating of x

P_{crox-1} = the probability of child c being given by rater r on occasion o a rating of $x-1$

B_c = the propensity to ask for help of child c

C_r = the sensitivity of rater r to noticing asking for help

D_o = the ease of asking for help on occasion o

F_x = the incremental psychological obstacle overcome in asking for help x times compared with $x-1$ times.

Equation (2) is algebraically simpler than G-Theory equation (1) because MFRM does not attempt to provide a detailed description of past data. MFRM extracts measures from those data that are as independent of the details of the data as statistically possible, i.e., measures that are likely to be the most useful for inference. MFRM specifies that each child, rater and occasion act independently (statistically) in generating the data. Raters do not collude, nor are they so tightly constrained by rating procedures that they are merely robot-like data coders. Inevitable random measurement error is incorporated explicitly into the model by the probability terms. Since the intention is to obtain individual child measures generalizable to any similar raters and occasions, interaction terms are not parameterized. This forces whatever interactions do occur to inflate the measurement error, and permits their detection by quality-control fit statistics.

In contrast to the G-Theory analysis, the MFRM analysis encourages substantive investigation into the behavior of individual children. Table 5.1 suggests several such questions. Are the raters exchangeable? Are they behaving consistently? Do any children ask for help significantly more or less than others? How is the children's asking behavior different on the second occasion?

Figure 5.1 summarizes the MFRM analysis of the data in Table 5.1. Equation (2) estimates a measure for each element (child, rater or occasion) of each facet (children, raters and occasions) located in a common frame of reference. Tables 5.4, 5.5, and 5.6 list the measures for the three facets, accompanied by their standard errors and local fit statistics. The linear unit of measurement is the logit (log-odds unit), whose size, in substantive terms, depends on the overall level of stochasticity in the data.

Figure 5.1 also provides the answers to our questions. The raters do exhibit a difference in sensitivity of 0.70 logits, but, in this small data

Linear scale in logits	Many-Facet Rasch Measurement Study Measurement Summary				Non-linear "asks for help" scale
Measures	Child	Total Asks:	Rater	Occasion	Count
4	Anne	*Asks most:* 15	*Notices more*	*More asking*	(4 at $+\infty$)
3					3.5
2	Betty	10			3
1				First	2.5
			Lucy		2
0					
-1	Charles	6	Sue	Later	1.5
-2	David Ethel Fred George Harriet Ida Jenny Kate Luke	5 4			1
-3	Mary	*Asks least:* 3	*Notices less*	*Less asking*	(0 at $-\infty$)

Figure 5.1. **Measures of "asking for help" constructed with a many-facet Rasch model.**

Table 5.4.   Many-Facet Rasch Measurement Study: Child Measurement Report

Child	Observed Score	Observed Count	Observed Average	Measure (Logits)	Stand Error of Measure	Fit Mean-Square
Anne	15	4	3.8	3.97	0.98	0.2
Betty	10	4	2.5	1.42	0.65	0.7
Charles	6	4	1.5	−0.68	0.83	1.0
David	5	4	1.3	−1.40	0.87	1.3
Ethel	5	4	1.3	−1.40	0.87	1.4
Fred	5	4	1.3	−1.40	0.87	1.1
George	5	4	1.3	−1.40	0.87	0.2
Harriet	5	4	1.3	−1.40	0.87	0.2
Ida	5	4	1.3	−1.40	0.87	0.6
Jenny	4	4	1.0	−2.17	0.89	2.3
Kate	4	4	1.0	−2.17	0.89	0.7
Luke	4	4	1.0	−2.17	0.89	1.8
Mary	3	4	0.8	−2.98	0.92	0.7
Mean:	5.8	4	1.5	−1.01	0.86	0.9
S.D.:	3.1	0	0.8	1.75	0.07	0.6

set, this difference is not statistically significant, $p > .1$. Among the children, Anne asks for help significantly more often than the other children. Betty also asks for help significantly more often than all others except Anne. In general, these children asked significantly less often on the second occasion, three weeks after the first. This intriguing result, buried in a variance component in Table 5.2, begs for further investigation. Do these children no longer need help? Have the children discovered that other children's "help" isn't helpful? Has the teacher requested the children not ask for help?

Are there are interactions? Does Figure 5.1 summarize the data?

Table 5.5.   Many-Facet Rasch Measurement Study: Rater Measurement Report

Rater	Observed Score	Observed Count	Observed Average	Measure (Logits)	Stand Error of Measure	Fit Mean-Square
Lucy	41	26	1.6	0.35	0.33	0.9
Sue	35	26	1.3	−0.35	0.34	1.0
Mean:	38.0	26	1.5	0.00	0.33	0.9
S.D.:	3.0	0	0.1	0.35	0.00	0.0

Table 5.6. Many-Facet Rasch Measurement Study: Occasion Measurement Report

Occasion	Observed Score	Observed Count	Observed Average	Measure (Logits)	Stand Error of Measure	Fit Mean-Square
First	45	26	1.7	0.80	0.33	0.8
3 weeks later	31	26	1.2	−0.80	0.34	1.1
Mean:	38.0	26	1.5	0.00	0.33	0.9
S.D.:	7.0	0	0.3	0.80	0.01	0.2

The "Fit Mean-square" columns in Tables 5.4, 5.5, 5.6 report, for each element, the extent to which the observations involving that element exhibit an average, modelled degree of randomness. Each fit mean-square is a summary of the difference between the observed data and the values expected given the parameter estimates, the MFRM measures. Each mean-square is a chi-square statistic divided by its degrees of freedom, so that its expectation is 1.0, and its range is 0 to infinity. Values greater than 1 indicate excess, unmodelled noise. Values less than 1 represent less than an average amount of stochasticity, e.g., dependency.

The fit mean-squares in Tables 5.5 and 5.6 are all close to 1.0, indicating no marked unmodelled within-rater or within-occasion behavior. The raters appear to be rating consistently, but independently, without collusion. Among the children in Table 5.4, however, there is considerable idiosyncratic behavior. Though, with only four observations per child, nothing is statistically significant, Jenny exhibits a mean-square of 2.3. There is 2.3 times more unpredictable randomness in her ratings than expected. Inspection of Table 5.1 indicates that she went against the trend by asking more often on the second occasion than on the first. Luke, with a mean-square of 1.8 (1.8 times more random), exhibited the opposite behavior, failing to ask for help at all on the second occasion. Anne, George and Harriet were the most predictable. They all asked slightly more often on the "easier to ask for help" first occasion than the "harder" second, and also were observed to ask more often by "more sensitive to asking behavior" rater Lucy than by Sue. This high degree of predictability is indicated by mean-squares of only 0.2, i.e., merely 20% of the modelled randomness. In G-Theory, less randomness is always preferred, but in MFRM less randomness is problematic as it may indicate unintended constraints on, or dependencies in, the data.

DESIGNS AND DECISIONS

Unlike G-Theory, MFRM does not require exactly formulated experimental designs. G-Theory requires these designs in order for the complete set of variance components to be estimable. The constraints on MFRM data collection designs are only that the measures be estimable unambiguously in one frame of reference or that the relationship between disjointed subsets of observations be specifiable. Unambiguous estimation implies that the measure of every element of every facet can be located unambiguously relative to that of every other element. This requirement is always met by fully crossed data designs, but can also be satisfied by surprisingly sparse designs.

Ambiguous estimates occur when subsets are disjointed. Suppose California raters rate California students, but New York raters rate New York students. If there is no crossing of students or raters across states, then we do not know whether the California students are more successful because they are more able or because their raters are more lenient. An obvious solution to this problem is to share raters or students across both states. Alternatively, we could assert that, as groups, California and New York students are equally able, so that any overall difference is due to overall differences in rater behavior across the two states. On the other hand, we could assert that California and New York raters are equally lenient, so that any overall difference is due to overall differences in student performance across the two states. This problem is usually overlooked in the raw score metric. In this example, since G-Theory reports uncorrected raw scores for the students, it automatically asserts that California and New York raters are equally lenient.

MFRM does not specify a separate D-Study because every G-Study is also a D-Study. Every data collection is for decision-making. The results of a study can also be used to guide the design of another study. If the spread of person measures is expected to be about the same in both studies, and each observation provides about the same statistical information, then the reliability of the new study can be computed from the Spearman-Brown prophecy formula:

$$R_T = \frac{C_T * R_O}{C_T * R_O + C_O * (1 - R_O)} \tag{3}$$

where

R_T = Target (wanted) reliability

R_O = Observed (previous) reliability

C_T = Target (wanted) average number of observations per examinee

C_O = Observed (previous) average number of observations per examinee,

and the average number of observations per examinee would be:

$$C_T = \frac{C_O * R_T * (1 - R_O)}{(1 - R_T) * R_O} \tag{4}$$

MFRM models the reliability of the new study to be independent of the source of the extra observations (e.g., more occasions or more raters, provided the extra observations are independently made and relevant). Consequently, the extra observations can be made in any way that is convenient. Further, there is no requirement that each examinee be observed the same number of times, or that a particular statistically motivated experimental design be fulfilled precisely.

GENERALIZABILITY

How generalizable are G-Theory and MFRM results? The distribution of child measures, reported in Table 5.4, do not display a statistically significant departure from normality. Dropping the two most frequent askers, Anne and Betty, from the data, however, improves the normality of the child effects, but reduces the observed child variance below the error variance. This happens in both MFRM and G-Theory analyses. In the MFRM analysis, this merely indicates how homogeneous most children are in asking for help. There are not enough observations of each child to distinguish their different proclivities to ask for help. In the G-Theory analysis, however, this produces components with *negative* variance, indicative of either model misspecification or sampling error. This G-Theory incongruity indicates the very restricted generalizability of G-Theory variance estimates. D-study data, yet to be collected, must include frequent askers similar to Anne and Betty, and in the same proportion, or else results may be paradoxical, exhibiting a theoretical impossibility (Shavelson & Webb, 1991, p. 39).

MFRM goes beyond G-Theory not only by estimating a measure and a standard error for each element, but also by reporting quality control fit statistics. An assumption of G-Theory is that the observed behavior is a random sample of all behavior. "To the extent that behavior is inconsistent across occasions, generalization from the sample of behavior collected on one occasion to the universe of behavior across all occasions is hazardous" (Shavelson and Webb, 1991, p. 7). G-Theory collects such inconsistency into variance components that are modelled to apply equally everywhere. In practice, inconsistent behavior is either local to particular observations or particular elements, or is systematic so that it has size and direction. In this data, most children were systematically inconsistent across occasions—they asked *less* the second time. But Jenny was locally inconsistent in that she asked conspicuously *more* the second time. The systematic effect is quantified by the difference between Rasch measures for the two occasions. Jenny's local inconsistency is detected by her fit statistics. In G-Theory, Jenny's behavior inflates the child–occasion interaction variance, but is not identified as individual to her. What is unusual about Jenny that prompts this locally inconsistent behavior? Can this behavior be expected in about 8% of the D-Study children, yet to come, in order to maintain the size of the child–occasion variance?

The aim of G-Theory is to estimate and optimize the reliability of decisions emanating from the data collection. For this data, the G-Theory reliability is the generalizability coefficient for relative child scores reported in the D-Study, Table 5.3, for two raters on two occasions. The G-Theory reliability value is 0.62. In contrast, the MFRM reliability coefficient is 0.87, when misfit is treated as random rather than structural (identifiable with particular elements). If, however, misfit is structural, then the MFRM reliability reduces to 0.46. G-Theory reliability falls between these two values because G-theory parameterizes interaction variance as structurally identifiable with groups of elements, not particular elements.

Interaction variance is a summary of many idiosyncratic outcomes, each the result of specific interaction between elements (e.g., a particular rater observing a particular child on a particular occasion). Such interaction activity cannot be expected to be homogeneous across D-Studies or even within a study. Consequently, regarding interaction as random error, except when identified otherwise by fit statistics, is the more consistent approach. Interaction identified by local misfit indicates a local inconsistency that falls outside the framework of both G-Theory and MFRM. In MFRM, the effect of element-related variance, local misfit, can be reduced by omission of misfitting elements or anomalous observations.

DISCUSSION

The view that G-Theory and MFRM are alternative solutions to the same measurement problem is seen to be an illusion. They embody very different conceptualizations of measurement. G-Theory provides a general summary, in an assumed linear raw score context, of a process that is hypothesized to continue into the future in exactly the same way apart from well-controlled alterations in experimental design. G-Theory has no implications for the individual examinee apart from the number of observations that will be made. For each examinee, the raw score is the measure estimate.

MFRM concentrates on the individual examinee. For each examinee, a deliberately linear measure is estimated that is corrected for, and is as independent as statistically possible of, the particularities of the raters, items, occasions, rating scale, etc., that the examinee encountered. MFRM thus provides a measure as fair and accurate as it is possible to derive from the data that were obtained. It is on such a measure that decisions relating to each examinee should be based.

REFERENCES

Andrich, D. (1988). *Rasch models for measurement*. Newbury Park, CA: Sage.

Cronbach, L.J., Gleser, G.C., Nanda, H., & Rajaratnam, N. (1972). *The dependability of behavioral measurements: theory of generalizability for scores and profiles*. New York: Wiley.

Linacre, J.M. (1989). *Many-facet Rasch measurement*. Chicago: MESA Press.

Shavelson, R.J., & Webb, N.M. (1991). *Generalizability theory: a primer*. Newbury Park, CA: Sage.

CHAPTER 6

The Invariance of Judge Severity Calibrations

Mary E. Lunz
American Society of Clinical Pathologists

John A. Stahl
Computer Adaptive Technologies, Inc.

Benjamin D. Wright
University of Chicago

It is often necessary to use judges to evaluate examinee performances. Unless the same judges assess all examinee performances, which is usually impractical, the varying severities of the judges may affect the scores awarded (Braun, 1989, Lunz, Wright and Linacre, 1990). Quantifying and accounting for differences in severity among judges can enable more precise and generalizable performance measures. An extended version of the Rasch model, the facets model, was developed for this purpose (Linacre, 1989).

For multiple-choice examinations that do not require judges, the Rasch model analyzes the interaction between examinee ability and item difficulty. Rasch item calibrations have been shown to be invariant across groups of examinees and examinee ability measures invariant across different subsets of items (Wright, 1967; Forsyth, 1981). When the data fit the model, the analysis of judges, as a third facet in the equation, should also provide statistically invariant estimates of judge severity. This study explores the invariance of judge severity calibrations across diverse strata of examinees and across two examination administrations.

For most examinations which require judges, the working assumption has been that when judges are qualified, pass/fail decisions are fair and generalizable beyond the particular judge/examinee interaction. The validity of the "equity" assumption has been studied with interjudge and, sometimes, intra-judge reliabilities yielding moderate correlations among or within judges (Michael, Cooper, Schaffer and Wallis 1980; Lunz and Stahl, 1990). But these correlation studies do not address variations in judge severity which may impact examinee scores.

In order to study the equity assumption with respect to judge-severity, a model that calibrates judge severities on an examination variable is needed. If differences in judge severity calibrations are *not* observed, then the equity assumption is validated. Conversely, observable differences among judges make the equity assumption suspect and point out the necessity of taking the differences in judge severity into account.

The assumptions from which the Rasch model is derived are that (a) the more able person has the higher probability of success on any item and (b) any person has a higher probability of success on an easy item than on a hard item (Rasch, 1960/1980). Many studies have demonstrated the utility of these Rasch specifications for a variety of tests. When judges are introduced into the examination process, the issue of whether the Rasch specifications continue to be met arises. Many studies report differences among judges (Cason & Cason, 1984; De Gruijter, 1984, Lunz and Stahl, 1993, Littlefield & Troendle, 1987). If these differences in judge severity can be calibrated and accounted for in the calculation of examinee measures, then some of the subjectivity inherent in the process of judgment may be controlled, thus improving the objectivity of measurement and supporting the generalization of pass/fail decisions beyond the particular judge/examinee interaction. Calibration of judge severity, however, assumes that judges are relatively consistent in the application of their expectations regardless of the difficulty of the items or the ability of the examinees.

The hypothesis is that differences among judge severities can be measured and that these differences remain statistically consistent across examination administrations and across different levels of examinee ability. Severity is defined as the level of expectations imposed by a judge when evaluating person performances. This suggests that individual judges have distinct tendencies toward leniency or severity.

The lenient judge tends to award higher scores on all items to all examinees while the more severe judge tends to award lower scores on all items to all examinees.

METHODS

Judge Mediated Examination Procedures

Data from two examination administrations six months apart were used in this study. The first administration required 17 judges, and the second administration required 14 judges. Eleven of these judges graded at both the first and second administrations. These judges take their responsibilities seriously, because the results affect the decision to certify the examinees. Most of the judges had previous judging experience prior to these two administrations; however, several were new. We have observed inexperienced judges to be more variable until they become familiar and comfortable with the rating system and the application of their expectations. All judges attended a three-hour training session designed to review the criteria for rating each item and to explain the details of the rating scale.

The certification examination is for histotechnology, the science of cell identification and classification. Histologic Technicians are responsible for the preparation and chemical staining of tissue samples for microscopic evaluation. The performance part of the certification examination is designed to assess their ability to perform this task.

Each candidate prepares 15 specifically defined tissue slides for microscope evaluations. The quality of slides is assessed by trained judges who are experienced in this field. Judges rate slides in batches of five so that three judges participate in the rating of each candidate's examination. A four-point rating scale is used (0 = unacceptable, 1 = marginal, 2 = acceptable and 3 = excellent). Three hundred and twenty-four (324) candidates submitted examinations (15 slides each) for the first administration and 260 candidates submitted examinations for the second administration.

Multi-Faceted Data Analysis

These data were analyzed with FACETS, a computer program for Rasch analysis of examinations with more than two facets (Linacre, 1988). The Rasch model $\log\{P_{ni}/(1 - P_{ni})\} = B_n - D_i$ (Rasch, 1960/1980) analyzes dichotomous data by estimating candidate ability

B_n and item difficulty D_i from the observed item responses so as to bring the probabilities of correct and incorrect responses as close to the observed responses as possible. This is a two "facet" application. The observed responses are modelled to depend upon the difference between the difficulty of the item (facet one) and the ability of the candidate (facet two). An examination which requires judges adds a third facet. In this example, the observed responses are modelled to depend upon the differences among the item difficulties, candidate abilities, and judge severities (facet 3).

The multi-facet Rasch model (Linacre 1989) can analyze all facets of a performance assessment examination. For this examination, the probability of person n with ability B_n achieving score x (rather than x-1) on item i with difficulty D_i from judge j with severity C_j was modeled as:

$$\log \left(\frac{P_{nijx}}{P_{nijx-1}} \right) = B_n - D_1 - C_j - F_x$$

where

P_{nijx} = Probability of candidate n being given score x by judge j on item i,

P_{nijx-1} = Probability of candidate n being given score x-1 by judge j on item i,

and

B_n = ability of candidate n − the candidate facet,
D_i = difficulty of item i − the item facet,
C_j = severity of judge j − the judge facet,
F_x = difficulty of achieving rating step x relative to step x-1 on the rating scale.

Candidate performance estimates, standard errors and fit statistics for candidate measures (B_n), item difficulties (D_i), judge severities (C_j), and rating scale step difficulties (F_x) are calculated from these data. Each facet on the examination variable is calibrated from the relevant observed ratings (responses) and all but the candidate measure facet are anchored at a common origin of zero.

The ratings awarded on all items by all of the judges are used to estimate individual judge severities and individual item difficulties using the unconditional maximum likelihood formula (UCON) (Wright and Stone, 1979). Candidate measures are calculated after the effects of the other examination facets have been subtracted. The resulting linear examination variable positions candidate measures (B_n) from highest to lowest, item difficulties (D_i) from most to least difficult and judge severities (C_j) from most to least severe (see Linacre, 1989 for description of the estimation process).

Sample Selection

The examinations from each administration were divided into three mutually exclusive ability strata based on candidate measures. The lower strata included the failures (16.6% first and 12.7% second administration). The upper strata included a comparable percentage of the most able candidates. The middle strata, the remainder of the candidates, was excluded from the study. The upper and lower strata were selected for study because they represented the most dramatic differences in candidate ability and would thus provide the most rigorous assessment of judge severity invariance.

These candidate strata differ substantially in ability. For the first administration, 54 candidates in the upper strata with a mean ability measure of 1.58 logits (SD = .68 logits) were three standard deviations above the lower ability strata with a mean ability measure of −.65 logits (SD = .61). For the second administration, 33 candidates in the upper strata with a mean ability measure of 1.44 logits (SD = .88) were substantially above the 33 candidates in the lower strata with a mean ability of −.13 logits (SD = .42).

Analysis of Judge Severity

Judge severity calibrations, standard errors and fit statistics were computed independently for each judge for each candidate group (upper and lower strata) and for each administration. Invariant judge severity calibrations should be statistically equivalent across these differing ability strata and examination administrations.

Fit Statistics

The fit statistics evaluate the suitability of these data for constructing a variable and making measures (Wright and Stone, 1979; Wright and Masters, 1982). The fit statistics for judges indicate the degree to which each judge is internally self-consistent and able to implement the rating scale to make distinctions among candidate performances. Two versions of fit to the expectations of the model are reported. The infit statistic is an information weighted mean-square residual which is sensitive to an accumulation of inlying deviations. The outfit statistic is an unweighted mean-square residual which is sensitive to outlying deviations. The expected value for the mean squares is one (1.0). Their asymptotic standard errors are approximately the square root of two divided by the number of independent replications on which the corresponding estimate is based. The region of acceptable fit that we have found useful is mean squares between 0.5 and 1.5. Judges with infit or outfit statistics outside of these criteria are flagged, and their ratings are reviewed for unexpected deviations on particular slides or candidate performances.

Reliability

The elements defining each facet of the examination variable are summarized by their mean, standard deviation, and internal separation reliability. In most examinations, variation in candidate performance is expected. Separation reliability, which is similar to the KR-20 internal consistency statistic, indicates the proportion of the observed variance not due to measurement error (Wright & Masters, 1982 pp 91–94). The spread or separation of judge severities should be within the error of measurement if judges meet the traditional assumption of equity. The assumption of equity among judges must be questioned if the variance exceeds that expected due to error of measurement.

Severity Calibration Comparisons

Judge severity calibrations were compared across ability strata (upper and lower) for each administration and within ability strata (upper to upper and lower to lower) across administrations. For each of these comparisons summary statistics and fit statistics are presented. In addition, judge severity calibrations are compared in terms of "standardized differences" (Wright, 1967; Forsyth, 1981). The formula used to obtain standardized differences for judge severity calibrations is:

$$Z_j = (C_{j1} - C_{j2})/(S_{j1}^2 + S_{j2}^2)^{1/2}$$

where C_{j1} and C_{j2} are judge severity estimates for the ability strata and S_{j1}^2 and S_{j2}^2 are the estimated error variances associated with these severity estimates.

RESULTS

Severity Calibrations

Tables 6.1 and 6.2 present the judge severity calibrations, standard errors, fit statistics and summary statistics for each judge for each ability strata for the two administrations. Variation in judge severity contradicts the equity assumption that the pass/fail decision is independent of judge/candidate interactions. There is clear evidence that these judges differ in severity beyond the variance that can be attributed to error. For example, in the first test administration, judge calibrations for the upper strata range from −1.60 to 1.60 logits. Even when the candidate abilities within each strata are similar due to stratification, the severities of the judges still differ significantly.

The reliability coefficient of judge separation for the first administration upper strata was .70 and for the lower strata .60. For the second administration, the reliability coefficient of judge separation for the upper strata was .47 and for the lower strata .69.

Analysis of Fit

Analysis of the fit statistics revealed fit statistics of less than .5 usually indicate restricted use of the rating scale. For example, judges award ratings in the middle of the scale to all or most performances (e.g., ratings 2). More severe judges with low fit statistics tend to award ratings of 0 or 1 consistently while more lenient judges may award ratings of 2 or 3 to all or most candidates. Of course, the expected ratings for the judge are summed with the overall difficulty of the slide before the fit is calculated. When a relatively severe judge encounters a group of less able candidates it is probable that lower ratings will be awarded consistently, causing the fit statistics for that judge, when assessing that group of candidates to appear more consistent than expected. Usually, the mean ability of the candidates is not known prior to the analysis; however, in this example, the candidates were grouped by ability, so a tendency toward over-consistency among judges is expected, and is demonstrated in Table 6.1. In fact, the fit statistics for judge 9 in the lower strata are least expected (fit = 1.5), as some candidates in the lower strata were awarded higher-than-expected ratings. This judge must have had some difficulty assessing the lower ability candidates, and therefore gave some of them "the benefit of the doubt" on several slides.

Table 6.1. Severity Calibrations, Standard Errors, Fit Statistics by Judge and Ability Strata
First Administration

Judge #	Upper Strata						Lower Strata					
	Score	N of Slides[c]	Severity[a] Calib	Model Error	Infit MnSq	Outfit MnSq	Score	N of Slides[c]	Severity[a] Calib	Model Error	Infit MnSq	Outfit MnSq
2	138	50	-0.14	0.31	1.3	0.9	36	20	0.06	0.30	0.9	0.9
3	121	45	0.41	0.28	0.8	0.7	91	45	0.30	0.19	0.8	0.7
4	197	75	0.60	0.20	0.8	0.7	191	90	-0.49	0.14	0.9	0.9
5	164	60	-0.04	0.27	1.3	1.3	127	60	-0.27	0.18	1.3	1.3
6	110	45	0.80	0.22	1.2	1.2	67	35	0.12	0.21	0.6	0.6
7	175	65	-0.09	0.24	1.5	1.1	74	35	-0.19	0.23	0.9	0.8
8	44	15	-1.60	1.02	0.9	0.5	77	35	-0.43	0.23	1.2	1.2
9	108	40	0.56	0.31	0.6	0.5	104	50	0.04	0.19	1.5	1.5
13	150	55	0.29	0.27	1.0	1.1	195	95	0.20	0.13	1.2	1.2
18	200	70	-0.69	0.33	1.1	1.0	106	45	-0.64	0.22	1.4	1.2
19	62	25	1.10	0.30	0.5	0.7	33	20	0.36	0.27	1.1	1.1
23	54	20	0.74	0.43	0.8	1.2	40	20	0.52	0.28	0.1	0.2
29*	75	25					28	15	0.62	0.34	0.8	0.8

34	216	75	−0.76	0.35	1.1	0.9	141	70	−0.22	0.16	0.7	0.7
36	207	75	0.22	0.25	1.0	1.1	103	55	0.23	0.17	1.0	1.0
46	48	20	1.60	0.31	0.9	0.8	88	50	0.05	0.17	0.6	0.5
62	144	50	−0.58	0.43	0.9	0.7	150	70	−0.27	0.16	1.4	1.3

Severity

Mean = 0.00[b]
SD = .77
SE = .41
RMSE = .53
Judge Separation R = .70

N candidates = 54
Mean candidate ability = 1.58

Severity

Mean = 0.00[b]
SD = .35
SE = .21
RMSE = .22
Judge Separation R = .60

N candidates = 54
Mean candidate ability = −.65

[a] High positive calibration = severe: High negative calibration = lenient.

[b] Rasch model calibration centers the judge severity facet at a mean of zero.

[c] Each examination included 15 slides. Slides were graded in batches of 5 by 3 different judges, so that 3 judges contributed to each candidate measure. The number of slides graded by each judge varied due to speed of grading and rotational pattern.

* Perfect rating given to a small sample. Judge severity calibration cannot be estimated (Wright & Stone, 1979).

Table 6.2. Severity Calibrations, Standard Errors, Fit Statistics by Judge and Ability Strata Second Administration

Judge #			Upper Strata						Lower Strata			
	Score	N of Slides[c]	Severity[a] Calib	Model Error	Infit MnSq	Outfit MnSq	Score	N of Slides[c]	Severity[a] Calib	Model Error	Infit MnSq	Outfit MnSq
2	24	10	-0.05	0.49	0.8	0.8	30	15	-0.18	0.31	0.4	0.4
5	78	30	0.43	0.35	1.1	0.7	107	60	0.04	0.14	1.2	1.2
6	192	75	0.06	0.21	0.9	0.9	51	25	-0.10	0.24	1.2	1.3
7	99	35	-0.32	0.44	0.8	0.6	69	35	-0.00	0.20	1.4	1.5
8	181	65	-1.36	0.30	0.9	0.7	51	30	0.85	0.20	0.5	0.5
9	139	50	0.18	0.34	0.8	1.1	98	55	0.56	0.15	0.9	0.9
12	51	20	0.99	0.40	0.7	0.8	39	15	-0.97	0.43	1.5	1.4
13	143	50	-0.17	0.41	1.1	0.8	139	75	0.18	0.13	1.3	1.3
16	42	15	0.33	0.61	0.8	0.7	45	20	-0.56	0.29	0.6	0.6
19	101	35	-0.65	0.52	0.8	1.1	72	30	-0.16	0.26	1.3	1.0
23	97	35	-0.07	0.40	1.3	1.0	72	35	0.19	0.22	0.8	0.7
29	42	15	-0.20	0.66	1.0	0.4	41	20	-0.35	0.26	0.4	0.4
46	67	25	0.49	0.41	0.9	1.0	67	35	0.29	0.20	1.0	1.0
52	90	35	0.98	0.31	1.7	1.5	90	45	0.21	0.18	0.7	0.7

Upper Strata:

Severity Mean = 0.00[b]
SD = .59
SE = .42
RMSE = .43
Judge Separation R = .47

N candidates = 33[c]
Mean candidate ability = 1.44

Lower Strata:

Severity Mean = 0.00[b]
SD = .44
SE = .23
RMSE = .24
Judge Separation R = .69

N candidates = 33[c]
Mean candidate ability = -.13

[a] High positive calibration = severe: High negative calibration = lenient.
[b] Rasch model calibration centers the judge facet at a mean of zero.
[c] Each examination included 15 slides. Slides were graded in batches of 5 by 3 different judges, so that 3 judges contributed to each candidate measure. The number of slides graded by each judge varied due to speed of grading and rotational pattern.

In the second administration (Table 6.2) the fit statistics for judges 2 and 29 were .4 when rating the lower strata. Review of their records revealed that ratings of 2 were given consistently. Judge 2 rated sets of 5 slides from three candidates, and judge 29 rated sets of 5 slides from 11 low ability candidates. Judge 52 had fit statistics of 1.7 and 1.5 when rating the upper strata. This suggests that some lower-than-expected ratings were given on some slides to these able candidate performances. This judge was relatively severe overall and graded slides from only seven candidates in the upper strata.

Standardized Differences

Across Ability Strata Within Administrations

Table 6.3 shows the standardized differences (Z_{j12}) in judge severity for the upper and lower ability strata within and across administrations. In the first administration, judges 4, 6, and 46 show significant variation (standardized difference > 2) in severity beyond that expected due to the error of measurement. All three judges appear to be significantly more lenient, when rating the lower strata. Judge 29 gave perfect scores to all candidates in the upper strata during the first administration which made it impossible to estimate his severity.

In the second administration judges 8, 12 and 52 show significant variation in severity beyond that due to the error of measurement. Judge 8 was significantly more severe when rating the lower strata while judges 12 and 52 were significantly more lenient when rating the lower strata. The majority of judges were consistent within the error of measurement when rating diverse ability strata.

Within Ability Strata Across Administrations

Invariance of judge severity can also be observed by tracking judge severity across examination administrations. The severities of the 11 common judges were compared for the upper and for the lower strata across the two administrations (See Table 6.3). Judge 19 is the only judge who altered in severity beyond the variance expected due to error of measurement for either the upper or lower strata across examinations administrations. Judge 19 graded for the first time at the first administration and was relatively severe overall and perhaps more severe than necessary when rating performances from able candidates. At the second administration this judge became more lenient overall. We have found changes of this type to be quite common for new

Table 6.3.   Standardized Differences[a] for Judge Severity Calibrations Across Ability Strata and Within Ability Strata Across Administration

Judges	Standardized Differences Within Administration		Standardized Differences Across Administrations	
	First Administration Upper/Lower	Second Administration Upper/Lower	1st to 2nd Upper/Upper	1st to 2nd Lower/Lower
2*	−.46	.22	.53	−.31
3	.33			
4	4.46**			
5*	.71	1.03	1.56	.47
6*	2.24**	.50	−1.71	−.35
7*	.30	−.66	−.02	.24
8*	−1.12	−6.13**	.43	1.78
9*	1.43	−1.02	−.35	.79
12		3.34**		
13*	.30	−.81	−.49	−.08
16		.34		
18	−.13			
19*	1.83	−.84	−2.55**	−.69
23*	.43	−.57	−1.00	−.45
29*		.21		−1.14
34	−1.40			
36	−.03			
46*	4.38**	.44	−1.73	.36
52		2.15**		
62	−.68			

[a] Standardized difference = 2.00 or more standard units (95% confidence that a difference exists) different than expected given the combined error of measure. Positive is more severe and negative is less severe for that sample.

* Judged both examination administrations.

** Significantly different in severity between ability strata or within ability strata across administrations.

judges. The other judge severities were statistically comparable across administrations supporting the concept that judges have a measurable level of severity that they apply regardless of the candidates or the examination administration.

Only three judges, in each administration apparently altered their severities significantly across ability strata, and only one judge altered severity significantly across administrations within ability strata. These changes in severity may be due to idiosyncratic factors like mood or fatigue rather than to any permanent alteration in expectations.

DISCUSSION

Significant differences among judge severities were found within each ability strata. This is evidence that even the most thoroughly trained judges remain unique persons, even when judging candidate performances of similar ability. Judges cannot be trained, cajoled or coerced into judging with exactly the same severity. The multi-facet Rasch analysis presented here shows that it is possible to describe the relative differences in judge severities. Calibrations of judge severity are shown to be generally invariant with respect to differing candidate ability strata. In two administrations, involving 20 judges and 31 comparisons, only 6 comparisons show significant variation in calibrated severity across ability strata. For 10 of the 11 judges common to both administrations or 20 of 21 comparisons, there were no statistically significant differences in calibrated severity. The number of rating points awarded to candidate performances was quite different across ability strata, but the pattern used by the judges for awarding rating points was generally comparable regardless of candidate ability. The fit statistics show that most of these judges make stable distinctions among candidates within ability strata. Significant variation could be caused by unfamiliarity with the rating scale, such as being a new judge, lack of experience, or fatigue.

The fact that most judge calibrations were invariant across ability strata for two examination administrations indicates the potential usefulness of these analyses. This kind of analysis adds an element of control to examinations that require judges. Adjusting candidate ability measures so that they become "judge-free" and generalize beyond particular judge/candidate interactions improves the objectivity and fairness of the examination. It may also be possible to equate examinations that require judges by anchoring on the severities of predictable judges. The infit and outfit statistics flag unexpectedly high or low ratings or over consistent use of a particular rating (e.g. 2), so that training can be targeted directly at the particular deviate rating patterns of individual judges. Our experience has been that judges who receive this type of information accept it and are often successful in improving their consistency.

The limitation of this study is the limited variance within the candidate samples precipitated by the research design. When the middle strata is included in the sample, the overconsistency demonstrated in the judge-fit statistics decreases. However, these data provide a good example of what to look for in judge-fit statistics so that the examination process can be improved. While the results are never perfect, these analyses provide new and extremely useful information for the individual judge and the testing agency which may lead to more control for examinations that require judges.

REFERENCES

Braun, H.I. (1989). Understand scoring reliability: Experiments in calibrating essay readers. *Journal of Educational Statistics, 13,* 1–18.

Cason, G.J. & Cason, C.L. (1984). A deterministic theory of clinical performance rating. *Evaluation and the Health Professions, 7,* 221–247.

DeGruijter, D.N.M. (1984). Two simple models for rates effects. *Applied Psychological Measurement, 8,* 2, 213–218.

Forsyth, R., Sarsangjan, V. and Gilmer, J. (1981). Some empirical results related to the robustness of the Rasch model. *Applied Psychological Measurement, 5,* 175–186.

Linacre, J.M. (1988). *FACETS, a computer program for the analysis of multifaceted data.* Chicago: MESA Press.

Linacre, J.M. (1989). *Multi-faceted Measurement.* Chicago: MESA Press.

Littlefield, J.H. and Troendle, G.R. (1987). *Effects of rating task instructions on consistency and accuracy of expert raters.* Paper presented at the American Educational Research Association, Washington, D.C.

Lunz, M.E. and Stahl, J.A. (1990). A comparison of intra- and interjudge decision consistency using analytic and holistic scoring criteria. *Journal of Allied Health, 19,* 173–179.

Lunz, M.E., Wright, B.D., Linacre, J.M. (1990). Measuring the impact of judge severity on examination scores. *Applied Measurement in Education, 3,* 331–345.

Lunz, M.E. and Stahl, J.A. (1993). Impact of examiners on candidate scores: An introduction to the use of multifacet Rasch model analysis for oral examinations. *Teaching and Learning in Medicine, 5,* 3, 174–181.

Michael, W.B., Cooper, T., Schaffer, P. and Wallis, E. (1980). A comparison of the reliability and validity of ratings of student performance on essay examinations by professor of English and by professors of other disciplines. *Psychological Measurement, 40,* 183–195.

Rasch, G. (1960/1980). *Probablistic models from some intelligence testing.* Chicago: University of Chicago Press.

Wright, B.D. (1967). *Sample free test calibration and person measurement.* Paper presented at the Invitational Conference on Testing Problems. Educational Testing Service, N.J.

Wright, B.D. and Masters, G.N. (1982). *Rating Scale Analysis.* Chicago: MESA Press.

Wright, B.D. and Stone, M.H. (1979). *Best Test Design.* Chicago: MESA Press.

chapter **7**

Judge Performance Reports: Media and Message

John A. Stahl
Computer Adaptive Technologies, Inc.

Mary E. Lunz
American Society of Clinical Pathologists

The purpose of this paper is to present a reporting system for evaluating judge performance when judge severity is calibrated using the many-facet Rasch model as a routine part of examination analysis. Judge severity is defined as all of the personal, social, educational, and experiential factors which may influence judge grading patterns. The philosophy behind the report is that judges are unique individuals who benefit from an analytical assessment of their judging patterns. Each judge has a unique level of severity that he or she applies consistently to all candidate performances graded. The many-facet Rasch analysis accounts for differences in judge severity, so it is important that the judge be relatively consistent when grading all items. Attempts to train judges to grade identically rarely have the degree of success expected (see Raymond, Webb and Houston, 1991).

An alternative approach is to accept the fact that judges implement somewhat different levels of severity, even when they use the same judging criteria, and then to account for the difference in severity among judges before making a final assessment of the candidate performance (Lunz, Wright and Linacre, 1990, Engelhard, 1992). The expectation is for judges to be relatively consistent internally—that is, to apply generally the same level of severity to each candidate performance they grade. Thus, a severe judge is expected to grade all performances using more rigorous expectations than a lenient judge.

The ability of judges to maintain internal consistency has been verified in previous studies. It has been observed that judges tend to be consistent (within the standard error of measurement) across candidate ability levels and different examination administrations (Lunz, Stahl and Wright, in press). A good example of this consistency can be found in a longitudinal study of judge severity across seven histotechnology performance assessment examinations conducted by the authors. The judges in the study graded on some or all of the seven administrations. Their severity calibrations were plotted for each examination at which they graded. Figure 7.1 presents the results for one of the judges who graded on all seven of the administrations.

The error bands in the figure represent two standard errors of measurement. When judge severity calibrations remain within the error bands across examinations there is evidence that judges are relatively consistent across candidate performances and across examination administrations. There is no significant difference in the severity demonstrated by the judge. The judge represented in Figure 7.1 may be

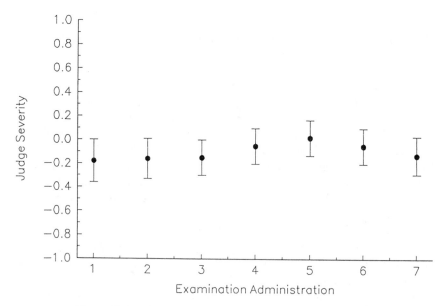

Figure 7.1. One Judge: Severity Over 7 Administrations

deemed internally consistent across administrations. With few exceptions, the other judges examined in the longitudinal study demonstrated comparable levels of consistency, regardless of their individual degrees of severity.

When emphasis is placed on maintaining internal grading consistency, it is important that the judges receive specific feedback on their grading patterns. This feedback must be in a form that is tailored to each individual judge. Reports based on summary statistics such as group means or judge means are frequently difficult to interpret and rarely provide the detailed information required for judges to evaluate their own performance. Ideally, a report must present information to the judges that will aid them in evaluating their grading patterns so that they may take corrective action, should that be necessary. The report should function as a strong motivator by stimulating the judge's interest in the grading process. The more detailed and personal the report, the more likely it is to be useful.

METHOD

The many-facet Rasch model allows for the systematic analysis of judge-mediated examinations (Linacre, 1989). The data examined in this study are from an examination in histotechnology. This examination required the 93 candidates to prepare 15 laboratory slides to defined specifications. The slides were graded by experienced, trained judges using very specific grading criteria. During the grading session a rotational system allowed all judges to grade three tasks on the 15 slide-items at some time during the grading session. Also, three judges had input into each candidate performance, so judges were linked through candidate performances. The grading session was two days in duration and included a two-hour training session. There were six experienced judges grading this examination.

In the many-facet Rasch model, the probability of a candidate achieving a particular score is modelled as follows:

$$\frac{P_{njix}}{P_{njix-1}} = B_n - C_j - D_i - F_x$$

where

P_{njix} = the probability of achieving a score of x by person n with ability B from judge j with severity C on item i with difficulty D

P_{njix-1} = the probability of achieving a score of x − 1 by person n with ability B from judge j with severity C on item i with difficulty D

B_n = the ability B of person n
C_j = the severity C of judge j
D_i = the difficulty D of slide-item i

and

F_x = the step difficulty F of step x on the rating scale

Because of the linking pattern, it is possible to assess the grading patterns of each judge on each slide-item during each grading session.

As a routine part of this analysis, a judge-by-item interaction is calculated to detect potential judge-by-item "bias". Bias is defined as unexpected severity or leniency on the part of a judge on particular items, regardless of his or her overall severity. The analysis first determines a judge's severity based on his or her grading of all items across all the candidate performances assessed. Item difficulty is calculated based on all grades given to all candidates on that item. The "expected score" is calculated for each judge on each item, given the calibrated severity of the judge and the calibrated difficulty of the item. This "expected score" is then compared to the observed score. A bias estimate and standard error are calculated by fixing the parameters of all facets (i.e., slide-items, judges, candidates, etc.) at their estimated values, adding a bias facet to the model and estimating the calibration of this added bias facet in an iterative process (Linacre and Wright, 1992, p. 30). This bias estimate is converted into a standardized z-score by dividing by the standard error. This bias analysis is accomplished using FACETS (Linacre, 1989) a computer program for the analysis of examinations with three or more facets.

Theoretically, the expected and observed scores should vary within the error of measurement. A standardized bias score that has an *absolute* value ≥2.0 (an approximate 95% confidence interval) indicates that the judge is grading an item significantly harder or easier than expected based on his or her grading across all slides. A significant deviation indicates that the judge has departed from his or her own level of severity on a particular item. This information is presented to the judges in a graph which aids them in identifying the inconsistencies in their grading patterns during an examination administration. The format of the report is designed to help judges assess their grading patterns objectively, item by item.

RESULTS

The first step in analyzing the examination data is to review the fit statistics. These statistics are very useful in identifying any particular slide or judge that performed in a manner different from that predicted by the measurement model used. Two fit statistics are reported. The infit statistic is an information-weighted mean-squared residual that is sensitive to the accumulation of central, inlying deviations (Wright and Stone, 1979). The outfit statistic is an unweighted mean-squared residual that is sensitive to occasional outlying deviations (Wright and Stone, 1979). Typical criteria for acceptable fit are mean-squared residuals between 1.5 and .6 (Lunz, Wright and Linacre, 1990). Judges and slide-items with fit statistics beyond these criteria are reviewed carefully for inconsistency. The slide difficulty calibrations with their accompanying fit statistics are presented in Table 7.1.

All of the slides demonstrate acceptable fit statistics with the exception of slide numbers 6, 8 and 12. Subsequent discussions with the judges revealed that slide 6, which had high infit and outfit statistics, is relatively easy; however, the results are either excellent or unaccept-

Table 7.1.   Slide Difficulty Calibrations

Slide	Score	Count	Difficulty	Error	Infit Mn. Sq.	Outfit Mn. Sq.
1	575	465	−0.32	0.12	0.8	0.6
2	534	465	0.20	0.10	1.0	1.2
3	537	465	0.17	0.11	1.0	1.0
4	565	465	−0.18	0.12	1.0	1.3
5	575	465	−0.32	0.12	0.8	0.8
6	608	465	−0.88	0.16	1.6	2.9
7	539	465	0.22	0.11	1.3	0.5
8	566	465	−0.12	0.12	0.9	0.4
9	430	465	1.21	0.09	1.1	0.9
10	559	465	−0.02	0.11	1.0	0.6
11	562	465	−0.17	0.12	1.3	0.7
12	575	465	−0.35	0.12	1.0	0.4
13	550	465	−0.01	0.11	1.1	0.9
14	516	465	0.36	0.10	0.9	0.7
15	530	465	0.22	0.10	1.1	1.0

Note: The count is based on grades for five tasks per slide for 93 candidates = 465 grades. Four of the task grades are based on 0–1 scales and the fifth is based on a 0–3 rating scale. The maximum score for a slide is 7. The judges in this study only graded three of the five tasks. The remaining two tasks were graded in a different part of the grading session by different judges.

able. There does not appear to be identifiable intermediate levels of performance in the preparation of this slide. As a result, candidates generally received perfect grades on this slide or zero grades. This slide was the easiest to prepare (-0.88 logits), so the strong misfit comes from the relatively few candidates who received the zero scores. This is some indication that the ability to obtain an adequate tissue sample also plays an important role in the successful preparation of the slide. It may be that this confounding factor would be sufficiently important to preclude using this particular slide on future examinations.

Slides 8 and 12 were also relatively easy slides to prepare. The low outfit statistics indicate that these slides were graded using a restricted portion of the rating scale. Since they were easy slides, most of the candidates received ratings of 2 or 3, producing a consistency in rating beyond that predicted by the stochastic nature of the model.

The judge severity calibrations with their accompanying fit statistics are presented in Table 7.2.

All six judges had acceptable fit statistics, suggesting that they were generally consistent across all slide-items and candidate performances.

The judge-by-slide "bias" analysis was conducted to gain detailed information for each judge, to monitor and, if necessary, to adjust, their grading patterns. The judge report is the method used to present this information to the judges in a way that is acceptable and informative to them.

A graphic representation of the standardized judge-by-slide bias was selected because it resembles the quality control charts familiar to laboratory personal. The 15 slide items are identified along the X-axis by the numbers 1 to 15. The standardized bias scores for that judge on each item is represented along the Y-axis. The bias analysis is independent of overall judge severity.

Table 7.2.   Judge Difficulty Calibrations

Judge	Score	Count	Severity	Error	Infit Mn. Sq.	Outfit Mn. Sq.
1	780	615	0.32	0.07	0.9	1.0
2	1141	825	−0.29	0.07	1.1	1.0
3	760	585	0.13	0.08	0.9	1.1
4	1066	795	−0.17	0.07	1.1	0.9
5	880	690	0.03	0.07	1.1	1.0
6	900	675	−0.02	0.07	1.2	1.0

Note: Each judge rated three tasks for each slide. The count represents the number of slides graded by each judge × 3. The judges were allowed to grade at their own pace which accounts for the difference in the number of slides graded.

Graphs from the reports for this examination are presented in Figures 7.2 through 7.7.

An introduction accompanies the graph to identify the judge by name and number. A severity classification is derived from the entire grading session and is reported in a five-step ordinal scale as follows: Easy–Moderate to Easy–Moderate–Moderate to Hard–Hard. Judges are cautioned that no particular level of severity is desirable but that internal consistency is the goal. The particular items that were graded more severely or leniently than expected are identified on the graph. A complete listing of the items on the test is presented to aid in the interpretation of the graph.

The graph is a plot of the standardized bias scores. A cover letter explains the interpretation of these scores. A copy of the cover letter is found in Appendix A. A negative bias score greater than −2.0 indicates a slide item was graded more leniently than expected while a positive bias score greater than 2.0 indicates a slide item was graded more severely than expected. In this examination, judge 1, a hard judge, graded slides 1 and 3 significantly harder than expected. Judge 3, a moderate-to-hard judge, graded slide 12 harder than expected.

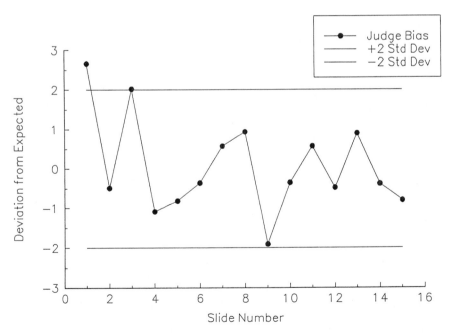

Figure 7.2. Judge Summary Report Judge 1: Hard Judge

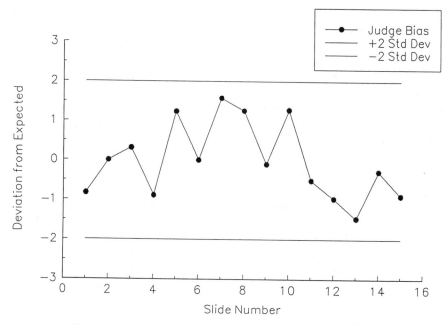

Figure 7.3.   Judge Summary Report Judge 2: Easy Judge

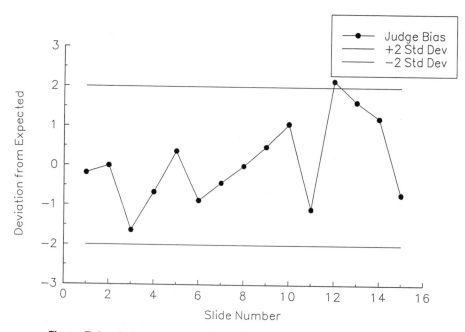

Figure 7.4.   Judge Summary Report Judge 3: Moderate to Hard Judge

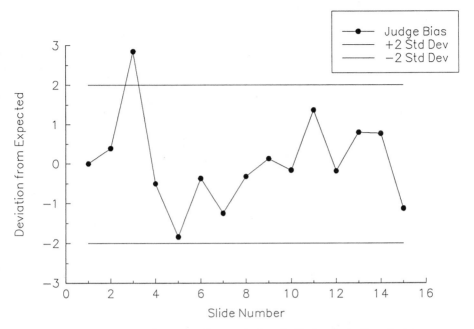

Figure 7.5.   Judge Summary Report Judge 4: Moderate to Easy Judge

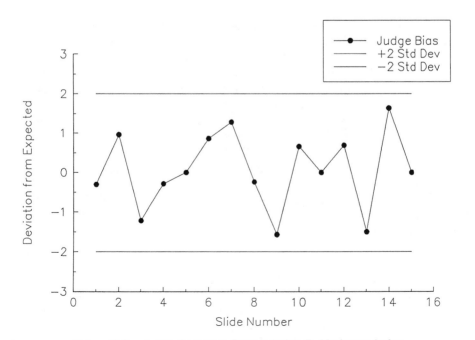

Figure 7.6.   Judge Summary Report Judge 5: Moderate Judge

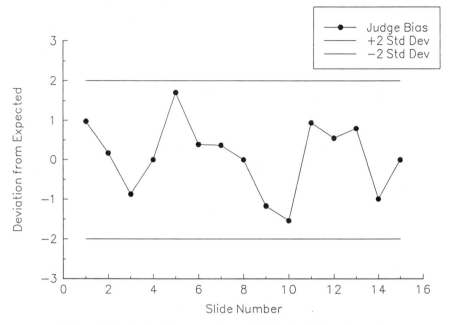

Figure 7.7.   Judge Summary Report Judge 6: Moderate Judge

Judge 4, a moderate-to-easy judge, graded slide 3 harder than expected. These judges differed in their overall level of severity, but were relatively consistent across items. The remaining three judges did not exhibit any significant deviations in their internal grading consistency. Experience has shown that there is no relationship between judge severity and unexpected grading of a particular item.

Monitoring the judges on subsequent examinations has shown that the feedback provided aided judges in improving and maintaining their own internal consistency. The judges become more focused on their own internal standards and worry less about how they compare to other judges. The judges in this study had received this type of feedback for several prior examination administrations, which accounts for the fact that the judges were internally consistent when grading 95% of the slide-items.

DISCUSSION

In all judge-mediated examinations, it is important that judges receive feedback on their performance, whether the goal is inter-judge consistency or intra-judge consistency. However, the format in which this feedback is presented will determine its usefulness. By focusing on judge-by-item interactions, unexpected grading patterns can be identified. These judges relate to information presented in a graphic format and are amenable to analyzing their grading patterns. The judge does not have to guess at the cause of inconsistency from an overall correlation or a comparison to other judges. The details of each judge's performance are available to them for their personal study.

The information in the report is not comparative, but rather is analytic. Judges do not seem to like being compared to others. In fact, they seem to take pride in their individual assessments. When unexpected severity or leniency on certain items is brought to their attention, judges have a focus for analyzing their own grading. Experience has shown that judges can often identify reasons for unexpected grading patterns and then take corrective action.

For example, judge 1 was particularly hard on slide 1. When asked about this pattern, the judge responded that the slide was one he frequently encountered during his normal work, and, as a result, his expectations for excellent performance on that slide were probably higher than for the other slides. He felt more attune to the fine points for quality on that particular slide and would tend to deduct points more readily on that slide than on slides with which he was less familiar. On other examinations we found that judges, unfamiliar with a particular slide, tended to grade more lenient than expected on that slide. Their inexperience with that particular slide caused them to give the examinee the benefit of the doubt. In addition, we have found that "first-time" judges are less consistent than experienced judges who have had the benefit of feedback.

Emphasis on intra- rather than inter-judge consistency removes a great deal of stress from the judging situation. Judges need not worry about whether they are too "hard" or too "easy", whether they are grading the same way as their peers or not. Rather, judges focus on applying their expertise as honestly as possible. We know that judges are generally consistent across examinations. The goal is to give them detailed reports so that they become more aware of their personal behavior and therefore more consistent in their grading patterns.

REFERENCES

Engelhard, G. (1992). The measurement of writing competence with a many-faceted Rasch model. *Applied Measurement in Education,* 5(3), 171–191.

Linacre, J.M. (1988). *FACETS, a computer program for the analysis of multi-faceted data.* Chicago: MESA Press.

Linacre, J.M. (1989). *Multi-faceted Measurement*. Chicago: MESA Press.

Linacre, J.M. and Wright, B.D. (1992). *A User's Guide to Facets,* Chicago: MESA Press.

Lunz, M.E., Wright, B.D., Linacre, J.M. (1990). Measuring the impact of judge severity on examination scores. *Applied Measurement in Education. 3,* 331–345.

Lunz, M.E., Stahl, J.A., Wright, B.D. (1996). The invariance of judge severity calibrations. In *Objective Measurement: Theory Into Practice Volume 3* G. Engelhard, Jr. and M. Wilson (Eds.), Norwood NJ: Ablex Press.

Raymond, M., Webb, L. & Houston, W. (1991). Correcting performance rating errors in oral examinations. *Evaluation and the Health Professions. 14,* 100–122.

Wright, B.D., & Stone, M.H. (1979). *Best test design: Rasch measurement*. Chicago: MESA.

APPENDIX A

Explanation of the Judge Summary Report

I. The first page of the report lists general information about the performance of the judge on the most recent practical. The judge's name and number appear at the beginning of the report, followed by an approximate evaluation of their relative severity. This evaluation is not meant to encourage the judge to change their level of severity. Each judge is encouraged to maintain his or her own individual standard and to consistently apply this standard whenever they participate in a grading session.

II. The next section reports unexpected grading patterns. This information is derived from a judge-by-slide analysis. In this analysis, the judge's severity is compared to his or her severity on all the other slides and the slide difficulty across all the other judges. The expected rating is based on the overall severity of the judge and the overall difficulty of the slide. For example, a more severe judge would be expected to give lower grades even on relatively easy slides. A significant difference between the expected and observed grade indicates that the judge treated that particular slide in a different manner than the other slides he or she graded.

III. The final section of the first page lists the names associated with the slide numbers on the graph on the second page.

IV. The graph on the second page indicates the standardized differences from the judge-by-slide analysis discussed above. The closer to zero the less difference between an observed score and the expected value. A *positive* value indicates a slide was graded harder than expected while a *negative* value indicates a slide was graded easier than expected. Slides that require particular attention are those with standardized differences greater than 2.00 or less than −2.00. These slides will be listed in Section II as Unexpected Grading Patterns. Some variation is expected and acceptable. This detailed information on your performance is only meant to assist you in the analysis of your individual grading patterns.

chapter **8**

Examining Changes in the Home Environment with the Rasch Measurement Model*

Judith A. Monsaas
North Georgia College

George Engelhard, Jr.
Emory University

Human development occurs within the context of a variety of social environments (Bronfenbrenner, 1979; Garbarino & Abramowitz, 1992). One of the most important contexts from an ecological perspective is the home environment. Because of the potential influences of the home environment on child development in general and on the development of school-related social skills and cognitive competencies in particular, a variety of early intervention programs have been proposed for changing the home environment in order to foster optimal development (Weiss & Jacobs, 1988; White, Taylor, & Moss, 1992). Many of these interventions are motivated by the desire to change the

* Earlier versions of this chapter were presented at the annual meeting of the Eastern Educational Research Association in Clearwater, FL (February, 1993), the Seventh International Objective Measurement Workshop in Atlanta, GA (April, 1993), and the European Meeting of the Psychometric Society in Barcelona, Spain (July, 1993).

home environments of children who are believed to be at-risk for school failure. The development of methodologically sound procedures for measuring and evaluating changes in the home environments related to these interventions has been challenging. This has been particularly true for addressing these issues with culturally diverse families (Slaughter, 1988). Procedures for examining changes in the home environment have ranged from qualitative (Gilgun, Daly, & Handel, 1992) to quantitative methods (Dunst & Trivette, 1992), as well as combined approaches (Rank, 1992; Sandelowski, Holditch-Davis, & Harris, 1992).

The purposes of this chapter are to describe and illustrate a new quantitative approach based on the Rasch measurement model that can be used for evaluating changes in selected aspects of the home environment (Linacre, 1992; Fischer & Parzer, 1991). This new Rasch method differs from previous quantitative approaches in several ways. First, much of the previous research has been based on subscale or total scores as the unit of analysis. With the Rasch method, changes in the home environment related to *individual* items can be examined in detail; although traditional analyses based on item p-values have been conducted, the Rasch model provides a coherent framework that is psychometrically defensible for examining change. This item-level analysis can provide a detailed framework for examining whether or not the influences of an intervention program are the same for all of the items in the instruments used to measure the home environment. Second, the statistical analyses typically used for analyzing scores are based on the group as the level of analysis and do not focus on changes within the home environments of *individual* families. For example, if a pretest/posttest design with no control group is used, then a standard statistical analysis would be to use a t-test for dependent groups to compare the means of the families at Time 1 and Time 2. Conclusions would then be drawn about overall group differences in the home environment over time rather than about changes in individual families. Finally, the Rasch method provides a framework for combining the psychometric analyses of items with the statistical analyses of time effects. In most traditional analyses, the reliability and validity analyses are conducted first, and then separate statistical analyses are performed. There are several psychometric, statistical, and substantive advantages that can be realized from combining the measurement and statistical analyses. The approach described here will yield results comparable to those described by Wilson (1992); the major difference is that in this chapter an overall time effect parameter is estimated prior to the analyses of the interaction effects. The advantages of using the

Rasch model are illustrated in this chapter with data from the evaluation of an early intervention program.

DESCRIPTION OF THE PROGRAM

The early intervention program examined here is called the Preschool
Parent Partners (PPP) program. The PPP program is a parent-training
program designed to improve the parenting skills of the parents of
three- and four-year-olds who are at risk for later school failure. The
PPP program was implemented in an urban school system in south-
west Georgia. The PPP program involved monthly interventions with
parents of at-risk preschoolers over a nine-month period. These
monthly interventions were conducted by three teachers. During the
nine-month period, parents alternated between five school and four
home sessions. The five school sessions were conducted at an elementary school; topics covered in these sessions included behavior management (discipline) techniques, school readiness, developmental characteristics of normal three- and four-year-olds, and self-esteem. On the
four alternate months, the teachers made visits to the families where
they reinforced skills discussed at the school sessions and demonstrated additional methods parents could use in interacting with their
children. This chapter focuses on the analysis of changes in parenting
skill from the beginning to the end of the PPP program.

DESCRIPTION OF THE RASCH MODEL FOR
EXAMINING CHANGE

The FACETS model is an extension of the Rasch measurement model
(Rasch, 1980; Wright & Stone, 1979; Wright & Masters, 1982) that can
be used for examining change due to a time or treatment effect (Linacre, 1992). The FACETS model can be written as follows:

$$\log [P_{nij1}/P_{nij0}] = \beta_n - \delta_i - \Delta_j - \delta\Delta_{ij}$$

where

P_{nij1} = probability of family n being rated 1 on item i at time j,
P_{nij0} = probability of family n being rated 0 on item i at time j,
β_n = Quality of home environment for family n,
δ_i = Difficulty of item i,

Δ_j = Time effect j (Δ_1 is anchored at zero),

$\delta\Delta_{ij}$ = Interaction between difficulty of item i and time j.

The home environment facet, β_n, provides a measure of the quality of a family's home environment on a linear logistic scale (logits). The difficulty of item i in logits is δ_i. The time effect facet, Δ_j, provides an estimate in logits of the overall changes in the quality of the home environment. The interaction term, $\delta\Delta_{ij}$, provides evidence of whether or not the time effects are statistically equivalent across the items in the subscale.

METHOD

Participants

All of the participants in this study took part in PPP. Preschool children were defined as being at-risk for school failure if their parents had one or more of the following characteristics: Received Aid to Families with Dependent Children (AFDC), had low socioeconomic status as measured by the eligibility of their child for free- or reduced-price lunch, was a teenage parent, had not completed high school or any combination of these. Pretest and posttest data were available on the home environments of 40 children. There were 23 males and 17 females in the study. Twenty-seven of the participants were black, and 13 were white. Although this sample size is somewhat small, it represents the actual data that were available to the evaluators and serves to illustrate the analytic framework available with the Rasch measurement model.

Instrument

The Home Observation for Measurement of Environment (HOME; Caldwell & Bradley, 1984) instrument was selected because it is widely used by researchers who study families, and also because it measured many of the specific aspects of the home environment that were the focus of the program. The HOME instrument is designed to describe the types of stimulation available in a child's home that facilitate cognitive development. It is a 55-item scale with the following 8 subscales: learning stimulation (LEARN, 11 items), language stimulation (LANG, 7 items), physical environment (PHYS, 7 items), warmth and acceptance (WARM, 7 items), academic stimulation (ACAD, 5 items), modeling (MODEL, 5 items), variety of experience (VARI, 9 items), and acceptance (ACCEPT, 4 items). Each of the items was scored dichotomously by a teacher who visited each family and observed the interactions between the parent (or primary caregiver) and the child. About two-thirds of the items involved the teacher observing and rating the interactions. The other third of the items involved parental reports of information that was not likely to occur during a home visit (e.g., family takes child on outing at least every other week).

Procedures

The three teachers who conducted the home visits gathered the HOME data. Before the program was implemented, the three teachers were trained in the use of the HOME instrument. Although parents were not assigned to teachers at random, there is no evidence of any systematic bias in these assignments. Families remained with the same teacher throughout the program, so the same teacher conducted the pretest and posttest evaluations for each family. The teacher rated the family using the HOME during the first and last home visits. The teachers obtained HOME information on the first (October) and last (April) home visits each year. The data were analyzed using the FACETS computer program (Linacre & Wright, 1992). Item-level changes in the home environment were examined using the approach described by Linacre (1992).

RESULTS

Each of the subscales of the HOME instrument was calibrated separately. The item separation reliabilities that are comparable to KR20 reliability coefficients are shown in Table 8.1. The reliabilities are quite high and range from a high of .97 on the WARM scale to .79 on the PHYS scale. The reliability coefficient for the TOTAL scale (55 items) is .94. The χ^2 tests indicate that the differences between the items within each subscale on the HOME instrument are statistically significant.

The time effects for each subscale and the TOTAL scale are presented graphically in Figure 8.1. The time effects are statistically significant for all of the subscales and the TOTAL scale. The smallest change in the quality of the home environment was observed for the PHYS scale with a time effect of .61 logits (SE = .12), while the largest change was on the WARM scale with an effect of 2.35 logits (SE = .21).

Table 8.1.   Item Reliability for Eight Scales

Scale	Number of Items	R	χ^2	df
Learning Stimulation (LEARN)	11	.94	154.6*	10
Language Stimulation (LANG)	7	.88	62.9*	6
Physical Environment (PHYS)	7	.79	21.4*	6
Warmth and Affection (WARM)	7	.97	192.6*	6
Academic Stimulation (ACAD)	5	.96	133.7*	4
Modeling (MODEL)	5	.95	65.7*	4
Variety in Experience (VARI)	9	.94	150.8*	8
Acceptance (ACCEPT)	4	.90	43.0*	3
TOTAL	55	.94	905.6*	54

* $p < .05$

Note: R is the reliability of item separation (comparable to KR20 reliability index); χ^2 provided a test of whether or not the differences between the items are statistically significant.

The change for the TOTAL scale was also statistically significant with a time effect of 1.05 logits (SE = .06).

Up to this point, the Rasch approach has combined into one integrated analysis the (a) examination of subscale reliabilities, and (b) the statistical analyses of the time effects. In addition to the advantages of combining these two steps that are generally done separately

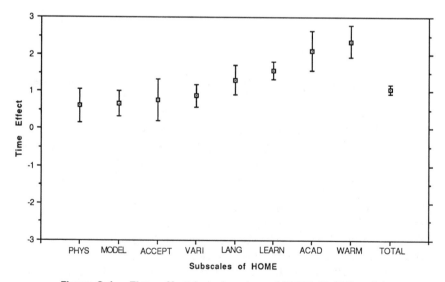

Figure 8.1.   Time effect by subscale and TOTAL (2 SE bands)

in traditional approaches to data analysis, the Rasch approach also provides additional information that contributes to the substantive interpretation of the data. For example, changes in the home environments of individual families on each item can be explored in detail. In order to illustrate some of the further advantages of the Rasch approach, the results for the ACAD scale are presented in detail. Comparable analyses can be conducted for the other subscales, as well as for the TOTAL scale.

Academic Stimulation (ACAD) Scale

The calibration of the five items in the ACAD scale are shown in Table 8.2.

The five items range in difficulty from Item 1 (Child is encouraged to learn colors) that is an easy item to Item 5 (Child is encouraged to learn to read a few words) that is a hard item. The items fit the Rasch model, and the reliability coefficient is high (R = .96). None of the z-score tests of the interation effects, $\delta\Delta_{ij}$, are statistically significant; this indicates that the time effect is consistent over the five items.

A map can be constructed to graphically illustrate the calibrations of the time effect, the five items, and the location of individual families on the ACAD scale. This map is shown in Figure 8.2.

The time effect is anchored at 0.0 for the pretest, and the size of the time effect is 2.10 logits (SE = .27). For the typical family at the time of the pretest, it is expected that they will have passed Items 1, 4 and 2, and not Items 3 and 5. The typical family at the time of the posttest is expected to have passed Items 1, 4, 2 and 3, and not to have passed Item

Table 8.2. Calibration of Items for the Academic Stimulation Scale

| Item | Difficulty | SE | FIT | Z-Scores | | Item (Child is encouraged to learn . . .) |
				Pre	Post	
5	3.81	.35	.37	−.1	0.1	to read a few words
3	0.43	.32	−1.47	0.3	−.4	spatial relationships
2	0.00	.34	−.35	−.6	0.9	patterned speech (songs, etc.)
4	−1.82	.51	1.58	−.2	0.3	numbers
1	−2.42	.06	−.61	0.8	−.7	colors
Mean	0.00	.42	−.10			
SD	2.18	.11	1.14			
Reliability = .96						

Note: The Z-scores test whether or not the interaction, $\delta\Delta_{ij}$, between time and item difficulty is statistically significant.

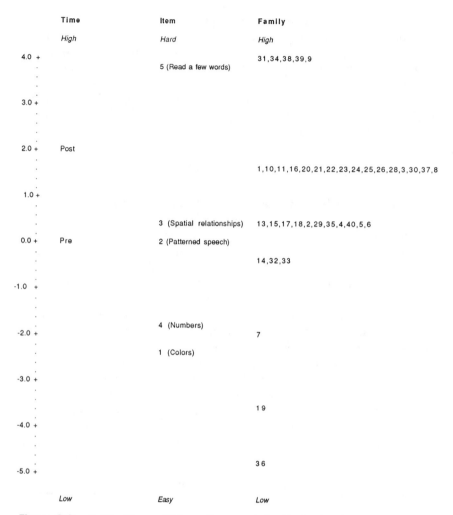

Figure 8.2. Calibrations of Time, Item, and Family for Academic Stimulation Scale

5. Families 31, 34, 38, 39 and 9 are expected to have passed all of the items, and they do in fact have observed scores of 5 on the ACAD scale.

In addition to constructing maps for each subscale, such as the one presented in Figure 8.2, it is also possible to examine in detail the effects of time on each of the items for a particular family. The rating patterns for Families 32, 1 and 21 are shown in Table 8.3.

For each of the families, there was a total of 10 observations (5 items at Time 1 and 5 items again at Time 2). The item difficulties for

Table 8.3. Observed and Expected Ratings for Selected Families

					Observations							Raw Score	FIT	Rasch Scale
	1	2	3	4	5	6	7	8	9	10			
Item(Time)	1(2)	4(2)	1(1)	2(2)	4(1)	3(2)	2(1)	3(1)	5(2)	5(1)			
Difficulty:	-4.52	-3.92	-2.42	-2.10	-1.82	-1.67	.00	.43	1.71	3.81			
Consistent Rating Patterns													
Family 32	1	1	1	1	1	1	0	0	0	0	6	-.92	-.48
	.98	.97	.87	.84	.79	.77	.38	.29	.10	.01			
Family 1	1	1	1	1	1	1	1	1	0	0	8	-.48	1.53
	1.00	1.00	.98	.97	.97	.96	.82	.75	.46	.09			
Misfitting Rating Pattern													
Family 21	0*	1	1	1	1	1	1	1	0	1*	8	2.01	1.53
	1.00	1.00	.98	.97	.97	.96	.82	.75	.46	.09			

Note: Each of the families has 10 observations (5 items in the Academic Stimulation Scale rated at two time points). The cell entries for each family are defined as follows: First row for each family is observed rating and the second row is expected rating. Asterisks indicate unexpected observed values.

these 10 observations range from −4.52 for Item 1 at Time 2 to 3.81 logits for Item 5 at Time 1. The item difficulties at Time 1 range from −2.42 logits for Item 1 to 3.81 logits for Item 5. Since the time effect is 2.10 logits, the adjusted difficulties for these five items at Time 2 ranges from −4.52 logits for Item 1 to 1.71 logits for Item 5. In other words, the item difficulties at Time 2 are simply obtained by subtracting the time effect from the item difficulties at Time 1.

The Rasch estimate for Family 32 is −.48 logits, and it is expected that items with difficulties less than −.48 would be passed, while items with difficulties above −.48 would not be passed. Family 32 has a consistent rating pattern. The agreement between the observed and expected ratings is quite high for Family 32 with a standardized fit statistic of −.92. The data for Family 32 can also be shown graphically in the form of a Family Characteristic Curve (FCC) as in Figure 8.3.

FCCs are similar to item or person characteristic curves and show graphically the probabilistic relationship between the observed and expected ratings for each family.

Families 1 and 21 have raw scores of 8, and Rasch estimates of 1.53 logits on the ACAD scale. Although these values are comparable, Family 1 has a consistent rating pattern (FIT = −.48), while Family 21 has an inconsistent and misfitting rating pattern (FIT = 2.01). Based on the Rasch model, it is expected that Family 21 would pass Item 1 at Time 2 which was not passed. It would also be expected that Item 5 at

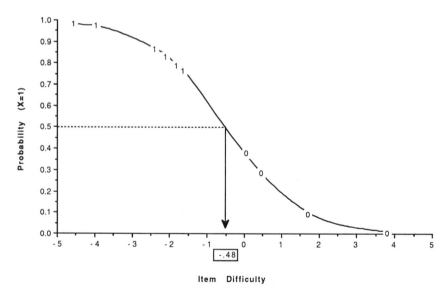

Figure 8.3.   Family Characteristic Curve (Family 32, B = −.48, Fit = −.92)

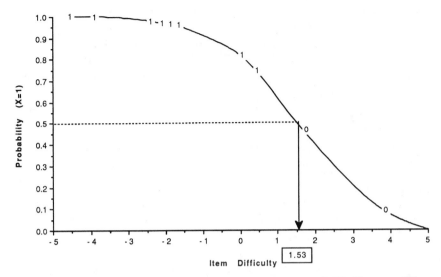

Figure 8.4. Family Characteristic Curve (Family 1, B = 1.53, Fit = −.48)

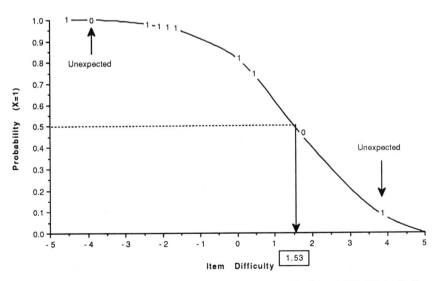

Figure 8.5. Family Characteristic Curve (Family 21, B = 1.53, Fit = 2.1)

Time 1 would not be passed, and this was passed. Inconsistent rating patterns can be detected, and examined in more detail to determine why these two unexpected ratings were observed for Family 21. The FCCs for Families 1 and 21 are shown in Figures 8.4 and 8.5 respectively.

TOTAL Scale

In addition to looking at the subscales individually, it is also informative to examine the calibration of the TOTAL scale (55 items) in terms of each subscale. The map for the TOTAL scale is presented in Figure 8.6.

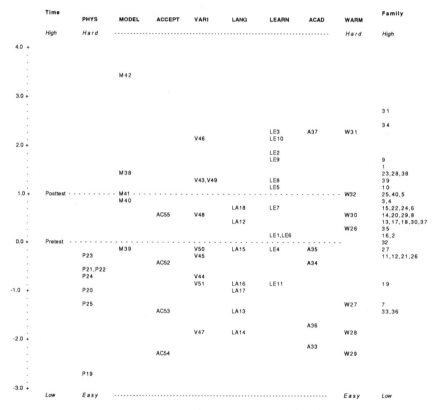

Figure 8.6. Calibrations of Time, Item (classified by subscale), and Families for Total Scale

The Time effect is 1.05 logits (SE = .06). It is clear that PHYS items tend to be easy to pass for these families, and that Item 42 (WARM scale) is hard to pass for these families. The typical family at Time 1 would pass items below the pretest line, and it would not pass items above this pretest line. At Time 2, a typical family would be expected to pass all of the items below the both the pretest and posttest lines shown in Figure 8.6. Items between the pretest and posttest lines are the most likely to change as a result of the program. Although not described in detail here, analyses similar to those presented for the ACAD scale can also be developed for the TOTAL scale.

DISCUSSION

The method proposed in this study contributes to our substantive understanding of home environments, as well as to our methodological understanding of how to quantitatively examine changes that may result from an intervention program. It also contributes to our understanding of the psychometric properties of the HOME instrument when used to measure the home environments of at-risk children. The Rasch analyses suggest that there were significant changes in the home environments of these families from the start to the end of the intervention program. The largest change was observed in the area of academic stimulation, while the smallest change was observed for the physical environment.

The Rasch model used to analyze the data in this study provides a useful framework for combining measurement with data analysis. Typically, researchers examine separately the psychometric characteristics of the instrument (reliability and validity of the scores), and then conduct the appropriate statistical analyses, such a t-tests or ANOVAs. This chapter illustrated some of the advantages of explicitly combining these two steps for analyzing data.

In summary, the purpose of this chapter was to examine changes in the home environment related to a parent training program. In order to examine these changes, a new procedure for quantifying time and treatment effects based on the Rasch measurement model was used (Linacre, 1992). Previous research on the influences of intervention programs on home environments typically treat the subscale or total scores as the unit of analysis. In this study, changes were examined with the item as the level of analysis. This item-level approach provides a detailed framework for examining whether or not the influences of the intervention program are the same for all of the items.

REFERENCES

Bronfenbrenner, U. (1979). *The ecology of human development: Experiments by nature and design.* Cambridge, MA: Harvard University Press.

Caldwell, B.M., & Bradley, R.H. (1984). *Home observation for measurement of environment.* Little Rock, Arkansas: University of Arkansas at Little Rock.

Dunst, C.J., & Trivette, C.M. (1988). Toward experimental evaluation of the family, infant, and preschool program. In H.B. Weiss and F.H. Jacobs (Eds.), *Evaluating family programs* (pp. 315–346). New York: Aldine de Gruyter.

Fischer, G., & Parzer, P. (1991). An extension of the rating scale model with an application to the measurement of change. *Psychometrika, 56*(4), 637–651.

Garbarino, J., & Abramowitz, R.H. (1992). The family as a social system. In J. Garbarino, (Ed.), *Children and families in the social environment* (pp. 71–98). Second Edition. New York: Aldine De Gruyter.

Gilgun, J. F., Daly, K., & Handel, G. (Eds.). (1992). *Qualitative methods in family research.* Newbury Park, CA: Sage Publications.

Linacre, J.M. (1992). Treatment effects. *Transactions of the Rasch Measurement SIG, 6*(2), 218–219.

Linacre, J.M., & Wright, B.D. (1992). *A user's guide to FACETS: A Rasch measurement computer program.* Chicago: MESA Press.

Pence, A.R. (Ed.). (1988). *Ecological research with children and families: From concepts to methodology.* New York: Teachers College Press.

Rank, M.R. (1992). The blending of qualitative and quantitative methods in understanding childbearing among welfare recipients. In J.F. Gilgun, K. Daly, and G. Handel (Eds.), *Qualitative methods in family research* (pp. 281–300). Newbury Park, CA: Sage Publications.

Sandelowski, M., Holditch-Davis, D., & Harris, B.G. (1992). Using qualitative and quantitative methods: The transition to parenthood of infertile couples. In J.F. Gilgun, K. Daly, and G. Handel (Eds.), *Qualitative methods in family research,* (pp. 301–322). Newbury Park, CA: Sage Publications.

Slaughter, D.T. (1988). Programs for racially and ethnically diverse American families: Some critical issues. In H.B. Weiss and F.H. Jacobs (Eds.), *Evaluating family programs,* (pp. 461–476). New York: Aldine de Gruyter.

Weiss, H.B., & Jacobs, F.H. (Eds.). (1988). *Evaluating family programs.* New York: Aldine de Gruyter.

White, K.R., Taylor, M.J., & Moss, V.D. (1992). Does research support claims about the benefits of involving parents in early intervention programs. *Review of Educational Research, 62*(1), 91–125.

Wilson, M. (1992). Measuring changes in the quality of school life. In M. Wilson (Ed.), *Objective Measurement I: Theory into Practice,* (pp. 77–96). Norwood, NJ: Ablex.

part three

The Random Coefficients Multinominal Logits (RCML) Model

chapter **9**

Formulating the Rasch Model as a Mixed Coefficients Multinomial Logit*

Raymond J. Adams
Australian Council for Educational Research

Mark Wilson
University of California, Berkeley

One popular class of qualitative response models that has found widespread application in psychometric research and practice has been labelled the Rasch family (Rasch, 1960/1980; Masters & Wright, 1984). This family of models includes the simple logistic model (SLM; Wright & Panchapakesan, 1969), the linear logistic model (Fischer, 1973), the rating scale and partial credit models (Andrich, 1978a; Masters, 1982; Glas, 1989), the partial order model (Wilson, 1990), the FACETS models (Linacre, 1989) and the multi-dimensional polytomous response model (Kelderman, 1989), to name a few.

Our purpose here is to present a random coefficients multinomial logit model (RCML) that encompasses many of the unidimensional

* The first author's work was partially supported by a research grant from the Graduate School of Education, University of California and a National Academy of Education Spencer Fellowship. The second author's work was supported by a National Academy of Education Spencer Fellowship.

143

Rasch models that have been previously proposed while allowing a flexible mechanism for generating and fitting additional models that belong to the Rasch family. Antecedents to this approach can be found in the work of Fischer (1973) and Glas (1990), who introduce the possibility of imposing linear models on the item difficulties.

We first present and describe the general form of the model as an extension of the fixed multinomial logit (Amemiya, 1981). We then illustrate how through appropriate parameterizations, the RCML encompass a range of alternative Rasch models. Conditional and marginal maximum likelihood estimation methods are described, and we fit some alternative forms of the model to an example data set.

A RANDOM COEFFICIENTS MULTINOMIAL LOGIT MODEL

The fixed multinomial logit is a regression model that is applicable when a dependent variable takes discrete values. Multinomial logit models have arisen in a range of contexts, including psycho-social models of judgment (Bock & Jones, 1968) and econometric models of probabilistic choice (McFadden, 1973).

Assuming that a dependent variable X_i takes K_i values 1, 2, . . . , K_i the multinomial logit is defined as:

$$\Pr(X_i = j) = \frac{\exp(\underline{z}'_{ij}\underline{\beta})}{\displaystyle\sum_{k=1}^{K_i} \exp(\underline{z}'_{ik}\underline{\beta})} \quad \cdot (1)$$

where the $\underline{z}'_{ij}$ are vectors of known constants and $\underline{\beta}$ is a vector of unknown (fixed) regression coefficients.

The model can be extended to a random coefficients model (or more correctly a mixed model) if a subset of the $\underline{\beta}$ parameters are considered to be random. In this paper we consider the case where $\underline{\beta} = (\theta, \underline{\xi}')'$ with θ random and $\underline{\xi}$ fixed so that letting $\underline{z}'_{ij} = (b_{ij}, \underline{a}'_{ij})$ model (1) becomes

$$\Pr(X_i = j) = \frac{\exp(b_{ij}\theta + \underline{a}'_{ij}\underline{\xi})}{\displaystyle\sum_{k=1}^{K_i} \exp(b_k\theta + \underline{a}'_{ik}\underline{\xi})} \quad (2)$$

In measurement contexts this model is suitable for the analysis of categorical response data that results from the interaction of a set of *cases* and a set of *items*. We use the terms items and cases because they are familiar in psychometrics but here they are very generally defined. A case is any object to be measured—it need not be a person. Items are defined as the instruments of measurement—they may be conventional test or questionnaire items or they may be rater-task combinations. The items are seen as fixed quantities, while the cases that are to be measured are regarded as random selections from a population. In (2) the cases are modelled with the random parameter θ, which represents the attribute being measured. The population distribution of the attribute is given by the density function $g(\theta; \underset{\sim}{\alpha})$ (with corresponding cumulative distribution function $G(\theta; \underset{\sim}{\alpha})$), where $\underset{\sim}{\alpha}$ is used to indicate a vector of parameters that characterizes the distribution.

The dependent variable X_i is the response of an individual to item i and it can take K_i values $1, 2, \ldots, K_i$. In the measurement context each of the K_i possible values for X_i are assigned a score or "level" which is given by a mapping function $B_i(k)$, which gives the performance level of the observed response k to item i. The scoring function is incorporated in (2) as the coefficient of θ, ie. $b_{ij} \equiv B_i(j)$.

In the majority of Rasch Model formulations there has been a one-to-one matching between the category to which an observation belongs and the score that is allocated to the observation. In the simple logistic model, for example, it has been standard practice to use the labels '0' and '1' to indicate both the categories of performance and the scores. A similar practice has been followed with the rating scale and partial credit models, where each category of performance is seen as indicating a different level of performance. The use of the mapping function allows a more flexible relationship between the quality of a response and the level of performance that it reflects. Examples of where this is applicable are given in Kelderman (1989), Wilson (1990) and Wilson and Adams (1992).

To describe the items we intoduce a vector of p free parameters $\underset{\sim}{\xi}' = (\xi'_1, \xi'_2, \ldots, \xi'_p)$—linear combinations of these parameters are used in the response probability model. The linear combinations are defined by design vectors $\underset{\sim}{a}'_{ik}$, $(i = 1, \ldots, I; k = 1, \ldots, K_i)$ which for notational convenience can be denoted collectively by the design matrix $\mathbf{A} = (\underset{\sim}{a}'_{11}, \underset{\sim}{a}'_{12}, \ldots, \underset{\sim}{a}'_{1k_1}, \underset{\sim}{a}'_{21}, \ldots, \underset{\sim}{a}'_{2k_2}, \ldots, \underset{\sim}{a}'_{1k_I})'$. The design matrix $\mathbf{A}$ has $\sum\limits_{i=1}^{I} K_i$ rows and p columns. The response probability model then gives the probability of a response in category x of item i as:

$$f_i(x \, ; \mathbf{A}, \underset{\sim}{\xi} \mid \theta) = \frac{\exp\{\theta B_i(x) + \underset{\sim}{a}'_{ix} \underset{\sim}{\xi}\}}{\sum\limits_{k=1}^{K_i} \exp\{\theta B_i(k) + \underset{\sim}{a}'_{ik} \underset{\sim}{\xi}\}}. \tag{3}$$

Model (3) gives the probability of observing each kind of response conditional upon a particular value of the attribute, θ. It is the specific definition of the function B_i and the vectors A that define the Rasch model for item i.

To distinguish between conditioning on specific values of random variables and dependence on known constants or unknown parameter values we use the notation $f_i(x ; A, \xi \mid \theta)$ to indicate that the distribution depends upon A and ξ and has been conditioned on the random variable θ. It will occasionally be convenient to drop the illustration of dependence on known constants or unknown parameter values and abbreviate the notation to $f_i(x \mid \theta)$.

Typically in the measurement context we model responses to a set of test items, if we consider I items (i = 1, . . . , I), then a response vector $\underset{\sim}{x} = (x_1, x_2, . . . , x_I)'$ can be constructed for each individual and a response vector scoring function can be defined as:

$$B(\underset{\sim}{x}) = \sum_{i=1}^{I} B_i(x_i).$$

Treating individual responses as conditionally independent we can write the conditional probability of observing response vector $\underset{\sim}{x}$ as:

$$f(\underset{\sim}{x} ; A, \xi \mid \theta) = \frac{\exp\{\theta B(\underset{\sim}{x}) + \underset{\sim}{a}'_{+x} \xi\}}{\Psi(\theta, \xi)}, \tag{4}$$

where $\underset{\sim}{a}'_{+x}$ is the vector sum of the design vectors corresponding to the response pattern $\underset{\sim}{x}$, and:

$$\Psi(\theta, \xi) = \prod_{i=1}^{I} \left[\sum_{k=1}^{K_i} \exp\{\theta B_i(k) + \underset{\sim}{a}'_{ik} \xi\} \right].$$

Equation (4) is a *conditional item response model* because it gives the probability of a response vector conditional upon a given level of the attribute. Note that this is a different use of the term *conditional* than that normally associated with the Rasch model where the conditional model usually refers to the result of conditioning on the sufficient statistics for θ values that are assumed fixed and not random.

A *marginal item response model* is written by combining the population model and the conditional item response model to give the probability of observing the response vector $\underset{\sim}{x}$ for a case selected at random from the population as:

$$f(\underset{\sim}{x} ; A, \underset{\sim}{\xi}, \underset{\sim}{\alpha}) = f(\underset{\sim}{x} ; A, \underset{\sim}{\xi} \mid \theta) \, dG(\theta ; \underset{\sim}{\alpha}). \tag{5}$$

The Stieljes integral is used because it reduces to the standard Riemann integral when G is continuous and to ordinary summation when G is discrete (Hewitt & Stromberg, 1965). We will also find it useful to consider a *joint item response model* which gives the probability of observing the response vector $\underset{\sim}{x}$ and the attribute value θ,

$$f(\underset{\sim}{x}, \theta; A, \underset{\sim}{\xi}, \underset{\sim}{\alpha}) = f(\underset{\sim}{x} ; A, \underset{\sim}{\xi} \mid \theta) \, g(\theta ; \underset{\sim}{\alpha}) \tag{6}$$

SOME EXAMPLE PARAMETERIZATIONS

In the usual parameterization of the SLM for a set of I dichotomous items there are I item easiness parameters, ξ. In this model the general form of the response probability function is

$$f_i(1 \mid \theta) = \frac{1}{1 + \exp\{\theta + \xi_i\}},$$

$$f_i(2 \mid \theta) = \frac{\exp\{\theta + \xi_i\}}{1 + \exp\{\theta + \xi_i\}}, \tag{7}$$

where for the purposes of identification constraints are applied to the distribution of θ—another alternative is to constrain the ξ_i. Each of the items has two response categories, $k = 1, 2$, and in this model the scoring function takes the form, $B_i(k) = K - 1$ for all i. This is consistent with a score of zero for the first category of each item and a score of one for the second category. The model is then specified by the scoring functions $B_i(k)$ matrix and the design matrix A

$$A = \begin{bmatrix} 0 & 0 & 0 & . & . & . & . & 0 & 0 \\ 1 & 0 & 0 & . & . & . & . & 0 & 0 \\ 0 & 0 & 0 & . & . & . & . & 0 & 0 \\ 0 & 1 & 0 & . & . & . & . & 0 & 0 \\ 0 & 0 & 0 & . & . & . & . & 0 & 0 \\ 0 & 0 & 1 & . & . & . & . & 0 & 0 \\ . & . & . & . & . & . & . & . & . \\ . & . & . & . & . & . & . & . & . \\ 0 & 0 & 0 & . & . & . & 0 & 1 & 0 \\ 0 & 0 & 0 & . & . & . & 0 & 0 & 0 \\ 0 & 0 & 0 & . & . & . & 0 & 0 & 1 \end{bmatrix} .$$

A has 2xI rows and I columns, the rows are grouped in pairs with the first of each pair corresponding to the first category of response to each item and the second corresponding to the second category of response. The first pair of rows in A correspond to the categories for item 1, the first row for the first category and the second row for the second. Setting the first row to all zeros, and coupling this with a scoring function that gives a score of zero for the first category, when substituted into (3) gives the numerator of the first part of (7). Similarly, setting a one in the first column of the second row and a scoring function that assigns a score of one to the second category, results in the numerator for the second part of (7).

Note also that if $\underset{\sim}{n} = (N_{11}, N_{12}, \ldots, N_{11}, N_{12})'$, where N_{ik} is the count of responses in category k for item i, then $\underset{\sim}{n}'A$ is the sufficient statistics vector for $\underset{\sim}{\xi}$. In this case

$$\underset{\sim}{n}'A = (N_{12}, N_{22}, \ldots, N_{12}),$$

showing that the sufficient statistics for ξ_i is simply the count of responses in the second category of item i. We will later show that this result holds for all of the models that we are considering.

As a second example consider the Andrich's (1978a) model for Likert-type rating scales in the form discussed by Wright & Masters (1982) and Masters & Wright (1984). For a test of I items each with K response categories this model describes the set of items with I item location parameters, δ_i (i = 1, ... , I), and K − 1 "threshold" parameters, τ_k (k = 1, ... , K − 1). (Identifying constraints normally need to be applied to both the item location and threshold parameters but we will ignore them here to simplify the discussion).

This model can be described by (3) noting that there are p = I + K − 1 free item parameters so that $\xi' = (\xi_1, \xi_2, \ldots, \xi_{I+K-1}) \equiv (-\delta_1, -\delta_2, \ldots, -\delta_I, \tau_1, \ldots, \tau_{K-1})$. The appropriate scoring function is $B_i(k) = k - 1$ for all items and the design matrix is:

Recognizing again that the sufficient statistics for $\underset{\sim}{\xi}$ are given by $\underset{\sim}{n}'A$ we see that for the item difficulty parameters the sufficient statistics are the "item scores" and for each of the category threshold parameters the sufficient statistic is the number of responses at or above that category (see Wright and Masters, 1982).

Now we consider the Binomial trials model (Andrich, 1978b) that may be appropriate when an item response format requires a number of independent attempts at each item, and the number of successes in the trials is counted (Masters and Wright, 1984). To fit the Binomial model with the multinomial logit, define $B_i(k) = k - 1$ for all items and define a parameter vector $\xi' = (\delta_1, \delta_2 \ldots \delta_I, \alpha_1, \alpha_2, \ldots \alpha_K)$ of length I + K, where I is the number of items and K is the maximum

$$A = \begin{bmatrix}
0 & 0 & 0 & . & . & . & 0 & 0 & 0 & 0 & . & . & 0 \\
1 & 0 & 0 & . & . & . & 1 & 0 & 0 & 0 & . & . & 0 \\
2 & 0 & 0 & . & . & . & 1 & 1 & 0 & 0 & . & . & 0 \\
3 & 0 & 0 & . & . & . & 1 & 1 & 1 & 0 & . & . & 0 \\
. & . & . & . & . & . & . & . & . & . & . & . & . \\
K-1 & 0 & 0 & . & . & . & 1 & 1 & 1 & 1 & . & . & 1 \\
0 & 0 & 0 & . & . & . & 0 & 0 & 0 & 0 & . & . & 0 \\
0 & 1 & 0 & . & . & . & 1 & 0 & 0 & 0 & . & . & 0 \\
0 & 2 & 0 & . & . & . & 1 & 1 & 0 & 0 & . & . & 0 \\
. & . & . & . & . & . & . & . & . & . & . & . & . \\
0 & K-1 & 0 & . & . & . & 1 & 1 & 1 & 1 & . & . & 1 \\
. & . & . & . & . & . & . & . & . & . & . & . & . \\
0 & 0 & 0 & . & . & 0 & 0 & 0 & 0 & 0 & . & . & 0 \\
0 & 0 & 0 & . & . & 1 & 1 & 0 & 0 & 0 & . & . & 0 \\
0 & 0 & 0 & . & . & 2 & 1 & 1 & 0 & 0 & . & . & 0 \\
0 & 0 & 0 & . & . & 3 & 1 & 1 & 1 & 0 & . & . & 0 \\
. & . & . & . & . & . & . & . & . & . & . & . & . \\
0 & 0 & 0 & . & . & K-1 & 1 & 1 & 1 & 1 & . & . & 1
\end{bmatrix}$$

number of observed response categories for any item. The delta parameters are item location (or difficulty) parameters and are free to be estimated, the alpha parameters are the binomial category parameters and their values are fixed at $\alpha_k = \log (k/(K - k + 1))$. The design matrix for this model is identical to that given for the rating scale model. The difference between the two models is then recognized in estimation where the alpha parameters are fixed and not estimated.

The flexibility of the RCML also allows the estimation of Rasch Models that has not previously been specifically considered. Consider, for example, a rating scale with items that fall into two subsets with the items in each subset having a different number of response alternatives. To encompass this situation, the RCML can be parameterized to estimate separate set of τ parameters for each of the item subsets. Other possibilities are illustrated in the examples that are presented at the end of the paper and in Wilson and Adams (1992) and in the chapters of this volume by Moore, Draney, and Wang and Wilson.

ESTIMATING THE RANDOM COEFFICIENTS MULTINOMIAL LOGIT MODEL

In the psychometric literature three different likelihood approaches for estimating models like those given by (4), (5), and (6) have attracted most attention. One method involves treating both the case attributes,

θ, and the item parameters, ξ, as constant but unknown parameters, and maximizing a likelihood based upon the conditional item response model. Of all the likelihood approaches, this approach, which is generally called joint maximum likelihood, leads to the simplest computational algorithms (Wright & Masters, 1982). Unfortunately, treating all parameters as fixed unknowns requires the addition of a new parameter for every additional observed case and, as Neyman and Scott (1948) have shown, under these circumstances it is possible for maximum likelihood estimators to fail to satisfy the usual asymptotic properties of efficiency and consistency. In fact, Andersen (1973) shows that for any fixed number of item parameters, MLEs of ξ will be inconsistent. For the simple logistic form of the dichotomous Rasch model Haberman (1977) has shown that if θ and ξ are treated as fixed unknowns and estimated jointly, the MLEs will be consistent and efficient when the number of items and the number of cases increases to infinity. Similar proofs for the more general forms of the Rasch model are yet to be produced. Because of these theoretical problems with this approach, we will not consider it further here.

An approach common in the Rasch modelling literature involves conditioning what we have called the conditional form of the model (ie the model given in (4)) on the sufficient statistics for the θ parameters. The resulting likelihood does not contain the θ parameters and allows consistent and efficient estimation of ξ (Andersen, 1970). Equation (4) gives the probability of observing the response vector $\underset{\sim}{x}$ given an attribute value of θ. If θ is treated as an unknown parameter to be estimated by maximizing (4), it is easy to show that $B(\underset{\sim}{x})$ is the sufficient statistic for θ. Conditioning (4) on the sufficient statistic produces an expression that does not involve the nuisance parameters, θ. The advantage of such approach is that it does not require assumptions to be made about the population distribution of θ.

For a fixed set of I items the response vector scoring function $B(\underset{\sim}{x})$ can take values $t_1, t_2, \ldots, t_s$ and if we define $\Omega_r = \{\underset{\sim}{x}: B(\underset{\sim}{x}) = r\}$ to be the set of response patterns that yield "score" r then using (3) we can write the probability of observing $B(\underset{\sim}{x}) = r$ as:

$$\text{Prob}(B(\underset{\sim}{x}) = r) = \sum_{\underset{\sim}{z} \in \Omega_r} \frac{\exp\{\theta r + \underline{a}'_{+\underline{z}}\underline{\xi}\}}{\Psi(\theta, \underline{\xi})},$$

$$= \frac{\exp(\theta r)}{\Psi(\theta, \underline{\xi})} \sum_{\underset{\sim}{z} \in \Omega_r} \exp(\underline{a}'_{+\underline{z}}\underline{\xi}),$$

so that

$$f(\underline{a} \; ; \mathbf{A}, \underline{\xi} \mid \theta, B(\underline{x}) = r) = \frac{\exp(\underline{a}'_{+x}\underline{\xi})}{\displaystyle\sum_{\underline{z} \in \Omega_r} \exp(\underline{a}'_{+z}\underline{\xi})} . \tag{8}$$

If we observe the response patterns of N individuals, the response pattern of individual n is denoted $\underline{x}_n$ and $B(\underline{x}_n) = r_n$. Then (8) can be used to construct the conditional likelihood:

$$\Lambda_c(\underline{\xi} \mid \mathbf{X}) = \prod_{n=1}^{N} f(\underline{x}_n; \mathbf{A}, \underline{\xi} \mid \theta, B(\underline{x}_n) = r_n),$$

$$= \frac{\exp\left(\displaystyle\sum_{n=1}^{N} \underline{a}'_{+x}\underline{\xi}\right)}{\displaystyle\prod_{n=1}^{N} \sum_{\underline{z} \in \Omega_{r_n}} \exp(\underline{a}'_{+z}\underline{\xi})}$$

The log likelihood is

$$\lambda_c(\underline{\xi} \mid \mathbf{X}) = \sum_{n=1}^{N} \underline{a}'_{+x}\underline{\xi} - \sum_{n=1}^{N} \log\left(\sum_{\underline{z} \in \Omega_{r_n}} \exp(\underline{a}'_{+z}\underline{\xi})\right),$$

from which we derive the likelihood equations,

$$\frac{\partial \lambda}{\partial \underline{\xi}} = \sum_{n=1}^{N} \left(\underline{a}_{+z} - \sum_{\underline{z} \in \Omega_{r_n}} \underline{a}_{+z} f(\underline{z} \; ; \mathbf{A}, \underline{\xi} \mid \theta, B(\underline{z}) = r_n\right)$$

$$= 0.$$

Conditional MLES for the $\underline{\xi}$ parameters can be obtained using a Newton-Raphson routine to solve the likelihood equations. The information matrix which is given by:

$$\frac{\partial^2 \lambda}{\partial \underline{\xi}' \partial \underline{\xi}} = -\sum_{n=1}^{N} \sum_{\underline{z} \in \Omega_{r_n}} \underline{a}_{+z} \frac{\partial f(\underline{z} \; ; \mathbf{A}, \underline{\xi} \mid \theta, B(\underline{z}) = r_n)}{\partial \underline{\xi}'}$$

$$= -\sum_{n=1}^{N} \sum_{\underline{z} \in \Omega_{r_n}} \underline{a}_{+z} \underline{a}'_{+z} f(\underline{z} \mid r_n)(1 - f(\underline{z} \mid r_n)),$$

can be used to provide asymptotic standard wrrors for the parameter estimates.

Andersen (1970) and Fischer (1981; 1983) have shown that maximum likelihood estimators of ξ based upon a conditioned likelihood are consistent and efficient. From our current perspective, however, this method of estimation has two disadvantages. First, as all information about the cases and population is conditioned out, it provides no information about the population parameters (see Andersen & Madsen, 1977). Second, despite recent advances in available technology and computing algorithms (Verhelst, Glas & van der Sluis, 1984), the computations involved in the estimation are very time-consuming. We will not consider this method of estimation further here but its use with the mixed multinomial logit will be considered in the future.

MARGINAL MAXIMUM LIKELIHOOD ESTIMATION

A third approach, that follows the work of Bock and Lieberman (1970) and Bock and Aitken (1981) involves estimating the distribution parameters $\underset{\sim}{\alpha}$ and the item parameters $\underset{\sim}{\xi}$ by maximizing a likelihood based upon the marginal multinomial logit model given by (5). This third approach has generally been called marginal maximum likelihood estimation (MML) and is the only one of the likelihood methods that makes use of the population model. The joint and conditional maximum likelihood do not require assumptions to be made with regard to the population distribution of the attribute θ.

The necessity of making assumptions about the population distribution of the attribute θ can be both an advantage and a disadvantage. The disadvantage is that the model is more stringent, in the sense that it relies on more assumptions about the data. From this perspective the joint and conditional approaches are more robust. Additionally Zwinderman and van den Wollenberg (1990) have argued that it is more difficult to diagnose sources of misfit in the marginal model. Fortunately Mislevy (1984, 1986) has shown that it is possible to make quite mild assumptions about the population distribution—one common method is to assume that the attribute distribution can be approximated by a step distribution with the density at each node estimated from the data. The advantage of estimating the population distribution in this way is that it enables direct inferences to be made about the attribute distribution in the population.

The estimation procedure that we will develop in detail is one that involves use of the marginal model. Using (5), if N individuals are drawn at random from the population, the likelihood of the observed set of response patterns is;

$$\Lambda(\underline{\alpha}, \underline{\xi} \mid \mathbf{X}) = \prod_{n=1}^{N} f(\underline{x}_n ; \mathbf{A}, \underline{\xi}, \underline{\alpha})$$

$$= \prod_{n=1}^{N} \int_{\theta} f(\underline{x}_n ; \mathbf{A}, \underline{\xi} \mid \theta) \, dG(\theta ; \underline{\alpha}).$$

The log likelihood is

$$\lambda(\underline{\alpha}, \underline{\xi} \mid \mathbf{X}) = \sum_{n=1}^{N} \left(\log \int_{\theta} f(\underline{x}_n ; \mathbf{A}, \underline{\xi} \mid \theta) \, d(G\theta ; \underline{\alpha}) \right), \tag{9}$$

from which we derive the likelihood equations,

$$\frac{\partial \lambda}{\partial \underline{\xi}} = \sum_{n=1}^{N} \left(\int_{\theta} \frac{\partial \log f(\underline{x}_n ; \mathbf{A}, \underline{\xi} \mid \theta)}{\partial \underline{\xi}} \, dH(\theta; \mathbf{A}, \xi, \underline{\alpha} \mid \underline{x}_n) \right)$$

$$= 0, \tag{10}$$

and

$$\frac{\partial \lambda}{\partial \underline{\alpha}} = \sum_{n=1}^{N} \left(\int_{\theta} \frac{\partial \log g(\theta; \underline{\alpha})}{\partial \underline{\alpha}} \, dH(\theta; \mathbf{A}, \xi, \underline{\alpha} \mid \underline{x}_n) \right)$$

$$= 0, \tag{11}$$

where $H(\theta; \mathbf{A}, \underline{\xi}, \underline{\alpha} \mid \underline{x}_n)$ is the distribution function for the marginal posterior density of θ given $\underline{x}_n$ which has the density:

$$h(\theta; \mathbf{A}, \xi, \underline{\alpha} \mid \underline{x}_n) = \frac{f(\underline{x}_n; \mathbf{A}, \underline{\xi} \mid \theta) \, g(\theta; \underline{\alpha})}{f(\underline{x}_n ; \mathbf{A}, \xi, \underline{\alpha})}.$$

THE EM ALGORITHM

Our method of maximizing (9) is not by directly solving (10) and (11) but to follow Bock and Aitken (1981) and apply the EM algorithm of Dempster, Laird, and Rubin (1977). The EM approach to estimating

the model is easy to derive and implement, but can take many iterations to converge. In practice we have found the estimation time tolerable, comparable to that required for, say, the two parameter logistic
model using BILOG (Mislevy and Bock, 1983).

In the following we describe the EM algorithm as applied to this
model in slightly more detail than is perhaps necessary. We do this for
two reasons: First, the EM algorithm when applied to Rasch models is
remarkably simple; and second, we have found that many existing
explications of the EM algorithm for IRT models do not distinguish
clearly between the nature of the estimators that are proposed, the
estimation algorithm, and the methods implemented as part of the
computational procedures.

Dempster et al. show that maximizing the expected value of the
likelihood of the joint item response model (the equivalent of their
complete data likelihood) will lead to the MLEs for the marginal item
response model (the equivalent of their incomplete data likelihood). If
we assume that, in addition to the response data $\mathbf{X}$, that the case
attributes θ have been directly observed then from (6), we can write a
joint data likelihood as:

$$\Lambda(\underset{\sim}{\alpha}, \underset{\sim}{\xi} \mid \mathbf{X}, \theta) = \prod_{n=1}^{N} f(\underline{x}_n, \theta_n; \mathbf{A}, \underset{\sim}{\xi}, \underset{\sim}{\alpha})$$

$$= \prod_{n=1}^{N} f(\underline{x}_n; \mathbf{A}, \underset{\sim}{\xi} \mid \theta_n) \, g(\theta_n; \underset{\sim}{\alpha}),$$

and the log-likelihood is:

$$\lambda(\underset{\sim}{\alpha}, \underset{\sim}{\xi} \mid \mathbf{X}, \theta) = \sum_{n=1}^{N} (\log f(\underline{x}_n; \mathbf{A}, \underset{\sim}{\xi} \mid \theta_n) + \log g(\theta_n; \underset{\sim}{\alpha})).$$

The joint log-likelihood cannot be directly maximized because it
depends upon the unknown values θ_n. But an alternative is to maximize its expectation given current estimates of the unknown values θ_n.
To do this, let $\underset{\sim}{\alpha}^{(t)}$ and $\underset{\sim}{\xi}^{(t)}$ be estimates of $\underset{\sim}{\alpha}$ and $\underset{\sim}{\xi}$ so that the marginal
posterior density of θ given x_n is estimated by:

$$h(\theta; \mathbf{A}, \underset{\sim}{\xi}^{(t)}, \underset{\sim}{\alpha}^{(t)} \underline{x}_n) = \frac{f(\underline{x}_n; \mathbf{A}, \underset{\sim}{\xi}^{(t)} \mid \theta) \, g(\theta; \underset{\sim}{\alpha}^{(t)})}{f(\underline{x}_n; \mathbf{A}, \underset{\sim}{\xi}^{(t)}, \underset{\sim}{\alpha}^{(t)})}. \tag{12}$$

The expected value of the joint log-likelihood is;

$$E_\theta(\lambda(\underset{\sim}{\alpha}, \underset{\sim}{\xi} \mid \mathbf{X}, \theta) \mid \underset{\sim}{\alpha}^{(t)}, \underset{\sim}{\xi}^{(t)}) = \sum_{n=1}^{N} \int_\theta \log f(\underset{\sim}{x}_n; \mathbf{A}, \underset{\sim}{\xi} \mid \theta_n \, dH(\theta; \mathbf{A}, \underset{\sim}{\xi}^{(t)}, \underset{\sim}{\alpha}^{(t)} \mid \underset{\sim}{x}_n)$$

$$+ \sum_{n=1}^{N} \int_\theta \log g(\theta_n; \underset{\sim}{\alpha}) \, dH(\theta; \mathbf{A}, \underset{\sim}{\xi}^{(t)}, \underset{\sim}{\alpha}^{(t)} \mid \underset{\sim}{x}_n),$$

which is by maximized by solving

$$\frac{\partial E_\theta(\lambda(\underset{\sim}{\alpha}, \underset{\sim}{\xi} \mid \mathbf{X}, \theta) \mid \underset{\sim}{\alpha}^{(t)}, \underset{\sim}{\xi}^{(t)})}{\partial \underset{\sim}{\xi}}$$

$$= \sum_{n=1}^{N} \left(\int_\theta \frac{\partial \log f(\underset{\sim}{x}_n; \mathbf{A}, \underset{\sim}{\xi} \mid \theta)}{\partial \underset{\sim}{\xi}} \, dH(\theta; \mathbf{A} \, \underset{\sim}{\xi}^{(t)}, \underset{\sim}{\alpha}^{(t)} \mid \underset{\sim}{x}_n) \right)$$

$$= \sum_{n=1}^{N} \sum_{i=1}^{I} \left[\underset{\sim}{a}_{ix_{ni}} - \int_\theta \sum_{k=1}^{K_i} (\underset{\sim}{a}_{ik} f_i(k \mid \theta) \, dH(\theta; \mathbf{A}, \underset{\sim}{\xi}^{(t)}, \underset{\sim}{\alpha}^{(t)} \mid \underset{\sim}{x}_n) \right]$$

$$= \sum_{n=1}^{N} [\underset{\sim}{a}_n - \int_\theta \underset{\sim}{a}(\theta, \underset{\sim}{\xi}) \, dH(\theta; \mathbf{A}, \underset{\sim}{\xi}^{(t)}, \underset{\sim}{\alpha}^{(t)} \mid \underset{\sim}{x}_n)]$$

$$= 0, \tag{13}$$

where $\underset{\sim}{a}_n = \Sigma_{i=1}^{I} \underset{\sim}{a}_{ix_{ni}}$ is the sum of the design vectors that correspond to the response vector of person n and $\underset{\sim}{a}(\theta, \underset{\sim}{\xi}) = \Sigma_{i=1}^{I} \Sigma_{k=1}^{K_i} (\underset{\sim}{a}_{ik} f_i(k \mid \theta)$ is the conditional expectation of $\underset{\sim}{a}_n$ given θ.

For the distribution parameters $\underset{\sim}{\alpha}$, the form of the likelihood equations depends upon the choice of population distribution. In this paper we consider the possibility of using a normal population distribution so that $\underset{\sim}{\alpha} = (\mu, \sigma^2)$, and:

$$g(\theta, \underset{\sim}{\alpha}) = \frac{1}{\sigma\sqrt{2\pi}} \exp\left\{ -\frac{1}{2} \left(\frac{\theta - \mu}{\sigma} \right)^2 \right\},$$

and, a step distribution with nodes $\theta_1, \ldots, \theta_Q$, so that $\underset{\sim}{\alpha} = (w_1, \ldots, w_Q)$ are the densities of the distribution at each node with

$$g(\theta_q, \underset{\sim}{\alpha}) = w_q \quad \text{for } q = 1, \ldots, Q \quad \text{and} \quad \sum_{q=1}^{Q} w_q = 1.$$

For both of the distributions we have chosen, direct estimates of the population parameters are available. The general form of the likelihood equation is:

$$\frac{\partial E_\theta(\lambda(\underset{\sim}{\alpha}, \underset{\sim}{\xi} \mid \mathbf{X}, \theta) \mid \underset{\sim}{\alpha}^{(t)}, \underset{\sim}{\xi}^{(t)}}{\partial \underset{\sim}{\alpha}} = \sum_{n=1}^{N} \left(\int_\theta \frac{\partial \log g(\theta; \underset{\sim}{\alpha})}{\partial \underset{\sim}{\alpha}} \, dH(\theta; \mathbf{x}, \underset{\sim}{\xi}^{(t)}, \underset{\sim}{\alpha}^{(t)} \mid \underset{\sim}{x}_n) \right)$$

$$= 0. \tag{14}$$

Solving this in normal case leads to:

$$\hat{\mu} = \frac{1}{N} \sum_{n=1}^{N} \int_\theta \theta \, dH(\theta; \mathbf{A}, \underset{\sim}{\xi}^{(t)}, \underset{\sim}{\alpha}^{(t)} \mid \underset{\sim}{x}_n),$$

$$\hat{\sigma}^2 = \frac{1}{N} \sum_{n=1}^{N} \int_\theta (\theta - \mu)^2 \, dH(\theta; \mathbf{A}, \underset{\sim}{\xi}^{(t)}, \underset{\sim}{\alpha}^{(t)} \mid \underset{\sim}{x}_n).$$

and for the step distribution we find that

$$\hat{w}_q = \frac{1}{N} \sum_{n=1}^{N} h(\theta_q; \mathbf{A}, \underset{\sim}{\xi}^{(t)}, \underset{\sim}{\alpha}^{(t)} \mid \underset{\sim}{x}_n), \qquad \text{for } q = 1, \ldots, Q.$$

The EM algorithm proceeds by using estimates $\underset{\sim}{\alpha}^{(t)}$ and $\underset{\sim}{\xi}^{(t)}$ to estimate the marginal posterior (12), (the E-step of the algorithm) and then maximizing the expected value of the joint likelihood by solving (13) and (14) (the M-step of the algorithm) which yields improved estimates $\underset{\sim}{\alpha}^{(t+1)}$ and $\underset{\sim}{\xi}^{(t+1)}$. The procedure is then repeated until convergence. Dempster et al. show that the final estimates $\hat{\underset{\sim}{\alpha}}$ and $\hat{\underset{\sim}{\xi}}$ are the MLEs for the marginal model (see also Glas, 1989).

Louis (1982) has shown that it is possible to estimate an asymptotic variance–covariance matrix for the parameter estimates from the joint likelihood. If we let χ denote a vector containing both $\underset{\sim}{\alpha}$ and $\underset{\sim}{\xi}$, Louis (1982, equation 3.2) shows that an asymptotic variance–covariance matrix for the parameter estimates is given by the inverse of:

$$\mathbf{I} = E_\theta \left(\frac{\partial^2 \lambda}{\partial \underset{\sim}{\zeta} \partial \underset{\sim}{\zeta}'} - \frac{\partial \lambda}{\partial \underset{\sim}{\zeta}} \frac{\partial \lambda}{\partial \underset{\sim}{\zeta}'} \,\Big|\, \hat{\underset{\sim}{\zeta}} \right), \tag{15}$$

evaluated at $\hat{\underset{\sim}{\zeta}}$ and where $\lambda \equiv \lambda(\underset{\sim}{\alpha}, \underset{\sim}{\xi} \mid \mathbf{X}, \theta)$.

For the normal population distribution the integration required for the solution of (13) and (14) is performed using quadrature. Equation (13) is replaced by a quadrature approximation

$$\sum_{n=1}^{N} \left[\underline{a}_n - \int_\theta \underline{\bar{a}} \, dH(\theta; \mathbf{A}, \underline{\xi}^{(t)}, \underline{\alpha}^{(t)} \mid \underline{a}_n) \right]$$

$$\approx \sum_{n=1}^{N} \underline{a}_n - \sum_{n=1}^{N} \sum_{q=1}^{Q} \underline{\bar{a}}(\theta_q, \underline{\xi}) \, h(\theta_q; \mathbf{A}, \underline{\xi}^{(t)}, \underline{\alpha}^{(t)} \mid \underline{a}_n)$$

$$= \sum_{n=1}^{N} \underline{a}_n - \sum_{q=1}^{Q} \underline{\bar{a}}(\theta_q, \underline{\xi}) \sum_{n=1}^{N} h(\theta_q; \mathbf{A}, \underline{\xi}^{(t)}, \underline{\alpha}^{(t)} \mid \underline{a}_n),$$

and for (14),

$$\mu^{(t+1)} = \sum_{n=1}^{N} \int_\theta \theta \, dH(\theta; \mathbf{A}, \underline{\xi}^{(t)}, \underline{\alpha}^{(t)} \mid \underline{x}_n)$$

$$\approx \sum_{q=1}^{Q} \theta_q \sum_{n=1}^{N} h(\theta_q; \mathbf{A}, \underline{\xi}^{(t)}, \underline{\alpha}^{(t)} \mid \underline{x}_n),$$

$$\sigma^{2(t+1)} = \sum_{n=1}^{N} \int_\theta (\theta - \mu)^2 \, dH(\theta; \mathbf{A}, \underline{\xi}^{(t)}, \underline{\alpha}^{(t)} \mid \underline{x}_n)$$

$$\approx \sum_{q=1}^{Q} (\theta_q - \mu)^2 \sum_{n=1}^{N} h(\theta_q; \mathbf{A}, \underline{\xi}^{(t)}, \underline{\alpha}^{(t)} \mid \underline{x}_n).$$

The algorithm proceeds by calculating $\sum_{n=1}^{N} h(\theta_q; \mathbf{A}, \underline{\xi}^{(t)}, \underline{\alpha}^{(t)} \mid \underline{x}_n)$ for q = 1, . . . , Q, which is then substituted into the likelihood equations which are solved to produce updated estimates $\underline{\xi}^{(t+1)}$ and $\underline{\alpha}^{(t+1)}$.

The likelihood equations for the item parameter estimates are solved using a Newton-Raphson routine. The quadrature form of the matrix of second derivatives required for this solution is:

$$I(\underline{\xi}) = -\sum_{q=1}^{Q} \left(\left(\sum_{i=1}^{I} \sum_{h=1}^{m_i} (\underline{a}_{ih}\underline{a}_{ih}f_i(h \mid \theta)) - \underline{\bar{a}}'(\theta_q, \underline{\xi})\underline{\bar{a}}(\theta_q, \underline{\xi}) \right) \sum_{n=1}^{N} h(\theta_q; \mathbf{A}, \underline{\xi}^{(t)}, \underline{\alpha}^{(t)} \mid \underline{x}_n) \right).$$

When there are a large number of item parameters to be estimated (more than 30), this matrix becomes too big to routinely calculate and invert. On these occasions, however, the off-diagonal elements tend to be small and can be ignored in searching for the updated estimates. Calculation and inversion need only occur once, after convergence. Standard errors are calculated using (15) by calculating the first and second derivatives of the joint log-likelihood at $\hat{\zeta}$ and then integrating over the posterior density.

EXAMPLE

To illustrate the RCML we fit the model to a small set of data collected from an administration of the International Language Testing System (IELTS), an essay test for academic purposes. Additional examples are provided in the chapters by Draney, Moore and Wang and Wilson.

The IELTS (Ingram, 1990) is a joint British-Australian test of English for Academic Purposes. It is primarily intended as a screening test for university selection. The skills of listening and speaking are tested in general, non-academic contexts, while modules assessing reading and writing are academically oriented and subject-area specific. There are separate modules for (broadly) Arts and Social Sciences, Medical and Life Sciences, and Science and Technology; there is also a General Training module for students coming on non-academic, training attachments in an English speaking environment.

The writing test in the academic modules comprises two tasks. The first task, the only one we use in our example, is an information transfer task. Candidates are required to produce a text of at least 100 words on the basis of a stimulus consisting of a diagram or other graphic representation of information. In the data that we analyze the performances on the task are rated on a five-point rating scale for each of three rating criteria: task fulfillment, coherence and cohesion, and sentence structure. For example, in the task fulfillment category, the rating descriptors range from "The seriousness of the flaws in this answer make it difficult to judge in relation to the task" at 0, to "This is an answer which fulfills the task in a way which the reader finds completely satisfactory" at 4. A common method of scoring the IELTS is to sum the scores on the three rating criteria and to produce an overall score. Such a procedure assumes the unidimensionality of the three rating criteria, an assumption that we will also make.

The data we use are from a study by McNamara and Adams (1991) in which 49 candidates taking the Arts and Social Sciences module were rated on the first written task. Note that this data set is very small, and would not usually be considered large enough for a "serious" analysis. It does however illustrate a useful potential application of the RCML. In the data we will analyze, each candidate was judged by two raters using the three criteria. In formulating the RCML for these data we consider the combination of two raters and three criteria as constituting six items.

A model that allows each item to have a unique difficulty, each rater to have a unique "harshness", and for a unique rating structure to be applied to each criteria-rater combination is a partial credit model and it is specified by the design matrix:

$A =$

0	0	0	0	0	0	0	0	0	0	0	0	0	0	0	0	0	0	0	0	0
1	0	1	1	0	0	0	0	0	0	0	0	0	0	0	0	0	0	0	0	0
2	0	2	1	1	0	0	0	0	0	0	0	0	0	0	0	0	0	0	0	0
3	0	3	1	1	1	0	0	0	0	0	0	0	0	0	0	0	0	0	0	0
4	0	4	0	0	0	0	0	0	0	0	0	0	0	0	0	0	0	0	0	0
0	0	0	0	0	0	0	0	0	0	0	0	0	0	0	0	0	0	0	0	0
0	1	1	0	0	0	1	0	0	0	0	0	0	0	0	0	0	0	0	0	0
0	2	2	0	0	0	1	1	0	0	0	0	0	0	0	0	0	0	0	0	0
0	3	3	0	0	0	1	1	1	0	0	0	0	0	0	0	0	0	0	0	0
0	4	4	0	0	0	0	0	0	0	0	0	0	0	0	0	0	0	0	0	0
0	0	0	0	0	0	0	0	0	0	0	0	0	0	0	0	0	0	0	0	0
-1	-1	1	0	0	0	0	0	0	1	0	0	0	0	0	0	0	0	0	0	0
-2	-2	2	0	0	0	0	0	0	1	1	0	0	0	0	0	0	0	0	0	0
-3	-3	3	0	0	0	0	0	0	1	1	1	0	0	0	0	0	0	0	0	0
-4	-4	4	0	0	0	0	0	0	0	0	0	0	0	0	0	0	0	0	0	0
0	0	0	0	0	0	0	0	0	0	0	0	0	0	0	0	0	0	0	0	0
1	0	-1	0	0	0	0	0	0	0	0	0	1	0	0	0	0	0	0	0	0
2	0	-2	0	0	0	0	0	0	0	0	0	1	1	0	0	0	0	0	0	0
3	0	-3	0	0	0	0	0	0	0	0	0	1	1	1	0	0	0	0	0	0
4	0	-4	0	0	0	0	0	0	0	0	0	0	0	0	0	0	0	0	0	0
0	0	0	0	0	0	0	0	0	0	0	0	0	0	0	0	0	0	0	0	0
0	1	-1	0	0	0	0	0	0	0	0	0	0	0	1	0	0	0	0	0	0
0	2	-2	0	0	0	0	0	0	0	0	0	0	0	1	1	0	0	0	0	0
0	3	-3	0	0	0	0	0	0	0	0	0	0	0	1	1	1	0	0	0	0
0	4	-4	0	0	0	0	0	0	0	0	0	0	0	0	0	0	0	0	0	0
0	0	0	0	0	0	0	0	0	0	0	0	0	0	0	0	0	0	0	0	0
-1	-1	-1	0	0	0	0	0	0	0	0	0	0	0	0	0	0	1	0	0	0
-2	-2	-2	0	0	0	0	0	0	0	0	0	0	0	0	0	0	1	1	0	0
-3	-3	-3	0	0	0	0	0	0	0	0	0	0	0	0	0	0	1	1	1	0
-4	-4	-4	0	0	0	0	0	0	0	0	0	0	0	0	0	0	0	0	0	0

The matrix contains 30 rows, one for each of the five possible responses to the six items. The categories of response to each item are fully ordered and this is reflected through the use of the scoring function, $B_i(k) = k - 1$. Column one of the matrix corresponds to the difficulty parameter for the first criterion, δ_1, column two to the diffi-

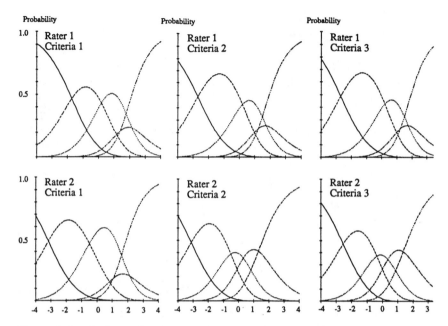

Figure 9.1. Estimated category characteristic curves for the partial credit model.

culty parameter of the second criterion, δ_2, and column three to the difference between the harshness of the two raters, ρ. The remaining 18 columns specify the rating structure parameters: τ_{ij}, $i = 1, \ldots, 6$, $j = 1, 2, 3$. For the purpose of model identification each set of parameters has been constrained to have a zero mean.

The results of fitting this model using a normal population distribution are shown in Figure 9.1 which illustrates the complete set of estimated category characteristic curves (CCCs) for the six items (rater criteria combinations) and Table 9.1, which gives the parameter estimates and their standard error estimates. To test the fit of the model, we use the Glas (1989) R_1 χ^2 statistic which for this model is 126.01 on 119 degrees of freedom indicating an acceptable fit of the model.

Interestingly the CCCs plotted in Figure 9.1 show that while there is an inconsistency between the raters in their use of the rating structure, there is more consistency within each rater. This is particularly true for rater 1. That is, the data may be fitted by a model that constrains the rating structure to be equal across criteria for each rater—we call this a fixed rater structure model. The design matrix necessary for fitting such a model is:

$$
\mathbf{A} =
\begin{bmatrix}
0 & 0 & 0 & 0 & 0 & 0 & 0 & 0 & 0 \\
1 & 0 & 1 & 1 & 0 & 0 & 0 & 0 & 0 \\
2 & 0 & 2 & 1 & 1 & 0 & 0 & 0 & 0 \\
3 & 0 & 3 & 1 & 1 & 1 & 0 & 0 & 0 \\
4 & 0 & 4 & 0 & 0 & 0 & 0 & 0 & 0 \\
0 & 0 & 0 & 0 & 0 & 0 & 0 & 0 & 0 \\
0 & 1 & 1 & 1 & 0 & 0 & 0 & 0 & 0 \\
0 & 2 & 2 & 1 & 1 & 0 & 0 & 0 & 0 \\
0 & 3 & 3 & 1 & 1 & 1 & 0 & 0 & 0 \\
0 & 4 & 4 & 0 & 0 & 0 & 0 & 0 & 0 \\
0 & 0 & 0 & 0 & 0 & 0 & 0 & 0 & 0 \\
-1 & -1 & 1 & 1 & 0 & 0 & 0 & 0 & 0 \\
-2 & -2 & 2 & 1 & 1 & 0 & 0 & 0 & 0 \\
-3 & -3 & 3 & 1 & 1 & 1 & 0 & 0 & 0 \\
-4 & -4 & 4 & 0 & 0 & 0 & 0 & 0 & 0 \\
0 & 0 & 0 & 0 & 0 & 0 & 0 & 0 & 0 \\
1 & 0 & -1 & 0 & 0 & 0 & 1 & 0 & 0 \\
2 & 0 & -2 & 0 & 0 & 0 & 1 & 1 & 0 \\
3 & 0 & -3 & 0 & 0 & 0 & 1 & 1 & 1 \\
4 & 0 & -4 & 0 & 0 & 0 & 0 & 0 & 0 \\
0 & 0 & 0 & 0 & 0 & 0 & 0 & 0 & 0 \\
0 & 1 & -1 & 0 & 0 & 0 & 1 & 0 & 0 \\
0 & 2 & -2 & 0 & 0 & 0 & 1 & 1 & 0 \\
0 & 3 & -3 & 0 & 0 & 0 & 1 & 1 & 1 \\
0 & 4 & -4 & 0 & 0 & 0 & 0 & 0 & 0 \\
0 & 0 & 0 & 0 & 0 & 0 & 0 & 0 & 0 \\
-1 & -1 & -1 & 0 & 0 & 0 & 1 & 0 & 0 \\
-2 & -2 & -2 & 0 & 0 & 0 & 1 & 1 & 0 \\
-3 & -3 & -3 & 0 & 0 & 0 & 1 & 1 & 1 \\
-4 & -4 & -4 & 0 & 0 & 0 & 0 & 0 & 0 \\
\end{bmatrix}
$$

The estimated parameter values for this model are given in Table 9.2. The fixed rater structure model is a sub-model of the partial credit model, which allows us to compare the fit of the two models using the change in the likelihood ratio χ^2. The likelihood ratio χ^2 for the partial credit model is 626.24 and for the fixed rater structure it is 649.12. The difference of 27.88 on 12 degrees of freedom is significant at the 5% level, indicating that the fixed rater structure model fits significantly worse than the partial credit model. The Glas R_1 χ^2 is 141.69 on 131 degrees of freedom so even though the likelihood ratio χ^2 indicates a significantly worse fit the absolute fit is still appears to be satisfactory.

An alternative sub-model to the fixed rater structure model is a

Table 9.1.   Estimates for the Partial Credit Model for the International Language Testing System

Parameter[1]		Estimate	Standard Error
Difficulty of Criterion one	δ_1	−0.20	0.03
Difficulty of Criterion two	δ_2	0.21	0.03
Rater of Harshness contrast	ρ	−0.31	0.03
Steps for Criterion One, Rater One	τ_{11}	2.22	0.31
	τ_{12}	0.32	0.29
	τ_{13}	−1.65	0.45
Steps for Criterion Two, Rater One	τ_{21}	2.83	0.33
	τ_{22}	−0.09	0.28
	τ_{23}	−1.63	0.40
Steps for Criterion Three, Rater One	τ_{31}	3.05	0.40
	τ_{32}	0.37	0.29
	τ_{33}	−2.25	0.52
Steps for Criterion One, Rater Two	τ_{41}	0.78	0.23
	τ_{42}	1.51	0.23
	τ_{43}	−1.74	0.31
Steps for Criterion Two, Rater Two	τ_{51}	2.63	0.35
	τ_{52}	0.00	0.28
	τ_{53}	−0.82	0.30
Steps for Criterion Three, Rater Two	τ_{61}	2.24	0.33
	τ_{62}	0.07	0.27
	τ_{63}	−0.66	0.30

[1] The model is identified by ensuring that the sum of criterion difficulties is zero and the sum of rater harshness is zero. It follows that the difficulty of the third criteria is the negative sum of the difficulties of the first two criterion and the harshness of the second rater is the negative of the harshness of the first rater.

Table 9.2.   Estimates for the Fixed Rater Structure Model for International Language Testing System Data

Parameter[1]		Estimate	Standard Error
Difficulty of Criterion one	δ_1	−0.20	0.03
Difficulty of Criterion two	δ_2	0.21	0.03
Rater Harshness contrast	ρ	−0.31	0.03
Steps for Criterion One	τ_{11}	2.59	0.08
	τ_{12}	0.24	0.23
	τ_{13}	−1.80	0.28
Steps for Criterion Two	τ_{21}	1.82	0.26
	τ_{22}	0.48	0.16
	τ_{23}	−1.01	0.20

[1] The model is identified by ensuring that the sum of criterion difficulties is zero and the sum of rater harshness is zero. It follows that the difficulty of the third criterion is the negative sum of the difficulties of the first two criteria and the harshness of the second rater is the negative of the harshness of the first rater.

Table 9.3. Estimates for the Fixed Criterion Structure Model for International Language Testing System Data

Parameter[1]		Estimate	Standard Error
Difficulty of Criterion one	δ_1	−0.20	0.03
Difficulty of Criterion two	δ_2	0.20	0.03
Rater Harshness contrast	ρ	−0.37	0.03
Steps for Criterion One	τ_{11}	1.65	0.22
	τ_{12}	0.79	0.28
	τ_{13}	−1.76	0.26
Steps for Criterion Two	τ_{21}	2.82	0.13
	τ_{22}	−0.08	0.71
	τ_{23}	−1.16	0.26
Steps for Criterion Three	τ_{31}	2.69	0.13
	τ_{32}	0.18	0.93
	τ_{33}	−1.30	0.28

[1] The model is identified by ensuring that the sum of criterion difficulties is zero and the sum of rater harshness is zero. It follows that the difficulty of the third criteria is the negative sum of the difficulties of the first two criterion and the harshness of the second rater is the negative of the harshness of the first rater.

fixed criterion structure that constrains the rating structures for a criterion to be the same regardless of the rater, although rater harshness is still allowed to vary. The parameter estimates and standard errors for this model are shown in Table 9.3. The Glas R_1 χ^2 is 148.77 on 128 degrees of freedom and the change in the likelihood ratio χ^2 is 25.24 on nine degrees of freedom. Our analysis appears to be giving some support to the notion that raters may have a scoring style, that is, they use the rating structure in a fixed way regardless of the criterion.

DISCUSSION

As Rasch models are applied in more complex situations, the problem of finding an appropriate model to suit the structure of the context has become a complex one. The tools available for creating and comparing alternative models in this family are few. Linacre's FACETS program (Linacre and Wright, 1992) can fit many, but not all, of the models available with the RCML. FACETS has proven to be a very useful and flexible piece of software but it is restricted to joint maximum likelihood estimation and will in general produce biased parameters estimates. Kelderman's program, LOGIMO (Kelderman & Steen, 1986), use a quasi-loglinear approach to estimate the SLM and partial credit models as well as the multidimensional polytomous response model, but does not allow cross-item constraints like those used in the rating scale model. Thissen's program MULTILOG (Thissen, 1985), estimates the SLM and partial credit models, as well as the rating scale model, using marginal maximum likelihood; but is not sufficiently flexible to estimate all of the models considered here. The lack of general analysis tools appears to have arisen because the various Rasch models have been developed relatively independently and, apart from FACETS, LOGIMO and MULTILOG, their chosen parameterizations have been "hard-wired" into software.

The RCML has been designed with this concern in mind. It prompts the analyst to consider particular models within a large class of multifaceted unidimensional Rasch models. The incorporation of a design matrix allows a flexible approach to model specification, including the consideration of related models created by constraining parameters to produce less complex models, and by building in extra parameters corresponding to unparameterized observational conditions to produce more complex models.

REFERENCES

Amemiya, T. (1981). Qualitative response models: A survey. *Journal of Economic Literature, 19,* 1483–1536.

Andersen, E.B. (1970). Asymptotic properties of conditional maximum likelihood estimators. *Journal of the Royal Statistical Society, Series B, 32,* 283–301.

Andersen, E.B. (1973). Conditional inference for multiple choice questionnaires. *British Journal of Mathematical and Statistical Psychology, 26,* 31–44.

Andersen, E.B., & Madsen, M. (1977). Estimating the parameters of the latent population distribution. *Psychometrika, 42,* 357–374.

Andrich, D.A. (1978a). A rating formulation for ordered response categories. *Psychometrika, 43,* 561–573.

Andrich, D.A. (1978b). A binomial latent trait model for the study of Likert-style attitude questionnaires. *British Journal of Mathematical and Statistical Psychology, 31,* 84–98.

Bock, R.D., & Aitken, M. (1981). Marginal maximum likelihood estimation of item parameters: An application of the EM algorithm. *Psychometrika, 46,* 443–459.

Bock, R.D., & Jones, L.V. (1968). *The measurement and prediction of judgement and choice.* San Francisco: Holden-Day.

Bock, R.D., & Lieberman, M. (1970). Fitting a response model for n dichotomously scored items. *Psychometrika, 35,* 179–187.

Dempster, A.P., Laird, N.M., & Rubin, D.B. (1977). Maximum likelihood from incomplete data via the EM algorithm. *Journal of the Royal Statistical Society, Series B, 39,* 1–38.

Draney, K. (1993). Measuring learning in LISP: An application of the random coefficients multinomial logit model. *In this volume.*

Fischer, G.H. (1973). The linear logistic model as an instrument in educational research. *Acta Psychologica, 37,* 359–374.

Fischer, G.H. (1981). On the existence and uniqueness of maximum likelihood estimates in the Rasch model. *Psychometrika, 46,* 59–77.

Fischer, G.H. (1983). Logistic latent trait models with linear constraints. *Psychometrika, 48,* 3–26.

Glas, C.A.W. (1989). *Contributions to estimation and testing Rasch Models.* Doctoral Dissertation. Universiteit Twente.

Haberman, S.J. (1977). Maximum likelihood estimates in exponential response models. *Annals of Statistics, 5,* 815–841.

Hewitt, E. & Stromberg, K. (1965). *Real and abstract analysis.* Berlin: Springer-Verlag.

Ingram, D.E. (1990, April). *The International English Language Testing System (IELTS): Its nature and development.* Paper presented at the RELC Seminar on "Language Testing and Language Program Evaluation," Singapore.

Kelderman, H. (1989). *Loglinear multidimensional IRT models for polytomously scored items.* Paper presented at the Fifth International Objective Measurement Workshop. University of California, Berkeley. March 25–26, 1989.

Kelderman, H., & Steen, R. (1986). *LOGIMO I* [computer program]. Enschede, The Netherlands: University of Twente, Department of Education.

Linacre, J.M. (1989). *Many faceted Rasch measurement.* Doctoral Dissertation. University of Chicago.

Linacre, J.M. & Wright, B.D. (1992). A user's guide to FACETS: A Rasch measurement program. Chicago: MESA Press.

Louis, T.A. (1982). Finding the observed information matrix when using the EM algorithm. *Journal of the Royal Statistical Society, Series B, 44,* 226–233.

McFadden, D. (1973). Conditional logit analysis of qualitative choice behaviour. In P. Zarembka (Ed.). *Frontiers in econometrics.* (pp. 105–142). New York: Academic Press.

McNamara, T.F., & Adams, R.J. (1991). *Exploring rater behaviour with Rasch techniques.* Paper presented at the 13th Language Testing Research Colloquium, Educational Testing Service, Princeton, NJ, 21–23 March 1991.

Masters, G.N. (1982). A Rasch model for partial credit scoring. *Psychometrika, 47,* 149–174.

Masters, G.N., & Wright, B.D. (1984). The essential process in a family of measurement models. *Psychometrika, 49,* 529–544.

Mislevy, R.J. (1984). Estimating latent distributions. *Psychometrika, 49,* 359–381.

Mislevy, R.J. (1986). Bayes modal estimation in item response models. *Psychometrika, 51,* 177–195.

Mislevy, R.J., & Bock, R.D. (1983). *BILOG: Analysis and Scoring of Binary*

Items with One-, Two-, and Three Parameter Logistic Models. Mooresville, IN: Scientific Software Inc.

Moore, S. (1996). Estimating differential item functioning in the polytomous case with the random coefficients multinomial logit model. In G. Engelhard, Jr. & M. Wilson (Eds.) *Objective Measurement: Theory Into Practice, Volume 3.* Norwood, NJ: Ablex, (219–238).

Neyman, J., & Scott, E.L. (1948). Consistent estimates based on partially consistent observations. *Econometrika, 16,* 1–32.

Press, W., Flannery, B., Teukolsky, S., & Vetterling, W. (1986). *Numerical recipes: The art of scientific computing.* New York: Cambridge University Press.

Rasch, G. (1980). *Probabilistic models for some intelligence and attainment tests.* (expanded ed.). Chicago: The University of Chicago Press. (Original work published 1960).

Thissen, D. (1985). *MULTILOG: Analysis and test scoring for multiple category items.* Mooresville, IN: Scientific Software Inc.

Verhelst, N.D., Glas, C.A.W., & van der Sluis, A. (1984). Estimation problems in the Rasch model: the basic symmetric functions. *Computational Statistics Quarterly, 1,* 245–262.

Wang, W.C., and Wilson, M. (1994). Comparing multiple choice and performance-based items using item response modelling. *In this volume.*

Wilson, M. (1989). *An extension of the partial credit model to incorporate diagnostic information.* Paper presented at the Fifth International Objective Measurement Workshop, University of California, Berkeley. March 25–26, 1989.

Wilson, M.R., & Adams, R.J. (1993). Marginal maximum likelihood estimation for the ordered partition model. *Journal of Educational Statistics, 18,* 69–90.

Wright, B.D., & Masters, G.N. (1982). *Rating scale analysis: Rasch measurement.* Chicago: MESA Press.

Wright, B.D. & Panchapakesan, N. (1969). A procedure for sample-free item analysis. *Educational and Psychological Measurement, 29,* 23–48.

Zwinderman, A.H., & van den Wollenberg, A.L. (1990). Robustness of marginal maximum likelihood estimation in the Rasch model. *Applied Psychological Measurement, 14,* 73–81.

chapter **10**

Comparing Multiple-choice Items and Performance-based Items Using Item Response Modeling*

Wen-chung Wang
National Taiwan University

Mark Wilson
University of California, Berkeley

The initial enthusiasm of multiple-choice testing can be attributed to Alpha Intelligence Test during World War I. Since then, multiple-choice items have been widely used in psychological and educational testing. The administrative convenience, computerized scoring (objective ranking), and economic character of multiple-choice items makes them an automatic choice for test developers. Each multiple-choice item is designed to tap some of the skills or knowledge required for success. A tendency to provide correct answers over many multiple-

_____

* The funding of this research was supported by NSF Grant RED-9255272. The first author's work was supported by a dissertation fellowship from the Chiang Ching-Kuo Foundation.

choice items adds up to a prediction of success along the underlying overall proficiency.

However multiple-choice items have been criticized as being inadequate to assess fully students' abilities. In addition, *test-wiseness* may seriously contaminate the measurement. Recently, there has been an increased emphasis on performance-based items (or constructed-response items). A performance-based item refers to any item format that requires the examinee to generate a response in any way other than selecting from a short list of alternative answers as in multiple-choice items (Pollack, Rock, and Jenkins, 1992).

The main advantages of performance-based items are as follows:

1. they can provide a more direct measure of content specifications (face validity and content validity);
2. they can provide more diagnostic information about students' learning difficulties from their responses;
3. students tend to appreciate them more than multiple-choice items; and indirectly
4. these test formats may stimulate the teaching of important skills, such as problem solving and essay writing (Grima & Liang, 1992).

Those in favor of multiple-choice items claim that the cost in dollars and human resources to develop and score performance-based items tend to be many times more than those for multiple-choice items. Furthermore, the reliability of performance-based items may be lower. If the performance-based item is highly dependent on language proficiency (as is often the case), it may not be fair for those students whose native language is not English. In such a case, the unidimensionality assumption is violated.

It is much more convenient and objective to score multiple-choice items than performance-based items since there are no variations in the rating process. That is, the scores of a multiple-choice item should always be identical even when different raters are employed. However, for a performance-based item, this is usually not the case. Thus, the scores of a performance-based item are rater-dependent. Lunz, Wright, & Linacre (1990) have pointed out that despite thorough training, raters still vary in severity. If an item is judged by a *severe* rater, the score will be lower than that by a *lenient* rater. It is obviously unfair for examinees if raters' severities vary significantly and we do not try to compensate for the differences of scores due to raters' severities. For a large-scale test where a great many raters are involved, we should try to ensure that the raters follow the same rating criteria and thus express similar rating severities, and also to estimate the values of their severities afterward and to compensate for any differences.

Traditionally, the assessment of interrater consistency has focused on the reliability of the rating instrument and procedure. The intraclass correlation coefficient has been used as a measure of average interrater reliability by several authors (Winer, 1962; Shrout & Fleiss, 1979). Coefficient alpha (Cronbach, 1951) is another estimate of average rater reliability. Dillon and Mulani (1984) have applied latent class analysis to estimate the probability of each response pattern across the raters. Van den Bergh and Eiting (1989) assume multiple quantitative ratings to be congeneric, tau-equivalent, or parallel and then employ LISREL (Jöreskog & Sorbom, 1988) to fit these models. Overall and Magee (1992) have proposed several simple models, such as the disattenuation model, the common factor model, the external criterion model, the treatment effects model, and the regression model, to estimate individual reliabilities of raters from simple bivariate correlations among their ratings. These methods for analyzing rater reliability are based on raw scores and their linear transformations rather than a nonlinear individual rating.

Item response theory provides an alternative unit of analysis, the logit, for rater reliability. For example, an extension of the Rasch model, the many-faceted model (FACETS, Linacre, 1988, 1989), has been applied to equate practical examinations with multiple facets, such as items, examinees, raters, tasks, and rating scales (Lunz, Wright, Stahl, & Linacre, 1989); to clarify and control the multiple facets of an oral examination involving protocols, raters, and candidates (Lunz, Stahl, Wright, & Linacre, 1989); to examine raters' severities in essay, clinical, and oral forms of tests and grading periods (Lunz and Stahl, 1990); and to measure writing ability, writing-task difficulty, domain difficulty, and rater severity (Engelhard, 1992). All of these papers conclude that rater severity plays a significant role in performance-based items and should not be neglected.

Given their advantages and disadvantages, test constructors sometimes try to incorporate multiple-choice items and performance-based items in a test. An issue of interest is whether a performance-based item provides more information about examinees' abilities than a multiple-choice item. If so, how much more? Furthermore, it is very common that a large-scale test contains several versions or forms. These forms may not be exactly parallel but are expected to be very similar. Traditionally, horizontal equating can be applied to calibrate item parameters and person parameters among these forms by common items or common examinees across forms. Assuming the parameters of these common items or common examinees remain stable in different forms, we can thus calibrate other parameters accordingly. It is also plausible to link different forms through common raters, assuming the raters' parameters to be unchanged across test forms. We will use both common items and common raters to link forms.

The purpose of this article is to illustrate how to (a) link different test forms through common items and common raters, (b) detect rater severity, and (c) compare item information between multiple-choice items and performance-based items through item response modeling.

THE MODEL

Suppose there are I items indexed $i = 1, \ldots, I$ and K_i response categories in item i. Let b_{ik} be the score of the response category k to item i, which is then collected into the scoring vector $b_i = (b_{i1}, b_{i2}, \ldots, b_{iKj})$, let $\xi = (\xi_1, \xi_2, \ldots, \xi_p)'$ denote a vector of p free item parameters, and let α'_{ik} denote their linear combinations for $i = 1, \ldots, I; k = 1, \ldots, K_i$. Under this setup, the probability a response in category x of item i is modeled as

$$f_i(x; \xi \mid \theta) = \frac{\exp[b_{ix}\theta + a'_{ix}\xi)]}{\sum\limits_{u=1}^{K_i} \exp[b_{iu}\theta + a'_{iu}\xi]}. \tag{1}$$

Model (1) is called the *random coefficients multinomial logit model* (RCML, Adams and Wilson, this volume). The RCML model is a generalized Rasch model that integrates many existing Rasch models. In addition, it also provides a great deal of flexibility to design customized models. It allows different numbers of categories in different items, and complex patterns of raters (Adams, Wilson, & Wu, 1993).

Item and Test Information Functions

The information function of the RCML model is as follows. Let $P_{ix}(\theta)$ denote $f_i(x; \xi \mid \theta)$, then the expected score of item i is

$$E_i(\theta) = \sum_{x=1}^{K_i} P_{ix}(\theta)b_{ix},$$

Since the variance of item i is

$$\sigma_i^2(\theta) = \left[\sum_{x=1}^{K_i} P_{ix}(\theta) b_{ix}^2 \right] - [E_i(\theta)]^2,$$

therefore, the information is thus

$$I_i(\theta) = [\partial E_i(\theta)/\partial \theta]^2 \, \sigma_i^2(\theta).$$

Note that

$$\frac{\partial E_i(\theta)}{\partial \theta} = \sum_{x=1}^{K_i} b_{ix} \frac{\partial P_{ix}(\theta)}{\partial \theta},$$

and applying the quotient rule,

$$\frac{\partial P_{ix}(\theta)}{\partial \theta}$$

$$= \frac{\left\{ \sum_{h=1}^{K_i} \exp[b_{ih}\theta + a_{ih}'\xi] \, b_{ix} \exp(b_{ix}\theta + a_{ix}'\xi) - \exp(b_{ix}\theta + a_{ix}'\xi) \sum_{h=1}^{K_i} \exp[b_{ik}\theta + a_{ih}'\xi] \right\}}{\left\{ \sum_{h=1}^{K_i} \exp[b_{ih}\theta + a_{ih}'\xi] \right\}^2}$$

$$= b_{ix} P_{ix}(\theta) - P_{ix}(\theta) E_i(\theta)$$

Therefore,

$$\frac{\partial E_i(\theta)}{\partial \theta} = \sum_{x=1}^{K_i} b_{ix}^2 P_{ix}(\theta) - E_i(\theta) \sum_{x=1}^{K_i} b_{ix} P_{ix}(\theta) = \sum_{x=1}^{K_i} b_{ix}^2 P_{ix}(\theta) - [E_i(\theta)]^2,$$

hence the information of item i is

$$I_i(\theta) = \sum_{x=1}^{K_i} b_{ix}^2 P_{ix}(\theta) - [E_i(\theta)]^2, \tag{2}$$

and the test information is

$$I(\theta) = \sum_{i=1}^{I} I_i(\theta). \tag{3}$$

Formulas (2) and (3) are applied to calculate the item information and test information in the example below.

Some Applications of the RCML Model

The RCML model can also be used in more complicated situations. For instance, if a test has several rating scales, where each rating scale has different number of response categories, Andrich's rating scale model (Andrich, 1978) cannot be used, because his model requires the same response alternatives and the same structure for all items. The RCML model is free of this constraint.

Consider furthermore a more complicated test, which contains several item bundles. Suppose there are a set of C bundles, let $\mathbf{a}_{ck}$ denote the design vector of their linear combinations on the item parameters for $c = 1, \ldots, C$; $k = 1, \ldots, m(c)$; and let $m(c)$ be the number of response categories in bundle c. Under this setup, the probability of a response in category k of bundle c can be expressed as

$$f_c(k; \xi \mid \theta) = \frac{\exp[b_{ck}\theta + a'_{ck}\xi]}{\sum_{u=1}^{m(c)} \exp[b_{cu}\theta + a'_{cu}\xi]}. \tag{4}$$

Comparing (4) with (1), we find that the difference is the specific term *item bundle* in the former and the generic term *item* in the latter. The item bundle models can be divided into the unrestricted bundle models and the strict bundle models. The former assume that the probability of a bundle response k_c is conditional on a vector of parameters ξ associated with bundle c (possibly with other bundles), while the later requires that ξ is associated with only bundle c. In other words, the parametric definition in the unrestricted bundle models may allow some *dependence* across bundles, whereas that of each bundle in the strict bundle models is independent of other bundles. Thus the unrestricted bundle model using fewer parameters is more parsimonious than the strict bundle model, if it fits the data. Wilson &

Adams (1995) have shown how the RCML model can be applied to analyze a bundled test using the Structure of the Learning Outcomes (SOLO) Taxonomy (Biggs & Collis, 1982).

Estimation of the RCML Model

Marginal maximum likelihood (MML) estimation is implemented in this volume the RCML computer program (Adams and Wilson, 1991). Although joint maximum likelihood estimation is widely applied by several well-known computer programs, such as BICAL (Wright, Mead and Bell, 1980) and LOGIST (Wingersky, Barton, and Lord, 1982), it need not be consistent as sample size increases. The MML approach alleviates this problem by integrating over the ability distribution and estimating the item parameters in the marginal distribution of ability.

In the item response model, the latent trait θ is associated with each case (or subject) in a certain population; as θ varies from individual to individual in the population, it has a distribution with a density function $g(\theta;\alpha)$, which contains a vector of parameters α to characterize the distribution. The density function g may be characterized as a step distribution with pre-specified nodes or is distributed as normal $N(0, 1)$ and approximated by a step distribution with pre-specified nodes.

We do not directly solve the likelihood equations, but follow Bock and Aitken's (1981) reformulation of the EM algorithm (Dempster, Laird, & Rubin, 1977). In a digital computer, where direct integration is difficult, the technique of quadrature is applied for approximating the integration. Using the quadrature approach, the area under a continuous curve can be approximated by the sum of the area of many small rectangles. The population distribution is known or is concurrently estimated. We take the expectation of the sufficient statistics, conditional on the observed data and the provisional parameter estimates (E step), substituting these conditional expectations into the maximization (M step), and carrying out a maximum likelihood estimation through Newton-Raphson iterations. After the change of parameter estimates between two EM iterations is smaller than some convergence criterion, the EM algorithm stops and then goes on to the estimation of person ability by treating these item parameters as true values.

Since the person parameters are integrated out, MML estimation does not directly provide estimates for each person. We employ EAP estimation (Expected a posteriori; Bock and Aitken, 1981) to calculate person parameters. For details about the estimation, see Adams and Wilson (this volume).

AN EXAMPLE

The data from the California Learning Assessment System (CLAS) 1992 Spring Field Test Grade 4 Mathematics Form M0423, Form M0424, and Form M0425 (hereafter are referred to Forms 3, 4, and 5, respectively) are used as an example. There were 435, 496, and 488 examinees who took these three forms, respectively. One of the main purposes of the test was to generate some approximate information on which to base a decision regarding the mixture of multiple choice and open-ended items that would satisfy some minimum requirements in terms of standard errors of student estimates. The items in these three different forms are designed to measure an underlying mathematics ability. Although they are not expected to be exactly parallel, they possess identical test formats. All of them contain 20 multiple-choice items, 2 open-ended items, and 1 investigation item.

The open-ended items require examinees to explain their reasoning processes in problem solving and were scored from 0 to 5 by two raters independently. The investigation items require examinees to work out three activities in about an hour and a half with a partner and to answer the questions given. The responses to the investigation item as a whole were scored from 0 to 5 by one rater only. Altogether there were 49 raters employed to score the open-ended and the investigation items in the three forms. Among them, 11 raters only scored the investigation items, 5 raters scored both the open-ended items and the investigation items, the remainder scored only the open-ended items.

Given that the three forms were taken by three separate samples of students, we need to establish link information among the three forms. There is only one common multiple-choice item across the three forms. Forms 4 and 5 have additional five common multiple-choice items. Thus, there are 53 distinct multiple-choice items in the three forms. On the other side, there are 8 common raters between Forms 3 and 4. Nothing else is common across the 3 forms. Under this circumstance, the major linking information used between Forms 4 and 5 is provided by the common items they share and that between Form 3 and 4 is provided by the common raters.

Prior to analyzing the data, we need to combine the 3 samples from Forms 3, 4, and 5 into a complete data set; altogether 1419 examinees. Each examinee could have only completed 20 multiple-choice items, 2 open-ended items, and 1 investigation item. The other 33 ($=53 - 20$) multiple-choice items are treated as *missing at random*. This is consistent with the testing arrangement because the forms were distributed randomly within class. Moreover, we need to change the open-ended and the investigation items from *item-oriented* organization into a *rater-oriented* format.

Since there are nine items (two open-ended and one investigation items per form) to be judged by some subset of the 49 raters, we can organize the data as 441 *rater-items* (=9 × 49). Each examinee could have only obtained five scores from raters (two scores from one of the two open-ended items and one score from the investigation item), the other 436 rater-items are treated as missing at random.

With this organization, and given sufficient data, we could in theory estimate parameters for 494 (= 53 + 441) items, but we actually estimated only 146 parameters because not every rater rated each open-ended and investigation item, and also because we assumed a somewhat simpler model than is theoretically possible. The scoring vector and the design matrix for these 146 parameters are shown in the Appendix.

RESULTS

Calibrations of Item Parameters

The calibrations for person ability distribution, item difficulties of the multiple-choice items, the open-ended items, the investigation items, and rater severities are shown graphically in Figure 10.1. The person ability estimates range from −1.37 logits to 2.71 logits, with mode .25, mean .23, and variance .61. The item difficulties of the 53 multiple-choice items range from −2.42 logits for Item 47 to 2.10 logits for Item 5. The 20 multiple-choice items in Form 3 are numbered from 1 to 20, those in Form 4 are numbered 16, and from 21 to 39, and those in Form 5 are numbered 16, 24, 36 to 39, and 40 to 53. The means and the variances of the item parameters of the 20 multiple-choice items are .19 logits and 1.33 logits, respectively in Form 3, −.18 logits and .74 logits, respectively in Form 4, and −.16 logits and 1.08 logits, respectively in Form 5. The item difficulties of the multiple-choice items in Form 3 are somewhat higher, and more dispersed than those of other two forms.

The item difficulties of the open-ended and the investigation items in Figure 10.1 have been transformed into what we call the *level thresholds* from overall difficulties and step difficulties in the original printout. The level threshold is the point on the ability continuum at which the probabilities of reaching and not reaching that level are both .5. Of the six open-ended items in the three forms, the second item

Person ability distribution (counts)		Logit	Multiple-choice	Open-ended A1	A2	B1	B2	C1	C2	Investigation A	B	C	Rater Severity
		3.25								5			
		3.00									5		
1		2.75											
2		2.50					5				4		
3		2.25		5				5				5	
5	x	2.00	3 5			5				4			46
18	xx	1.75	17										21 35
57	xxxxxxxx	1.50	7 49 52		5				5			4	8 24 27 29
68	xxxxxxxxxx	1.25	1 30 53	4							3		5 7 9 10 17 19 20 23 26 30 31 32 34 37 43
101	xxxxxxxxxxxxx	1.00	9 29				4	4	4	3			2 3 4 6 16 22 25 28 33 36 42 45 49
127	xxxxxxxxxxxxxxxx	0.75	13 15 33 37 45 46			4							3 15
198	xxxxxxxxxxxxxxxxxxxxxxxxxxx	0.50	19 23 36				3						11 12 14 18 38
246	xxxxxxxxxxxxxxxxxxxxxxxxxxxxxxxxx	0.25	6 28 35	3	4		2					3	
152	xxxxxxxxxxxxxxxxxxxx	-0.00	10 18 20 24 32 51			3		3					1 39 40 44 47
130	xxxxxxxxxxxxxxxx	-0.25	26 34 40 41 43 44		3				3	2	2		41
107	xxxxxxxxxxxxx	-0.50	2 11 21 48	2									48
122	xxxxxxxxxxxxxxx	-0.75	8 16 27					2					
73	xxxxxxxxx	-1.00	12 22 38 42		2								
9	x	-1.25	31										
		-1.50	50			2			2				
		-1.75	25 39				1	1					
		-2.00	14									2	
		-2.25	4										
		-2.50	47							1	1		
		-2.75			1								
		-3.00											
		-3.25		1									
		-3.50				1			1				
		-3.75											
		-4.00											
		-4.25										1	

Note: Form 3 (A), Form 4 (B), and Form 5 (C). 53 multiple-choice items, 6 open-ended items, 3 investigation items, and 49 raters.

Raters: Format **Bold:** investigation items only; Format *Italic*: Both Open-ended and investigation items; Format Plain: open-ended items only.

Figure 10.1. Person ability distribution, item and rater parameters of the multiple-choice, the open-ended and the investigation items.

of Form 4 (refer to B2 in Figure 1) and the first item of Form 5 (refer to C1 in Figure 1) are the most difficult and least dispersed ones respectively. In summary, the level thresholds of the investigation items are more difficult and more dispersed than those of the open-ended items. The investigation item of Form 5 (refer to C in Figure 10.1) is the easiest of the three investigation items.

Comparing the person ability distribution and the item difficulties of the multiple-choice, the open-ended, and the investigation items, we find that all of the examinees have probabilities greater than a half of answering correctly the multiple-choice items 47, 4, 14 25, 39, 50, and 31, and obtaining one point on both the open-ended and the investigation items, assuming a standard rater severity of zero logit. Multiple-choice items 17, 3, and 5 and the highest score (5) of all the open-ended and the investigation items are very difficult for most examinees.

In sum, the item difficulties of three forms are not exactly equivalent. Form 3 has somewhat more difficult multiple-choice items and an easier investigation item. Most item difficulties of the multiple-choice items in the three forms cluster between −1.00 logits to 1.00 logits, which correspond to those of Levels 2, 3, and 4 in the open-ended items and the investigation items. The investigation items are more difficult than the open-ended items.

Rater Severity

Interrater correlations (Pearson's correlation) of the open-ended items in three forms are shown in Table 10.1. The interrater correlations of the three forms are between .63 and .81, which reflect some inconsistency between raters. Even though the correlations are reasonably high, we cannot detect whether one examinee was judged by two severe raters while another examinee judged by two lenient raters. If this is the case, the scores derived from two raters may be very consistent and thus the interrater correlation would be quite high. Only when we are able to estimate rater severities and if they are not significantly dif-

Table 10.1. Interrater Correlations of the Open-Ended Items in Three Forms

Forms	1st Item	2nd Item
Form 3	.66	.81
Form 4	.63	.71
Form 5	.79	.67

ferent can we use the raw scores to represent examinees' abilities. Otherwise, the same raw scores derived from two raters may reflect different degrees of ability.

The range of the rater severities of the 49 raters is 2.67 logits, from −.61 logits for Rater 48 to 2.06 for Rater 46, and their mean and the standard deviation are .94 logits and .56 logits, respectively. There are 11 raters (bold format in Figure 10.1) who only judged the investigation items. The severities of these 11 raters tend to be somewhat dispersed, for example, Raters 48, 41, 39, 40, 44, and 47 are relatively lenient, while Rater 46 is the most severe. Figure 10.2 shows the 95% confident intervals for these 49 rater severities in logits. The intervals do not all overlap and the chi-squared statistic for testing equal severity is 771.14 with 48 degrees of freedom. Therefore, we conclude that,

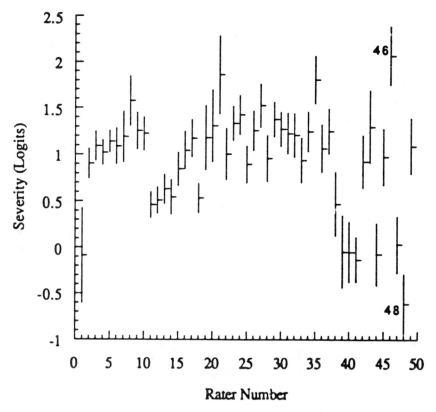

Figure 10.2.   Ninety five percents confidence intervals of the 49 rater severities.

subject to the existing information and with standard levels of statistical confidence, the raters were rating with different severity. This is an important finding in the present context as to date CLAS has tended to simply add together rater judgments without making any adjustments for rater variation except when the raw scores are very different (and the "adjustment" was to have a third rating).

Defining *severe* raters and *lenient* raters as those severities in logits located one standard deviation (= .56 logits) above and below the mean respectively, we obtain 4 severe raters and 7 lenient raters. Suppose these 49 raters are sampled uniformly, then the probability that examinee is judged by a severe rater on an investigation item is 8.2% (= 4/49), and by a lenient rater it is 14.3% (= 7/49). Similarly, the probability of an examinee being judged by two severe raters on an open-ended item is 1.0% and by two lenient raters on an open-ended item it is 3.6%. Since we define severe and lenient raters as at least one standard deviation away from the mean severity, the *rating bias* causes at least .56 logits difference compared to when examinee is judged by average raters.

To further illustrate the impact of this disparity in rater severity, we consider the following. Figures 10.3a and 10.3b show item characteristic curves (ICCs) of the investigation item of Form 3 rated by Raters 48 (the least severe rater) and 46 (the most severe rater), respectively. Comparing these two figures, we see that the ICCs shift toward right-hand side from Figures 10.3a to 10.3b. It is much more difficult for examinees to obtain higher scores from Rater 46 than from rater 48.

Figure 10.4 shows the expected scores of this item rated by Raters 46 and 48. An examinee with ability 0.0 logits will be expected to have a score of about 2.2 from Rater 48, and a score of about .7 from Rater 46. An examinee with ability 2.0 logits will have a score of about 3.7 from Rater 48, and about 1.7 from Rater 46. The maximum difference of the expected scores derived from these two raters is about 2 points when examinees' abilities are located between .5 logits and 2.5 logits. Since all of the open-ended items and the investigation items are judged by a 6-point scale, a difference of 2 points is a large bias. Alternatively, a raw score of 2 derived from Rater 48 represents ability estimate of − .3 logits, but 2.4 logits if the score derived from Rater 46. Therefore, the same raw scores derived from two raters do not necessarily result in the same ability estimates. In other words, raw scores are no longer sufficient statistics for ability estimates as in the Rasch models.

Note that in Figures 10.3 and 10.4 we compare two extreme raters, the influence of rater severities as a whole in the test is much smaller. Because not only a few raters differ in severity but also these extreme

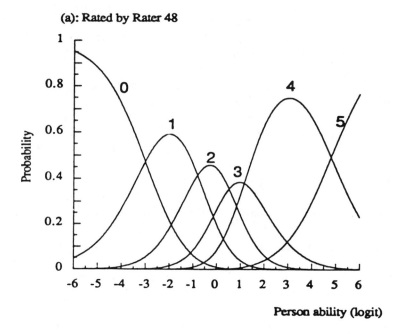

(a): Rated by Rater 48

Person ability (logit)

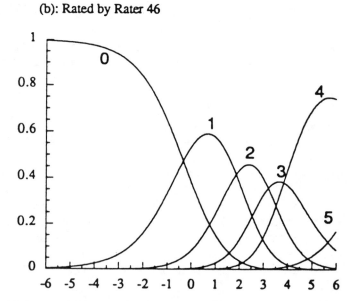

(b): Rated by Rater 46

Figure 10.3.   Probability distribution of the investigation item of Form 3 judged by Raters 48 and 46.

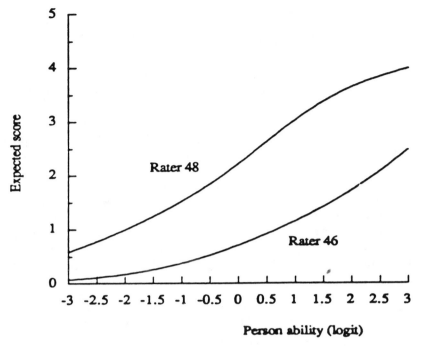

Figure 10.4. Expected scores on the investigation item of Form M0423 when examinees judged by Raters 48 and 46.

raters judged mainly on the investigation items (this may be due to the lack of a second rating for the investigation items, which was used as a quality control method in the open-ended items). If we constrain all of the rater severities to be the mean severity (.94 logits), the mean and the standard deviation of the absolute value of differences in person ability estimates between with and without this constraint is only .08 logits. We find that the mean of the absolute difference in person ability estimates between these two models is .08 and .06 logits respectively with the maximum difference .35 logits. Although only a small amount of examinees are affected, it spoils fairness.

In sum, the rater severities are not equal and should not be treated as such. Those who only judged the investigation items tend to have extreme severities. If we do not take the variation of the rater severity into account, a small amount of examinees will be affected significantly on their relative position to other examinees. They are not treated fairly.

Information and Standard Errors

Figures 10.5 and 10.6 show the information and the standard errors of the person ability estimates for the three forms, respectively. With respect to the person ability distribution where most examinees locate between -1.0 and 2.0 logits, Form 3 has the most accurate in the estimation of the person abilities in the three because it provides the largest information in that range. Form 4 provides greatest information where person abilities are around 1.5 logits, whereas Form 5 around .5 logits. The standard errors of the three forms in the range of the person ability distribution are between .3 and .4 logits. There are only small differences among three forms. Note that since the standard errors are the square root of the inverses of the information, one can gain accurate interpretation by comparing Figures 10.5 and 10.6.

Averaging the information in the three forms, we derive Figure 10.7, which shows the average information of the multiple-choice, the open-ended, and the investigation items. The maximum information

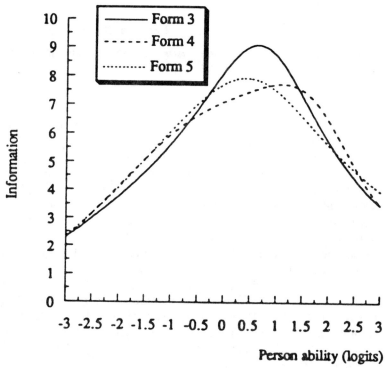

Figure 10.5.   Information of Forms 3, 4, and 5.

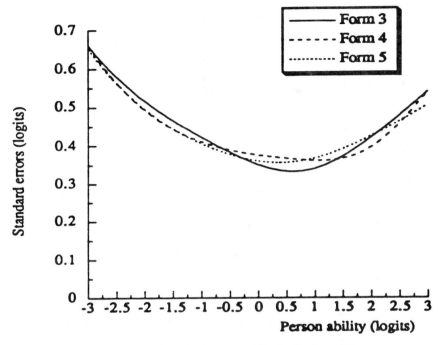

Figure 10.6.   Standard errors of Forms 3, 4, and 5.

for a multiple-choice item is approximately .2 at about .0 logits; the maximum information for an open-ended item is approximately .95 at about 1.0 logits; the maximum information for a investigation item is approximately .65 at about 1.5 logits.

The differences in information reflect the maximum scores available to the three item types. The difference in location of the maximum points on the variable may be taken as evidence that the item constructors were successful in creating the investigation items and the open-ended items that were targeted at a higher level than were the traditional multiple-choice items. In order to calculate a typical standard error for the students in the sample, the information is averaged across the range of the sample (-1.25 to 2.75 logits), weighted by the distribution of the student estimates, and then converted into the standard errors. The results of this averaging process are shown in Table 10.2.

Examining Table 10.2, we see that an average open-ended item provides about 4.5 times as much information about a typical student as a multiple-choice item, while an investigation item provides about 3.2

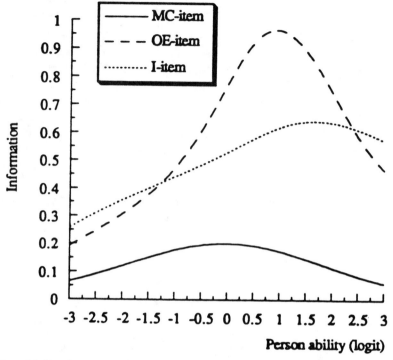

Figure 10.7.   Average information of each of the multiple-choice, the open-ended, and the investigation items.

Table 10.2.   Information and Standard Errors of Average Item and Item Combinations (logits)

	Information	Standard Error
Single		
Multiple-choice item	.177	2.377
Open-ended item	.793	1.123
Investigation item	.564	1.332
Item combinations*		
20MC + 2 × 20E + 1I (reference)	6.543	.391
2 × 40E + 1I	6.908	.380
40MC + 1I	7.644	.362
5MC + 2 × 20E + 1I	4.438	.475
5MC + 4 × 20E PL 1I	7.610	.362
30MC + 1 × 20E + 1I	6.361	.396

*Note: MC: multiple choice item, OE: open-ended item, I: investigation item.

times. Based on this information, we can calculate projections of information available from different arrangements of the multiple-choice, the open-ended and the investigation items, assuming that the examinee distribution remains the same. The second panel of the Table 10.2 gives the information and the standard error for the actual arrangement in this Field Trial (20 multiple choice items, 2 open-ended items rated twice, and 1 investigation item), as a reference. In the rows that follow, these same statistics are shown for a variety of other arrangements that have been suggested as alternatives.

For instance, if we leave out all the multiple choice items and double the number of the open-ended items, the information and the standard error are about the same. One may consider leaving out all the open-ended items and doubling the number of multiple-choice items, and deriving somewhat larger information and smaller standard error. Thirty multiple-choice items, one open-ended item, and one investiga-

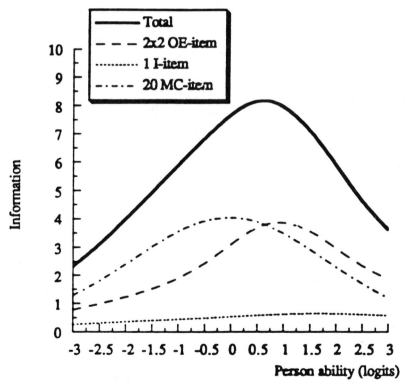

Figure 10.8.   Information of the average mode: 20 multiple-choice, 2 open-ended, and 1 investigation items.

tion item provide almost identical information to the reference item combination. These alternatives are informative because test users may gain insight of organizing different item formats and controlling the minimum accuracy of the test for the coming year.

As stated above, each open-ended item was rated twice by two raters. Therefore, it actually provides twice as much information as if the item is rated once. Based on this assumption, we define an average mode of the test as the combinations of 20 average multiple-choice items and 2×2 average open-ended items (each item rated twice) and 1 average investigation item, shown in Figure 10.8. The maximum information of the single investigation item is approximately .5 and it does not change much across the person ability distribution. The maximum information of the 20 multiple-choice items is approximately 4.0 at around .0 logit, that of the 4 ($= 2 \times 2$) open-ended items is also approximately 4.0 but at around 1.0 logits. In total, the maximum information of the average mode is approximately 8.0 at around .5 logits. Again we find that the open-ended items are more accurate in detecting abler persons than the multiple-choice items.

One may feel dissatisfied that the investigation items provide much less information regarding the approximately 90 minutes needed to answer an investigation item. This is because so far the test constructors have developed only one rating scale (0 to 5) to judge the investigation items. It can be improved if more insight of these items is gained. For example, they can be scored on several domains, with 0 to 5 per domain, or their rating scales can be elaborated and extended into a larger one, say from 0 to 20.

DISCUSSION

Nowadays, a large-scale test tends to incorporate several item formats, such as multiple-choice items, essay questions, or open-ended items. The standard computer programs usually do not offer the flexibility to deal with different formats in a test. The newly developed RCML program can provide users a great deal of flexibility to design customized models by manipulating the scoring functions and the design matrix. Although the flexibility seems powerful in practice, the user may feel it is complicated and difficult to create his own models. As he gains more insight of the RCML model, however, he will come to appreciate the flexibility it offers.

Usually, test equating is based on common items or common examinees across different tests. In the example, the item parameters of both the open-ended and the investigation items are decomposed into linear combinations of overall item difficulties, step difficulties and rater severities. We then use common items to link Forms 4 and 5, and common raters to link Forms 3 and 4. Therefore, all three forms are linked together. The item parameters of three forms are estimated simultaneously rather than separately.

There are always pros and cons about multiple-choice and performance-based items. A test user usually considers various aspects in order to choose the proper test format. Based on the information gain of this particular data set, we find that an open-ended item provides about 4.5 times more information than a multiple-choice item on average. Since an open-ended item is rated twice, the information gain becomes 9 times in total. The information gain, however, does not suffice to justify its desirability in practice, because a great many factors should be considered, such as economic factors and rater's objectivity. In the research, the most criticized issue of performance-based items, rater's severity, is well-handled by introducing rater parameters. The range of rater severities is as large as 2.5 logits, thus any procedure without taking rater severities into account may be misleading.

In general, as the number of response categories to an item increases, its information tends to increase as well. Dichotomous items such as multiple-choice items provide much less information than polytomous items. Extending the range of the rating scale or applying more than one domain will improve the information gain of an item. An alternative is through statistical treatment, weighting on items or examinees, because the items or examinees may not be sampled by simple random sampling method, say stratified sampling, and they may represent different degrees of importance to the users. Therefore different weights should be allowed for different items or examinees. The effects of different weights on the estimations of items and persons are left for further research.

REFERENCES

Adams, R.J., & Wilson, M.L. (1991). A random coefficients multinomial logit: generalizing Rasch models. G. Engelhard, Jr. & M. Wilson (Eds.) In *Objective Measurement: Thoery Into Practice, Volume 3,* Norwood, NJ: Ablex.

Adams, R.J., Wilson, M.L., & Wu, M.L. (in press). *Multilevel item response models: An approach to errors in variables regression. Journal of Educational Behavioral Statistics.*

Andrich, D. (1978). A rating formulation for ordered response categories. *Psychometrika, 43,* 561–573.

Biggs, J.B., & Collis, K.F. (1982). Evaluating the quality of learning: The SOLO taxonomy. New York: Academic Press.

Bock, R.D., & Aitken, M. (1981). Marginal maximum likelihood estimation of item parameters: an application of the EM algorithm. *Psychometrika, 46,* 443–459.

Cronbach, L.J. (1951). Coefficients alpha and the internal structure of tests. *Psychometrika, 16,* 297–334.

Dempster, A.P., Laird, N.M., & Rubin, D.B. (1977). Maximum likelihood from incomplete data via the EM algorithm. *Journal of the Royal Statistical Society, Series B, 39,* 1–38.

Dillon, W.R., & Mulani, N. (1984). A probabilistic latent class model for assessing interjudge reliability. *Multivariate Behavioral Research, 19,* 438–458.

Engelhard, G. Jr. (1992). The measurement of writing ability with a many-faceted Rasch model. *Applied Measurement in Education, 5,* 171–191.

Grima, A., & Liang, J. (1992). The effect of response rate to multiple-choice and open-ended items on differential item functioning. Paper presented at the Annual Meeting of the American Educational Research Association, San Francisco.

Jöreskog, K.G., & Sorbom, D. (1988). *LISREL VII: A guide to program applications.* Chicago: SPSS, Inc.

Linacre, J.M. (1989). *Many-faceted Rasch measurement.* Chicago: MESA Press.

Lunz, M.E., & Stahl, J.A. (1990). Severity of grading across time periods. Paper presented at the Annual Meeting of the American Educational Research Association, Boston.

Lunz, M.E., Stahl, J.A., Wright, B.D., & Linacre, J.M. (1989). Variation among examiners and protocols oral examinations. Paper presented at the Annual Meeting of the American Educational Research Association, San Francisco.

Lunz, M.E., Wright, B.D., & Linacre, J.M. (1990). Measuring the impact of judge severity on examination scores. *Applied Measurement in Education, 3,* 331–345.

Lunz, M.E., Wright, B.D., Stahl, J.A., & Linacre, J.M. (1989). Equating practical examinations. Paper presented at the Annual Meeting of the National Council on Measurement in Education, San Francisco.

Overall, J.E., & Magee, K.N. (1992). Estimating individual rater reliabilities. *Applied Psychological Measurement, 16,* 77–85.

Pollack, J.M., Rock, D.A., & Jenkins, F. (1992). Advantages and disadvantages of constructed-response item formats in large-scale surveys. Paper presented at the Annual Meeting of the American Educational Research Association, San Francisco.

Shrout, P.E., & Fleiss, J.L. (1979). Intraclass correlations: Uses in assessing rater reliability. *Psychological Bulletin, 86,* 420–428.

Van den Bergh, H., & Eiting, M.H. (1989). A method of estimating rater reliability. *Journal of Educational Measurement, 26,* 29–40.

Wilson, M.L., & Adams, R.J. (1995). *Rasch models for item bundles. Psychometrika,* 60(2), 181–198.

Winer, B.J. (1962). *Statistical principles in experimental design.* New York: McGraw-Hill.

Wingersky, M.S., Barton, M.A., & Lord, F.M. (1982). *LOGIST User's Guide.* Princeton, NJ: Educational Testing Service.
Wright, B.D., Mead, R.J., & Bell, S.R. (1980). *BICAL: Calibrating items and scales with the Rasch model.* (Research Memorandum NO. 23C). Chicago, IL: University of Chicago, Statistical Laboratory.

APPENDIX

Scoring Vector

The scoring vector for these 53 multiple-choice items is the same as that for Rasch dichotomous model and we constrain the sum of item difficulties of the 53 multiple-choice items to be zero. There are only two response categories, either right or wrong, in these 53 multiple-choice items. Let the first response category (incorrect answer) be scored 0 and the second category (correct answer) be scored 1. Therefore, the scoring vector of the first multiple-choice item is $\mathbf{b}_{m1} = (0,1)'$, where the subscript m denotes multiple-choice items. The scoring vectors of all other 52 multiple-choice items are identical to that of the first multiple-choice item. Accordingly, the first 106 elements in the scoring vector are as follows:

$$\mathbf{B_m} = (\mathbf{b}'_{m1}, \mathbf{b}'_{m2}, \ldots, \mathbf{b}'_{m53})' = (0\ 1\ 0\ 1\ \ldots\ 0\ 1)'. \qquad (A1)$$

Consider the 441 rater-items. Each item has 6 response categories scored from 0 to 5 respectively. The scoring function of the first rater-item is defined as follows:

$$\mathbf{b}_{r1} = (0\ 1\ 2\ 3\ 4\ 5)',$$

where the subscript r denotes rater-items. The scoring functions of the other 440 rater-items are identical to that of the first rater-item. Therefore, we can collect them into a 2,646 (= 441 × 6) element scoring vector as follows:

$$\mathbf{B_r} = (\mathbf{b}'_{r1}, \mathbf{b}'_{r2}, \ldots, \mathbf{b}'_{r441})' = (0\ 1\ 2\ 3\ 4\ 5\ 0\ 1\ 2\ 3\ 4\ 5$$
$$\ldots\ 0\ 1\ 2\ 3\ 4\ 5)'. \qquad (A2)$$

The first six elements correspond to the first rater-item, the second six elements to the second rater-item, and so on. The vectors given in (A1) and (A2) are collected into the scoring vector $\mathbf{B} = (\mathbf{B}'_m, \mathbf{B}'_r)'$, with 2,752 (= 106 + 2,646) elements.

Design Matrix

We construct the design matrix **A** using the following order of item parameters: (a) 52-item difficulty parameters, one for each of the first 52 multiple-choice items; (b) nine-item difficulty parameters, one for each of the open-ended items and the investigation items; (c) nine sets of rating-scale style step difficulties, one set of four for each open-ended item and the investigation item; (d) 49 rating severity parameters, one for each rater. There are 146 parameters in total. Since there are 2,752 elements in the scoring vector **B** and 146 item parameters to be estimated, the design matrix **A** is a 2,752 by 146 matrix.

Because we constrain the sum of the 53 multiple-choice item difficulty parameters to be zero, the item difficulty parameter of the 53rd multiple-choice item is minus the sum of the first 52 multiple-choice item difficulty parameters. The other 94 $(= 146 - 52)$ parameters pertain to the 441 rater-items. Since in the data set these 441 rater-items are arranged in the sequence of rater number, the first nine rater-items belong to the first rater, the second nine rater-items belong to the second rater, and so on. Among those nine rater-items, the first two belong to the first and the second open-ended items of Form 3, respectively, the third to the investigation item of the same form. Similarly, the subsequent three rater-items belong to the first, the second open-ended and investigation items of Form 4, respectively, the last three rater-items to those of Form 5, respectively.

In order to obtain multiple facets, we need to manipulate the design matrix **A**. For illustration, let's partition the design matrix into four parts:

$$\mathbf{A}_{(2752 \times 146)} = \begin{bmatrix} \mathbf{A}_{1_{(106 \times 52)}} & \mathbf{A}_{2_{(106 \times 94)}} \\ \mathbf{A}_{3_{(2646 \times 52)}} & \mathbf{A}_{4_{(2646 \times 94)}} \end{bmatrix}$$

where $\mathbf{A}_1$ corresponds to the 53 multiple-choice items and their 52 free item parameters, $\mathbf{A}_4$ to the 441 rater-items and their 94 free parameters; $\mathbf{A}_2$ and $\mathbf{A}_3$ are both zero matrices because we do not model the *dependency* between multiple-choice items and rater-items.

Matrix $\mathbf{A}_1$ is as follows:

$$\begin{bmatrix} 0 & 0 & 0 & . & . & . & 0 & 0 & 0 \\ 1 & 0 & 0 & . & . & . & 0 & 0 & 0 \\ 0 & 0 & 0 & . & . & . & 0 & 0 & 0 \\ 0 & 1 & 0 & . & . & . & 0 & 0 & 0 \\ 0 & 0 & 0 & . & . & . & 0 & 0 & 0 \end{bmatrix}$$

$$\mathbf{A}_{1_{(106\times52)}} = \begin{bmatrix} 0 & 0 & 1 & \dots & 0 & 0 & 0 \\ & & & \ddots & & & \\ & & & & & & \\ & & & & & & \\ 0 & 0 & 0 & \dots & 0 & 0 & 0 \\ -1 & -1 & -1 & \dots & -1 & -1 & -1 \end{bmatrix} .$$

The first row vector in $\mathbf{A}_1$ represents the linear combinations of the item parameters as they relate to the first response category (incorrect response) of the first multiple-choice item. They are all zeros because we treat that category as a reference. The second row vector corresponds to the linear combinations of the item parameters as they relate to the second response category (correct response) of the first multiple-choice item. The third and the fourth row vectors pertain to the first and the second categories of the second multiple-choice item, respectively, and so on until the second last row vector. The last row vector accomplishes the constraint of making the parameters of the last multiple-choice item equal minus the sum of the item difficulties of the other 52 multiple-choice items.

$\mathbf{A}_4$ is a 2646 by 94 matrix. For simplicity, let $\mathbf{A}_4$ be partitioned as follows:

$$\mathbf{A}_{4_{(2646\times94)}} = \begin{bmatrix} D & S & R & O & & O & O \\ D & S & O & R & \dots & O & O \\ D & S & O & O & & O & O \\ & & & \vdots & & & \\ & & & & & & \\ D & S & O & O & & O & O \\ D & S & O & O & \dots & R & O \\ D & S & O & O & & O & R \end{bmatrix} ,$$

where $\mathbf{D}$ is a 54 by 9 matrix, $\mathbf{S}$ is a 54 by 36 matrix, $\mathbf{R}$ is a 54 by 1 matrix, and $\mathbf{O}$ is a 54 by 1 zero matrix. Every $\mathbf{R}$ corresponds to a specific rater. Since there are 49 raters, matrix $\mathbf{A}_4$ contains 49 $\mathbf{D}$, $\mathbf{S}$, and $\mathbf{R}$ sub-matrices. for mnemonics, matrix $\mathbf{D}$ can be viewed as a sub-design matrix pertaining to overall item difficulty, matrix $\mathbf{S}$ to step difficulties, and matrix $\mathbf{R}$ to rater severity. Next we partition matrix $\mathbf{D}$ into

$$D = \begin{bmatrix} C & O & O & O & O & O & O & O & O \\ O & C & O & O & O & O & O & O & O \\ O & O & C & O & O & O & O & O & O \\ O & O & O & C & O & O & O & O & O \\ O & O & O & O & C & O & O & O & O \\ O & O & O & O & O & C & O & O & O \\ O & O & O & O & O & O & C & O & O \\ O & O & O & O & O & O & O & C & O \\ O & O & O & O & O & O & O & O & C \end{bmatrix}, $$

where $C = (0\ 1\ 2\ 3\ 4\ 5)'$, O is a 6 by 1 zero matrix. Matrix S can be partitioned into:

$$S = \begin{bmatrix} T & O & O & O & O & O & O & O & O \\ O & T & O & O & O & O & O & O & O \\ O & O & T & O & O & O & O & O & O \\ O & O & O & T & O & O & O & O & O \\ O & O & O & O & T & O & O & O & O \\ O & O & O & O & O & T & O & O & O \\ O & O & O & O & O & O & T & O & O \\ O & O & O & O & O & O & O & T & O \\ O & O & O & O & O & O & O & O & T \end{bmatrix}, $$

where O is a 6 by 4 zero matrix, and

$$T = \begin{bmatrix} 0 & 0 & 0 & 0 \\ 1 & 0 & 0 & 0 \\ 1 & 1 & 0 & 0 \\ 1 & 1 & 1 & 0 \\ 1 & 1 & 1 & 1 \\ 0 & 0 & 0 & 0 \end{bmatrix}.$$

Again, for mnemonics, matrix C can be viewed as a sub-design matrix pertaining to the overall item difficulty of its corresponding rater-item, and S to its step difficulties. Therefore, matrices C and S in the first row of matrix D correspond to the first rater-item, which is the first open-ended item of Form 3; similarly, those in the second row and third row of matrix D correspond to the second open-ended item and the investigation item of Form 3, respectively. The following three rows correspond to Form 4, and the last three to Form 5, respectively.

Next back to matrix R, a sub-design matrix pertaining to rater severity. In this study, we assume that rater severities remain stable across the open-ended items, the investigation items, and different forms (Forms 3, 4, and 5). This is because the item difficulties and the step difficulties remain relatively constant for each rater. Therefore, matrix **R** is defined as

$$\mathbf{R} = (0\ 1\ 2\ 3\ 4\ 5\ 0\ 1\ 2\ 3\ 4\ 5\ \ldots 0\ 1\ 2\ 3\ 4\ 5)',$$

where the first six elements correspond to the first rater-item, the second six elements to the second rater-item, and so on.

Note that in this example we make two assumptions about rater severities. We assume that rater severities remain unchanged across items, that is, the rater holds the same severity no matter which item he or she judges, the open-ended items or the investigation items, the first open-ended item or the second, in Forms 3, 4, or 5. This seems to us to be a desirable formulation, as it corresponds to standard notions of how one might model raters. However, one may argue that this assumption is too strict. For instance, each rater-item might be modeled to have different step difficulties, or raters might express different severities between the nine rater-items. The availability of data can impose severe limits on the estimability of these more complex models. For instance, to estimate the last model, every rater would have to rate several students on each of the nine rater-items, which was not the case here.

chapter 11

Measuring learning in LISP: An application of the random coefficients multinomial logit model*

Karen L. Draney, Mark Wilson and Peter Pirolli
University of California, Berkeley

The Random Coefficients Multinomial Logit (RCML) model (Adams & Wilson, 1991, this volume) is a general, flexible Rasch family model which allows the user to specify and estimate a wide variety of logistic-type models. Models in which the probability of a particular response to a task situation may be expressed in terms of a linear combination of a person characteristic and various characteristics of the task may be estimated using this model. Thus, this model incorporates as a special case Fischer's Linear Logistic Test Model or LLTM (Fischer, 1983), which breaks down the difficulty of an item into a number of component subtasks, such that the item's difficulty is a sum of difficulties of components the item contained, weighted by the number of times each component had to be performed in order to correctly answer

* Acknowledgement: We would like to thank Margaret Recker and Katherine Bielaczyc for sharing their data with us, and for aiding in the analysis. This research was supported by Office of Naval Research, Cognitive Science Program, grant no. N00014–91J-1523.

the item. For the RCML, the probability of responding in category x to task i is:

$$P(X_i = x; A, \xi \mid \theta) = \frac{\exp\{\theta B_i(x) + a_{ix}'\xi\}}{\displaystyle\sum_{k=1}^{K_i} \exp\{\theta B_i(k) + a_{ik}'\xi\}} , \tag{1}$$

where θ is person proficiency. The vector ξ contains p free parameters describing the task situations. A is a design matrix made up of the vectors a_{ix}, which define linear combinations of the parameters in ξ that correspond to a response in category x to task i. $B_i(x)$ is the scoring function that maps response x onto its corresponding level of performance. A more complete description of the RCML may be found in Adams & Wilson (this volume).

Current research in the field of cognitive science has led to the development of complex theories to describe student performance and learning. These theories seek to understand student performance in terms of a number of factors. In addition to various task characteristics, student grouping factors such as strategy usage, level of metacognitive behavior, and variations in the learning material to which the students are exposed are predicted to have an effect on student performance. In-depth study of the factors affecting student performance when learning complex material have been undertaken in such fields as economics (Shute & Glaser, 1990) and computer programming (Anderson, Conrad, & Corbett, 1989; Pirolli, 1986; Pirolli & Recker, 1991). Data from such studies often include a large amount of rich information, such as indicators of global versus local planning and level and amount of self-explanation used, as well as measures of success or failure on a variety of tasks. A general model such as the RCML is potentially very useful in analyzing effects and relationships among these pieces of information. As an example of the types of models that may be explored using the RCML, this chapter examines the relationship between item difficulty, exposure to an example, and learning effects in data gathered using a computerized tutoring system designed to teach the computer programming language LISP.

METHODS

Data Sources

The data set which will be used in the example analysis was compiled from studies by Pirolli (1986), Pirolli (1988), Pirolli & Recker (1991), and Bielaczyc, Pirolli, & Brown (1991), involving the use of a computerized tutoring system known as the LISP Tutor (Anderson, Farrell, & Sauers, 1984). This system is designed to teach the programming language LISP. The four studies were conducted in different years and at different universities; however, the studies were deliberately designed to be very similar, enough so that the data from the studies may be combined for the purposes of this analysis. College-age students worked through several introductory sessions with the LISP Tutor. They were then given a text and one of several examples explaining the use of the programming technique recursion. As they read and tried to understand the explanatory material, they were asked to reason aloud. These sessions were videotaped, and later coded for, among other things, the number of times a student made a self-explanation statement attempting to relate the text to the example.

After finishing the explanatory material, the student then worked through the LISP Tutor lesson on recursion. The lesson consisted of a number of problems, each of which involved writing a LISP function to perform some task. The LISP Tutor automatically records each keystroke, and the time between each keystroke, as well as coding student performance on a number of tasks in terms of whether or not students appeared to have used correct *production rules*. The concept of a production rule is rather complex, and different researchers have put forth different definitions, but for the purposes of this investigation, it will be sufficient to define a production rule as a condition-action pairing. The condition specifies a particular programming goal and the problem specifications that apply. The action tells the subject how to proceed and may involve writing LISP code, embellishing the problem specifications, or setting a subgoal. The following example of a production rule is given in Anderson, Farrell, and Sauers (1984):

IF   the goal is to add List1 and List2
THEN   write (APPEND List1 List2).

All production rules for the data in this example involved writing LISP code. There were multiple opportunities for subjects to use each of the production rules recognized by the LISP Tutor. Each attempt to use a production rule will be referred to as an *instance*. If the subject made one or more errors during an attempt to use any production rule, this was coded as a 1 for that instance of that production rule. If the subject used the production rule without making errors, this was coded as a 0.

Part of the design of these four studies included a variation of the example seen by students as part of the explanatory material. Some students saw a recursion example involving numerical recursion, and others saw an example involving list recursion. The researchers hypothesized that seeing one of the two examples would affect student performance on some of the productions. Several productions were used in the list recursion example, several others were used in the number recursion example, one production was used in both examples, and the rest were directly related to neither example. It was hypothesized that subjects would do relatively better on production rules that had been used in the example they had seen than they would on production rules that were not directly related to an example, and that subjects who had seen a particular example would do relatively better on production rules directly related to that example than would subjects who had not seen that example.

As mentioned previously, each production rule could be attempted multiple times during the course of a tutor session. If a production rule was attempted and performed incorrectly, the tutor responded with feedback designed to help the subject learn to use the production rule correctly. It was therefore expected that the probability of error would decline steadily with each successive attempt by a subject to use a production rule.

The first of the four LISP tutor studies was undertaken to investigate basic declarative and procedural transfer effects from examples (Pirolli & Recker, in press). Twenty subjects from this study will be included in the analysis. The second study was an exploratory study of self-explanation (Pirolli & Recker, in press), and included 12 subjects. The third study explored the relationship between self-explanation and the use of a computerized instructional environment (Recker & Pirolli, in press) and included 17 subjects. The fourth study investigated pedagogical manipulation of self-explanation (Bielaczyc, Pirolli, & Brown, 1991) and included 27 subjects. Subjects for these four studies were recruited from undergraduate college student populations at Carnegie Mellon University and at the University of California—Berkeley. Subjects were recruited via posted announcements and were paid for their participation in the studies. There were a total of 76 subjects in all four studies.

There were originally 25 productions that were of interest, and each production could be attempted many times. However, some productions were never attempted by most subjects, and the number of instances of each production varied. It was decided to use only those productions for which at least two-thirds of the persons (about 50 of the 76) attempted the production at least once. This resulted in the selection of 4 production rules associated with example 1 (number recursion), 5 production rules associated with example 2 (list recursion), 12 production rules directly associated with neither example, and 1 production rule associated with both example 1 and example 2.

In order to decide how many instances of each production should be used, the number of subjects attempting the production at each trial was examined. It was noted that there was a clear pattern of missing data across all productions: For one or more instances, two-thirds or more of the subjects would respond, and then at some point, the number of respondents would fall sharply, usually to almost none. All instances of a particular production up to this drop-off point were used in the analysis. This resulted in the use of as few as one or as many as 10 instances.

Model Specification

In this analysis of the LISP Tutor data, we were interested in the effect of several characteristics of the task setting on student performance. The first was the relative difficulty of each of the production rules. This is similar to a classic, Rasch-type item difficulty, except for the existence of multiple observations for each subject on each item. In addition, the researches wished to examine the effect of the example seen by a particular subject group on that group's performance of productions related to that example. Finally, researchers wished to determine the effects of practice across repeated instances of the productions. Two models were fitted to the data. In Model 1, the effect of practice was assumed to be the same across all productions with multiple instances. In Model 2, a separate practice effect parameter was estimated for each production with multiple instances.

It should be noted that the LISP Tutor is a highly complex environment. The current analyses in no way take into consideration all of the factors which may affect the performance of students in this environment. The major purpose of these analyses is to illustrate how RCML models may be used to understand the influence of various factors on person performance. It would be possible to specify still other parameters which might affect student performance, and to use other, related data to better understand the behavior which takes place in this environment. We intend to do this in later studies, for which the current one is only a beginning.

The RCML assumes a single underlying distribution of ability in the population of persons. In this example, there may actually be two ability distributions, one for each example group. In addition, the group effect parameters refer only to the performance of one of the groups on a set of items. The RCML may be used to estimate person group effects on item difficulties in the case where there are two person groups; however, because of the assumption of only one distribution of person ability, the following device must be used to estimate group effect parameters: Each item is divided into two separate items, one for each person group. Each person, then, takes only one of these items, the one which corresponds to that person's group membership, and has missing data for the other. Each response to one of these items contributes, via the design matrix, to the estimation of the original item's difficulty; in addition, a response by a person in person group 2 to an item in item group 2 contributes to the group difference parameter. (This scheme could be extended to more than two groups, but it becomes considerably more complicated). An illustration of data resulting from the use of this scheme is given in Figure 11.1. In this illustration, items labeled (a) are items as seen by person group 1, and items labeled (b) are the same items as seen by person group 2. Persons 001 and 002 obtained the same original response patterns, but were in different groups.

The probability of error for Model 1 on a given instance of a particular production may be written as:

$$P(X_{ij} = 1; \beta_j, \tau, \alpha \mid \theta_i, \phi) = \frac{\exp\left(\theta_i - \beta_j + (t - 1)\alpha + \sum_{h=0}^{2} \phi_{ih}\tau_{hk}\right)}{1 + \exp\left(\theta_i - \beta_j + (t - 1)\alpha + \sum_{h=0}^{2} \phi_{ih}\tau_{hk}\right)}, \quad (2)$$

original data

Person ID	Person Group	Item 1	Item 2	Item 3
001	1	1	0	1
002	2	1	0	1
003	1	1	1	1
004	2	0	0	0

rescored data

Person ID	Person Group	Item 1a	Item 1b	Item 2a	Item 2b	Item 3a	Item 3b
001	1	1		0		1	
002	2		1		0		1
003	1	1		1		1	
004	2		0		0		0

Figure 11.1.   Illustration of missing data patterns.

where X_{ij} is the response of person i to production rule j, and is coded 1 for error and 0 for no error. θ_i is the proficiency of person i, ϕ is an indicator vector whose entries ϕ_{ih} are equal to 1 if person i is a member of group h and zero otherwise, β_j is the difficulty of production j, t is the number of the current instance, with 1 indicating the first instance, and α is the practice effect. τ_{hk}, h = 1,2 and k = 0, . . ,2 are the effects that seeing example h has on productions related to example k (k = 0 indicates a production related to neither example), and which are collected into the matrix τ. In this case, τ_{hk} is assumed to be zero for all productions associated with neither example, and also assumed to be zero for the effect of example 1 on example 2 productions and conversely. Thus, τ_{hk} = 0 except in the case where h = k; that is, when a person in a particular example group attempts a production rule which relates to the example they saw. This reflects the assumption that seeing one example will only have an effect on production rules directly related to that example, and not on any of the other productions.

For Model 2, the probability of error on a given instance of a production is:

$$P(X_{ij} = 1; \beta_j, \tau, \alpha_j \mid \theta_i, \phi) = \frac{\exp\left(\theta_i - \beta_j + (t - 1)\alpha_j + \sum_{h=0}^{2} \phi_{ih}\tau_{hk}\right)}{1 + \exp\left(\theta_i - \beta_j + (t - 1)\alpha_j + \sum_{h=0}^{2} \phi_{ih}\tau_{hk}\right)}, \quad (3)$$

where all variables are the same as before, except that α_j is now indexed by item, since there is now, at least potentially, a separate practice effect for each item.

Appendix A shows an illustration of the RCML design matrices for these analyses of the LISP Tutor data.

RESULTS

Parameter estimates and standard errors for Model 1, which contains only one practice effect across all productions, are given in Table 11.1. Because standard errors for each parameter are available, a t-test may be used to determine whether a particular parameter is significantly different from zero. In our case, we are interested in testing the significance of α and τ. Both estimated example effects for this model are statistically significant. The estimated practice effect is also statis-

Table 11.1. Parameter Estimates and Standard Errors for Single Practice Effect

Parameter	Example	Number of Instances	Estimate	Standard Error
code-add1	neither	1	0.435	0.084
code-add1-on-recursive-result	neither	1	−0.361	0.084
code-car	list	9	−0.631	0.071
code-cdr	list	10	−0.461	0.071
code-cons-on-recursive-result	list	5	0.739	0.071
code-difference	neither	1		0.077
code-equal-test	neither	2	0.999	0.077
code-greater-test	neither	1	−0.417	0.084
code-list-recursion	list	6	−1.538	0.084
code-member-test	neither	2	−0.789	0.077
code-mod	neither	1	0.370	0.077
code-not-test	neither	1	1.675	0.084
code-null-test	list	6	0.004	0.071
code-number-recursion	number	6	−0.812	0.077
code-number-test	neither	1	−0.815	0.084
code-oddp-test	neither	1	−0.421	0.084
code-plus-on-recursive-result	number	2	0.595	0.077
code-smaller-test	neither	1	−0.873	0.084
code-sub1	number	8	0.843	0.063
code-times-on-recursive-result	neither	2	−1.233	0.084
code-zerop-test	number	6	0.712	0.063
recursive-call	both	10	0.838	*
Group effect 1	number		−0.313	0.077
Group effect 2	list		−0.278	0.063
Practice effect	both		−0.100	<0.001

* Note: Parameter constrained to negative sum of other population difficulties.

tically significant. The two example effect parameters are about the same for each group, suggesting that each example has approximately the same effect on the error rates for productions associated with it. Example effects are approximately three times the size of the estimated practice effect, suggesting that seeing an example related to the ask is more effective in reducing error than is practice, especially on the first few instances. The relationship between the difficulties of the productions, the size of the practice effect, the abilities of subjects in each example group, and the size of the example effect, is shown graphically in Figure 11.2. This figure illustrates the relative positions of the production rules on the logit scale, with the most difficult productions (i.e. the ones on which most errors were made) at the top of the page, and the easier productions near the bottom. Ability estimates

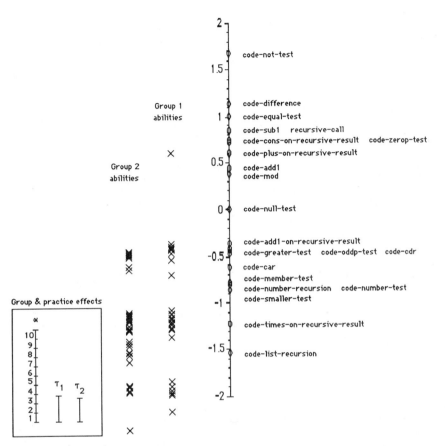

Figure 11.2.   Distribution of item estimates and person abilities with representation of example and practice effects.

for the two person groups are shown in the two columns on the left-hand side of the page, each person being represented by an X. A person has a greater than 50% chance of making an error on any production whose location on the logit scale is above their position, and a less than 50% chance of error for any production whose location is below theirs. The box in the lower left-hand corner of the figure contains "rulers" representing the effects of practice and examples on the performance of production rules. The example effect rulers are labeled τ_1 and τ_2 for the effects of example 1 and example 2, respectively, and the length of these rulers represents the boost in ability for a person in that group when the person encounters production rules related to the example seen by that group. This could also be thought of as a drop in the difficulty of items related to each example; however, it is easier to illustrate graphically by referring to person ability. The practice effect is represented as a segmented line at the far left side of the box. For each subject, each successive attempt to use one of the production rules results in an increase in that person's ability equal to the length of one segment. To determine the effects of practice and example on a person's ability, simply begin at that person's location on the scale, and move up the scale the length of the appropriate ruler. This new location is the person's ability to perform the task when practice and example have been taken into consideration.

Parameter estimates and standard errors for Model 2, which contains multiple practice effects, are given in Table 11.2. Practice effects are statistically significant for the production rules code-list-recursion,

Table 11.2.   Parameter Estimates and Standard Errors for Multiple Practice Effects

Production	Difficulty Estimate	Standard Error	Slope Estimate	Standard Error
code-add1	0.556	0.084	—	—
code-add1-on-recursive-result	0.127	0.084	—	—
code-car	−1.246	0.071	0.004	0.266
code-cdr	−0.404	0.071	−0.141	0.266
code-cons-on-recursive-result	0.206	0.071	0.067	0.266
code-difference	0.037	0.077	—	—
code-equal-test	0.687	0.077	−0.261	0.278
code-greater-test	1.205	0.077	—	—
code-list-recursion	−0.526	0.077	−0.628	0.278
code-member-test	−0.992	0.077	−0.044	0.278
code-mod	−0.271	0.077	—	—
code-not-test	0.611	0.077	—	—
code-null-test	1.563	0.071	−0.797	0.266
code-number-recursion	−1.477	0.077	−0.004	0.278
code-number-test	−0.354	0.077	—	—
code-oddp-test	−0.731	0.084	—	—
code-plus-on-recursive-result	−0.373	0.077	0.894	0.278
code-smaller-test	0.082	0.077	—	—
code-sub1	0.186	0.063	0.020	0.251
code-times-on-recursive-result	0.120	0.077	−1.294	0.278
code-zerop-test	0.540	0.063	−0.154	0.251
recursive-call	−0.454	*	−0.085	<0.001
Group effect 1	0.053	0.063		
Group effect 2	0.013	0.071		

* Note: Parameter constrained to negative sum of other production difficulties.

code-null-test, code-times-on-recursive-result, and recursive-call. All other productions showed nonsignificant practice effects. For this model, both of the example effects are very small, and neither effect reaches statistical significance.

Since these models deal with relative probabilities of error, comparison of the parameters estimated by the two models is facilitated by examining the probability that a person with ability estimate equal to the mean ability for each group makes an error on the first instance of each production rule. This information is given in Tables 11.3 and 11.4. In order to evaluate the performance of the two models relative to one another, observed proportions of persons in each group who performed each task correctly are given in Table 11.5.

The probabilities of error on the first instance of each production for Model 1 are given in Table 11.3. Although many of the modeled probabilities of error on the first instance of a production are quite close to the observed values, several of the modeled probabilities of error are quite a bit higher than the observed proportions of error (see, for example, code-car). Others are quite a bit lower than the observed (see,

Table 11.3.   Probability of Error on the First Trial of Each Production for Single Practice Effect

Parameter	P(Error | Group = 1)	P(Error | Group = 2)
code-add1	0.355	0.315
code-add1-on-recursive-result	0.199	0.172
code-car	0.160	0.107
code-cdr	0.184	0.125
code-cons-on-recursive-result	0.428	0.321
code-difference	0.528	0.483
code-equal-test	0.492	0.447
code-greater-test	0.190	0.164
code-list-recursion	0.071	0.046
code-member-test	0.140	0.119
code-mod	0.341	0.302
code-not-test	0.656	0.614
code-null-test	0.264	0.185
code-number-recursion	0.104	0.117
code-number-test	0.136	0.117
code-oddp-test	0.190	0.164
code-plus-on-recursive-result	0.321	0.351
code-smaller-test	0.130	0.111
code-sub1	0.378	0.409
code-times-on-recursive-result	0.094	0.080
code-zerop-test	0.347	0.378
recursive-call	0.376	0.343

Table 11.4. Probability of Error on the First Trial of Each Production for Multiple Practice Effects

Parameter	P(Error I Group = 1)	P(Error I Group = 2)
code-add1	0.388	0.347
code-add1-on-recursive-result	0.293	0.257
code-car	0.095	0.081
code-cdr	0.196	0.171
code-cons-on-recursive-result	0.309	0.275
code-difference	0.274	0.240
code-equal-test	0.420	0.377
code-greater-test	0.549	0.504
code-list-recursion	0.177	0.154
code-member-test	0.119	0.101
code-mod	0.217	0.188
code-not-test	0.402	0.359
code-null-test	0.635	0.595
code-number-recursion	0.081	0.065
code-number-test	0.204	0.176
code-oddp-test	0.149	0.128
code-plus-on-recursive-result	0.209	0.173
code-smaller-test	0.283	0.248
code-sub1	0.316	0.268
code-times-on-recursive-result	0.291	0.255
code-zerop-test	0.397	0.343
recursive-call	0.377	0.327

for example, code-cdr). This is because the modeled difficulty of each production is based on person performance across repeated instances of the production. In other words, whenever the modeled probability of error on the first instance is lower than the observed proportion, the proportions of error on subsequent instances tend to be quite a bit lower than on the first instance. Similarly, if the modeled probability of error on the first instance appears too high, observed proportions of errors on the next several instances will be as high as or higher than on the first instance.

The probabilities of error on the first instance of each production rule for Model 2 are more difficult to interpret. For several of the productions, there are striking differences between the observed and expected proportions of error on the first instance. As for Model 1, this tends to occur in productions with multiple instances for which the proportions of error on the first instance are much higher or much lower than on subsequent instances. In the case of the code-number-recursion production, for example, the modeled probability of error on the first instance is less than .10 for Model 2. The observed proportion

Table 11.5.   Observed Proportion of Error on the
First Trial of Each Production

Parameter	Group 1	Group 2
code-add1	0.33	0.31
code-add1-on-recursive-result	0.21	0.18
code-car	0.06	0.05
code-cdr	0.25	0.32
code-cons-on-recursive-result	0.53	0.32
code-difference	0.52	0.48
code-equal-test	0.29	0.11
code-greater-test	0.17	0.19
code-list-recursion	0.19	0.07
code-member-test	0.34	0.32
code-mod	0.35	0.3
code-not-test	0.54	0.69
code-null-test	0.78	0.39
code-number-recursion	0.25	0.16
code-number-test	0.16	0.11
code-oddp-test	0.19	0.18
code-plus-on-recursive-result	0.22	0.34
code-smaller-test	0.05	0.17
code-sub1	0.41	0.59
code-times-on-recursive-result	0.13	0.11
code-zerop-test	0.34	0.55
recursive-call	0.25	0.41

of error is .25, which is quite a bit higher. However, on the next four instances of this production, the observed proportion of error for both groups drops to below .10. The model is giving less weight to extreme proportions of error at the first or last trial, and more weight to instances at the center of the time interval. Model 2 probabilities also do not reflect large group differences in error rates for the productions related to an example. This suggests that either the example effects seen in Model 1 really had something to do with differing practice effects for the productions, or that the estimation of multiple practice effects has hidden the effects of the examples.

Although tests of fit have been developed for the RCML model, based on the work of Glas (1989), these tests may no longer be valid when the model is used to estimate group effects in the manner described above. Tests of fit for models involving more than one latent ability distribution have yet to be developed. The fit of the two RCML models may be examined to a certain extent by comparing predicted to expected probability of success across all instances for the various productions. This may be done graphically, by plotting the expected curves and the observed proportions together. Figures 11.3 through 11.6 show such curves for four selected productions, one set for each model. These productions were selected to show the range of diagnostic information obtained, from those that fit well with one model or another to those that showed poor fit with both models.

Figure 11.3 shows an example 2 production, code-null-test. The modeled probabilities for Model 1 seem reasonable in that the probability of error is always higher for group 1 than for group 2, and the distances between the modeled curves and the observed curves for the two groups seem fairly consistent. Model 1 seems to describe this data quite well in that sense. However, it appears that, for this production, the single time effect across all instances is not a good estimate of the practice effect for this production; the decrease in the error rate is much steeper for this production than for the average across all productions. The modeled probabilities for Model 2, in contrast, seem to have captured the slope of the practice effect quite accurately. However, Model 2 does not reflect the noticeable difference between the performance of the two groups on this production.

Figure 11.4 shows modeled versus empirical curves for the recursive-call production, which is associated with both examples. The modeled curves for both Model 1 and Model 2 are quite similar. Neither shows a particularly large group difference. This seems to agree with the pattern in the empirical curves, which cross several times and tend to bounce back and forth around the modeled curves. The downward trend in the error rates is approximately the same for both models, and seems to capture the general decrease in error shown in the empirical curves. However, the data in this picture show quite a bit of what seems like random noise in the empirical error rates.

Figure 11.5 shows the modeled and empirical curves for code-sub1, a group 1 production. The first instance shows a much larger proportion of error for group 2 than for group 1; however, this effect largely disappears over the next several instances. The last two instances show a marked increase in the proportion of error for both groups, which is a cause for concern. It may be that there is something different about these last two instances that is causing people to make more errors than they had previously done. The practice effect for Model 2 shows a slight, but nonsignificant, increase over time for this production.

Figure 11.6, which shows the modeled and empirical curves for the code-car production, is perhaps the most worrisome of these graphs. Although group 2 consistently outperforms group 1, as predicted, there seems to be no consistent practice effect. Again, the proportion of errors made increases on the last two instances of the production, and the regularity with which the proportion of errors made increases and

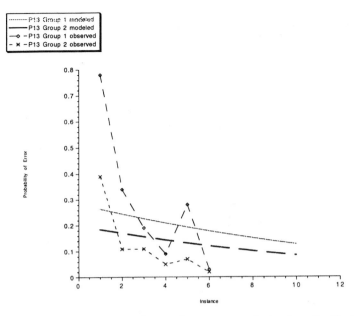

Figure 11.3a.   Code null test observed versus expected values for Model 1.

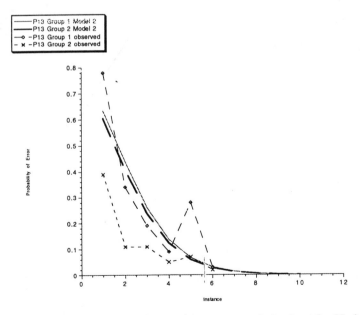

Figure 11.3b.   Code null test observed versus expected values for Model 2.

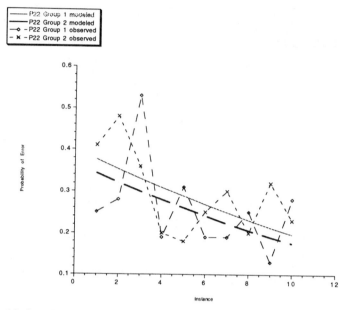

Figure 11.4a.   Recursive call observed versus expected values for Model 1.

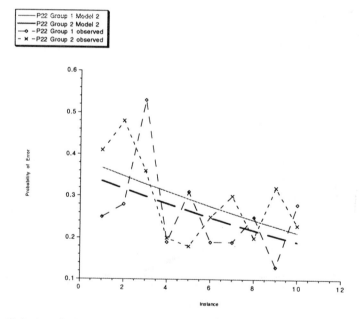

Figure 11.4b.   Recursive call observed versus expected values for Model 2.

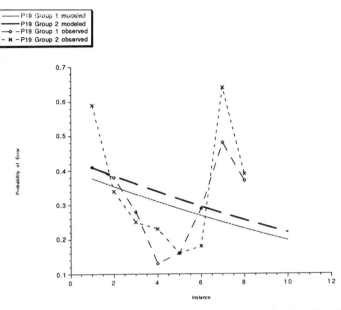

Figure 11.5a.   Code sub1 observed versus expected values for Model 1.

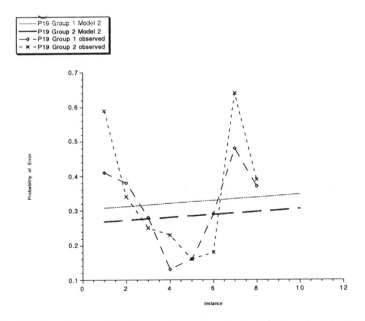

Figure 11.5b.   Code sub1 observed versus expected values for Model 2.

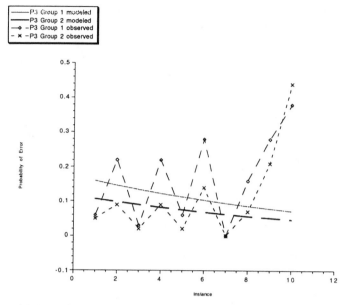

Figure 11.6a.   Code car observed versus expected values for Model 1.

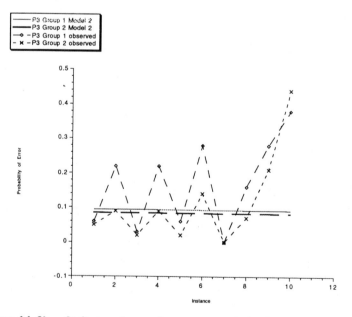

Figure 11.6b.   Code car observed versus expected values for Model 2.

decreases for both groups seems suggestive of something other than random noise. The modeled curves for Model 2 are horizontal lines, showing the complete lack of a decrease in error rate over time.

These examples suggest that seeing the two examples does affect performance on some of the productions in the manner predicted by theory. However, some of the productions show no discernible example effect, and others are actually easier for the group for which they should be more difficult. This may be part of the reason why Model 2, which took into account a practice effect for all items with multiple instances, failed to show a clear example effect. Model 2 did seem to be successful in separating those productions that showed a clear practice effect from those that did not. The productions for which the practice effect were statistically significant tended to show patterns like code-null-test, shown in Figure 11.3. The productions with nonsignificant practice effects tended to show patterns more like those in Figures 11.5 and 11.6.

DISCUSSION

The above examples illustrate how the RCML may be used to understand the effects of a variety of complex factors on student performance. In addition to examining the relative difficulty of the various production rules, we were able to investigate the effects of experimental manipulations and practice on student learning. We can conclude that both examples and practice have a significant effect on student error rates in this environment. In addition, it seems clear that practice does not affect all of the production rules in the same way. The patterns that were observed when plotting curves of observed versus expected error rates across several of the production rules suggest that our two models have not taken into account all relevant information, and that more exploration is necessary. Based on our examination of the results so far, and our knowledge about the LISP Tutor data, a number of directions for future research are possible.

The finding that not all of the slopes of the learning curves are equal, or in other words that some error curves show steep decline with practice and some do not, leads us to question whether or not there might be subgroups of production rules with equal practice parameters. Some production rules are new to the current lesson and some were learned in previous lessons. It is possible that newly learned production rules would show roughly equal, steep learning rates, while previously learned production rules would not. This possibility will be investigated in later studies.

The appearance of systematic patterns of error such as those in Figure 11.6 needs to be explained. Further investigation of the structure of the LISP Tutor reveals that different instances of the same production are embedded within different problems. In other words, the first instance of a production may occur when writing a LISP function to perform one task, the second instance when writing a function to perform a completely different task, and so on. Also, the sequence of the productions within each problem changed from problem to problem. A particular production might be the first thing a subject would need to do in writing one function, but near the end of a group of things that would need to be done to write another function. It is quite possible that the difficulty of the problem in which the production appears may account for some of the regularity observed in the fluctuations of difficulty across instances with several of the productions. It is also possible that a production's position within the sequence of steps necessary to solve a problem could affect that production's difficulty. It may, for example, be more likely that subjects make errors when executing the first production in a problem solution than when executing productions near the end of the solution. This information is available in the datasets used for this analysis, and parameters for such effects could be estimated by the RCML. However, such an analysis is beyond the scope of the current paper.

For the example that has been addressed in this chapter, estimation of group effects was relatively straightforward, since the group membership of each person was known. In many cases, however, person group membership is latent rather than observed. For example, with the LISP Tutor data, researchers have theorized that aspects of student metacognition may strongly affect student learning and performance within a tutoring session. In particular, students who use a self-explanation strategy, which involves making links between the text to explain a particular aspect of programming, and an illustrative example of that aspect, tend to perform better than students who do not construct such links for themselves (Pirolli & Recker, 1991). Similar effects have been noted in studies like that by Shute and Glaser (1990), in which students who use a global planning approach to problem solving learn concepts of economics more quickly than do students who do not do such planning. In the case of the LISP Tutor, evidence of self-explanation is available via protocol analysis from the videotapes of each tutoring session. However, such analysis is quite difficult, time-consuming, and expensive. It would be much more efficient if tasks could be constructed such that performance on some tasks was affected by a strategy of interest, while performance on others tasks was not.

Such data could then be used to estimate strategy class membership for each subject.

Examples of models that estimate latent class membership are discussed by Wilson (1989), and Mislevy and Verhelst (1990). These particular models, however, lack the generality necessary to estimate practice effects and other complexities of data such as that from the LISP Tutor studies. This suggests that it would be very useful to have a model that combines the generality and flexibility of the RCML with the ability to estimate latent group membership as well as latent ability for each person. Such a model has in fact been suggested by Pirolli and Wilson (1992), and estimation software is currently under development. A model that allowed the estimation of latent group membership as well as proficiency level for each person would allow the researcher to test theories about such things as developmental stages, differences in learning styles, or experimental interventions. The effects of these classes on human behavior in a wide variety of situations may be investigated, leading to a better understanding of human development and learning.

REFERENCES

Adams, R., & Wilson, M. (1991). *The random coefficients multinomial logit model: A general approach to fitting Rasch models.* Paper presented at the annual meeting of the American Educational Research Association, Chicago, April.

Adams, R., & Wilson, M. (1996). Formulating the Rasch model as a mixed coefficients multinomial logit. In G. Engelhard Jr., & M. Wilson, (Eds.). *Objective measurement: Theory into practice, Volume 3.* Norwood, NJ: Ablex.

Anderson, J.R., Conrad, F.G., & Corbett, A.T. (1989). Skill acquisition and the LISP Tutor. *Cognitive Science, 13,* 467–505.

Anderson, J.R., Farrell, R., & Sauers, R. (1984). Learning to program in LISP. *Cognitive Science, 8,* 87–129.

Bielaczyc, K., Pirolli, P., & Brown, A. (1991). *The effects of training in explanation strategies on the acquisition of programming.* (Tech. Rep. CSM-3). Berkeley, CA: University of California.

Fisher, G. (1983). Logistic latent trait models with linear constraints. *Psychometrika, 48,* 3–26.

Gitomer, D.H., & Yamamoto, K. (1990). Performance modeling that integrates latent trait and class theory. *Journal of Educational Measurement, 28,* 173–189.

Glas, C.A.W. (1989). *Contributions to estimation and testing Rasch models.* Doctoral Dissertation, Universiteit Twente.

Mislevy, R.J., & Verhelst, N. (1990). Modeling item responses when different subjects employ different solution strategies. *Psychometrika, 55,* 195–215.

Pirolli, P. (1986). A cognitive model and computer tutor for programming recursion. *Human-Computer Interaction, 2,* 319–355.

Pirolli, P., & Recker, M. (1991). *Knowledge construction and transfer using an intelligent tutoring system: The role of examples, self-explanation, practice, and reflection.* (Tech. Rep. No. CSM-1). University of California.

Pirolli, P., & Wilson, M. (1992). Measuring learning strategies and understanding: A research framework. In C. Frassen, G. Gauthier, & G.I. McCalla (Eds.), *Intelligent tutoring systems, Proceedings of the Second International Conference,* Montreal, Canada, June 1992. Berlin: Springer-Verlag.

Shute, V., & Glaser, R. (1990). A large-scale evaluation of an intelligent discovery world: Smithtown. *Interactive Learning Environments, 1,* 51–77.

Wilson, M. (1989). Saltus: A psychometric model of discontinuity in cognitive development. *Psychological Bulletin, 105,* 276–289.

Wilson, M. (1990). *A mixture model approach to the measurement of stage-like development.* Paper presented at the Berkeley-Stanford Quantitative Methods Colloquium, Berkeley, CA.

APPENDIX A

Figure 11.A1 shows the design matrix used to estimate a uniform practice effect across all productions. Items one and two do not have multiple instances—each person attempted these items only once. Performance on these items was also not thought to be affected by example group membership—these items are unrelated to either example. Thus, errors on these two items by persons in either group contribute only to their respective difficulty parameters, β_1 and β_2, and not to the practice effect parameter α or the group effect parameters τ_1 and τ_2. Item three was attempted five times by each subject, and was also an item thought to be associated with example 1. An error by either group on each instance of this item contributes to the item's difficulty parameter, β_3. In addition, an error on each instance by a person in group 1 contributes to the example 1 effect parameter τ_1. Also, since this item was attempted multiple times, errors on instances other than the first contribute to the practice effect parameter α. Item four is similar to item three, except that it is related to example 2 instead of to example 1, and thus contributes to τ_2 instead of τ_1.

Figure 11.A2 shows the design matrix for the RCML analysis that includes multiple practice effects, one for each item with multiple

item	group	instance	response	β_1	β_2	β_3	β_4	...	α	τ_1	τ_2
1	1	1	0	0	0	0	0	...	0	0	0
1	1	1	1	1	0	0	0	...	0	0	0
1	2	1	0	0	0	0	0	...	0	0	0
1	2	1	1	1	0	0	0	...	0	0	0
2	1	1	0	0	0	0	0	...	0	0	0
2	1	1	1	0	1	0	0	...	0	0	0
2	2	1	0	0	0	0	0	...	0	0	0
2	2	1	1	0	1	0	0	...	0	0	0
3	1	1	0	0	0	0	0	...	0	0	0
3	1	1	1	0	0	1	0	...	0	1	0
3	2	1	0	0	0	0	0	...	0	0	0
3	2	1	1	0	0	1	0	...	0	0	0
3	1	2	0	0	0	0	0	...	0	0	0
3	1	2	1	0	0	1	0	...	1	1	0
3	2	2	0	0	0	0	0	...	0	0	0
3	2	2	1	0	0	1	0	...	1	0	0
3	1	3	0	0	0	0	0	...	0	0	0
3	1	3	1	0	0	1	0	...	2	1	0
3	2	3	0	0	0	0	0	...	0	0	0
3	2	3	1	0	0	1	0	...	2	0	0
3	1	4	0	0	0	0	0	...	0	0	0
3	1	4	1	0	0	1	0	...	3	1	0
3	2	4	0	0	0	0	0	...	0	0	0
3	2	4	1	0	0	1	0	...	3	0	0
3	1	5	0	0	0	0	0	...	0	0	0
3	1	5	1	0	0	1	0	...	4	1	0
3	2	5	0	0	0	0	0	...	0	0	0
3	2	5	1	0	0	1	0	...	4	0	0
4	1	1	0	0	0	0	0	...	0	0	0
4	1	1	1	0	0	0	1	...	0	0	0
4	2	1	0	0	0	0	0	...	0	0	0
4	2	1	1	0	0	0	1	...	0	0	1
4	1	2	0	0	0	0	0	...	0	0	0
4	1	2	1	0	0	0	1	...	1	0	0
4	2	2	0	0	0	0	0	...	0	0	0
4	2	2	1	0	0	0	1	...	1	0	1
4	1	3	0	0	0	0	0	...	0	0	0
4	1	3	1	0	0	0	1	...	2	0	0
4	2	3	0	0	0	0	0	...	0	0	0
4	2	3	1	0	0	0	1	...	2	0	1
4	1	4	0	0	0	0	0	...	0	0	0
4	1	4	1	0	0	0	1	...	3	0	0
4	2	4	0	0	0	0	0	...	0	0	0
4	2	4	1	0	0	0	1	...	3	0	1
4	1	5	0	0	0	0	0	...	0	0	0
4	1	5	1	0	0	0	1	...	4	0	0
4	2	5	0	0	0	0	0	...	0	0	0
4	2	5	1	0	0	0	1	...	4	0	1

Figure 11.A1. Example design matrix for RCML analysis with single practice effect.

instances. This design matrix is very similar to the one in Figure 11.A1, except that, for each item that was attempted multiple times, there is a separate practice effect parameter.

item	group	instance	response	β_1	β_2	β_3	α_3	β_4	α_4	...	τ_1	τ_2
1	1	1	0	0	0	0	0	0	0	...	0	0
1	1	1	1	1	0	0	0	0	0	...	0	0
1	2	1	0	0	0	0	0	0	0	...	0	0
1	2	1	1	1	0	0	0	0	0	...	0	0
2	1	1	0	0	0	0	0	0	0	...	0	0
2	1	1	1	0	1	0	0	0	0	...	0	0
2	2	1	0	0	0	0	0	0	0	...	0	0
2	2	1	1	0	1	0	0	0	0	...	0	0
3	1	1	0	0	0	0	0	0	0	...	0	0
3	1	1	1	0	0	1	0	0	0	...	1	0
3	2	1	0	0	0	0	0	0	0	...	0	0
3	2	1	1	0	0	1	0	0	0	...	0	0
3	1	2	0	0	0	0	0	0	0	...	0	0
3	1	2	1	0	0	1	1	0	0	...	1	0
3	2	2	0	0	0	0	0	0	0	...	0	0
3	2	2	1	0	0	1	1	0	0	...	0	0
3	1	3	0	0	0	0	0	0	0	...	0	0
3	1	3	1	0	0	1	2	0	0	...	1	0
3	2	3	0	0	0	0	0	0	0	...	0	0
3	2	3	1	0	0	1	2	0	0	...	0	0
3	1	4	0	0	0	0	0	0	0	...	0	0
3	1	4	1	0	0	1	3	0	0	...	1	0
3	2	4	0	0	0	0	0	0	0	...	0	0
3	2	4	1	0	0	1	3	0	0	...	0	0
3	1	5	0	0	0	0	0	0	0	...	0	0
3	1	5	1	0	0	1	4	0	0	...	1	0
3	2	5	0	0	0	0	0	0	0	...	0	0
3	2	5	1	0	0	1	4	0	0	...	0	0
4	1	1	0	0	0	0	0	0	0	...	0	0
4	1	1	1	0	0	0	0	1	0	...	0	0
4	2	1	0	0	0	0	0	0	0	...	0	0
4	2	1	1	0	0	0	0	1	0	...	0	1
4	1	2	0	0	0	0	0	0	0	...	0	0
4	1	2	1	0	0	0	0	1	1	...	0	0
4	2	2	0	0	0	0	0	0	0	...	0	0
4	2	2	1	0	0	0	0	1	1	...	0	1
4	1	3	0	0	0	0	0	0	0	...	0	0
4	1	3	1	0	0	0	0	1	2	...	0	0
4	2	3	0	0	0	0	0	0	0	...	0	0
4	2	3	1	0	0	0	0	1	2	...	0	1
4	1	4	0	0	0	0	0	0	0	...	0	0
4	1	4	1	0	0	0	0	1	3	...	0	0
4	2	4	0	0	0	0	0	0	0	...	0	0
4	2	4	1	0	0	0	0	1	3	...	0	1
4	1	5	0	0	0	0	0	0	0	...	0	0
4	1	5	1	0	0	0	0	1	4	...	0	0
4	2	5	0	0	0	0	0	0	0	...	0	0
4	2	5	1	0	0	0	0	1	4	...	0	1

Figure 11.A2.   Example design matrix for RCML analysis with multiple practice effects.

chapter **12**

Estimating Differential Item Functioning in the Polytomous Case with the Random Coefficients Multinomial Logit (RCML) Model

Stephen Moore
University of California at Berkeley

Using standardized testing, decision makers can compare members of a large population on a common scale. Such a capability is considered all but essential in the process of placement and screening in a number of assessment contexts in education, business, the military, and many other areas. A population of potential test takers may be broken down into groups according to factors such as gender, race, or ethnicity. If the probability of success on a test item differs statistically by group for examinees at the same level of ability on the latent dimension tapped by the item, then that item exhibits differential item functioning (DIF) and may bias test results in favor of one group over another (Berk, 1982). The primary purpose of this paper is the demonstration of the random coefficients multinomial logit (RCML) model (Adams &

Wilson, 1991, in this volume) as a method for detecting DIF in standardized test items.

When a test is functioning as intended, all examinees at the same level of ability will have scores that center on the same value. If some of the test items are easier for boys, as an example, than for girls of equal ability, then those girls will have lower test scores, on average, than their male counterparts. In order for any measurement model to place examinees on an interval scale that validly assesses the latent dimension of interest, the raw scores of the test must at least preserve the relative order of their respective true scores on that dimension (Thorndike, 1982). In general, scores on a test that include one or more biased items are not order-preserving transformations of examinee true scores because a higher score can result simply from being a member of the advantaged group. Thus, the validity of such a test is abrogated to some extent, regardless of its other merits.

This is not to say that a test comprising bias-free items is necessarily a valid measure of the trait of interest. Bias is not the only threat to test validity; in a particular test, it may not even be the most important threat to validity. From the foregoing, however, it does follow that freedom from biased items is a necessary, if not sufficient, condition for a test to be valid.

Although closely related, the terms *DIF* and *bias* have distinct meanings. DIF exists when an item is shown statistically to function differently by group, but bias exists only when an item actually gives an unfair advantage to a group. Statistical DIF is not sufficient to establish that the item is biased. Only a substantive analysis conducted by experts in the domain tapped by the item can do that.

THE DICHOTOMOUS RASCH MODEL AND TWO POLYTOMOUS EXTENSIONS

The Rasch model is commonly expressed according to equation 1 below:

$$P(x_{ni} = 1 \mid \theta_n) = \frac{\exp(\theta_n - \delta_i)}{1 + \exp(\theta_n - \delta_i)}, \tag{1}$$

where $P(x_{ni} = 1 \mid \theta_n)$ is the probability of the nth examinee responding correctly to the ith item given θ_n, the parameter associated with the level of ability for the nth examinee, and where δ_i is the parameter associated with the difficulty of the ith item. The examinee ability parameter θ_n and the item difficulty parameter δ_i both represent locations on the same dimension: the latent construct tapped by the items.

Equation 1 expresses the Rasch model as it is applied only to dichotomous items. Dichotomous items are those for which an examinee's responses are scored in one of only two categories, for example, correct and incorrect. Polytomous items are those for which an examinee's responses are scored according to more than two categories, for example, correct, partially correct, and incorrect. In general, polytomous items may have as many as 10 scoring categories. The two most common extensions of the Rasch model to the polytomous case are the partial credit (PC) model and the rating scale (RS) model (Wright & Masters, 1982).

The PC model is the more general of these two polytomous Rasch models. In the dichotomous case, there is only one difficulty parameter, δ_i, where the subscript i stands for item. In the PC model, the difficulty parameters are doubly subscripted, δ_{im}, where the subscript i is as above and the subscript m is for the item "step". The number of steps associated with an item is one less than its number of scoring categories. For example, a dichotomous item has only one step: the step from incorrect to correct (i.e., from a score of 0 to a score of 1). A polytomous item with 3 scoring categories has 2 steps: from 0 to 1 and from 1 to 2. The logic underlying the PC model is analogous to modeling a polytomous item as if it were a series of dichotomous items, one for every step in the polytomous item, each successive one of which being conditional on having answered correctly the one for the preceding step. The PC model is commonly expressed according to equation 2 below

$$P(X_{nim} = x \mid \theta_n) = \frac{\exp \sum_{m=0}^{x} (\theta_n - \delta_{im})}{\sum_{0}^{m} \exp \sum_{m=0}^{x} (\theta_n - \delta_{im})}, \qquad (2)$$

where the terms are defined as above.

The rating scale (RS) model is a less general application of the Rasch model to polytomous items. The RS model is less general than the PC model in that the RS model assumes that the relation among the step parameters for a given item is the same for all items. With the PC model, the distances separating the m item step parameters are free to vary and are estimated individually for each item. With the RS model, however, those distances are constrained to be equal for all items and a single common set of distances separating the item steps is estimated and applied to all items alike. The additional constraint imposed with RS would be appropriate if, for example, the same Likert-type scale were to underlie the responses to all of the items—in the case of an attitude survey, perhaps. The RS model is commonly defined according to equation 3 below:

$$P(X_{nim} = x \mid \theta_n) = \frac{\exp \displaystyle\sum_{m=0}^{x} [\theta_n - (\delta_i + \tau_m)]}{\displaystyle\sum_{0}^{m} \exp \displaystyle\sum_{m=0}^{x} [\theta_n - (\delta_i + \tau_{im})]}. \tag{3}$$

A comparison of the PC model of equation 2 and the RS model of equation 3 indicates that, whereas there is a unique item parameter for each step of every item in equation 2 (δ_{im}), such is not the case in equation 3. Instead, there is only one parameter (δ_i) that is unique for every item in equation 3. The other class of parameter in equation 3 is the set of τ_m. These are the threshold parameters for the m item steps. They show the common separation among the item steps for all items. The threshold parameter for step 1 (τ_1), for example, may differ from the other τ_m for the other steps but it would be the same for the first step of every item; likewise for the rest of the τ_m.

As stated above, the δ_{im} of the PC model is defined to represent the locations of the item steps as if those steps were separate dichotomous items in a conditional sequence. That is, if an examinee had successfully taken the first step of a given polytomous item, then the probability of taking the second step would be the same as if that examinee were facing a dichotomous item with a difficulty equal to the δ_{im} for that step. With the PC model, those conditional item difficulties, the δ_{im} for the steps, are free to vary both from item to item and from step to step. With the RS model, however, only the item locations parameter values (δ_i) may vary from item to item. The conditional difficulty of going, say, from a score of 1 to a score of 2 is not free to vary from item to item because each of the step parameter values (τ_m) are constrained to be the same for every item. Therefore, the RS model is a special case of the PC model and the parameters of the RS model are defined in terms of the parameters of the PC model. Computationally, the τ_m values under RS represent deviations from the δ_i values that are averaged across all items separately for each step. In a polytomous item with two steps (three score categories), for example, the standard definitions for the parameters of the RS model are as follows:

$$\delta_i = (\delta_{i1} + \delta_{i2})/2, \quad \tau_1 = \sum_{i=1}^{I} (\delta_{i1} - \delta_{i2})/2I, \quad \text{and} \quad \tau_2 = -\tau_1,$$

where I is the number of items on the test.

RANDOM COEFFICIENTS MULTINOMIAL LOGIT MODEL

The random coefficients multinomial logit (RCML) model (Adams & Wilson, 1991) is based upon a generalization of the Rasch model of equation 1 above. Using the RCML model, it is possible to fit any of the unidimensional logistic models that are based on simple sufficient statistics, including the dichotomous Rasch model itself, its poly-tomous extensions (e.g., the partial credit (PC) and rating scale (RS) models), and many more. In fact, all such models are special cases of RCML. The RCML model is expressed according to equation 4 below:

$$P(X_i = x_i \mid \theta_n) = \frac{\exp\{\theta_n B_i + \mathbf{a}_i' \boldsymbol{\xi}\}}{\displaystyle\sum_{m=0}^{M} \exp\{\theta_n B_i + \mathbf{a}_i' \boldsymbol{\xi}\}}, \tag{4}$$

where $P(X_i = x_i \mid \theta_n)$ is the probability of a particular response to item i given some ability, θ_n; B_i is the score associated with the response of interest; $\mathbf{a}_i$ is the vector of the design matrix (**A**) that relates the response of interest to the vector of parameters for item i; and $\boldsymbol{\xi}$ is the vector of item parameters. See the Adams and Wilson chapter for further description of the RCML model.

DIF Detection for Dichotomous Rasch Items Using RCML

The RCML model is extremely flexible. The parameters might be de-fined in any number of ways. When applied to detecting DIF, the model must accommodate information about group membership. Ac-cordingly, in the dichotomous case, two parameters are estimated for each item: $\boldsymbol{\xi}_i = (\delta_i, \gamma_i)$. The first element, δ_i, is defined as the negative of the standard Rasch model item difficulty parameter from equation

1 for item i in group 1 (the group thought to be advantaged with respect to the item). The second element of ξ_i is γ_i, the bias parameter. It is defined as the difference between the difficulty parameters for the two groups: $\gamma_i = \delta_i$ (group 1) $- \delta_i$ (group 2).

The fact that δ_i is defined for RCML (equation 4) as the negative of the corresponding parameter in the standard Rasch model (equation 1) stems from the fact that the more general RCML model is expressed in terms of a linear combination of exponents: one due to the person (θ_n) and a vector of others due to the item (ξ_i). For the sake of generality and convenience, the elements of ξ_i are all expressed as positive quantities. Because the Rasch model is a special case of RCML, however, the specific linear combination of exponents in equation 1 can be expressed in a more intuitively meaningful way: as the simple difference between the location of the person and the location of the item.

An example of the design matrix, that parameterizes RCML to estimate Rasch model bias, is shown in Figure 12.1 for the 3-item case. Running across the top of the matrix are column headings for B_i and ξ,

Item	Group	B_i	$\xi =$ (δ_1	γ_1	δ_2	γ_2	δ_3	γ_3)
1	1	0	0	0	0	0	0	0
1	1	1	-1	0	0	0	0	0
1	2	0	0	0	0	0	0	0
1	2	1	-1	1	0	0	0	0
2	1	0	0	0	0	0	0	0
2	1	1	0	0	-1	0	0	0
2	2	0	0	0	0	0	0	0
2	2	1	0	0	-1	1	0	0
3	1	0	0	0	0	0	0	0
3	1	1	0	0	0	0	-1	0
3	2	0	0	0	0	0	0	0
3	2	1	0	0	0	0	-1	1

Figure 12.1.   Rasch model.

the score function and the vector of difficulty and bias parameters from equation 4.

In this example, there is a difficulty parameter and a bias parameter estimated for every item. Depending on the nature of the case, however, a different parameterization may be appropriate. For example, by leaving δ_3 out of ξ and by setting equal to 1 the element for item 3 in the rows corresponding to a correct response and in the columns corresponding to the δ_i for the other items, δ_3 would automatically equal the negative sum of the other δ_i parameters when the recoded vectors for item 3 were substituted into equation 4. Doing so would constrain the entire set of δ_i parameters to sum to zero. Fixing the scale of the item parameters in this way may be appropriate to anchor the ability scale. In the illustrative analyses in this chapter, however, the center of the distribution of person abilities is fixed at zero, so all parameters are estimated as a demonstration.

By including the B_i term in equation 4, RCML allows item responses to be scored in any number of ways. In order not to complicate matters unnecessarily, however, the B_i scoring functions for the items used as examples in this paper are defined to be simply 0 and 1 in the dichotomous case and 0, 1, and 2 in the polytomous case. Substituting a score of 1 from the dichotomous scoring scheme for B_i in equation 4 and substituting the appropriate elements of the design matrix and parameter estimates defined above, the probability of responding correctly to item i for an examinee in group 1 can be expressed in the following simplified form:

$$P(X = 1; g = 1 \mid \theta) = \frac{\exp\{(1)\theta + [(-1)\delta_i + (0)\gamma_i]\}}{1 + \exp\{(1)\theta + [(-1)\delta_i + (0)\gamma_i]\}}.$$

Likewise, the corresponding probability for group 2 is:

$$P(X = 1; g = 2 \mid \theta) = \frac{\exp\{(1)\theta + [(-1)\delta_i + (1)\gamma_i]\}}{1 + \exp\{(1)\theta + [(-1)\delta_i + (1)\gamma_i]\}}.$$

Given the definitions of the parameters stated above and given the different vectors from **A** that are applied to the two different groups, the probability for group 1 is equivalent to the Rasch model in equation 1, which is a function of the difference in location between the examinee (θ_n) and the item (δ_i). The probability for group 2 is the same except that the item difficulty for that group is altered by the addition of the bias term, γ_i. The bias term is positive when the item is more difficult for group 2. In such circumstances, γ_i acts to increase item difficulty selectively for those examinees and is thus consistent with the above definition of bias.

Estimating the PC and RS Models Using RCML Without Examining DIF

The design matrix A that parameterizes RCML to fit the PC model is given in Figure 12.2. In this case, the elements of the vector of RCML parameters (ξ), are the item step parameters (δ_{im}) of the PC model. Defining ξ in this way, using the examinee responses of 0, 1, and 2 as the RCML scoring function B_i, using the elements of the above design matrix, and substituting into equation 4 above, the RCML expressions for the probabilities associated with a given item response become equivalent to the corresponding probabilities obtained from the definition of the PC model given above in equation 2.

The numerators of the expressions for the probabilities of the three possible scores (0, 1, and 2) will vary according to how the model parameters were multiplied by the elements of the design matrix. The denominators for each of the three score probabilities would always be the same: The sum of the three possible numerators. If X = 0, the numerator becomes

$$\exp\{(0)\theta_n + [(0)\delta_{i1} + (0)\delta_{i2}]\} = 1$$

Item	B_i	$\xi=$ (δ_{11}	δ_{12}	δ_{21}	δ_{22}	δ_{I1}	δ_{I2})
1	0	0	0	0	0	0	0
1	1	-1	0	0	0	0	0
1	2	-1	-1	0	0	0	0
2	0	0	0	0	0	0	0
2	1	0	0	-1	0	0	0
2	2	0	0	-1	-1	0	0
3	0	0	0	0	0	0	0
3	1	1	0	1	0	1	0
3	2	1	1	1	1	1	1

Figure 12.2. Partial credit model.

The foregoing expression is shown to equal 1 because the linear combination of model parameters equals zero and $\exp(0) = 1$. If $X = 1$, the numerator becomes

$$\exp\{(1)\theta_n + [(-1)\delta_{i1} + (0)\delta_{i2}]\}$$

If $X = 2$, the numerator becomes

$$\exp\{(2)\theta_n + [(-1)\delta_{i1} + (-1)\delta_{i2}]\}$$

Therefore, the expression for the probability that an examinee would obtain a score of two, for example, becomes

$$P(X = 2 \mid \theta_n) = \frac{\exp\{(2)\theta_n + [(-1)\delta_{i1} + (-1)\delta_{i2}]\}}{\Psi}$$

where Ψ is the denominator in equation 4:

$$\Psi = \sum_{m=0}^{M} \exp\{\theta_n B_i + \mathbf{a}_i'\xi\}.$$

In this case,

$$\Psi = 1 + \exp\{(1)\theta_n + [(-1)\delta_{i1} + (0)\delta_{i2}]\} + \exp\{(2)\theta_n + [(-1)\delta_{i1} + (-1)\delta_{i2}]\}$$

This expression is equivalent to the standard definition of the PC model shown in equation 2 above.

The design matrix that parameterizes RCML to fit the RS model is given in Figure 12.3.

As with the PC model shown above, when the RCML version of the RS model is substituted into equation 4, the numerators of the expressions for the RS probabilities of the three possible scores (0, 1, and 2) vary according to how the model parameters are multiplied by the elements of the design matrix. As with PC, the denominators for each of the three RS score probabilities are always the same: The sum of the three possible numerators. If $X = 0$, the RS numerator becomes

$$\exp\{(0)\theta_n + [(0)\delta_i + (0)\tau]\} = 1$$

Like the corresponding expression for PC, this expression equals 1 because the linear combination of model parameters equals zero and $\exp(0) = 1$. If $X = 1$, the RS numerator becomes

$$\exp\{(1)\theta_n + [(1)\delta_i + (1)\tau]\}$$

		$\xi=$			
<ins>Item</ins>	B_i	$(\delta_1$	δ_2	δ_3	$\tau)$
1	0	0	0	0	0
1	1	1	0	0	1
1	2	2	0	0	0
2	0	0	0	0	0
2	1	0	1	0	1
2	2	0	2	0	0
3	0	0	0	0	0
3	1	0	0	1	1
3	2	0	0	2	0

Figure 12.3.   Rating scale model.

If X = 2, the RS numerator becomes

$$\exp \{(2)\theta_n + [(2)\delta_i + (0)\tau]\}$$

Using the same example shown above for PC, the expression for the probability that X = 2 in the RS model is

$$P(X = 2 \mid \theta_n) = \exp \frac{\{(2)\theta_n + [(2)\delta_i + (0)\tau]\}}{\Psi}$$

where Ψ is as defined above. In this case,

$$\Psi = 1 + \exp \{(1)\theta_n + [(-1)\delta_i + (1)\tau]\} + \exp \{(2)\theta_n + [(-2)\delta_i + (0)\tau]\}$$

With the above RCML design matrix for the RS model, the threshold parameter τ is not expressly included when X = 2 (i.e., τ is multiplied by a zero element when X = 2). In the RS model defined in equation 3, however, although both τ_1 and τ_2 are included in the computation when X = 2, they cancel since $\tau_2 = -\tau_1$. Thus, the RS design matrix shown here is consistent with equation 3 and the standard RS parameterization.

Differing Views of Bias Under the PC and RS Models

Implicit in deciding whether the PC model or the RS model is more appropriate for analyzing one's test items is a decision about how one conceptualizes bias. As stated, the values of the parameters of the PC model (δ_{im}) are free to vary by item and by step. Under the RS model, however, only the item location parameter (δ_i) may vary across items; the step threshold parameters (τ_m) are constrained to be equal for all items. If DIF in dichotomous items is defined as a difference in Rasch-model item difficulty parameters for two groups and if the amount of that group difference is estimated separately for every item, then the extension of this definition to polytomous items under the PC model would be straightforward. A separate PC bias parameter would be estimated for every item step: $\gamma_{im} = \delta_{im}(\text{group 1}) - \delta_{im}(\text{group 2})$.

DIF under the RS model, however, is slightly more complicated. The relationship between the parameters of the PC and RS models may be expressed as follows: $\delta_{im} = \delta_{i.} + \tau_{.m} + \epsilon_{im}$ where $\epsilon_{im} = \delta_{im} - \tau_{.m}$ is a residual item term, defined as the difference in locations for a given item step under the two models—due to the equality constraint across items imposed on the τ_m with RS. To emphasize the fact that $\delta_{i.}$ applies only at the item level and that $\tau_{.m}$ applies only at the step level, a period has been added to the subscripts as a place marker, indicating that all categories of the index for which a period is substituted are equally represented by that parameter. Using this notation, γ_{im}, DIF or group difference for a particular step of a given item under the PC model, may be partitioned into two RS bias components and a residual. One RS bias component is due to a difference in that item's group $\delta_{i.}$ values ($\gamma_{i.} = \delta_{i.}[\text{group 1}] - \delta_{i.}[\text{group 2}]$) and the other RS bias component is due to a difference in that step's group $\tau_{.m}$ values ($\gamma_{.m} = \tau_{.m}[\text{group 1}] - \tau_{.m}[\text{group 2}]$). The residual bias component is due to a group difference in the residual item terms defined at the beginning of the paragraph: $E_{im} = \epsilon_{im}[\text{group 1}] - \epsilon_{im}[\text{group 2}] = \gamma_{im} - \gamma_{i.} - \gamma_{.m}$, such that $\gamma_{im} = \gamma_{i.} + \gamma_{.m} + E_{im}$.

In these terms, bias might exist solely because of a group difference in overall item difficulty ($\gamma_{i.}$), solely because of a group difference across all items at a particular step ($\gamma_{.m}$), solely because of a group difference in the residual terms (E_{im}), or because of any combination of these factors operating together. Because the residual bias component E_{im} is not expressly estimated in a bias analysis based upon the RS model, however, the possibility exists that bias detected by a given γ_{im} estimate using PC would be missed by both of the bias components that are estimated with RS: $\gamma_{i.}$ and $\gamma_{.m}$. Such a situation might arise, for example, if the response data for one group adequately fit the RS model while the data for the other group did not, requiring instead the more general PC model. That is, perhaps the ϵ_{im} for one group might be zero for all items but not so for the other group.

Although detecting bias of this type constitutes a potential advantage of using PC instead of RS, the RS parameters also provide information that PC does not: the relative magnitude of bias effects due to items versus bias effects due to steps. Along with all of the other factors distinguishing PC and RS, this issue warrants consideration when a practitioner decides which model is most appropriate for bias detection with polytomous items.

RCML can be used to estimate the bias parameter γ_{im} under the PC model and $\gamma_{i.}$ and $\gamma_{.m}$ under the RS model. Both the item residual (ϵ_{im}) and the bias residual (E_{im}) can be computed by fitting PC and RS in two separate RCML analyses, obtaining the respective parameter estimates, and solving in the appropriate expression above.

DIF Detection in the PC and RS models Using RCML

The design matrix for fitting the PC version of RCML for estimating DIF in polytomous items is given in Figure 12.4.

As stated, the PC model polytomous bias parameter is defined as the difference between item step parameters for the two groups: $\gamma_{im} = \delta_{im}(\text{group 1}) - \delta_{im}(\text{group 2})$. The probability of a score of 2, for example, for an examinee in group 1 is:

$$P(X = 2; g = 1 \mid \theta) = \frac{\exp\{(2)\theta + [(-1)\delta_{i1} + (0)\gamma_{i1} + (-1)\delta_{i2} + (0)\gamma_{i2}]\}}{\Psi}$$

The probability of the same score for an examinee in group 2 is:

$$P(X = 2; g = 2 \mid \theta) = \frac{\exp\{(2)\theta + [(-1)\delta_{i1} + (1)\gamma_{i1} + (-1)\delta_{i2} + (1)\gamma_{i2}]\}}{\Psi}$$

The expression for group 1 is equivalent to the corresponding expression for the RCML version of the PC model shown above. The expression for group two is the same except that the bias terms (γ_{im}) are added in, effectively modifying the item step difficulties (δ_{im}) by an amount on the logit scale equal to group 1's advantage (or disadvantage), thus modifying the probability of obtaining, in this case, a score of X = 2. The probabilities of the scores X = 0 and X = 1 are found in like manner.

The design matrix for fitting the RS version of RCML for estimating DIF in polytomous items is given in Figure 12.5.

$$\xi =$$

Item	Group	B_i	δ_{11}	γ_{11}	δ_{12}	γ_{12}	δ_{11}	γ_{11}	δ_{12}	γ_{12}	δ_{31}	γ_{31}	δ_{32}	γ_{32}
1	1	0	0	0	0	0	0	0	0	0	0	0	0	0
1	1	1	-1	0	0	0	0	0	0	0	0	0	0	0
1	1	2	-1	0	-1	0	0	0	0	0	0	0	0	0
1	2	0	0	0	0	0	0	0	0	0	0	0	0	0
1	2	1	-1	1	0	0	0	0	0	0	0	0	0	0
1	2	2	-1	1	-1	1	0	0	0	0	0	0	0	0
2	1	0	0	0	0	0	0	0	0	0	0	0	0	0
2	1	1	0	0	0	0	-1	0	0	0	0	0	0	0
2	1	2	0	0	0	0	-1	0	-1	0	0	0	0	0
2	2	0	0	0	0	0	0	0	0	0	0	0	0	0
2	2	1	0	0	0	0	-1	1	0	0	0	0	0	0
2	2	2	0	0	0	0	-1	1	-1	1	0	0	0	0
3	1	0	0	0	0	0	0	0	0	0	0	0	0	0
3	1	1	0	0	0	0	0	0	0	0	-1	0	0	0
3	1	2	0	0	0	0	0	0	0	0	-1	0	-1	0
3	2	0	0	0	0	0	0	0	0	0	0	0	0	0
3	2	1	0	0	0	0	0	0	0	0	-1	1	0	0
3	2	2	0	0	0	0	0	0	0	0	-1	1	-1	1

Figure 12.4.   Partial credit model with DIF parameters.

With the RS version of RCML for DIF detection, the expression for $X = 1$ in group 1 is:

$$P(X = 1; g = 1 \mid \theta_n) = \frac{\exp\{(1)\theta_n + [(-1)\delta_i + (0)\gamma_i + (1)\tau + (0)\gamma_1]\}}{\Psi}$$

The corresponding expression for group 2 is:

$$P(X = 1; g = 2 \mid \theta_n) = \frac{\exp\{(1)\theta_n + [(-1)\delta_i + (1)\gamma_i + (1)\tau + (1)\gamma_1]\}}{\Psi}$$

The case where $X = 1$ is shown here as an example because only where $X = 1$ are both bias parameters, $\gamma_{i.}$ and $\gamma_{.1}$, included together. The RS bias expression for group 1 is equivalent to the corresponding expression for the non bias RS model shown earlier. For group 2, however, both the δ_i and the τ values may be modified by their respective bias

$$\xi =$$

Item	Group	B_i	(δ_1	γ_1.	δ_2	γ_2.	δ_3	γ_3.	τ_1	$\gamma_{.1}$)
1	1	0	0	0	0	0	0	0	0	0
1	1	1	-1	0	0	0	0	0	1	0
1	1	2	-2	0	0	0	0	0	0	0
1	2	0	0	0	0	0	0	0	0	0
1	2	1	-1	1	0	0	0	0	1	1
1	2	2	-2	2	0	0	0	0	0	0
2	1	0	0	0	0	0	0	0	0	0
2	1	1	0	0	-1	0	0	0	0	1
2	1	2	0	0	-2	0	0	0	0	0
2	2	0	0	0	0	0	0	0	0	0
2	2	1	0	0	-1	1	0	0	1	1
2	2	2	0	0	-2	2	0	0	0	0
3	1	0	0	0	0	0	0	0	0	0
3	1	1	0	0	0	0	-1	0	0	0
3	1	2	0	0	0	0	-2	0	1	0
3	2	0	0	0	0	0	0	0	0	0
3	2	1	0	0	0	0	-1	1	1	1
3	2	2	0	0	0	0	-2	2	0	0

Figure 12.5.   Rating scale model with DIF parameters.

terms, $\gamma_{i.}$ and $\gamma_{.1}$. The subscript for the second bias component is 1 because it pertains to the first threshold step for item i.

ILLUSTRATIVE ANALYSES

The DIF detecting parameterizations of RCML for the dichotomous Rasch (DR) model, the partial credit (PC) model, and the rating scale (RS) model are applied to two computer-simulated data sets, one dichotomous and one polytomous. The polytomous items simulated here have three response levels (two item steps). Both data sets have 20 items. The generating values for the item location parameters are given in Table 12.1 below.

In both data sets, item number three is biased by an amount equal to 0.50 logit in favor of group 1. The expected values for the RCML bias parameter estimates under the DR model are $\gamma_i = 0.00$ for unbiased items and $\gamma_i = -0.50$ for the biased item (item 3). The negative sign on the bias estimate simply indicates that group 1 is the advantaged group.

In the data generation step for the polytomous data set, the bias of -0.50 logit is simulated separately for both item steps. Under the PC and RS models, the expected bias parameter values for the unbiased items are zero, as in the dichotomous case. For PC item 3, however, the corresponding expected values are $\gamma_{31} = -0.50$ and $\gamma_{32} = -0.50$. Even though both of the steps of polytomous item 3 individually manifest a bias of -0.50 logit, the RS bias parameter for the item as a whole is

Table 12.1. Fixed Item and Item Step Location Values for the 20 Simulated Dichotomous and Polytomous Items

Item	Dichotomous Values δ_i	Polytomous Values δ_{i1}	δ_{i2}
1	−1.35	−1.35	−1.10
2	−1.20	−1.20	−0.95
3	−1.05	−1.05	−0.80
4	−0.90	−0.90	−0.65
5	−0.75	−0.75	−0.50
6	−0.60	−0.60	−0.35
7	−0.45	−0.45	−0.20
8	−0.30	−0.30	−0.05
9	−0.15	−0.15	0.10
10	0.00	0.00	0.25
11	0.00	0.00	0.25
12	0.15	0.00	0.25
13	0.30	0.05	0.30
14	0.45	0.20	0.45
15	0.60	0.35	0.60
16	0.75	0.50	0.75
17	0.90	0.65	0.90
18	1.05	0.80	1.05
19	1.20	0.95	1.20
20	1.35	1.10	1.35

expected to be $\gamma_{1.} = -0.50$. The RS bias parameter is defined as the average bias across the steps:

$$\gamma_1 = \delta_i^{G1} - \delta_i^{G2}$$

$$= \frac{1}{2}[\delta_{i1}^{G1} - \delta_{i2}^{G1}] - \frac{1}{2}[(\delta_{i1}^{G1} + 0.50) - (\delta_{i2}^{G1} + 0.50)]$$

$$= \frac{1}{2}[\delta_{i1}^{G1} - \delta_{i1}^{G1} + \delta_{i2}^{G1} - \delta_{i2}^{G1} - 0.50 - 0.50]$$

$$= \frac{1}{2}[-1.00] = -0.50,$$

where the superscripts on the item and step parameters denote group—G1 for group 1 and G2 for group 2. In the above expression, the step difficulties cancel leaving only the average of the biases added to them.

When bias takes the form simulated here in the polytomous case, both item steps are shifted by the same amount. As a result, the location for the item as a whole (δ_i) is shifted by that amount but the relative distance between the steps $(\tau_{.m})$ is not affected at all. For this reason, the expected value of the bias component pertaining to τ, the step structure common to all items under the RS model, would be $\gamma_{.m} = 0.00$. In general, the value of $\gamma_{.m}$ would be affected by group differences in step structure only as the average of those fluctuations. Thus, biases affecting the steps differently in different items would be confounded, possibly canceling each other and giving the erroneous impression that no bias exists. Therefore, if the practitioner suspected that groups are likely to differ by step as well as by item, then the PC model might be more appropriate for investigating DIF—even where the data for the advantaged group is known to fit the RS model.

RESULTS

The bias parameters estimated by RCML for the simulated data sets are given below, dichotomous Rasch (DR) in Table 12.2, partial credit (PC) in Table 12.3, and rating scale (RS) in Table 12.4. The estimates of item or step parameters are presented, along with the estimates of the bias parameters, to indicate the degree to which RCML recaptured all of the generating values from Table 12.1.

For item 3 in both data sets, dichotomous and polytomous, group 2 had a simulated disadvantage relative to group 1 of −0.50 logit. RCML recaptured this value almost exactly in the dichotomous model (DR: $\gamma_3 = -0.491$) and came fairly close in both polytomous models

**Table 12.2.   Results of the RCML
Dichotomous Rasch Estimation**

Item	Item Location Parameters (δ_i)	Item Bias Parameters (γ_i)
1	−1.399	−0.048
2	−1.203	−0.023
3	−1.053	−0.491 *(DIF = −0.50)
4	−0.963	0.033
5	−0.739	0.120
6	−0.519	0.171
7	−0.429	0.133
8	−0.174	0.267
9	−0.208	0.035
10	0.021	−0.058
11	−0.115	−0.116
12	0.108	0.083
13	0.339	0.074
14	0.617	0.228
15	0.545	0.055
16	0.797	0.015
17	0.967	0.104
18	1.129	0.138
19	1.183	−0.038
20	1.385	0.126

(PC: $\gamma_{31} = -0.342$, $\gamma_{32} = -0.351$ and RS: $\gamma_{3.} = -0.351$). For all models, the DIF estimates for the items where no group differences were simulated always were smaller than the DIF estimate for item 3, although some were far enough from their expected value of zero to cause some concern with the possibility of false positive results. For all three models, RCML recaptured quite closely the generating values for the item location parameters. To examine the stability of DIF estimates in RCML, particularly with respect to the danger of false positive results, the author is conducting Monte Carlo studies to compare RCML estimates to those obtained using the Mantel-Haenszel procedure (Holland, 1985).

CONCLUSIONS

The versatility of RCML allows the practitioner to conceive and estimate polytomous DIF, using any of the polytomous Rasch models, as a simple extension of the dichotomous case. As the questions concerning the stability of estimates are addressed, and as the capability of statis-

Table 12.3.　Results of the RCML Partial Credit
Estimation

Item	Step	Item-Step Parameters (δ_{im})	Item-Step Bias Parameters (γ_{im})
1	1	−1.393	0.100
	2	−1.189	0.024
2	1	−1.294	−0.065
	2	−1.111	0.042
3	1	−1.116	−0.342 *(DIF = −0.50)
	2	−0.811	−0.351 *(DIF = −0.50)
4	1	−0.878	0.087
	2	−0.765	−0.013
5	1	−0.865	−0.130
	2	−0.525	0.199
6	1	−0.905	0.041
	2	−0.453	0.122
7	1	−0.513	0.107
	2	−0.190	0.222
8	1	−0.208	0.277
	2	−0.102	0.049
9	1	−0.161	0.142
	2	0.007	−0.084
10	1	−0.181	0.021
	2	0.232	−0.039
11	1	−0.138	0.073
	2	0.135	−0.053
12	1	−0.173	0.033
	2	0.107	−0.035
13	1	−0.106	0.014
	2	0.301	0.039
14	1	0.180	0.051
	2	0.245	0.157
15	1	0.330	0.084
	2	0.586	0.022
16	1	0.220	−0.066
	2	0.798	0.193
17	1	0.488	−0.009
	2	0.869	0.072
18	1	0.566	−0.307
	2	1.020	0.130
19	1	0.803	−0.038
	2	1.350	0.280
20	1	0.931	−0.111
	2	1.305	0.078

Table 12.4.   Results of the RCML Rating Scale Estimation

Item	Item Location Parameters (δ_i)	Item Bias Parameters (γ_i)
1	-1.292	0.045
2	-1.205	-0.008
3	-0.952	-0.351 *(DIF = -0.50)
4	-0.824	0.024
5	-0.681	0.050
6	-0.658	0.081
7	-0.338	0.166
8	-0.143	0.159
9	-0.064	0.028
10	0.037	-0.009
11	0.011	0.011
12	-0.020	-0.002
13	0.108	0.025
14	0.233	0.103
15	0.473	0.057
16	0.503	0.046
17	0.685	0.026
18	0.791	-0.130
19	1.057	0.084
20	1.121	-0.038

Item	Tau (τ_m)	Tau Bias Parameter (γ_m)
All	0.155	-0.022

tical tests of DIF parameters is developed, RCML will be a mainstay of the effort to detect DIF in test items.

REFERENCES

Adams, R., & Wilson, M. (1991). *The random coefficients multinomial logit model: A general approach to fitting Rasch models.* Paper presented at the annual meeting of the American Educational Research Association, Chicago, April.

Adams, R., & Wilson, M. (1996). The random coefficients multinomial logit model. In G. Engelhard Jr., & M. Wilson (Eds.), *Objective measurement: Theory into practice, Volume 3.* Norwood, NJ: Ablex.

Berk, R.A. (Ed.). (1982). *Handbook of methods for detecting item bias.* Baltimore: Johns Hopkins University Press.

Holland, P.W. (1985). *On the study of differential item difficulty.* Princeton, NJ: Educational Testing Service.

Thorndike, R.L. (1982). *Applied psychometrics.* Boston: Houghton Mifflin.

Wright, B.D., & Masters, G.N. (1982). *Rating scale analysis.* Chicago: MESA Press.

part four

Measurement Theory

chapter **13**

Composition Analysis

Benjamin D. Wright
University of Chicago

Why do some organizations succeed while others fail? Why do groups of a particular kind work well in some situations but poorly in others? The psychology of group organization is rich but qualitative (Freud, 1921). Questions about how groups work seem non-mathematical. Nevertheless, algebra undertaken to obtain hierarchically stable measurement leads to a mathematics of group productivity.

Groups are composed of subgroups, subgroups of elements, elements of parts. Aggregations separate into sub-aggregations and come together into super-aggregations. The "entities" we experience become understood and useful as we learn how to see down into their substructures and up into the compositions they construct.

We know from experience that the way group members work together affects group success. But we do not know how to measure these effects, nor how to calculate effective group organizations. Quantification requires models that measure group strength as functions of member strengths. These models must be hierarchically robust. They must maintain their metric across descending and ascending levels of composition. Can a mathematics be developed which defines the different ways group members might work together such that their individual measures can be combined mathematically to calculate an expected measure for the group?

COMPOSITION ANALYSIS

Composition analysis is our name for the mathematics of how component measures combine to produce composite measures. Our deliberations will lead to measurement models that are infinitely divisible and, hence, inferentially stable. The models will compose and decompose smoothly from one level of aggregation to another. When the models work for groups of individuals, they will work for individuals within groups. When they work for individuals, they will work for parts within individuals. Although presented here as groups of persons, these models apply to groups of any kind: ideas, problems, cells.

Composition Rules

Bookstein (see Appendix A) shows that any distribution function that reduces to

$$G(x + y) = G(x) + G(y) \qquad \text{or} \qquad H(x \times y) = H(x) \times H(y)$$

will be indifferent to the intervals used for grouping and hence resilient to aggregation ambiguity. Bookstein's functions specify the divisibility needed for composition analysis. They also specify the arithmetic needed for quantitative comparisons. To relate these functions to the procedures of measurement, we enlarge the $+$ and $\times$ arithmetic *inside* functions G and H to include "procedural" compositors $\oplus$ and $\otimes$. These procedural "additions" and "multiplications" represent whatever empirical procedures are discovered to operationalize measurement, as in "aligning sticks end-to-end" to "add" length, and "piling bricks top-to-bottom" to "add" weight.

Two composition rules follow:

A *Procedural Addition* rule:	$G(x \oplus y) = G(x) + G(y),$
A *Procedural Multiplication* rule:	$H(x \otimes y) = H(x) \times H(y).$

These rules compose and decompose ad infinitum, as in:

$$\begin{aligned} G(x \oplus y \oplus z) &= G(x \oplus y) + G(z) \\ &= G(x \oplus z) + G(y) \\ &= G(y \oplus z) + G(x) \\ &= G(x) + G(y) + G(z). \end{aligned}$$

To discover the consequences for composition analysis, we will apply each rule to observation probabilities. Observation probabilities are addressed because we intend to use these rules on data in order to estimate measures for empirical compositions. These probabilities will be expressed as odds because $0 < P < 1$ is an awkward measure while $0 < [P/(1 - P)] < \infty$ maintains equal ratios, and log odds maintain equal differences. Our application of Bookstein's functions to odds will determine what compositions compositors $\oplus$ and $\otimes$ imply and hence what compositions are quantifiable.

Three compositions will result:

1. a TEAM *union* of *perfect agreement,*
2. a PACK *collection* of *helpful disagreements* and
3. a CHAIN *connection* of *imperfect agreements.*

We will deduce measurement models for these compositions, which, because of their divisibility, are indifferent to composition level and resilient to aggregation ambiguity. The resulting models will be the stable laws of composition analysis.

Finally we will place divisibility in the theory of inference that motivates these deductions and venture some interpretations of the three compositions.

THE MEASUREMENT MODEL

In order to apply the composition rules, we need a stochastic measurement model with parameters that follow the rules of arithmetic and estimates that enable comparisons between strengths B_n and B_m of objects n and m which are invariant with respect to whatever relevant, but necessarily incidental, measuring agents are used to manifest the comparison.

Measurement means quantitative comparison. Quantitative comparison means differences or ratios. Since odds are ratios, ratios are their comparison. The procedural comparison $\oplus$ of objects n and m is:

$$H(n \oplus m) \equiv H(n)/H(m).$$

Defining H as odds $[P/(1 - P)]$ gets:

$$[P_{n \oplus m}/(1 - P_{n \oplus m})] \equiv [P_n/(1 - P_n)]/[P_m/(1 - P_m)]$$

Estimation requires that strengths B_n and B_m be manifest by a relevant measuring agent i of difficulty D_i. Inferential stability requires that the comparison $(B_n - B_m)$ be independent of task difficulty D_i.

The *necessary* and *sufficient* model is:

$$[P_{ni}/(1 - P_{ni})]/[P_{mi}/(1 - P_{mi})] = [\exp(B_n - D_i)]/[\exp(B_m - D_i)]$$
$$= \exp(B_n - B_m)$$

because task difficulty D_i cancels so that the n $\oplus$ m comparison maintains the same difference of strengths regardless of which tasks are convenient to manifest these strengths (Rasch, 1960).

THREE COMPOSITIONS

Team Union of Perfect Agreement

Applying *procedural multiplication* to success odds defines group success odds, when group members work according to the procedural operator $\otimes$, as the following *product* of group member success odds:

$$\left(\frac{P_{n \otimes m}}{1 - P_{n \otimes m}}\right) = \left(\frac{P_n}{1 - P_n}\right) \times \left(\frac{P_m}{1 - P_m}\right) = \frac{P_n P_m}{(1 - P_n)(1 - P_m)}.$$

The group composition specified by this *first law of stable measurement* can be seen by applying probabilities P_n and P_m to the outcomes possible when persons n and m work on a task according to the multiplication of their success odds. Figure 13.1 shows the two outcomes which occur in this composition.

Agreement (11) wins or agreement (00) loses. Disagreements (10) and (01) are absent because they do not occur in the equation which defines TEAM composition. TEAMs work as *unions* of *perfect agreement*.

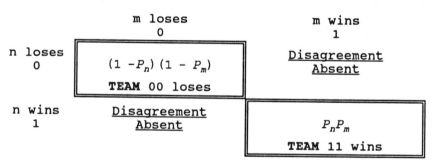

Figure 13.1. Outcomes Occurring for a TEAM.

Applying Rasch odds to TEAM work with group strength represented by $B_{n\otimes m}$ gets:

$$\exp(B_{n\otimes m} - D) = [\exp(B_n - D)] \, [\exp(B_m - D)]$$
$$= \exp[(B_n - D) + (B_m - D)].$$

Taking logs and generalizing to any size group defines N-member TEAM strength as:

$$(B_T - D) = \sum_n^N (B_n - D).$$

The strengths of TEAM members, relative to task difficulty $(B_n - D)$, *add* up to TEAM strength, relative to task difficulty $(B_T - D)$. TEAMs are concatenations of *relative* strengths, accumulated in *linear* form.

Pack Collection of Perfect Disagreements

Applying *procedural addition* to *success* odds defines group success odds, when group members work according to the procedural operator $\oplus$, as the following *addition* of group member success odds:

$$\left(\frac{P_{n\oplus m}}{1 - P_{n\oplus m}} \right) = \left(\frac{P_n}{1 - P_n} \right) + \left(\frac{P_m}{1 - P_m} \right) = \frac{P_n(1 - P_m) + P_m(1 - P_n)}{(1 - P_n)(1 - P_m)}.$$

The group composition specified by this *second law of stable measurement* can be seen by applying probabilities P_n and P_m to the outcomes possible when persons n and m work on a task according to the addition of their *success* odds. Figure 13.2 shows the three outcomes which occur in this composition.

Helpful disagreements (10) and (01) win. Unhelpful disagreement (00) loses. Agreement (11) is absent because it does not occur in the equation which defines PACK composition. PACKs work as *collections* of *perfect DISagreements*.

Applying Rasch success odds to PACK work gets:

$$\exp(B_{n\oplus m} - D) = \exp(B_n - D) + \exp(B_m - D)$$

or
$$\exp(B_{n\oplus m}) = \exp(B_n) + \exp(B_m).$$

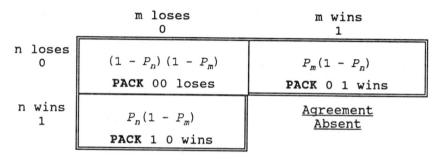

Figure 13.2.   Outcomes Occurring for a PACK.

This is also a *concatenation*, but of *absolute* (not relative to problem difficulty) strengths, accumulated in *exponential* form.

Taking logs and extending to a group of any size defines N-member PACK strength B_P as:

$$B_P \equiv \log \left(\sum_n^N \exp(B_n) \right) = \sum_n^N B_n/N + \log(NW) = \bar{B} + \log(NW)$$

with
$$W = 1 + \sigma_B^2 \left[\frac{1}{2} + \frac{\sigma_B \gamma_1}{6} + \frac{\sigma_B^2 \gamma_2}{24} + \cdots \right]$$

(For derivation see Appendix B).

Log (NW) is the amount PACK strength increases with PACK size N and member heterogeneity W. W brings in member heterogeneity through member strength variance σ_B^2, skew γ_1, kurtosis γ_2, etc. Positive skew and kurtosis amplify the impact of stronger members.

The homeostasis of most groups induces homogeneity. When heterogeneity emerges, members regroup toward homogeneity. As long as member strength variance σ_B^2 stays small, so that $\sigma_B < .3$ for $1 < W < 1.1$ or $\sigma_B < .5$ for $1 < W < 1.2$, then $W \approx 1$ and PACK strength can be modelled as:

$$B_P \approx \bar{B} + \log N.$$

The *perfect disagreements* of PACK members *collect to benefit* the PACK. As PACK size increases so does PACK strength. Unlike TEAMs, PACK strength is independent of task difficulty.

Chain Connections of Imperfect Agreements

Applying *procedural addition* to *failure* odds defines group failure odds, when group members work according to the procedural operator $\oplus$, as the following addition of group member *failure* odds:

$$\left(\frac{1 - P_{n\oplus m}}{P_{n\oplus m}}\right) = \left(\frac{1 - P_n}{P_n}\right) + \left(\frac{1 - P_m}{P_m}\right) = \frac{P_m(1 - P_n) + P_n(1 - P_m)}{P_n P_m}$$

The group composition specified by this *third law of stable measurement* can be seen by applying probabilities P_n and P_m to the outcomes possible when persons n and m work on a task together according to the addition of their *failure* odds. Figure 13.3 shows the three outcomes which occur in this composition.

Perfect agreement (11) wins. Disagreements (10) or (01) lose. Outcome (00) is absent because it does not occur in the equation that defines CHAIN composition. CHAINs work as *connections* of *IMperfect* agreements.

Applying Rasch failure odds to CHAIN work gets:

$$\exp(D - B_{n\oplus m}) = \exp(D - B_n) + \exp(D - B_m)$$

or

$$\exp(-B_{n\oplus m}) = \exp(-B_n) + \exp(-B_m),$$

a concatenation of absolute *weaknesses* in exponential form.

Taking logs and extending to a group of any size defines N-member CHAIN strength B_c as:

$$B_C \equiv -\log\left(\sum_n^N \exp(-B_n)\right) = \sum_n^N B_n/N - \log(NW') = \bar{B} - \log(NW')$$

with

$$W' = 1 + \sigma_B^2\left[\frac{1}{2} - \frac{\sigma_B \gamma_1}{6} + \frac{\sigma_B^2 \gamma_2}{24} + ..\right]$$

which member homogeneity simplifies to:

$$B_C \simeq \bar{B} - \log N.$$

The *imperfect agreements* of CHAIN members *connect against* the danger of harmful disagreement. Like PACKs, CHAIN strength is

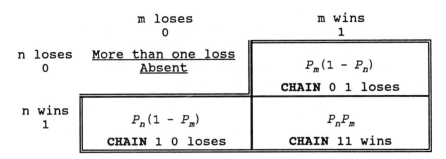

Figure 13.3. Outcomes Occurring for a CHAIN.

independent of problem difficulty. Unlike PACKs, as CHAIN size increases, CHAIN strength *de*creases.

COMPARING COMPOSITIONS

To see the differences among TEAMs, PACKs and CHAINs consider the possibilities for groups of three in Figure 13.4 and for groups of any size in Figure 13.5.

TEAMs are united in perfect agreement. Win or lose, no disagreement is permitted to occur. PACKs and CHAINs distinguish disagreement, but conversely. PACKs win by a single *winning* disagreement. CHAINs lose by a single *losing* disagreement. To help a TEAM, a member's strength must be stronger than problem difficulty. Members weaker than problem difficulty decrease TEAM strength. Adding to a

	TEAM	**PACK**	**CHAIN**
WIN	Agreement 111	Helpful Disagreement 100,010,001	Agreement 111
LOSE	Agreement 000	Disagreement 000	Harmful Disagreement 011,101,110
ABSENT	100,010,001 110,101,011	111 110,101,011	000 100,010,001

Figure 13.4. Outcomes for Three Member Groups.

	AGREE	DISAGREE
WINS	**TEAM** all 1's	**PACK** a single 1
LOSES	**TEAM** all 0's	**CHAIN** a single 0

or

	TEAM	PACK	CHAIN
all 1's	WINS	★★★	WINS
both 0's & 1's	★★★ ★★★	One 1 WINS	One 0 loses
all 0's	loses	loses	★★★

★★★ Absent

Figure 13.5.   Outcomes for Any Size Group.

PACK always increases PACK strength. Adding to a CHAIN always *decreases* CHAIN strength.

The measurement models for composition analysis in Figure 13.6 enable us to deduce which of these compositions works best against problems of different difficulties.

TEAMs vs PACKs

When is one united TEAM agreement on what is *best* more effective than a collection of PACK *dis*agreements?

Since $B_T = B_P$ when $(\bar{B} - D) = (+\log N)/(N - 1)$,
$B_T > B_P$ requires $(\bar{B} - D) > (+\log N)/(N - 1)$.

TEAMs:
$$B_T = D + \sum_{n}^{N} (B_n - D)$$
$B_n > D$ helps
$B_n < D$ hurts

PACKs:
$$B_P = \log\left(\sum_{n}^{N} \exp(B_n)\right) = \bar{B} + \log(N)$$
more N helps

CHAINs:
$$B_C = -\log\left(\sum_{n}^{N} \exp(-B_n)\right) = \bar{B} - \log(N)$$
more N hurts

Figure 13.6.   Measurement Models for Composition Analysis.

Group More Able
Problem Easier

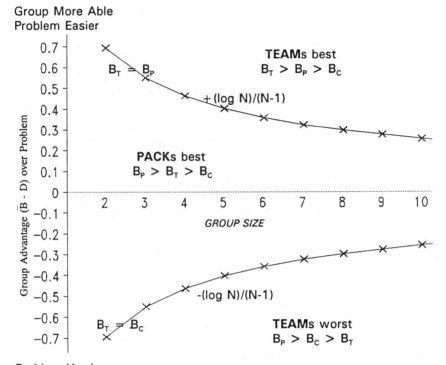

Figure 13.7. PACK vs TEAM vs CHAIN Strength by Group size and Problem Difficulty.

TEAMs do better than PACKs when average group strength is greater than problem difficulty by [(+log N)/(N − 1). This defines the upper curve in Figure 13.7.

TEAMs vs CHAINs

When is TEAM organization better than CHAIN organization?

Since $B_T = B_C$ when $(\bar{B} - D) = (-\log N)/(N - 1)$,
$B_T > B_C$ requires $(\bar{B} - D) > (-\log N)/(N - 1)$.

This is the lower curve in Figure 13.7.

To read Figure 13.7, find group size N = 4 on the horizontal axis. Go up to the upper curve and left to the vertical axis to read that a group of four must average half a logit *more* strength than problem difficulty to do better as a TEAM than a PACK.

When problem D is harder than $[\bar{B} - (\log N)/(N - 1)]$, PACK disagreement is more productive than TEAM agreement. As relative problem difficulty (D − B) increases, the value of TEAM work declines. The turning point at which PACKs become better than TEAMs is *always greater than zero*. Below $(B - D) = (-\log N)/(N - 1)$, a TEAM becomes the *least* productive group organization. Figure 13.8 formulates the relative strengths of TEAMs, PACKs and CHAINs.

Figure 13.9 uses Figure 13.7 to show how relationships between problem difficulty, group size and group organization can be used to design optimal work groups. The upper group of five, averaging .56 logits more able than their problem, should work best in TEAM agreement. The middle group of three, averaging only .18 logits more able than their problem, should work better in PACK *dis*agreement. The bottom group of seven, averaging .64 *less* able than their problem, however, encounter an additional consideration. Optimal organization for this group depends on the cost/benefit balance between success and failure. When opportunity invites, PACK disagreements should be more productive. When danger looms, however, CHAIN commitment to maintain agreement may be safer.

Visualizing Group Mixtures

When empirical measures B_G are estimated from group performance, we can see where each B_G fits on the line of TEAM, PACK and CHAIN compositions implied by its member measures $\{B_n$ for n $=$ 1,N$\}$ by plotting B_G at:

$$X_G = (B_G - \bar{B})/\log N \qquad \text{and} \qquad Y_G = (B_G - B_T)/\log N$$

WHEN:	THEN:
$(+\log N)/(N - 1) < (\bar{B} - D)$	$B_T > B_P > B_C$
$(-\log N)/(N - 1) < (\bar{B} - D) < (+\log N)/(N - 1)$	$B_P > B_T > B_C$
$(\bar{B} - D) < \cdot (-\log N)/(N - 1)$	$B_P > B_C > B_T$

Figure 13.8.   Relative Strengths of TEAMs, PACKs and CHAINs.

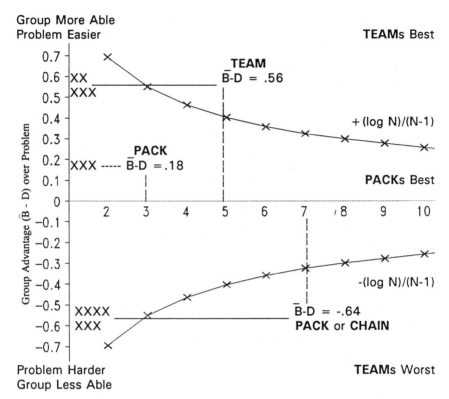

Figure 13.9.   Plotting Member Strength and Group Size on a PACK/TEAM/CHAIN Locator.

in an XY-plot benchmarked by a TEAM, PACK, CHAIN line with intercept (A_{ND}, 0), slope one and composition reference points:

$$X_T = (\bar{B} - D)[(N - 1)/\log N] = A_{ND}, \qquad Y_T = (B_T - B_T)/\log N = 0,$$
$$X_P = (B_P - \bar{B})/\log N = +1, \qquad Y_P = (B_P - B_T)/\log N = +1 - A_{ND},$$
$$X_C = (B_C - \bar{B})/\log N = -1, \qquad Y_C = (B_C - B_T)/\log N = -1 - A_{ND}.$$

GENERALIZING THE MEASUREMENT MODEL

To expand probability $P = \exp Q/(1 + \exp Q)$ in Q, write its log odds $\log[P/1 - P)] = Q$. Subscripting P and $(1 - P)$ to P_1 and P_0 for $\log(P_1/P_0) = Q_1$ leads to $\log(P_x/P_{x-1}) = Q_x$, a Rasch model for any number of ordered steps: x = 1, 2, 3, , , m − 1, m, . . . , ∞. This model constructs additive conjoint measurement from data obtained through any orderable categories: dichotomies, ratings, grades, partial credits (indexing x_i and Q_{ix} to item i), comparisons, ranks, counts, proportions, percents.

We can use this model to articulate a variety of frequently encountered facets. To represent a measure for person n, we introduce person parameter B_n. To produce an observable response x_{ni}, we provoke person n with item i designed to elicit manifestations of the intended variable. To calibrate item i, and so construct a quantitative definition of the variable, we introduce item parameter D_i. To calibrate the resistance against moving up in item i from category $x - 1$ to x, we add item step parameter F_{ix}. With D_i and F_{ix} in place, we can estimate *test-free* person measures which, for data which follow the model, are stable with respect to item selection.

When person n responds directly to item i, producing response x_{ni}, we can collect x_{ni}'s over persons and items and construct person measures on the item-defined variable. However, when persons are observed through performances that are not self-scoring, then we need a rater j to obtain rating x_{nij} of person n's performance on item i. But we know that even the best trained raters vary in the level at which they use rating scales. To calibrate raters, we add rater parameter C_j. With C_j in place, we can estimate *rater-free,* as well as test-free, person measures that, for data that fit, will be stable with respect to rater selection as well as item selection.

As comprehension of the measurement context grows, we can add more facets, a task parameter A_k for the difficulty of the task on which person n's performance is rated by rater j on item i to produce x_{nijk} and so on.

In order to obtain inferential stability (Fisher sufficiency (1920), Thurstone invariance (1925), a *stochastic* Guttman scale (1944), Rasch objectivity (1960), and Luce and Tukey conjoint additivity (1964)) we need only combine these parameters *additively* into a many-facet model (Linacre, 1989) such as:

$$\log\left[\frac{P_{nijkx}}{P_{nijkx-1}}\right] = Q_{nijkx} = B_n - D_i - C_j - A_k - F_{ix},$$

where B_n is the *person* parameter, D_i is the *item* parameter, C_j is the *rater* parameter, A_k is the *task* parameter and F_{ix} is the *item step* parameter.

Compositions can be studied in any facet of a many-facet model. Consider:

$$\log\left[\frac{P_{nijk1}}{P_{nijk0}}\right] = Q_{nijk1} = B_n - D_i - C_j - A_k,$$

Group Type	Measurement Model
Person **TEAM** n = 1,...,N	$B_T = \bar{B} + (N - 1)(\bar{B} - D - C - A)$
Item BLOCK i = 1,...,L	$D_B = \bar{D} - (L - 1)(B - \bar{D} - C - A)$
Rater **TEAM** j = 1,...,M	$C_T = \bar{C} - (M - 1)(B - D - \bar{C} - A)$
Task BLOCK k = 1,...,H	$A_B = \bar{A} - (H - 1)(B - D - C - \bar{A})$

Figure 13.10.   Facet Measures for TEAMs and BLOCKs.

rewritten for x = 0,1 to simplify presentation. The measurement models for TEAMs of animate elements, persons and raters, and for BLOCKs of inanimate elements, items and tasks, are listed in Figure 13.10.

For TEAM and BLOCK measures to increase with group size, the average measure of the grouped facet must exceed:

$$\bar{B} > D + C + A \qquad \bar{D} > B - C - A$$
$$\bar{C} > B - D - A \qquad \bar{A} > B - D - C$$

The PACK and CHAIN formulations in Figure 13.11 are simpler. For PACKs and CHAINs the levels of other facets do not matter. More persons make person PACKs stronger but person CHAINs weaker. More items, raters or tasks make PACKs easier to satisfy but CHAINs more difficult.

	PACKs	**CHAINs**
Persons	$B_P = \bar{B} + \log(N)$	$B_C = \bar{B} - \log(N)$
Items	$D_P = \bar{D} - \log(L)$	$D_C = \bar{D} + \log(L)$
Raters	$C_P = \bar{C} - \log(M)$	$C_C = \bar{C} + \log(M)$
Tasks	$A_P = \bar{A} - \log(H)$	$A_C = \bar{A} + \log(H)$

Figure 13.11.   Facet Measures for Homogeneous PACKs and CHAINs.

NECESSITIES FOR INFERENCE

Four problems interfere with inference:

Uncertainty is the motivation for inference. We have only the past by which to infer the uncertain future. Our solution is to contain uncertainty in *probability* distributions that regularize the irregularities that disrupt connections between what seems certain now but must be uncertain later.

Distortion interferes with the transition from data collection to meaning representation. Our ability to figure out comes from our faculty to visualize. Visualization evolved from the survival value of safe body navigation. Our solution to distortion is to represent data in bilinear forms that make the data look like the two-dimensional plane in front of us. To "see" what experience "means", we "map" it.

Confusion is caused by interdependency. As we look for tomorrow's probabilities in yesterday's lessons, interactions intrude and confuse us. Our solution is to force the complexities of experience into few enough invented "dimensions" to make room for clear thinking. The authority of these fictions is their utility. We will never know their "truth". But, when our fictions "work", they are usually useful.

The logic we use to control confusion is enforced singularity. We investigate the possibilities for, define and measure *one* dimension at a time. The necessary mathematics is parameter separability. Models that introduce putative "causes" as separately estimable parameters are the founding laws of quantification. They define measurement. They determine what is measurable. They decide which data are useful, and which are not.

Ambiguity is the fourth problem of inference. We control hierarchical ambiguity by using measurement models which embody *divisibility*.

Bookstein's functions:

$$H(x \times y) = H(x) \times H(y) \qquad \text{and} \qquad G(x + y) = G(x) + G(y)$$

for resilience to aggregation ambiguity contain the divisibility necessary to stabilize quantitative inference (Feller, 1966). They also contain the parameter separation and linearity necessary to alleviate confusion and distortion. Models which follow Bookstein's functions implement:

1. The *concatenation* and *conjoint additivity* that Norman Campbell (1920) and Luce and Tukey (1964) require for *fundamental measurement*,

PROBLEMS	SOLUTIONS	PARENTS
UNCERTAINTY have ⇒ want now ⇒ later statistic ⇒ parameter	**PROBABILITY** distribution regular irregularity misfit detection	Bernoulli 1713 De Moivre 1733 Laplace 1774 Poisson 1837
DISTORTION non-linearity unequal intervals incommensurability	**ADDITIVITY** linearity arithmetic concatenation	Luce/Tukey 1964 Fechner 1860 Helmholtz 1887 N.Campbell 1920
CONFUSION interdependence interaction confounding	**SEPARABILITY** sufficiency invariance conjoint order	Rasch 1960 R.A.Fisher 1920 Thurstone 1925 Guttman 1944
AMBIGUITY arbitrary grouping ambiguous hierarchy	**DIVISIBILITY** stability reproducibility	Kolmogorov 1932 Levy 1924 Bookstein 1992

For Bernoulli, De Moivre, Laplace and Poisson see Stigler (1986).
For Kolmogorov and Levy see Feller (1966).

Figure 13.12.   Foundations of Inference.

2. The *exponential linearity* that Ronald Fisher (1920) requires for *estimation sufficiency* and
3. The *parameter separation* that Thurstone (1925) and Rasch (1960) require for *objectivity*.

The measurable compositions are TEAMs, PACKs and CHAINs. The measurement models necessary and sufficient for quantitative composition analysis are linear mixtures of the Rasch models for measuring these compositions. Figure 13.12 summarizes the problems of inference and their current solutions.

The prevalence, history and logic of Bookstein's laws of addition and multiplication rules establish Rasch measurement models as the necessary and sufficient foundations for measurement. Models that contradict the inferential necessities of probability, linearity, separability and divisibility cannot survive the vicissitudes of practice. Only data that can be understood and organized to fit a Rasch model can be useful for constructing measures.

CONNOTATIONS, PROPERTIES AND STORIES

Mathematics leads to three reference compositions that empirical composites must mix to be measurable. We can use group member measures to calculate TEAM, PACK and CHAIN expectations. We can use these expectations and empirical group measures to study TEAM/PACK/CHAIN mixtures. So much for mathematics. What can TEAMs, PACKs and CHAINs say about everyday life? How might we bring these mathematical ideas to practice as useful formulations for better living? Can these abstractions help us manage our infinitely complex experiences with living compositions, hierarchies of functioning, families of ideas and sets of tasks? Can we construct maps by which to "see" how the compositions of which we are, by which we think and within which we live, might be better worked? Figure 13.13 lists some connotations that TEAMs, PACKs and CHAINs bring to mind. Figure 13.14 lists some properties that they imply. Here are some stories in which these compositions might participate.

Football

When a TEAM of players huddle to call a play, win or lose, they intend to act united. Should one of them err, he will hurt the TEAM. TEAM success is jeopardized by weak links in its CHAIN of players.

	SAFE SURE	DANGEROUS UNSURE
AGREE	**TEAM** government formality convention	**CHAIN** survival security discretion
DISAGREE	**PACK** science opportunity invention	chaos anarchy

	TEAM	**PACK**	**CHAIN**
WIN	virtue satisfaction justice	pride triumph progress	safety relief security
LOSE	guilt indignation worry	shame frustration disappointment	fear recrimination despair

Figure 13.13. Connotations of TEAM, PACK and CHAIN.

TEAM	PACK	CHAIN
unite	collect	connect
consolidate	accumulate	protect
evaluate	explore	preserve
unify	discover	secure
agree	attack	defend
uphold ground	gain ground	guard ground
capitalize consensus	optimize difference	survive together
play safe	take chance	hang on
smug secure	daring hopeful	cautious worried
virtue disapproval	pride shame	safety danger
usual events	rare events	dangerous events
easy problems	hard problems	risky problems
successful jury	missing key	mountain climbing

Figure 13.14. Properties Implied by TEAM, PACK and CHAIN.

Lost Keys

What is the best way to look for a lost key? Should we all agree to look in the same place? Or, should we all agree to disagree as to where to look and spread out? The tactic of sending each to a different place has the better chance of success. PACK work is the best way to look for lost keys.

Mountain Climbing

Climbers rope for safety. As one climbs, everyone else hangs on. Then, should a climber slip, his anchored mates may be able to save him. When, however, a supposedly anchored mate is not hanging on or moves out of turn, then all may fall. CHAIN work is the best way to climb mountains.

Cops and Robbers

When a crime is reported, the perpetrator is often unknown. Solving the problem is difficult in the beginning. PACKs of detective TEAMs fan out to search for suspects. As evidence accumulates, however, deciding who's guilty becomes easier. The PACK of TEAMs converges in their solutions to one TEAM agreement and detains the one most likely suspect.

Should the suspect go to trial, judgement will depend on a jury TEAM decision. But, if one jurist holds out, the jury TEAM may become a failing CHAIN.

A Common Source of Misapprehension

A weak shooter, in solitude, misses repeatedly. But then, in sudden company, is seen to *hit* on what is now his Nth try. His PACK ability: $B_{PN} = B + \log N = > B_{P1} = B' + \log 1 = B'$, when only his finally successful shot is seen, will appear to be the ability B' of a stronger shooter who hits on his first try.

A strong shooter, in solitude, hits repeatedly. But then, in sudden company, is seen to *miss* on what is now her Nth try. Her CHAIN ability: $B_{CN} = B - \log N = > B_{C1} = B'' - \log 1 = B''$, when only her finally unsuccessful shot is seen, will appear to be the ability B'' of a weaker shooter who misses on her first try.

Solving Problems

When problems are easy, TEAMing ideas into one course of action works best. When problems are hard, however, putting every egg in a single basket is not as productive as deploying a PACK of diverse undertakings. When a mistake is fatal, however, then PACK diversity risks CHAIN weakness.

REFERENCES

Bookstein, A. (1992). Informetric Distributions, Parts I and II, *Journal of the American Society for Information Science*, 41(5): 368–88.

Campbell, N.R. (1920). *Physics: The elements*. London: Cambridge University Press.

Fechner, G.T. (1860). *Elemente der psychophysik*. Leipzig: Breitkopf & Hartel. [Translation: Adler, H.E. (1966). *Elements of Psychophysics*. New York: Holt, Rinehart & Winston.].

Feller, W. (1966). *An introduction to probability theory and its applications, Volume II*. New York: John Wiley.

Fisher, R.A. (1920). A mathematical examination of the methods of determining the accuracy of an observation by the mean error and by the mean square error. *Monthly Notices of the Royal Astronomical Society*, (53), 758–770.

Freud, S. (1921). *Group psychology and the analysis of the ego*. New York: Norton.

Guttman, L. (1944). A basis for scaling quantitative data. *American Sociological Review*, (9), 139–150.

Helmholtz, H.V. (1887). Zahlen und Messen erkenntnis-theoretisch betrachet. *Philosophische Aufsatze Eduard Zeller gewidmet*. Leipzig. [Translation: Bryan, C.L. (1930). *Counting and measuring*. Princeton: van Nostrand.].

Linacre, J.M. (1989). *Many-facet Rasch measurement*. Chicago: MESA Press.

Luce, R.D. & Tukey, J.W. (1964). Simultaneous conjoint measurement. *Journal of Mathematical Psychology*, (1), 1–27.

Rasch, G. (1960). *Probabilistic models for some intelligence and attainment tests*. [Danish Institute of Educational Research 1960, University of Chicago Press 1980, MESA Press 1993] Chicago: MESA Press.

Stigler, S.M. (1986). *The history of statistics*. Cambridge: Harvard University Press.

Thurstone, L.L. (1925). A method of scaling psychological and educational tests. *Journal of Educational Psychology*, (16), 433–451.

APPENDIX A

Properties of Robust Functions

A. Bookstein
University of Chicago

The concern of this appendix is our ability to observe and describe regularities in the face of ambiguity. Since much of social science data are based on ill-defined concepts, this ability has serious practical implications.

Policy decisions are often based on assumptions about how certain characteristics are distributed over an affected population. Such assumptions tend to be expressed in terms of functions describing statistical distributions. Although these functions critically influence our decisions, they are usually created ad hoc, with little or no theoretical support. We are interested in situations in which the particular values entering the function could be quite different, given a plausible redefinition of the concepts being probed. In such situations, it is reasonable to demand of the functions involved that reasonable redefinition of key concepts not result in new functions that change the decisions being made.

We examine one case in which counts were described in terms of an unknown function, $f(x)$ (Bookstein, 1992). We had a population of items, each with an associated latent parameter, x, indicating its potential for producing some yield over a period of time. The number of items with values of x between x_0 and $x_0 + \delta$ is given by $f(x)*\delta$. It is convenient to let $f(x) = A*h(x)$, with $h(x)$ defined so $h(1) = 1$.

The function, $h(x)$ is unknown, but we would like the form that it takes not to depend on the size of the interval chosen. Demanding this constraint led to the condition that $h(x)$ must obey: $h(xy) = h(x)h(y)$. This functional constraint in many cases determines the function itself. For example, for $h(x)$ a "smooth" function, only the form $h(x) = A/x^\alpha$ is permitted.

The functional constraint, $h(xy) = h(x)h(y)$, also resulted from examining a wide range of other ambiguities in counting. Similar requirements occur in other contexts. In an interesting and important example, Shannon, in defining the properties of a measure of information, first considers the uncertainty of which of M equally likely events will occur. He argues that, if this is given by a function $f(M)$, this function must obey $f(MN) = f(M) + f(N)$. A discussion of the consequences of this assumption is found in Ash (1965).

In the example of information, a transition is made between discrete counts and continuous variables, the probabilities of events. But the constraint also plays a critical role in number theory, where a number of key "number theoretic" functions have a similar property (though it is usually assumed that the values corresponding to M and N are relatively prime.) For example, the function $\tau(n)$ giving the number of integer divisors of an integer n satisfies this condition. An excellent treatment of number theoretic functions from this point of view may be found in Stewart (1952).

Thus we find that the constraint is both strong, in the sense of determining the form of the functions satisfying it, and widespread. Both information and counts are central to much of social science policy making. It is the purpose of this appendix to show that other types of commonly occurring constraints are simply related to the one given above.

OTHER FORMS

The previous section defined a key relation that it is attractive for our functions to obey $h(xy) = h(x)h(y)$. Given such a function, we can define other functions with interesting functional properties. For example, $k(x) = \log(h(\exp(x)))$. Using the properties of log, h, and exp, it is easy to see that k obeys $k(x + y) = k(x) + k(y)$. Similarly, given such a function $k(x)$, we could define a function $h(x) = \exp(k(\log(x)))$, which obeys the initial condition.

EVALUATING k(x)

We have some freedom in evaluating $k(x)$, but not much. We can now list some consequences of the constraint.

1. We immediately see that, if $k(x)$ satisfies the additivity condition, so does $A*k(x)$, for any constant A. This allows us to choose k for which: $k(1) = 1$.
2. But if so, we can evaluate $k(1/m)$, for any integer m, $1 = k(1) = k(\{1/m + 1/m + \ldots + 1/m\}^m) = m*k(1/m)$, so, $k(1/m) = 1/m$.
3. Similarly, $k(mx) = m*k(x)$, so given any positive rational number, m/n, we have, $k(m/n) = mk(1/n) = m/n$.
4. Since $k(x) = k(x + 0) = k(x) + k(0)$, we must necessarily have, $k(0) = 0$.
5. Also, since $0 = k(0) = k(x + (-x)) = k(x) + k(-x)$, we can conclude that, $k(-x) = -k(x)$, for arbitrary x.

Thus we see that the additivity condition strictly imposes values that k can take on the rational numbers, a set dense in the real number line. If $k(x)$ is smooth, then, in general, we must have $k(x) = Ax$. We can make a stronger statement: If $k(x)$ is monotonic, say monotonically increasing, in any interval I, no matter how small, then it must be continuous in that interval and throughout its range. Thus, $k(x) = Ax$. If $k(x)$ is monotonic in a small interval including the irrational value x_0. Then we can find rational numbers r_1 and r_2, also in I, for which $r_1 < x_0 < r_2$. Thus, we have $k(r_1) < k(x_0) < k(r_2)$. This is true even if we choose a sequence of r_1 and r_2 increasingly close to x_0. For such values, $k(r_1) = r_1$ and $k(r_2) = r_2$ both approach x_0, so $k(x_0)$ must itself equal x_0. Thus, at least in I, $k(x) = x$, for irrational as well as rational x.

But now consider any x. Certainly $k(x) = k(r + (x - r)) = r + k(x - r)$, for r a rational number near enough to x that there exist values x_1 and x_2, both in I, for which $x_1 - x_2 = x - r$. Then, $k(x - r) = k(x_1 - x_2) = k(x_1) - k(x_2)$. But in this interval, we saw $k(x) = x$. Thus we have $k(x) = r + x_1 - x_2 = r + (x - r) = x$, as it was intended to prove.

REFERENCES

Ash, R. (1965) *Information Theory*, New York: Wiley.
Bookstein, A. (1992) Informetric Distributions, Parts I and II, *Journal of the American Society for Information Science*, 41(5): 368–88.
Stewart, B.M. (1952) *Theory of Numbers*, New York: MacMillan.

APPENDIX B

Derivation of PACK and CHAIN measure approximations from their exponential (ratio) parameter definition.

PACK definition:

$$b_P = \sum_i^N b_i = \bar{b} \sum_i^N (b_i/\bar{b})$$

where $\quad b_P = \exp(B_P) \qquad \bar{b} = \exp(\bar{B}) \qquad b_i/\bar{b} = \exp(B_i - \bar{B})$

so that $\qquad B_P = \bar{B} + \log \left[\sum_i^N \exp(B_i - \bar{B}) \right].$

Since

$$\exp(B_i - \bar{B}) = 1 + (B_i - \bar{B}) + (B_i - \bar{B})^2/2 + (B_i - \bar{B})^3/6 + \ldots,$$

$$\sum_i^N \exp(B_i - \bar{B}) = N[1 + \sigma_B^2/2 + \sigma_B^3 \gamma_1/6 + \sigma_B^4 \gamma_2/24 + \ldots] = NW$$

PACK measure becomes

$$B_P = \bar{B} + \log(NW) \approx \bar{B} + \log(N) \qquad \text{as} \qquad \sigma_B \to 0.$$

CHAIN definition:

$$1/b_C = \sum_{i}^{N} (1/b_i) = (1/\bar{b}) \sum_{i}^{N} (\bar{b}/b_i)$$

so that

$$B_C = \bar{B} - \log\left[\sum_{i}^{N} \exp(\bar{B} - B_i) \right].$$

Since

$$\exp(\bar{B} - B_i) = 1 + (\bar{B} - B_i) + (\bar{B} - B_i)^2/2 + (\bar{B} - B_i)^3/6 + \ldots,$$

$$\sum_{i}^{N} \exp(\bar{B} - B_i) = N[1 + \sigma_B^2/2 - \sigma_B^3\gamma_1/6 + \sigma_B^4\gamma_2/24 - \ldots] = NW'$$

CHAIN measure becomes

$$B_C = \bar{B} - \log(NW') \approx \bar{B} - \log(N) \qquad \text{as} \qquad \sigma_B \to 0.$$

chapter **14**

Theoretical and Empirical Evidence on the Dichotomization of Graded Responses

David Andrich
Murdoch University

It is common in educational and other kinds of social measurement to collect data in the form of graded responses. This is common in performance assessment and in the assessment of attitude. Data are collected in the form of graded responses where there is no measuring instrument of the kind found in the physical sciences, but the collection reflects physical measurement in important ways. In physical measurement the amount of the property is measured by mapping it onto a continuum that has been divided in units of equal length, and then the measure of the property of the entity (often termed simply the measure of the entity) is the count of the number of units from the origin that the entity passes. This chapter draws on this prototype of measurement.

In elementary treatments of graded responses, the prototype of physical measurement is followed closely in that the count of the categories is taken as the measure of the entity. In more advanced treatments, two modifications are made. First, it is not presumed that the categories that correspond to the units are of equal length, and second, a random component is built into the model that expresses the probability that an entity will be located in a particular category as a function of its location and characteristics of the categories. Then the estimate of the location of the entity from the data and according to the model is taken as the entity's measure. Different kinds of models of measurement have been proposed for such data, and two important and qualitatively distinguishable and incompatible ones are those based on the work of Thurstone in the 1920s and 1930s (e.g. Thurstone, 1927), and those based on the work of Rasch in the 1950s and 1960s (e.g. Rasch, 1960). This chapter focuses on the latter.

After data are collected in the form of graded responses, it is common to collapse responses in adjacent categories for one reason or another depending on the particular situation, with dichotomization being the extreme case of collapsing categories. Often this collapsing is motivated by a belief that the categories are not working quite as well as intended, and that this malfunctioning is less likely to be manifested with a smaller number of categories. That the collapsing of categories in general, and *dichotomization* in particular, should be permitted after the data have been collected has generally been seen as no more than commonsense, and indeed, this perspective has been formalized as a condition for selecting among models that might be used for analyzing graded responses. Jansen and Roskam (1986) present an argument for this condition and therefore conclude that because the Rasch model for graded responses does not permit this routine dichotomization, it should effectively be rejected for analyzing graded responses. They reject it because they argue that because the model does not permit dichotomization after the data are collected, or the collapsing of adjacent categories in general, that this implies a *redefinition* of the variable of measurement. The purpose of this chapter is to show that the violation of the joining assumption by the Rasch model does not involve a redefinition of the variable, *but reflects an implied change in precision of measurement and a possible redefinition of the relative meaning of the categories on the continuum that reflects this change in precision.* Whether or not the relative meanings of the categories are redefined without changing the nature of the variable itself is an empirical question. The paper presents an empirical example in which persons were asked to partition a continuum into three categories and four categories with respect to the same variable where the fourth category was defined operationally to be a subset of the third category, and shows that the relative location of all categories is changed with the addition of the fourth category.

DICHOTOMIZING GRADED RESPONSES

Dichotomization is the extreme case of collapsing adjacent categories, and because it is simpler to deal with dichotomization and to then generalize to any collapsing, Jansen and Roskam (1986) concentrate on this case. In order to make clear the principles on which Jansen and Roskam make their case a number of their principles and conclusions are analyzed. The principles are considered first. These are considered within the general understanding that the use of graded responses involves locating entities on a latent unidimensional continuum and that the response categories partition that continuum into adjacent and mutually exclusive categories (Jansen and Roskam, 1986, pp. 70–71). This, of course, is just as in the prototype of measurement referred to earlier.

Central to Jansen and Roskam's argument is the joining assumption:

> The probability of subject's responding with category j or category k is equal to the probability of responding with category h if category h replaces the categories j and k. Mild and obvious though this assumption may seem, it has the strong implication that there is no difference between dichotomization before the fact and dichotomization after the fact. (p. 73)

Clearly they mean that if the data were collected with a set of M categories, and the categories were subsequently dichotomized, then the distribution of responses should be the same as if the categories were dichotomized in the same way before the data were collected. If it were not, then they infer that the variable of measurement is different in the two dichotomizations. Thus, "In particular we address ourselves to . . . compatibility with dichotomizing the responses, either in constructing the response format (before the fact), or after having collected graded response data (after the fact)" (Jansen and Roskam, 1986, p. 70). They formalize this contention by a principle of ξ-invariance:

> As a necessary requirement, we will introduce ξ-invariance between graded and dichotomized responses, meaning, essentially, that the same person parameter, ξ, is reflected in either response format. The relation between graded and dichotomized responses is expressed in a *joining assumption*.
>
> Let **P** and **P'** be two partitionings of the responses, and let **M** and **M'** be two measurement models. We will assume that **M** and **M'** have the

same structure, that is, that models of the same structure apply to both **P** and **P'**. Otherwise, the structure of the model would depend in an ad hoc way on the response format.

So if **M** is the unidimensional polychotomous Rasch model holding for **P**, and **P'** is a dichotomization, we expect the dichotomous Rasch model, **M'**, to hold for **P'**. (p. 70, 73)

It is important to recognize this equivalence Jansen and Roskam make between the joining assumption and ξ-invariance, as it is this equivalence which is reexamined.

Jansen and Roskam's conclusions about the Rasch model are equally clear: "Insofar as it may be argued that dichotomization before the fact is not essentially different from dichotomization after the fact, the value of the unidimensional polychotomous Rasch model is consequently questionable" (Jansen and Roskam, 1986, p. 69). Also with respect to a particular rendition of the model which they term the Rating Rasch Model (RRM), they conclude:

Insofar as the joining assumption . . . applies to partitioning of the response continuum before the fact, the construction of graded responses interferes with the measurement outcome in the RRM. Since the property of ξ-invariance is seen to be essential for rating data, (the RRM) can not be considered as a measurement model for rating data. (p. 81)

This conclusion, if correct, would have a serious constraint on the use of the ubiquitous graded responses, which are expected to elicit more precise measurement than dichotomous responses without a change of variable. It is shown that this constraint is not necessary.

THE RASCH MODEL FOR GRADED RESPONSES

This section reviews briefly the development of some key points in the Rasch model for graded responses, highlighting those features central to appreciating why it violates the joining assumption. Rasch (1961) abstracted the following principles for specifically objective comparisons, and set them as *criteria for measurement*:

The comparison between two stimuli should be independent of which particular individuals were instrumental for the comparison; and it should also be independent of which other stimuli within the considered class were or might also have been compared.

Symmetrically, a comparison between two individuals should be independent of which particular stimuli within the class considered were

instrumental for comparison; and it should also be independent of which
other individuals were also compared, on the same or on some other
occasion. (p. 322)

Rasch termed such comparisons to be specifically objective: objective
because the comparison are invariant, and specifically objective because they are invariant with respect to a specified frame of reference.
It seems rather surprising that Jansen and Roskam articulated
ξ-invariance in terms of the joining assumption and do not seem to
appreciate explicitly that the essential basis of the Rasch class of models parallels their ξ-invariance. For if the location of the individual
and that of the stimuli (items) is characterized as unidimensional,
then conformity to the model implies invariance of the location of the
parameter of individuals with respect to different items that may involve different partitions of the continuum. This is elaborated in the
paper—especially how this invariance is incompatible with the joining
assumption.

Before proceeding, two points of convention in this chapter and one
of argument are clarified. First, in studying the process and models
arising from Rasch's specification, the focus in the rest of the chapter,
as has been so far, is on a particular person p responding to a specific
stimulus i. Thus the chapter is not concerned with various parameterizations that might arise in the context of many items. Second, while
Jansen and Roskam use the parameter ξ to indicate the location of a
person, this is not conventional in the additive or logarithmic metric,
and so rather than continuing to refer to ξ-invariance, in the rest of the
paper this property is referred to more concretely as *location-invariance.*
It is appreciated that Jansen and Roskam imply more by their term
than simply the location per se, that is, that the property characterized
by ξ under two partitions is the same, and not just that the location is
the same, but ξ is a parameter in the model that has a value. It will be
argued that if the data conform to the Rasch model, then both the
location and the property must be the same. The demonstration that
the data do conform to the model depends on the demonstration that
under the model, the location values of the same variable are the same,
and therefore ξ-invariance is identical to *location-invariance.* Third, it
is entirely possible that when one proceeds from collecting data with
dichotomous responses to graded responses that the variable definition
is changed. However, that is an empirical matter, and not a necessary
feature of the Rasch model as such. This chapter is about the inherent
properties of the Rasch model with which Jansen and Roskam were
also concerned.

The Mathematical Formulation of Specific Objectivity and Location Invariance

The necessary and sufficient mathematical expression of the Rasch's criteria for dichotomous responses in a stochastic context is given by

$$\Pr\{x_{pi}\} = \frac{1}{\gamma_{pi}} \exp\{(\beta_p - \delta_i)x_{pi}\}, \quad -\infty < \beta_p < \infty, \quad -\infty < \delta_i < \infty, \quad (1)$$

where β_p is the location parameter of person p, δ_i is the location parameter of some stimulus i usually termed an item, X_{pi}, $x_{pi} \in \{0, 1\}$, is the random variable characterizing the responses and $\gamma_{pi} = \Sigma^1_{x_{pi}=0}$ $\exp\{(\beta_p - \delta_i)x_p\}$ is a normalizing factor, ensuring $0 < \Pr\{x_{pi}\} < 1$. Because γ_{pi} always has this role and always takes the form of being the sum of the numerators, it will not be defined in other expressions of the class of Rasch models.

In this, and all probabilistic models that follow from specific objectivity, *sufficient statistics* play a central role, because it is through the sufficient statistics that one set of parameters can be eliminated while the other set is being estimated: specific objectivity is logically equivalent to the existence of sufficient statistics in stochastic models (Rasch, 1977; Wright, 1985), and is so well documented now that it is not explained further. Furthermore, the model exemplifies the kind of measurement found in physics, sometimes termed additive conjoint measurement (Perline, Wright and Wainer, 1979, Wright, 1985).

Generalization to the Unidimensional Case With More Than Two Categories

Rasch (1961) originally specified the case of more than two categories in a multidimensional form, and then specialized it to the case where the categories reflected a unidimensional continuum, and in this way presented the model in the form equivalent to

$$\Pr\{x_{pi}\} = \frac{1}{\gamma_{ni}} \exp\{\kappa_{xi} + \phi_{xi}(\beta_p - \delta_i)\}, \quad (2)$$

where $x_{pi} \in \{0,1,2,....m\}$ represents $m + 1$ successive categories beginning with 0. In empirical applications of the model to categories ordered in some sense, efforts have been made to estimate the parameters of (2), in particular the parameters ϕ_x (Andersen, 1972; Fischer, 1977).

However, Andersen (1977) showed that if one began with the model expressed in this form, then in order for the parameters to have sufficient statistics, the scoring functions had to have the special relationship $\phi_{(x+1)i} - \phi_{xi} = \phi_{xi} - \phi_{(x-1)i}$. Andrich (1978) constructed the κs and ϕs by making an essential connection to the prototype of measurement relevant to this chapter. Specifically, if $\tau_{1i}, \tau_{2i}, \tau_{3i}, ..., \tau_{xi}, ... \tau_{mi}$ are m ordered thresholds that divide the continuum into m + 1 categories, and $\alpha_{1i}, \alpha_{2i}, \alpha_{3i}, ..., \alpha_{xi}, ... \alpha_{mi}$ are discriminations at these thresholds, then the scoring functions and the category coefficients are defined by the recursive relationships

$$\phi_{0i} = 0 \quad\quad\quad and \quad \kappa_{0i} = 0$$
$$\phi_x = \alpha_1 + \alpha_2 + ... + \alpha_x$$
$$\kappa_{xi} = -\alpha_i\tau_{1i} - \alpha_{2i}\tau_{2i} .... - \alpha_{xi}\tau_{xi}, x = 1, ..., m.$$
$$and -\infty < \tau_{xi} < \infty, x = 1, ..., m; \tau_{(x+1)i} > \tau_{xi}.$$

Thus the scoring functions ϕ are the sums of the successive discriminations at the thresholds, beginning with the first threshold, and if all discriminations are positive, $\alpha_x > 0, x = 1, ..., m$, as would normally be required, then the scoring functions will increase so that $\phi_{x+1} > \phi_x$ $x = 1, ..., m$. If the discriminations at the thresholds are constrained to be *equal*, for example, $\alpha_1 = \alpha_2 = \alpha_3 = ... \alpha_x = ...\alpha_m = \alpha > 0$, then the scoring functions and the category coefficients become

$$\phi_{0i} = 0 \quad and \; \kappa_{0i} = 0$$
$$\phi_{xi} = x\alpha_i \quad\quad \kappa_{xi} = -\alpha_i(\tau_{1i} + \tau_{2i} .... + \tau_{xi}), x = 1, ..., m.$$

It can now be seen that the successive scoring functions have the property $\phi_{(x+1)i} - \phi_{xi} = \phi_{xi} - \phi_{(x-1)i} = \alpha_i$ specified by Andersen (1977). Thus the mathematical requirement of sufficient statistics, which in turn rests on the requirement of invariant comparisons, leads to the requirement of *equal discriminations at the thresholds,* something familiar in the prototype of measurement. The importance of reviewing this interpretation is that it emphasizes that the continuum is divided into mutually exclusive adjacent categories in which only the location of the thresholds (together with the location of the person and the item) play a role. No other parameters, such as discriminations at thresholds, need to be interpreted.

Finally, the single discrimination parameter α can be absorbed into the other parameters without loss of generality, giving the model

$$\Pr\{x_{pi}\} = \frac{1}{\gamma_{ni}} \exp\{\kappa_{xi} + x_{pi}(\beta_p - \delta_i)\} \tag{3}$$

where the scoring functions now are simply the successive integers $x_{pi} \in \{0,1,2,....m\}$ that are conveniently also the values of the random variable X_{pi}, and where the category coefficients are the opposite of the sums of the thresholds up to the category of the coefficient x:

$$\kappa_{0i} = 0; \kappa_{xi} = -\tau_{1i} - \tau_{2i} - \tau_{3i} \ldots\ldots\ldots -\tau_{xi}, \quad -\infty < \tau_{xi} < \infty, x = 1, ..., m.$$

Thus the scoring functions become the *counts* x of the numbers of thresholds exceeded by the response of the person, with x = 0 indicating that no threshold has been exceeded so that the response is in the first category, and x = m indicating that all thresholds have been exceeded, so that the response is in the last category. In this way, the model is consistent with the prototype of measurement in that *the relevant number locating a response is the count of the number of thresholds passed* when the discrimination at the thresholds are the same. However, while the logic above leads to equal discriminations at thresholds, it does not lead to equal distances between thresholds. Instead, the locations of the thresholds can be estimated from the data, which gives a kind of weighting to the distances between thresholds. In addition, the count is not taken directly as an estimate of the location, but instead is estimated from the count, which is the sufficient statistic.

Figure 14.1 shows the familiar probability curves for the responses in each of five categories as a function of the location of the person β. Clearly, as β increases, so the probability of a higher score increases.

Finally, Andrich (1978) showed that in the form of equation (3), the location of the parameter δ and the thresholds τ contain an arbitrariness so that without loss of generality, the thresholds may be mean deviated about δ_i giving $\Sigma_{x=1}^{m} \tau_{xi} = 0$. In order to focus exclusively on the thresholds, taking the reverse parameterization and adding the value δ_i to each of the threshold parameters gives the exponent of (3) in the form:

$$\begin{aligned}
&\kappa_{xi} + x(\beta_p - \delta_i) \\
&= -\tau_{1i} - \tau_{2i} \ldots\ldots -\tau_{xi} + x(\beta_p - \delta_i) \\
&= -(\tau_{1i} + \delta_i) - (\tau_{2i} + \delta_i) + \ldots\ldots\ldots -(\tau_{xi} + \delta_i) + x(\beta_p) \\
&= -\tau_{1i}^* - \tau_{2i}^* \ldots\ldots - \tau_{3i}^* + x(\beta_p) \\
&= \kappa_{xi}^* + x(\beta_p)
\end{aligned}$$

where $\tau_{ji}^* = \tau_{ji} + \delta_i, j = 1, \ldots x$, and $\kappa_{xi}^* = -\tau_{1i}^* - \tau_{2i}^* \ldots -\tau_{xi}^*$,

thereby eliminating the parameter δ_i. Dropping the notation (*), it being understood that the new thresholds have the location parameter

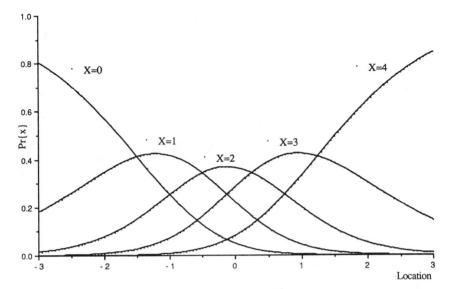

Figure 14.1. Category characteristic curves for the Rasch model for ordered response categories.

of the item absorbed in them, gives the simpler expression, which is the form similar to that of Wright and Masters (1982):

$$\Pr\{x_{pi}\} = \frac{1}{\gamma_{ni}} \exp(\kappa_{xi} + x_{pi}\beta_p). \tag{4}$$

This makes the interpretation even simpler in that it involves only the location of the person and the location of the thresholds that partition the continuum, which is the concern of this chapter.

Two issues may now be broached. First, it is opportune to see why the Rasch model for ordered categories cannot satisfy the joining assumption. If two adjacent categories x and $x + 1$ in a set of m categories are combined into a category x in a set of m-1 categories, and if the probabilities of these responses is given by equation (3), then in a set of m-1 categories it is not possible to write $\Pr\{x'_{pi}\} = \Pr\{(x_{pi})\} + \Pr\{(x + 1)_{pi}\}$ in the form of equation (3), that is

$$\Pr\{x'_{pi}\} = \Pr\{(x_{pi})\} + \Pr\{(x + 1)_{pi}\}$$

$$\neq \frac{1}{\gamma'_{pi}} \exp\{\kappa'_{xi} + x'(\beta_p - \delta_i)\}, \text{ for any } \gamma'_{pi}, \kappa'_{xi}.$$

It is this feature that lead Jansen and Roskam to conclude that the violation of the joining assumption also violates location-invariance. Second, although Jansen and Roskam refer to the model of equation (2) as the Rasch model for graded responses and then consider different specializations, because of the property of sufficiency and the rather unlikely degenerate cases that they consider, it is this model of equation (3) or (4) that will be termed the Rasch model for graded response categories. The model of equation (2) was indeed presented by Rasch, but it does not subscribe to the principle of invariance through sufficiency, the cornerstone of Rasch models (Rasch, 1960/1980), and so is not classed here as a *Rasch model*.

LOCATION INVARIANCE AND CHANGE IN THE DISTRIBUTION AND PRECISION AS A FUNCTION OF THE NUMBER OF CATEGORIES

Although the invariance properties of the Rasch class of models are well established, because of the point of the chapter, they are reviewed briefly here.

Location-Invariance

Suppose there are two items i and j, with m_i and m_j thresholds respectively, that are supposed to elicit the same property in any person p with $m_i \neq m_j$ and that the responses conform to the model of equation (4). Thus the two items must partition the continuum in two different ways. If the responses conform to the model, then for any person p

$$\Pr\{(x_{pi}, x_{pj}) \mid r_p = x_{pi} + x_{pj}\} = \frac{1}{\gamma_{rpij}} \exp\{\kappa_{xi} + \kappa_{xj}\} \qquad (5)$$

where $\gamma_{rpij} = \Sigma_{x_{pi}+x_{pj}=r} \exp\{\kappa_{xi} + \kappa_{xj} - x_{pi}\delta_i - x_{pj}\delta_i\}$ and $\Sigma_{x_{pi}+x_{pj}=r}$ denotes the sum over all possible pairs of responses (x_{pi}, x_{pj}) that have the same total r. The key point from equation (5) is that it does not involve the location parameter of the person, and so from a set of data, the parameters of the items—that is the thresholds into which the continuum has been partitioned—can be estimated independently of the unknown location parameters of the persons. However, the parameter eliminated is the *same* single parameter of the person with respect to the contact with the two items that have different numbers of categories. Therefore, the contact between the items and the persons, despite the different numbers of categories, provides a realization of the same property, that is the same variable. When equation (5) is generalized, it permits the estimation of the location parameters of different items with different numbers of categories and the thresholds so estimated reflect the *different partitions of the same continuum.*

A symmetrical argument can be presented for a single person responding to two items, though it is a little more complex. Consider first two persons p and q responding to one item i with m_i categories. Then if the outcome space of all possible pairs of responses is partitioned into subspaces $S(x_{pi}, x_{qi}) = \{(x_{pi}, x_{qi}), (x_{qi}, x_{pi})\}$ of pairs of pairs for $x_{pi} \neq x_{qi}, x_{pi}, x_{qi} \in \{0, 1, 2, \ldots, m_i\}$, then it can be shown readily that:

$$\Pr\{(x_{pi}, x_{qi}) \mid S(x_{pi}, x_{qi})\} = \frac{1}{\gamma_{pqi}} \exp\{x_{pi}\beta_p + x_{qi}\beta_q\}, \tag{6}$$

where $\qquad \gamma_{pqi} = \exp\{x_{pi}\beta_p + x_{qi}\beta_q\} + \exp\{x_q\beta_p + x_{pi}\beta_q\},$

which is independent of the parameters of item i. If the two people respond to other items with their values m_i different from the first item, that is with different numbers of thresholds and therefore different partitions of the continuum, then a likelihood equation may be written for the estimate of the person parameters, the solution equation for which is given by:

$$\sum_{i,x_{pi} \in \{S(x_{pi}, x_{qi})\}} - \sum_{i,x_{pi} \in \{S(x_{pi}, x_{qi})\}} \Pr\{(x_{pi}, x_{qi}) \mid S(x_{pi}, x_{qi})\}, \qquad p = 1, \ldots, P.. \tag{7}$$

The equation can in principle be generalized to many people, although it usually is not because usually there are many more persons than items, and therefore alternate methods are used to estimate the person parameters. However, the key point from equation (7) is that it is not constrained by the value m_i of the different items; the only criterion is that the data conform to the model, and if they do, then location invariance is assured.

Explicit Distributions With Different Partitions of the Continuum

If location-invariance does hold in the Rasch model, which has been illustrated to be the case by the very construction of the model, then the focus on the argument of Jansen and Roskam must be on the joining assumption and their equating it with location-invariance. It has already been broached that with an increase in the number of categories an increase in the precision is expected, and that it is this increase in precision which changes the response distribution. To get an appreciation of this argument, two concrete examples are provided. In both examples, the two partitions involve one item with three thresholds, and the other with four. In the first example, the partition with four thresholds has three thresholds exactly the same as for the three threshold case, and one extra threshold that extends the coverage of the continuum. In the second example, the partition with four thresholds has the thresholds closer together than the partition with three thresholds, but spans the same range of the continuum. In each case the probability of the distribution of the responses for a specified location of the person are shown. Note that these probabilities are generated by equation (4), and so the distributions of the responses are exactly in accord with the model. The parameters in the examples are summarized in Table 14.1.

The distributions for these examples are shown in Table 14.2 and they are respectively displayed graphically in Figures 14.2 and 14.3. For the graphical displays, the probabilities of each value $x, x \in \{1, 2, .. m_i - 1\}$ is placed at the midpoint between the thresholds. To locate the extreme points for the probabilities of 0 and m_i, a conversion to the multiplicative metric was taken, the point located, and then reconverted to the additive metric. For example, consider the case of the first item in the first example in which the first threshold has the value -1.0, and the task is to locate the probability of 0 on the continuum. This has to be somewhere between $-\infty$ and -1.0 in the logarithmic metric. Because $\exp(-\infty) = 0$ and $\exp(-1.0) = 0.3679$, the mid point between 0 and 0.3679 is 0.1840, and reconverting back to the logarithmic gives $\log(0.1840) = -1.69$: this is the point at which the probability of 0 is displayed. It can be shown easily that this reasoning to find the point is always equivalent to substracting $\log(2)$ from the

Table 14.1. Parameters in the Construction of Distributions with Different Partitions of the Continuum

		Thresholds (τ)			
		1	2	3	4
Example 1	(a)	−1.00	−0.25	0.50	
	(b)	−1.00	−0.25	0.50	1.25
Example 2	(a)	−1.50	0.00	1.50	
	(b)	−1.50	−0.75	0.75	1.50

Table 14.2. Distributions of Responses with Different Thresholds for a Single Person Location $\beta = -0.50$

		Probabilities in Categories (χ)				
		0	1	2	3	4
Example 1	(a)	.227	.374	.292	.107	
	(b)	.223	.367	.286	.105	.018
Example 2	(a)	.179	.486	.295	.040	
	(b)	.120	.326	.418	.120	.016

first threshold. Analogously, to find the point for locating the probability of the complementary maximum response m_i, log(2) is added to the threshold m_i.

Construction of the Distributions

The construction of the distributions for the first example will now be shown in detail, with attention being paid especially to the features that affect the probability distribution and that destroy the joining assumption. Because the two examples permit a highlighting of differ-

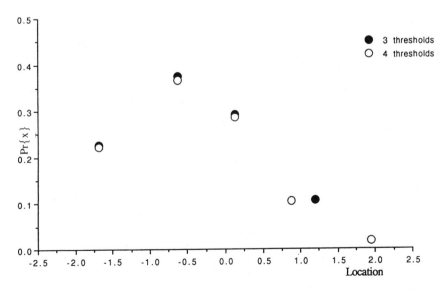

Figure 14.2. Distributions of responses with three and four thresholds where three thresholds are identical in the two sets and location = -0.5.

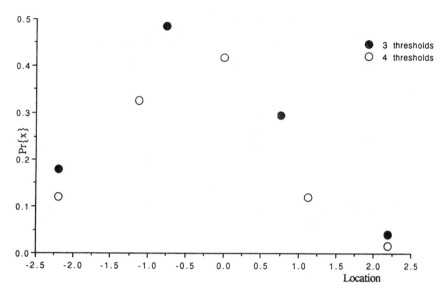

Figure 14.3.   Distributions of responses with three and four thresholds where the thresholds span the same range of the continuum and location = −0.5.

ent points, each is considered separately. In each case, only one person parameter is considered, $\beta_p = -0.5$.

Increasing the number of categories over a new region of the continuum

The equations for the build up of the probabilities are shown explicitly for the case of three thresholds of the first example. First, consider the dichotomous case: the two probabilities then take the form:

$$\text{Pr}\{0\} = \frac{1}{\gamma_{pi}} = \frac{1}{2.6487} = 0.3775$$

$$\text{Pr}\{1\} = \frac{1}{\gamma_{pi}} \exp[-\tau_1 + 1(\beta_p - \delta_i)] = \frac{1.6487}{2.6487} = 0.6225$$

where $\gamma_{pi} = 1 + \exp[-\tau_1 + 1\beta_p] = 1 + 1.6487 = 2.6487$ is simply the sum of the numerators which ensures that the sum of the probabilities is unity. If another category is added, that is, another thresholds is inserted that partitions the continuum, then the numerator of the probability of the first two categories remains the same, and the probability of a response in the third category is given by taking the numerator of the response in the second category and substracting the new threshold in the exponent and increasing the scoring of the coefficient of $(\beta_p - \delta_i)$ by 1. This gives:

$$\Pr\{0\} = \frac{1}{\gamma_{pi}} = \frac{1}{3.9327} = 0.2543$$

$$\Pr\{1\} = \frac{1}{\gamma_{pi}} \exp[-\tau_1 + 1\beta_p] = \frac{1.6487}{3.9327} = 0.4192$$

$$\Pr\{2\} = \frac{1}{\gamma_{pi}} \exp[-\tau_1 - \tau_2 + 2\beta_p] = \frac{1.2840}{3.9327} = 0.3265$$

where $\gamma_{pi} = 1 + \exp[-\tau_1 + 1\beta_p] + \exp[-\tau_1 - \tau_2 + 2\beta_p]$
$= 1 + 1.6487 \qquad\qquad + 1.2840 \qquad\qquad = 3.9327$

However, while the numerators relating to the first two categories have remained the same, it can be seen that the addition of the new category has changed the denominator, and therefore the probabilities of the first two categories have changed.

To add a fourth category, which implies another threshold, the numerators of the first three probabilities remains the same, and another term that involves simply subtracting another threshold in the exponent of the equation and increasing the coefficient of by 1 is included. This gives:

$$\Pr\{0\} = \frac{1}{\gamma_{pi}} = \frac{1}{4.4051} = 0.2270$$

$$\Pr\{1\} = \frac{1}{\gamma_{pi}} \exp\{[-\tau_1 + 1\beta_p] = \frac{1.6487}{4.4051} = 0.3742$$

$$\Pr\{2\} = \frac{1}{\gamma_{pi}} \exp\{[-\tau_1 - \tau_2 + 2\beta_p] = \frac{1.2840}{4.4051} = 0.2914$$

$$\Pr\{3\} = \frac{1}{\gamma_{pi}} \exp\{[-\tau_1 - \tau_2 - \tau_3 + 3\beta_p] = \frac{0.4724}{4.4051} = 0.1072$$

where

$$\gamma_{pi} = 1 + \exp[-\tau_1 + 1\beta_p] + \exp[-\tau_1 - \tau_2 + 2\beta_p] + \exp[-\tau_1 - \tau_2 - \tau_3 + 3\beta_p]$$

$$= 1 + 1.6487 + 1.2840 + 0.4724 = 4.4051.$$

Again, the denominator has a term corresponding to the numerator of the new category, and therefore, while the numerator of the equations for the first three categories does not change, the addition of an extra term changes the probabilities. This change in probabilities again accommodates the fact that the distribution involves four categories and not just three, and therefore each of the former categories in principle has its probability decreased.

As is evident from the above development, the sum of the probabilities of categories scored 2 and 3 is not the same as the probability of the category previously scored 2, nor is the sum of the probabilities of 0 and 1 the same as when there were only three categories. Given that the insertion of the extra category forces a redistribution of responses in all categories, this does not seem surprising. However, even with a change in the distribution by the addition of a threshold, if data were simulated according to the model for two items, one with three and one with four thresholds where the first two thresholds were the same, then by definition, in any estimation of the thresholds, they would be estimated to be the same for the first two thresholds in both the three and the four category items. Thus while the distribution changes, and the joining assumption is violated, the estimation of the thresholds, which partition the continuum, would not change. Thus the invariance of the partitioning is not related to the joining assumption. Further, if the locations of the persons were estimated, then the estimates of their locations would not be affected by the differences in the thresholds, only the precision of the estimates would be affected. Although the probabilities change as each new threshold is added, it is the *relative* probability of the original categories that remains invariant. For example if τ_1 remains the same, then $\Pr\{1\}/\Pr\{0\} = \exp\{[-\tau_1 + 1(\beta_p - \delta_i)]$, which is invariant no matter how many further categories are added. This leads to a closer analysis of the second example.

Increasing the number of categories over the same range of the continuum

In the second example, an extra category is added by adding an extra threshold within the same span of the continuum. As in the first example, the addition of the extra category changes the probabilities of responses in all categories, and in particular, notice that it reduces the probabilities of a response in the extreme categories. In fact, as the number of categories increases, so the proportion of responses in each category is reduced, and the distribution of these responses becomes narrower. This narrowing of the distribution reflects the increase in precision as the number of categories is increased. And it is this increase in precision that is incompatible with the joining assumption, but while it destroys the joining assumption, the different partionings of the continuum would not change the estimate of the location of the person parameters providing, of course, that the data conformed to the model.

To consolidate the effect of increasing precision by increasing the number of thresholds over the same continuum, Table 14.3 shows two further partitions of the same range of the continuum, with corresponding probabilities. Figure 14.4 shows the resultant distributions. Clearly, the effect identified above, the narrowing of the distribution with an increase in the number of categories, is manifested in these distributions.

Jansen and Roskam stress that they expect that the collapsing of categories, before the fact and after the fact, should not change the distribution. However, this would also imply that adding numbers of categories would not necessarily increase the precision. For example, it would imply that collecting data with units of 1 cm and then collapsing the categories into units of 2 cm would be the same as collecting the data in units of 2 centimeters in the first place. If this were the case, it would compromise the increase in precision in using 1 cm units rather than 2 cm units. Physicists know that the units in which they collect their data do make a difference to their information and that is why in order to get precision they construct more and more sensitive instruments that measure in smaller units. This example is elaborated in the last section.

Table 14.3. Further Partitions of the Continuum in Example 2 Showing Thresholds and Probabilities of Responses in Categories Partitioned by Them

No. of thresholds	Thresholds ($\beta = -0.5$.)					
	1	2	3	4	5	6
3	−1.50	0.0	1.50			
4	−1.50	−0.75	0.75	1.50		
5	−1.50	−.75	0.00	0.75	1.50	
6	−1.50	−.75	−0.25	0.25	0.75	1.50

	Probabilities in Categories (x)						
	0	1	2	3	4	5	6
3	.179	.486	.295	.040			
4	.120	.326	.418	.120	.016		
5	.010	.271	.349	.211	.061	.008	
6	.086	.234	.300	.234	.110	.032	.004

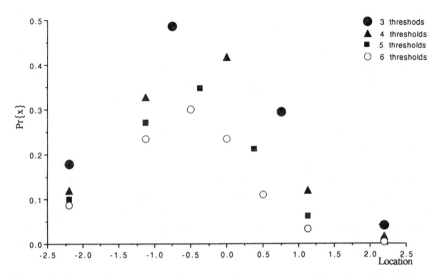

Figure 14.4.   Distribution of responses with three, four, five and six thresholds where the thresholds span the same range of the continuum and location = −0.5.

AN EMPIRICAL EXAMPLE

Jansen and Roskam's interpretation of the joining assumption gives the clear impression that they expect the original categories to remain fixed in some sense if extra categories are added.

> It would seem only reasonable that it does not matter whether the subject must choose his response from one set of graded responses or from another set of graded responses (both pertaining to the same response continuum). . . . In particular, this concerns response formats which differ only with respect to the quantifiers used to express degrees of, for example, acceptance, agreement, and the like. Exchanging one set of quantifiers in the response format for another set of quantifiers should be immaterial . . .
>
> For example, suppose we have four response categories:
> 'strongly agree,'   'mildly agree,'   'mildly disagree,'   'strongly disagree.'
>   If these were replaced by:
>   'agree,'   'mildly disagree,'   'strongly disagree'
> we would not expect that the subject's probability of choosing a 'disagree' response is not affected by joining the two "agreeing" categories into a single "agree" category. (Jansen and Roskam, 1986, p. 71)

It is accepted that it would be expected that exchanging quantifiers should not materially affect the location of the persons, but as indicated above, this is not equivalent to having the joining assumption hold. In addition, if the location of the categories changes in the presence of other categories, then this in itself would prevent the joining assumption from holding. However, from the perspective of the Rasch model, even the relative meaning of the categories does not have to be the same in the presence of other categories, the only requirement is that the data accord with the model. Juxtaposing Jansen and Roskam's joining assumption and the implication of the Rasch model in this regard leads to the following experiment, which is concerned with a different but related kind of joining assumption. It is a joining assumption at the level of the continuum. The central aspect of this experiment is that the relevant variable was operationalized abstractly, so that it was not changed substantively when more or fewer categories were used.

Data Collection

A class of 36 students in Social Research Methods at Murdoch University was asked to partition a finite length of a continuum into categories that reflected, in one case, three levels of achievement and in the other four levels. These are shown in Figures 14.5a and 14.5b respectively. It is evident that the levels form a hierarchy, with the fourth category in the 4-category set being a subset of the third category in the 3-category set. Thus the 3 levels in the 3-category set have explic-

---

Below is a line segment which represents a scale. Suppose you are to divide the line segment to represent levels of achievement in a unit in the study of English according to the following critria.

Fail: Has not achieved the objectives of the unit.

Pass: Has just achieved the objectives of the unit but **cannot proceed** to the next unit in the sequence of English studies.

Credit: Has achieved the objectives of the unit comfortably, and **can proceed** to the next unit in the sequence of English studies.

Place two lines on the segment to divide it into three regions, where each region represents one of these levels, with Fail on the left and Credit on the right. Put your two lines in between the points shown

Figure 14.5a.   Scaling levels of achievement

Below is a line segment which represents a scale. Suppose you are to divide the line segment to represent levels of achievement in a unit in the study of English according to the following critria.

Fail: Has not achieved the objectives of the unit.

Pass: Has just achieved the objectives of the unit but **cannot proceed** to the next unit in the sequence of English studies.

Credit: Has achieved the objectives of the unit comfortably, and **can proceed** to the next unit in the sequence of English studies.

Distinction: Has achieved the objectives of the unit with distinction, and **can proceed** to the next unit in th sequence.

Place three lines on the segment to divide it into four regions, where each region represents one of these levels, with Fail on the left and Distinction on the right. Put your three lines in between the points shown

Figure 14.5b. Scaling levels of achievement

itly different implications from each other, though the same implications in both sets, and the fourth category has the same implication as the third category, but the achievement is at a higher level. 19 of the students were given the 3-category set first, and 17 were given the 4-category first.

If the joining assumption held at the level of the continuum, it would be expected that the lengths of the continuum corresponding to each level would be the same under the two conditions, and that the addition of the fourth level would simply divide the third level in the 3-category set. Table 14.4 below shows the results. The length of each category was recorded to the nearest half unit shown on the line representing the continuum, and then doubled for convenience. No formal statistical tests have been carried out, and with the given sample sizes, they may prove to be statistically insignificant. However, it is evident that what changes there are in going from three to four levels, and the other way around, are in the expected direction of the probabilities of the Rasch model when adding successive categories. Thus even though the first two categories are identically defined operationally in the two sets, when the fourth category is present, their lengths are smaller than when the fourth category is not present—they have a different relative meaning in the two sets. It is inferred further that when the length is smaller, the probability of an entity being classified in it would be smaller, thus violating Jansen and Roskam's joining assumption.

Table 14.4.   Lengths of Line Segments Representing Each Level of Classification

	Fall	Pass	Credit	Distinction	
3 category first	15.63	12.63	19.74		19 cases
	14.68	9.10	13.00	11.21	
4 category first	15.71	14.47	17.23		17 cases
	13.71	12.82	12.64	8.23	
Total group	15.67	13.50	18.56		36 cases
	14.22	10.86	12.85	9.81	

SUMMARY AND DISCUSSION

It is common in the social sciences to collect data in the form of graded responses, which is envisaged as the partitioning of a latent unidimensional continuum into contiguous intervals. One view seems to be that because the graded responses partition the continuum more or less arbitrarily, that the distribution of responses should be invariant under different partitions of the continuum. Jansen and Roskam (1986) articulate this view persuasively, and central to their argument is the so-called joining assumption, which states that the probability of the responses in two adjacent categories should be the same as the probability of the response in the one category if the two categories are combined. A significant corollary to the joining assumption is that it should be immaterial whether two adjacent categories are combined before the data are collected or after they are collected.

This argument and perspective is not consistent with the Rasch model for graded response categories that explicitly has the feature that if the data fit the model with one set of categories, then when the data are collapsed, they will not fit the model with the new set of categories. Jansen and Roskam therefore reject the Rasch model for graded response categories. However, the Rasch model is derived from the principle of invariance of location parameters of items with respect to persons and vice versa, and therefore it seems necessary to understand why it has the property that the adjacent categories cannot be collapsed after the data are collected.

This chapter shows that the reason that the categories cannot be so collapsed is that the distribution of responses characterizes the precision of measurement, and that the precision of measurement is an integral part of the distribution. Thus with an increase in the number of categories, the distribution is changed—it is made narrower, reflecting the increase in precision. Although the probabilities of the responses in all categories change as each new category is added, if the original thresholds defining the categories are the same when another category is added, then the relative probabilities of the original categories remain the same.

It seems that the persistence of the view that the joining assumption should hold arises from a confusion between the invariance of the continuum, and the distribution of responses that pertain to the location of an object on the continuum in the presence of error. Although the continuum is invariant, the increase in precision in the location of a single object should provide a narrower distribution of the responses with respect to this single location.

A counter example might be useful: consider a continuum partitioned into units of a centimeter. Then, according to the joining assumption and its corollary that it should not matter whether the categories are collapsed before or after the data are collected, if one wanted to measure the length of some object to the nearest 1/1000th of centimeter, one could simply measure the object to the nearest centimeter and divide by 1000. This would clearly be unconvincing to physicists who spend a great deal of their time constructing instruments to increase the precision of their measurements. It does make a difference to the precision of the location of the object whether the measurements are made in smaller or larger units, and with smaller units, the error distribution should be narrower—otherwise there would be no increase in precision. The Rasch model for ordered response categories characterizes this change in distribution as a function of the change in the number of categories, from which it follows that neither the joining assumption nor its corollary can hold.

The conclusion therefore is that the process of data collection, including the number of categories, is an integral part of the data including their precision. Although the joining assumption cannot hold in the presence of adding or collapsing categories after the fact, it is possible to add categories before the data are collected. As categories are added, the relative meaning of the original categories may even change, so that their location on the continuum changes relative to each other; that is, the length on the continuum that they represent may become narrower. However, even in the presence of this possible change, if the data fit the model, then the *locations* of the persons will be invariant under the two sets of categories. Thus in this sense the Rasch model provides a greater flexibility regarding the distributions than does any model which satisfies the joining assumption. The argument presented here regarding the implications of the Rasch model was directed toward an empirical example, with some concrete illustrations to show the mutual effects of numbers of categories on locations of thresholds and probabilities. A more theoretical analysis can be found in Andrich (1995) and Roskam (1995).

REFERENCES

Andersen, E.B. (1972). The numerical solution of a set of conditional estimation equations. *Journal of the Royal Statistical Society* (Series B), *34* (1), 42–54.

Andersen, E.B. (1977) Sufficient statistics and latent trait models. *Psychometrika, 42,* 69–81.

Andrich, D. (1978). A rating formulation for ordered response categories. *Psychometrika, 43,* 357–374.

Andrich, D. (1995). Models for measurement, precision, and the nondichotomization of graded responses. *Psychometrika, 60,* 7–26.

Fischer, G. (1977) Some probabilistic models for the description of attitudinal and behavioral changes under the influence of mass communication. In W.F. & R. Repp (Eds.), *Mathematical models for social psychology* (pp. 102–151). Berne: Huber.

Jansen, P.G.W. & Roskam, E.E. (1986) Latent trait models and dichotomization of graded responses. *Psychometrika, 51 (1),* 69–91.

Perline, R., Wright, B.D. & Wainer, H. (1979). The Rasch model as additive conjoint measurement. *Applied Psychological Measurement, 3,* 237–256.

Rasch, G. (1960/80). *Probabilistic models for some intelligence and attainment tests.* (Copenhagen, Danish Institute for Educational Research), expanded edition (1980) with foreword and afterword by B.D. Wright. Chicago: The University of Chicago Press.

Rasch, G. (1961). On general laws and the meaning of measurement in psychology. In J. Neyman (Ed.) *Proceedings of the Fourth Berkeley Symposium on Mathematical Statistics and Probability. IV,* 321–334. Berkeley, CA: University of California Press.

Rasch, G. (1977) On specific objectivity: an attempt at formalizing the request for generality and validity of scientific statements. *Danish Yearbook of Philosophy 14,* 58–94.

Roskam, E.E. (1995). Graded responses and joining categories: A rejoinder to Andrich "Models for measurement, precision, and nondichotomization of graded responses." *Psychometrika, 60,* 27–35.

Thurstone, L.L. (1927) A law of comparative judgment. *Psychological Review, 34,* 278–286.

Wright, B.D. (1985). Additivity in Psychological Measurement. In E.E. Roskam (Ed.) *Measurement and Personality Assessment.* Selected papers, XXIII International Congress of Psychology, Volume 8, 101–111.

Wright, B.D. & Masters, G.N. (1982). *Rating Scale Analysis.* Chicago: MESA.

chapter 15

Item Component Equating

Richard M. Smith
Rehabilitation Foundation Inc.
Marianjoy Rehabilitation Hospital and Clinics

In recent years, the body of literature pertaining to research in the area of test equating has grown substantially. This literature reflects a variety of theoretical frameworks underlying the process of test equating, as well as the accompanying practical considerations involved in the actual equating of test forms. One theoretical framework that can be used for test equating is the Rasch model (Choppin, 1968; Rasch, 1960/1980; Wright and Bell, 1984; and Wright and Stone, 1979).

In the dichotomous Rasch model, the probability of a correct response to an item is given by the equation:

$$P\{x_{ni} = 1|\beta_n, \delta_i\} = [\exp(\beta_n - \delta_i)]/[1 + \exp(\beta_n - \delta_i)], \tag{1}$$

where β_n is the ability parameter for person n and δ_i is the difficulty parameter for item i (Wright and Stone, 1979). Under the condition that the data fit the model, the estimated logit item difficulties are freed from the distribution of the ability parameter in the sample of persons. However, in the item calibration process there is an indeterminacy in the logit metric. In most Rasch calibration programs, this is removed by setting the local origin equal to the average item difficulty. Calibrations of the same item set based on different samples will have the same local origin. Calibrations of different item sets will have different origins even if they are administered to the same sample of persons.

Traditional methods of test equating with the Rasch model have used common (linking) items or persons to place items from different tests and different calibrations onto a common metric (Choppin, 1968; Wright and Bell, 1984; and Wright and Stone, 1979). Recent developments in Rasch calibration programs (Wright, Linacre, and Schulz, 1989; Wright and Linacre, 1991) make it possible to exclude unadministered items from the unconditional (UCON) estimation procedure and allow the simultaneous calibration of multiple forms with common items on a common metric. This can also be accomplished with marginal maximum likelihood estimation (Adams and Wilson, in press). The pairwise estimation procedure developed by Choppin (1968) can also be used to provide a common origin, however, this procedure lacks asymptotic standard errors for the item difficulty estimates. However, estimates of the item difficulty standard errors can be obtained by using the pairwise item difficulties in a UCON procedure (Wright and Stone, 1979). Computer programs using the pairwise procedure are not commonly available in the United States.

Test equating using common items within the Rasch model is based on the distribution-free property of the item difficulty estimation. The only difference between two administrations of an item on different test forms should be the local origin (sum of the item difficulties set to zero), which must be specified in order to remove the indeterminacy of the logit scale in any calibration. The effect of the difference in local origins is removed by calculating the difference in difficulties between the common items from two or more forms. A weighted or unweighted average of the difference may be used as the link or shift-constant necessary to place the items on a common metric. This may be accomplished with a single item; however, most authors (Wright and Stone, 1979; Wright and Masters, 1982; Wright and Bell, 1984) recommend from 5 to 15 items to form the links. The larger the number of items, the less likely it is that local measurement disturbances and estimation error will affect the link constant.

The quality of the item pairs (common items) that comprise the link constant can be evaluated individually using a t-statistic based on the difference between the estimates of the item difficulties and the standard errors of estimate for these difficulties. Item pairs with significantly different item calibrations can be removed to improve the quality of the link constant. This allows a means of quality control that is not available if the simultaneous calibration and linking approach, using the missing data feature, is employed, although different item difficulty estimates for the same item appearing on different forms may be detected by the item fit statistics. Smith (1994) has shown that the total item fit statistics lack power in this situation.

Test equating using common persons requires that a set of common persons take two forms of an examination. In this method, the two test forms are not required to contain common items (Wright and Stone, 1979; Wright and Masters, 1982; Smith, 1992). When the two forms are calibrated separately, the differences in the mean ability of the person-measures for the persons taking both forms can be used as the difference in the local origins for the tests resulting from differences in the distribution of item difficulties on the two forms. The two tests can also be combined into a single calibration of the entire set of items.

In the common person separate calibration approach, a t-statistic can be used to determine if the person ability estimates are statistically equivalent. It is possible to exclude persons who have statistically different ability estimates from the linking process, just as misfitting item pairs are deleted in the common item-linking approach. This method of quality control over person performance on the two separate occasions is not easily available in the single calibration approach. Although a between fit statistic could be used to detect and delete these persons, this statistic is not commonly available in calibration programs. However, the between fit statistic is available in a Rasch item analysis program, IPARM (Smith, 1991).

The single calibration approach utilizes the missing data feature of recent Rasch calibration programs to estimate the difficulties directly from the total data matrix, treating unadministered items as missing data. However, this procedure also requires either common persons, common items, or assumptions about the ability distributions in the samples taking the different forms. None of the methods discussed above will allow the equating of test forms that lack either common items or persons without making assumptions about the distributions of person abilities.

The common component difficulty approach proposed in this paper is an outgrowth of Fischer's linear logistic test model (LLTM) (Fischer, 1973). In this model, the difficulties of the items are of secondary interest to the difficulties of the components that make up the items. Fischer estimates the component difficulties directly from the data and the item difficulties are then constructed from the component difficulties according to the presence or absence of the component in the item. This method confuses the issue of the fit of the data to the model with the misspecification of the underlying components.

Further work on this model (Green and Smith, 1987) compared the results of LLTM with a regression approach that used the item difficulties estimated with the dichotomous Rasch model and component frequencies to estimate the component difficulties. This method allows the separation of the fit of the data to the model from the fit of the specification of the components to the item difficulties. Using a variety of item fit statistics (Smith, 1991) available within the framework of the Rasch model, it is possible to identify and eliminate misfitting items from regression analysis.

Since the same set of components are generally specified for two different forms of a test, though not necessarily represented in the same frequency or combination for mutually exclusive sets of items, it should be possible to use the common components as a means of removing the local origin differences that would result from separately calibrating two test forms lacking either common items or common persons. This difference can be estimated by differences in the constant in the regression equations produced by regressing the estimated item difficulties on the component frequencies for each item.

INSTRUMENT

The tests used in this study were experimental forms of a paper-folding test. These items are designed to measure perceptual ability, more specifically the ability to manipulate objects mentally in a three-dimensional space. A total of 45 paper-folding items were designed according to a structural model developed from the component analysis of an earlier set of paper folding items (Smith, Kramer, and Kubiak, 1992; Smith and Kramer, 1992).

Ten item components were used in the study (e.g., position of hole, vertical fold, symmetrical fold, etc.). A definition of each component and the number of occurrences of each in the item set are found in Table 15.1. Figure 15.1 contains a diagram of each component and Figure 15.2 contains an example of a paper-folding item.

Table 15.1. Definition of Item Components

Variable	Definition	Number of Occurrences
1	Position of hole: other (POH)	23
2	Vertical symmetric fold (VS)	8
3	Horizontal symmetric fold (HS)	7
4	Diagonal symmetric fold (DS)	11
5	Vertical asymmetric visible fold (VAV)	11
6	Horizontal asymmetric visible fold (HAV)	12
7	Diagonal asymmetric visible fold (DAV)	15
8	Vertical asymmetric hidden fold (VAH)	5
9	Horizontal asymmetric hidden fold (HAH)	10
10	Diagonal asymmetric hidden fold (DAH)	11

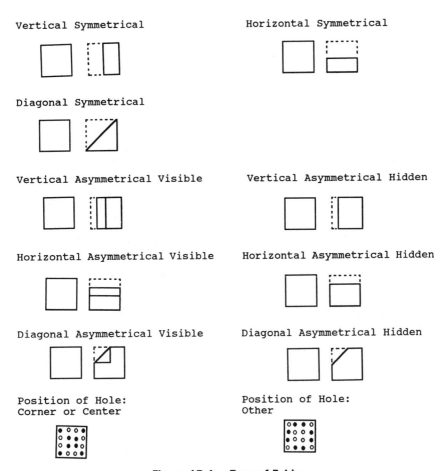

Figure 15.1. Type of Folds

The 45 items were arranged into eight tests. Six of the tests were of approximately equal difficulty containing eight easy items and seven difficult items each, for a total of 15 items each. The six forms were sequentially linked, sharing either the easy or hard item set with the adjacent form. This form structure is shown in Figure 15.3. Of these six forms, three share no common item. These three forms, Forms 1, 3, and 5, will be used in the simulated data analysis. The entire set of six linked forms will be used in the real data analysis.

Each of the three easy and hard subtests was balanced so as to have approximately the same distribution of item components. The last two tests were an easy form composed of the entire set of 24 easy items and a hard form composed of the entire set of 21 difficult items. These two

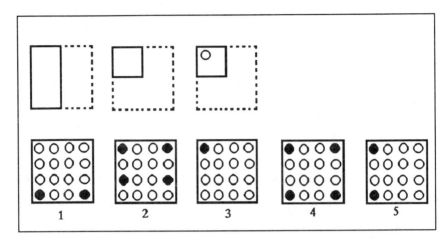

Figure 15.2.   Example of Paper-folding Item

forms had no common items and were used only in the simulated data analysis.

The theoretical difficulty of each item was calculated using regression weights estimated in an earlier study (Smith, Kramer and Kubiak, 1992). Thus, all 45 items had theoretical difficulties based on the combination of components present in each item.

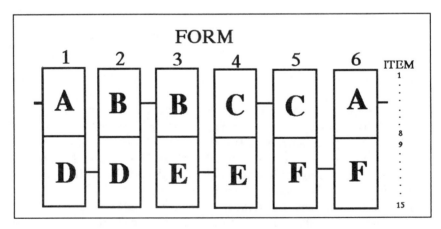

Figure 15.3.   Common Item Linking Structure

METHODS

Since the evaluation of the component equating method must be based on known item difficulties that share a common metric, simulated data and linked real data were used in this study. Each of the five tests in the simulated section was replicated three times with 2,000 persons simulated in each replication. The item difficulties used in the simulations were based on the generating component difficulties. There was a wide range of difficulties, ranging from −5.18 logits to 7.43 logits, and the mean of the item difficulty distribution was 0.11 logits. Thus, a comparison of generating to estimated item difficulties and component difficulties is possible. In each instance, a different distribution of normally distributed person abilities was used, subject to the constraint that the distributions have a mean of 0 and a standard deviation of 1. Using the simulated item responses, the item difficulties for each of three data sets for the five tests were estimated separately using BIGSCALE (Wright, Linacre, and Schulz, 1989).

The estimated item difficulties were then regressed on the component frequencies for each item on a test-by-test basis to recover the component difficulties. The results estimated from the simulated data were then compared to the generating values to determine the accuracy of the estimated values. In addition, the regression constant was used to estimate the link constant between the various forms.

The regression constant represents the difference between the mean of the independent variables, frequency counts in these data, and the dependent variable, item difficulties with a mean of 0.0 due to the calibration process. The difference between the regression constant for two sets of items represents an estimate of the link constant for those two sets of items. The regression constants will always be negative. The difference between the two regression constants is opposite in sign to the difference between the mean item difficulties. To place the two sets of items on a scale defined by the first set of items, the difference in the regression weights must be added to the item difficulties from the second test.

Since the generating item difficulties on a common metric were known in the simulated data analyses, the differences in local origins for separately calibrated subsets of items can be calculated. The differences in the generating item sets were used to evaluate the regression constant as an estimator of differences in local origins.

For the three 15-item tests with similar, though not equal, distributions of item difficulties, a situation much like that found in constructing roughly parallel forms of an examination, there are three equating possibilities, Form 1 with Form 3, Form 1 with Form 5, and Form 3 with Form 5. For the 24-item easy test and 21-item hard test, similar to the situation that might be encountered in vertical equating, there was only one possible equating, Form 7 with Form 8. The other comparisons would involve tests that share common items and were not investigated in the simulated data part of this study.

In the real data section of this study, the item difficulties for each of the six forms were estimated separately using BIGSTEPS (Wright and Linacre, 1991). Forms 1 to 6 were spiraled and administered to 2,750 examinees as an experimental section of a perceptual abilities test. The estimated item difficulties were used in estimating the unweighted link constants between the six forms. The estimated item difficulties were also regressed on the component frequencies for each item to estimate the component difficulties. The regression constants were used to estimate the equating constant between the various forms. The common item equating constants obtained from the real data were used to evaluate the regression constant as an estimator of differences in local origins.

RESULTS

Table 15.2 lists the generating component difficulties and those recovered from the simulated data for the five tests discussed above, aver-

Table 15.2. Generating and Estimated Component Difficulties

| Component | Generating Difficulty | Estimated Difficulty* | | | | |
		Form 1	Form 3	Form 5	Form 7	Form 8
01	1.63	1.47	1.72	1.65	1.61	1.46
02	1.63	1.61	2.00	1.91	1.48	1.61
03	1.33	1.02	0.88	1.61	1.11	1.50
04	1.96	1.65	1.99	2.34	1.41	2.12
05	0.20	0.18	0.07	0.47	0.00	0.13
06	2.24	2.41	2.07	2.29	2.11	2.13
07	1.41	1.40	1.41	1.58	1.26	1.25
08	3.68	4.27	3.81	3.65	3.55	3.73
09	3.66	3.70	3.68	3.77	3.55	3.52
10	5.28	5.33	5.30	5.50	—	5.26
Constant	−5.38	−5.27	−5.37	−5.74	−2.80	−7.83
Corr. with Generating (Constant excluded)		.9994	.9985	.9985	.9975	.9959

* Averaged over three replications

aged over three replications. Although the standard errors of the estimated component difficulties are not shown, only one of the estimated component difficulties was more than two standard errors from the generating value (component 3 on Form 7). The component difficulty for component 10 on Form 7 could not be estimated because there were no easy items that contained this type of fold (diagonal asymmetric hidden). The correlations between the generating and estimated values are 0.99 or higher. The standard errors for the component difficulties ranged from .10 to .51 with approximately 2/3 of the values below .30. As a check on the data simulation program, the correlation between the generating and estimated item difficulties were also calculated. For the 15 simulations all values were 0.994 or higher.

The correlation and plots of the component difficulties from each of the four equating pairs are shown in Figure 15.4. The correlation

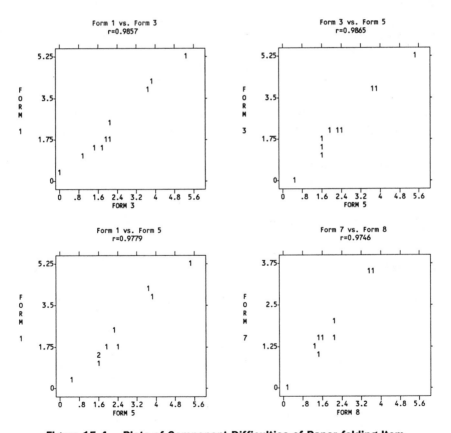

Figure 15.4.   Plots of Component Difficulties of Paper-folding Item

between the two sets of estimated item component difficulties was 0.97 or higher, indicating that the estimation of the components was very stable over the different equating pairs. For each of the four pairs of tests, a t-test was used to evaluate whether the estimated component difficulties were within two standard errors of each other. Only one of the 39 pairs tested (component 4 on the Form 7–8 equating pair) had a t-value indicating significance at $\alpha = 0.05$.

The regression constants, averaged over the three replications, for the five tests are estimates of the differences in the local origins of the five forms introduced by the indeterminacy in the estimation when the tests are calibrated separately. The standard errors of the constants, as shown in Table 15.3, ranged from .11 to .55, with 8 of the 15 standard errors below .20.

Differences between the regression constants estimate the link constant used in common item or common person equating for any pair of forms. In this case, differences between the regression constant across linked forms fell within two standard errors of the differences in the average generating item difficulties for all of the three replications and the mean of the replications in each of the four equating pairs described above. The regression constant for each equating pair, averaged over the three replications, and the differences in the generating values, are shown in Table 15.4.

The next section contains the details of the analysis of the real data responses to Forms 1 to 6. Recall that these data were administered to 2,750 examinees and as a result there were approximately 460 examinees per form (See Table 15.8 for the exact counts per form). This

Table 15.3. Generating and Estimated Regression Constants

	Form Number				
Replication	**1**	**3**	**5**	**7**	**8**
1	−5.39	−5.29	−5.86	−2.75	−7.96
	(.51)*	(.31)	(.19)	(.14)	(.39)
2	−5.06	−5.44	−5.65	−2.86	−7.58
	(.33)	(.36)	(.11)	(.19)	(.14)
3	−5.35	−5.37	−5.71	−2.78	−7.96
	(.55)	(.40)	(.12)	(.14)	(.11)
Mean	−5.27	−5.37	−5.74	−2.80	−7.83
	(.46)	(.36)	(.14)	(.16)	(.21)

* Standard error of estimate

Table 15.4.   Generating and Estimated Link Constants

Equating Pair	Generating	Sim 1	Sim 2	Sim 3	Mean	SE
1–3	−.369	−0.10	0.38	0.02	0.10	0.58
1–5	−.223	0.47	0.59	0.36	0.47	0.48
3–5	.146	0.57	0.21	0.34	0.37	0.39
7–8	4.951	5.21	4.72	5.18	5.03	0.26

number is less than one-fourth the sample size used in the simulations previously reported.

The results of the common item linking are shown in Table 15.5 and graphically displayed in Figure 15.5. These link constants result in a calibrated item bank with difficulties similar to those obtained from the common calibration of the 45-item set utilizing the missing data feature in BIGSCALE reported in Smith and Kramer (1992). These link constants were used to calculate the form difficulty translations reported in Table 15.7. The sum of the six link constants is expected to be 0.0, in this case the sum is −0.16. This value is within two standard errors of the expected value (Wright and Bell, 1984). To illustrate the fit of the items to the link constants, the plots of the linked item difficulties (LID) and the separate calibration item difficulties (SCID) for the six forms are shown in Figure 15.6. As these plots illustrate, with items relatively close to the offset unit slope line, there were few items that misfit the link constant. This fit can be determined with a t-test or by drawing the 95% confidence bands around the offset unit slope line.

The component difficulty estimates (the unstandardized regression weights derived from regressing the item difficulties on the component frequencies) for the six separate forms are found in Table 15.6. Even though these six forms contain common items that were used in

Table 15.5.   Common Item Link Constants

Link	Constant	S.E.
Form 1 to Form 2	−0.12	0.07
Form 2 to Form 3	0.21	0.07
Form 3 to Form 4	0.36	0.07
Form 4 to Form 5	−0.06	0.06
Form 5 to Form 6	−0.48	0.09
Form 6 to Form 1	−0.07	0.07

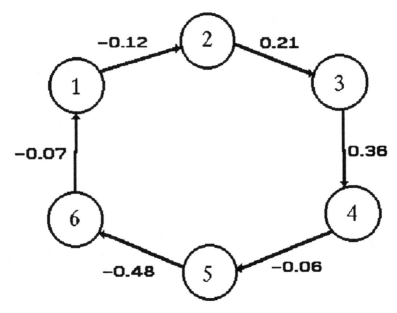

Figure 15.5. Common Item Form Equating Constants

the common item equating, this does not effect the common component equating procedure. The final column of Table 15.6 represents the regression weights for the entire data 45-item data set using the common-item-equated item difficulties as the dependent variable in the regression.

There are several features of these results that must be noted. First, there is great variability in the component estimates across the six forms, and in one case a component is unrepresented on Form 6. For the six forms, the degrees of freedom (df = 14) is very close to the number of independent variables. Earlier research indicated that there is a moderate degree of colinearity between the independent frequency variables. The results based on simulated data presented in Table 15.2 showed less variation. Second, there is large variation in the estimated regression constant, which was not observed in the simulated data. Third, the standard errors of the regression constants are considerably larger than those observed in the simulated data. Only the standard error for Form 4 approximates that found in the simulated data. The extent to which these results are due to sample size (2,000 for the simulated data and approximately 460 for the real data) can not be determined from these analyses.

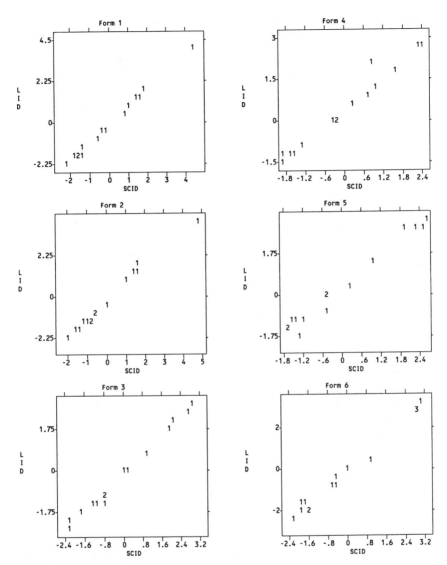

Figure 15.6.   Item Difficulty Plots Linked vs. Separate Calibration Difficulties

Table 15.7 contains the estimated form link constants for the real data based on the common item and common component linking approaches. For the common component approach, the number in parentheses represents the difference between the regression constant for Form 1 (arbitrarily chosen as the origin) and the other five forms. In

Table 15.6. Estimated Item Component Difficulties

Component		1	2	3	4	5	6	Total Item Set
1	POH	0.76	1.15	0.39	−0.03	0.64	−0.01	0.25
2	VS	0.92	0.45	0.27	1.00	0.71	0.93	0.55
3	HS	0.38	2.10	3.30	1.13	−0.03	−0.83	0.43
4	DS	1.73	2.34	3.23	1.14	1.71	1.94	1.52
5	VAV	1.30	1.71	2.80	1.54	1.47	0.52	1.06
6	HAV	0.29	0.92	2.32	0.78	0.48	0.44	1.79
7	DAV	1.46	1.76	2.02	0.78	0.42	0.87	0.57
8	VAH	0.82	−0.27	0.86	2.22	1.93	—	1.81
9	HAH	2.76	1.95	1.47	2.12	1.95	2.85	1.79
10	DAH	2.79	3.07	3.14	1.76	1.75	2.26	2.65
Constant		−3.21	−4.01	−4.70	−2.71	−2.49	−2.50	−2.56
S.E.		0.77	1.51	1.26	0.33	0.78	1.00	0.43
R Square		0.98	0.90	0.94	0.99	0.93	0.95	0.85

addition the mean of the replications of the three corresponding regression constants using simulated data and reported in Table 15.2 are repeated. Based on the unweighted link constants, the maximum difference in origins between the forms is approximately 0.67 logits (between Forms 2 and 5). Based on the regression constants, the maximum difference is 1.99 logits (between Forms 3 and 4). The standard errors for the regression constants range from 0.33 to 1.51. Given the size of these standard errors, all of the differences between the constants are within ±1 standard error of the values suggested by the common item equating. Unfortunately, except for Form 4, which has a

Table 15.7. Estimated Form Difficulty

	Equating Method			
	Real Data			Simulated Data
Form	Common Item	(Links)	Common Component	Common Component
Form 1	0.00		−3.21 (0.00)	−5.27 (0.00)
Form 2	−0.12	(1–2)	−4.01 (−0.80)	
Form 3	0.09	(1–2, 2–3)	−4.70 (−1.49)	−5.37 (−0.10)
Form 4	0.45	(1–2, 2–3, 3–4)	−2.71 (0.50)	
Form 5	0.55	(6–1, 5–6)	−2.49 (0.72)	−5.74 (−0.47)
Form 6	0.07	(6–1)	−2.50 (0.71)	

standard error of 0.33, the standard errors of the estimates appear to be too large to be practically useful.

The use of actual rather than simulated responses clearly has a marked effect on the stability of the estimates. In an attempt to investigate the reason for this instability, the actual linked item difficulties

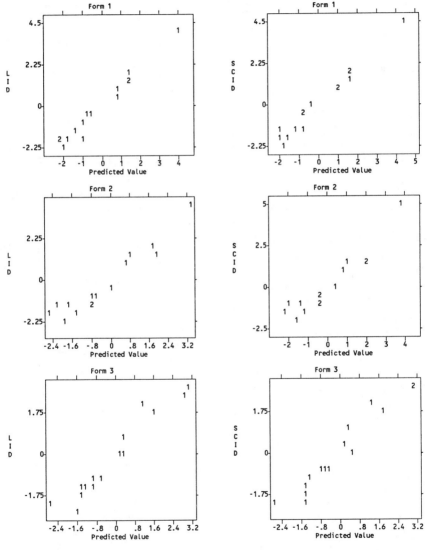

Figure 15.7a.   Item Difficulty Plots Separate Calibration vs. Regression Predicted

(LID) and separate calibration item difficulties (SCID) were plotted against the item difficulty values predicted from the regression equation using those two sets of item difficulties as dependent values. These plots are shown in Figures 15.7a and 15.7b. Each row of plots represents a single form. The plot on the left shows the linked item

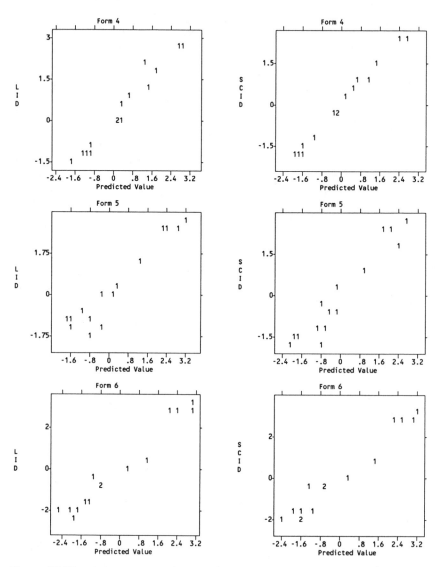

Figure 15.7b. Item Difficulty Plots Separate Calibration vs. Regression Predicted

difficulty. The plot on the right shows the separate calibration item difficulty. The slopes of the pairs of plots for each form are quite similar.

Since one possible source of error in the use of real data was the lack of fit of certain persons to the model, two editing strategies were developed and tested to determine if the person misfit was contributing to the size of the error in the regression weights. In the first procedure the response patterns were edited for patterns that would indicate guessing, such as a string of similar responses at the end of the response record, or a repeating pattern of responses at the end of the record. This procedure resulted in the deletion of approximately 15% in each of the samples. In the second procedure all persons with a raw score of five or less were deleted without regard to the pattern of responses. This procedure resulted in approximately 15% of the samples being deleted.

The analysis was rerun with these two revised sets of data. The results indicated that the editing process served only to increase the range of the observed constants estimated for the six forms. The estimation of some of the generating parameters improved while others were less accurately estimated. Thus removal of the misfitting response patterns or low scores had no systematic effect on the results.

To further illustrate the problem of the instability of the regression constant, the linked item difficulties, which have had the effect of the different local origins removed, were regressed on the component difficulties. The results are presented in Table 15.8 along with the link constants and the unedited unlinked regression results from Table 15.7. In the linked columns, the first represents the regression weight.

Table 15.8.   Estimated Form Difficulty

		Equating Method				
		Common Component				
		Unedited Unlinked		Unedited Linked		
Form	Common Item	Reg. W.	Link	Reg. W.	Link	S.E.
Form 1	0.00	−3.21	(0.00)	−3.44	(0.00)	0.74
Form 2	−0.12	−4.01	(−0.80)	−4.21	(−0.77)	1.35
Form 3	0.09	−4.70	(−1.49)	−4.30	(−0.86)	1.43
Form 4	0.45	−2.71	(0.50)	−2.38	(1.06)	0.60
Form 5	0.55	−2.49	(0.72)	−1.95	(1.49)	0.81
Form 6	0.07	−2.50	(0.71)	−2.77	(0.67)	1.00

The second column, in parentheses, is the difference between the regression weight for that form and the first form, which was arbitrarily chosen as the origin of the metric. Since the effect of the local origin has already been removed, these values should be within ±2 standard errors of 0.0. Given the standard errors shown in the third column all of these values are within that range. Thus, the estimated regression constants are not significantly different from zero. However, they show considerable variability when compared to the common item equating constants.

CONCLUSIONS

The preliminary results based on simulated data suggest that common component equating is possible. However, the standard errors of the regression weights are somewhat larger than the standard errors attached to common item link constants in these simulations. In the case where there are no common items or persons across tests, as is often the case in published standardized tests, this procedure is a possible alternative. The limiting factor is the identification of item components that account for significant proportions of the variance of the item difficulties, no small task in most tests.

As this study was somewhat limited in the number of items and the number of components used in equating, there is a need for further study to determine how many items or components are needed for stable results. In the simulated data the linking of Forms 7 and 8 (24 and 21 items) appear more stable than those based on Forms 1, 3, and 5 (15 items each).

In the real data analyses, the decreased sample size (460 vs. 2,000) appears to have had a significant effect. Editing for misfitting data does not appear to improve significantly the estimates. Statistically, the procedures appear to work as most of the estimated link constants were within ±2 standard errors of the expected values. However, the large standard errors make the procedures impractical for sample sizes in this range. More simulation studies are necessary to determine whether the large standard errors are due to the small sample size, or whether they conceal other problems.

In summary, this study details a method of creating a common metric for items from test forms that do not share a common set of items or persons through the use of the component difficulties that underlie the items. This can be important in synthesis research that seeks to combine the results of different samples taking different tests. Of particular importance would be the possibility of placing items from various standardized tests covering the same subject—such as reading, vocabulary or mathematics—on the same metric, based on the norming data, without having to administer the different tests to the same individuals. The utility of this technique depends on the ability to identify item components that account for a large portion of the variance in the difficulty of the items. This is a new area of research in measurement. Further study is needed before practical applications can be made, but the potential benefits are considerable.

REFERENCES

Adams, R. and Wilson, M. (1996). Formulating the Rasch model as a mixed coefficients multinomial logit. In G. Engelhard, Jr. and M. Wilson (Eds.). *Objective Measurement: Theory into Practice, Volume 3*. Norwood, NJ: Ablex.

Choppin, B. (1968). An item bank using sample-free calibration. *Nature, 219,* 870–872.

Fischer, G.H. (1973). The linear logistic test model as an instrument in educational research. *Acta Psychologica, 37,* 359–374.

Green, K.E. and Smith, R.M. (1987). A comparison of two methods of decomposing item difficulties. *Journal of Educational Statistics, 12,* 369–381.

Rasch, G. (1960, 1980). *Probabilistic models for some intelligence and attainment tests*. Copenhagen: Danish Institute for Educational Research, 1960. (Expanded edition, Chicago: The University of Chicago Press, 1980.)

Smith, R.M. (1991). *IPARM: Item and person analysis with the Rasch model*. Chicago: MESA Press.

Smith, R.M. (1992). *Applications of Rasch Measurement*. Chicago: MESA Press.

Smith, R.M. (1994). A comparison of the power of Rasch total and between fit statistics to detect measurement disturbances. *Educational and Psychological Measurement, 42–55.*

Smith, R.M. and Kramer, G.A. (1992). A comparison of two methods of test equating in the Rasch model. *Educational and Psychological Measurement, 52,* 835–846.

Smith, R.M., Kramer, G.A., and Kubiak, A.T. (1992). A confirmatory analysis of factors influencing the difficulty of paper-folding items. A paper presented at the Annual Meeting of the American Educational Research Association, San Francisco.

Wright, B.D. and Bell, S.R. (1984). Item banks: What, why, how. *Journal of Educational Measurement, 21,* 331–345.

Wright, B.D. and Linacre, J.M. (1991). BIGSTEPS: Rasch analysis for all two-facet models. Chicago: MESA Press.

Wright, B.D., Linacre, J.M., and Schulz, M.E. (1989). BIGSCALE: A Rasch program for rating scale analysis. Chicago: MESA Press.

Wright, B.D. and Masters, G.N. (1982). *Rating scale analysis*. Chicago: MESA Press.

Wright, B.D. and Stone, M.H. (1979). *Best test design*. Chicago: MESA Press.

chapter **16**

A Multidimensional Scaling, Paired Comparisons Approach to Assessing Unidimensionality in the Rasch Model

Tsuey-Hwa Chen
American Guidance Service

Mark L. Davison
University of Minnesota

The notion of an unobservable latent attribute, or trait, underlying a set of items forming an instrument is a critical one in the psychometric literature. This is because the assumption of unidimensionality not only makes applications of psychological measurement in describing individual differences more sensible, but it also provides the basis for development of many mathematical measurement models. For instance, the calibration techniques of the most widely used item response theory (IRT) models to date depend, to a large extent, on the evidence of one single underlying latent ability among the set of items.

A wide array of indices for assessing the unidimensionality assumption, each developed under different conceptual and theoretical frameworks, have been proposed. Hattie (1985) reviewed a total of over 30 such indices. Among these indices, there are many that lack adequate theoretical rationale, proper decision criteria or both for determining the existence of one underlying latent attribute.

The recent upsurge of interest in IRT highlights the importance of the dimensionality issue. Although not to be confused with the assumption of unidimensionality, the principle of local independence, which leads to the mathematical formulation of the IRT models, underlines the importance of identifying dimensionality. Lord (1980), for instance, emphasized the need for an index of unidimensionality; Hambleton, Swaminathan, Cook, Eignor, and Gifford (1978) argued that the unidimensionality assumption should be addressed before other goodness-of-fit tests take place.

Using a combination of item parameters in the model (i.e., difficulty, discrimination and guessing), various IRT-based methodologies for assessing unidimensionality have been proposed. Among the most commonly used techniques are the chi-square based fit measures for the one-parameter logistic model (i.e., the Rasch model), such as the mean-squared residual statistic (Mead 1976a, 1976b; Wright, Mead & Draba, 1976; Wright & Panchapakesan, 1969; Martin-Löf's T statistic (1973, discussed in Gustafsson, 1980); the van den Wollenberg Q1 statistic (1982); and measures based on the t-distribution, such as total-t and between-t statistics for items (Wright & Stone, 1979). Bock and Lieberman (1970) developed a procedure for estimating item parameters and assessing unidimensionality in the two-parameter model.

These methods are not without obstacles. The chi-square and t-statistic based indices have been criticized as lacking sound theoretical bases for their assumed sampling distributions, and for their sensitivity to sample size (Hattie, 1985). The Bock and Lieberman method, on the other hand, was found to be cumbersome. Other approaches are also available. Tucker and Lewis (1973) discussed a factor analysis (FA) based goodness-of-fit test for assessing the assumption of unidimensionality. Hulin, Drasgow and Parsons (1983) proposed a procedure that combined the IRT methods and factoring tetrachoric correlations for the two- and three-parameter IRT models. Finally, Stout (1987) suggested a theory-based nonparametric procedure to test the unidimensionality assumption. However, the efficacy of these methods for determining unidimensionality remains inconclusive in the literature (Hattie, 1985).

In summary, despite the well-documented importance of the assumption, there seem to be no satisfactory indices of unidimensionality. The purpose of this chapter is to propose a heuristic approach, in the context of the Rasch model and multidimensional scaling (MDS) theory, as an alternative to assessing the assumption of unidimensionality. The method utilizes a paired comparisons (PC) statistic derived from direct response data for dichotomous test items that satisfy the Rasch model. We begin by deriving the PC statistic for the Rasch model. Then an extension of a nonmetric MDS procedure to the analysis of the Rasch PC statistic is described. Application of the method in assessing unidimensionality in the Rasch model is explained, and its strengths and limitations are discussed. Finally, examples using real and simulated data are presented to illustrate the application of the procedure and examine its efficacy.

THE PAIRED COMPARISONS STATISTIC

Several authors (Andrich, 1978; Chen, 1991; Choppin, 1968; Davison & Chen, 1991; Rasch 1960; Wright & Masters, 1982) have described a pseudo pairwise comparisons statistic (here referred to as the "PC statistic") for analysis of dichotomously scored item pairs that satisfy the Rasch model. The term *pseudo* stems from the fact that the development is based on comparison of item pairs taken from direct response data. That is, unlike the classical choice models, the data collection strategy for the pseudo-PC experiment requires the subject to respond to each stimulus (item) directly without reference to other stimuli in the set. Our development of the PC statistic closely follows the earlier work and is presented only for completeness.

Let the discrete random variable a_{vj} take the value 1 when person v answers item j correctly and take the value 0 otherwise. Then according to the Rasch model

$$\pi\{a_{vj} = 1 \mid \theta_v, b_j\} = \frac{\exp(\theta_v - b_j)}{1 + \exp(\theta_v - b_j)}, \text{ and}$$

$$\pi\{a_{vj} = 0 \mid \theta_v, b_j\} = \frac{1}{1 + \exp(\theta_v - b_j)}, \tag{1}$$

where θ_v is the ability parameter for person v, and b_j is the difficulty parameter for item j.

Defined over item pairs, the PC statistic is a function of two joint probabilities, the probability that person v passes item j and fails item k, and the probability that person v fails item j and passes item k: $\pi\{a_{vj} = 1, a_{vk} = 0\}$ and $\pi\{a_{vj} = 0, a_{vk} = 1\}$. In terms of these two joint probabilities, the PC statistic is defined as:

$$\pi_{jk}(\theta_v) = \pi\{a_{vj} = 1, a_{vk} = 0 \mid a_{vj} + a_{vk} = 1, b_j, b_k, \theta_v\}$$

$$= \frac{\pi\{a_{vj} = 1, a_{vk} = 0 \mid b_j, b_k, \theta_v\}}{\pi\{a_{vj} = 1, a_{vk} = 0 \mid b_j, b_k, \theta_v\} + \pi\{a_{vj} = 0, a_{vk} = 1 \mid b_j, b_k, \theta_v\}}. \qquad (2)$$

In words, the PC statistic for item pair (j, k) is the probability that person v passes item j and fails item k, given that he or she passes only one item of the pair.

From the assumption of local independence in the Rasch model, these two joint probabilities have the following form:

$$\pi\{a_{vj} = 1, a_{vk} = 0 \mid b_j, b_k, \theta_v\} = \frac{\exp(\theta_v - b_j)}{[1 + \exp(\theta_v - b_j)][1 + \exp(\theta_v - b_k)]}, \text{ and}$$

$$\pi\{a_{vj} = 0, a_{vk} = 1 \mid b_j, b_k, \theta_v\} = \frac{\exp(\theta_v - b_k)}{[1 + \exp(\theta_v - b_j)][1 + \exp(\theta_v - b_k)]}. \qquad (3)$$

Inserting Equation 3 into the definition in Equation 2 yields

$$\pi_{jk} = \frac{\exp(b_k - b_j)}{1 + \exp(b_k - b_j)}, \text{ in which the dependence on } \theta_v \text{ is removed.} \qquad (4)$$

Readers familiar with the Bradley-Terry-Luce (BTL) model (Bradley & Terry, 1952; Luce, 1959) will recognize that the logistic function of π_{jk} in Equation 4 stands in the same relationship to item difficulties, b_k and b_j, as do the choice probabilities in the BTL model to the stimulus scale values. It is well known that, with a constant adjustment (1.7) for the arbitrary unit, this model yields virtually identical parameter estimates to Thurstone's Case V specialization of the law of comparative judgment for paired comparison responses (Andrich, 1978).

As can be seen from Equation 4, the person parameter θ_v is removed from the conditional probability π_{jk}. Therefore, the PC statistic depends only on the item difficulties, b_j and b_k, and is independent of the person ability parameters. It is thus a matter of irrelevance which set of individuals provide the data; subjects who score a total of 1 on an item pair contribute to the estimation of the PC statistic, regardless of their ability level. Consequently, a sample estimate of π_{jk}, say P_{jk}, can be computed by counting the number of subjects who passed item j but not k, and dividing that count by the number who passed exactly one of the two items.

Table 16.1 shows the PC statistics from a 10-item test. Each data point shows the proportion of students who passed the row item among

Table 16.1. Paired Comparisons Statistics for 10 Items

Item	1	2	3	4	5	6	7	8	9
2	0.039								
3	0.364	0.918							
4	0.029	0.469	0.022						
5	0.042	0.515	0.036	0.537					
6	0.119	0.839	0.244	0.904	0.865				
7	0.184	0.876	0.341	0.913	0.876	0.618			
8	0.750	1.000	0.864	1.000	0.990	0.955	0.897		
9	0.089	0.784	0.152	0.877	0.813	0.397	0.317	0.034	
10	0.052	0.756	0.115	0.844	0.803	0.333	0.273	0.016	0.415

the students who passed exactly one of the two items. For instance, the data point in row 1, column 1 equals .039, because 4 subjects passed item 2 but not item 1 and 103 subjects passed either item 1 or item 2 but not both. Hence $P_{jk} = 4/103 = .039$.

THE MULTIDIMENSIONAL SCALING APPROACH

Davison and Wood (1983) described a simple nonmetric MDS method to estimate stimulus scale values from choice data that satisfy the unidimensionality axiom. They argued that when a general class of choice models satisfying Equations 5 to 7 below are considered, then a specified, nonmonotone transformation of the choice probabilities is itself a dissimilarity measure that meets the fundamental assumption of nonmetric MDS in a one-dimensional solution.

Let b_j and b_k be the scale values for stimuli j and k, respectively, along a specified attribute continuum, and let π_{jk} be the population choice probabilities. Then the class of choice models considered in the Davison and Wood (1983) paper satisfies Equation 5:

$$\pi_{jk} = f(b_k - b_j), \tag{5}$$

where f is a monotone nondecreasing function such that,

$$(b_k - b_j) > (b_k' - b_j') \Rightarrow f(b_k - b_j) \geq f(b_k' - b_j'), \text{ for all } j, j', k, k', \tag{6}$$

and such that,

$$f(0) = .50. \tag{7}$$

Now, let

$$\delta_{jk} = |\ \pi_{jk} - .50\ |. \tag{8}$$

Davison and Wood (1983) demonstrate that when the choice probabilities satisfy Equations 5 through 7, then δ_{jk} is a monotone nondecreasing function of the distances $|\ b_k - b_j\ |$ between stimuli k and j along the psychological continuum under investigation. That is, if the model satisfies Equations 5 through 7, then:

$$|\ b_k - b_j\ | > |\ b_k{}' - b_j{}'| \Rightarrow \delta_{jk} \geq \delta_{j'k}{}', \text{ for all } j, j', k, k'. \tag{9}$$

The authors further suggest that when the data satisfy the unidimensionality assumption and that reasonably good sample estimates of the choice probabilities P_{jk} are available, it should be possible to estimate the scale values b_j and b_k using the dissimilarity estimates, $\delta_{jk} = |\ P_{jk} - .50\ |$ and a nonmetric MDS analysis in one dimension. The dissimilarity matrix, $\Delta = \{\delta_{jk}\}$ should be unidimensional.

Note that the Rasch PC statistic in Equation 4 is one example of such general choice models. That is, when the data satisfy the unidimensionality axiom, then given some rational sample estimates of the probability function:

$$\pi_{jk} = \frac{\exp(b_k - b_j)}{1 + \exp(b_k - b_j)},$$

it is possible to scale the stimuli along a one-dimensional continuum through a nonmetric MDS procedure using the dissimilarity measures δ_{jk}. The implication is that if the stimuli are scalable in one dimension, then it is reasonable to assume that the complete latent space is unidimensional. What is needed, then, is a decision criterion that will provide a good rationale to verify the existence of unidimensionality among the stimulus set.

It has been shown by several researchers (Davison, 1983; also cited in Davison & Hearn, 1989) that when a unidimensional set of stimuli are scaled in two dimensions, the stimuli often form a very distinctive C- (U-) or S-shaped configuration with the ordering of the stimuli along the C (U) or S corresponding to their ordering along the one dimension. Davison & Hearn (1989) use simulated data to demonstrate that a unidimensional stimulus set forms a C- or U-shaped structure in two dimensions when the monotone transformation relating distances to the dissimilarity measures is negatively accelerating and that it forms an S-shaped structure when the monotone function is positively accelerating. Given values of π_{jk} conforming to Equation 4 and proximities computed as in Equation 8, then the monotone function relating the proximity data, δ_{jk}, to distances $|\,b_k - b_j\,|$ should be negatively accelerating, and a C or U shape is expected in a nonmetric MDS.

Finally, Davison and Wood (1983) showed that when the nonmetric estimates in a one-dimensional solution were obtained for dissimilarity data δ_{jk} derived from Equation 11 below which satisfy a unidimensional distance model, the estimated stimulus coordinates closely approximated the scale values generated from Thurstone's Case V method. The correlations between the two sets of estimates were generally close to perfect (e.g., .98, .99). As a consequence, unlike other assessment methods that are usually carried out as preliminary assumption-testing techniques before the scaling takes place, the present approach can also be utilized as a scaling method in its own right.

The findings presented by Davison and Wood (1983) and others shed light on a potentially promising direction for addressing the issue of unidimensionality from the point of view of MDS. The theory suggests that the nature of the two-dimensional configuration is indicative of the sufficiency of a single trait in explaining the subjects' performances on or judgments about the stimulus set. If a C- (U-) or S-shaped configuration is observed for the data, one can safely confirm the existence of such an underlying latent attribute. If, on the other hand, the structure of the configuration plot departs from a C (U) or S shape and the ordering of the stimuli along each dimension appears to correspond to some important, identifiable stimulus feature, one has evidence that there is more than one attribute defining the latent space.

In the Rasch formulation, the empirical sample estimate of the population value π_{jk} can be derived from the observed matrix of dichotomous responses. In particular, the proportion of persons in the calibration sample passing item j but not item k, given that they have passed exactly one of the two items, can be taken as P_{jk}. That is,

$$P_{jk} = P\{a_{vj} = 1, a_{vk} = 0 \mid a_{vj} + a_{vk} = 1\}. \tag{10}$$

The dissimilarity measures δ_{jk} can be estimated by

$$\delta_{jk} = |\,P_{jk} - .50\,|. \tag{11}$$

The resulting dissimilarity measures form a square matrix (Δ) with one row and one column for each item and with the diagonal entries equal to zero. Since J items only define $J(J-1)/2$ unique item PC statistics, we need only work with the lower triangular portion of the dissimilarity matrix. The element of the matrix in row j column k ($j > k$) is the dissimilarity transformation of the proportion of persons passing row item (j) but not column item (k), given that the persons have passed exactly one of the two items.

The matrix Δ of the dissimilarity data can then be submitted to any computer program that executes nonmetric MDS analysis, such as KYST (Kruskal, J.B., Young, F.W., & Seery, J.B., 1973), ALSCAL (Young & Lewyckyj, 1979) or the nonmetric algorithm in SYSTAT (Wilkinson, 1989). The resulting configuration plot of the two-dimensional solution can be visually examined and conclusions about dimensionality can be reached on the basis of the stimulus structure appearing in the plot, the fit measure, and other criteria such as the Shepard diagrams (Davison, 1983; Davison & Hearn, 1989) which provide pictorial representations of the inverse of the monotone function relating the estimated distances and the original data.

EXAMPLES

The Real Data Analysis

The first example used data from a mathematics test developed by a large suburban school district. The data contained binary responses of 178 examinees to 50 mathematics items. First, a FORTRAN computer program was used to convert the direct responses to a lower triangular matrix of dissimilarity measures, which in turn was submitted to the KYST program for nonmetric MDS analysis.

A maximum of two dimensions was specified. The value of STRESS Formula 1 for the one-dimensional solution was .111, indicating a fairly high degree of fit between the data and the one-dimensional parameter estimates (Davison, 1983). Increasing the number of dimensions by one reduces the STRESS value to .069, suggesting the adequacy of the two-dimensional solution in representing the underlying structure of the items. Columns 2 and 4 in Table 16.2 show the results of the MDS parameter estimates. Note that the items were re-sequenced according to their one-dimensional MDS calibration order. For comparison purposes, item parameter estimates and their corresponding standard errors obtained from the unconditional maximum likelihood procedure (UCON), described in Wright and Stone (1979), via the BIG-STEPS (Linacre & Wright, 1993) computer software, are also presented in Table 16.2 (columns 6 and 7).

Note that all three procedures constrained the center of the scale to zero (means = 0.00). The one-dimensional MDS procedure went a step

Table 16.2. Item Parameter Estimates for Real Data

Item #	MDS Estimates				UCON Estimates			
	One-Dimensional		Two-Dimensional					
	Original	Re-Scaled*	Original	Re-Scaled*	Par. Est.	Std. Err.	95% CI	Abs. Diff**
1	-2.12	-2.92	-0.75	-1.03	-2.96	0.51	-3.96 ~ -1.96	0.04
2	-1.74	-2.41	-0.93	-1.28	-2.53	0.42	-3.35 ~ -1.71	0.12
3	-1.61	-2.22	-1.04	-1.43	-2.20	0.37	-2.93 ~ -1.47	0.02
4	-1.52	-2.10	-1.04	-1.44	-2.22	0.37	-2.95 ~ -1.49	0.12
5	-1.46	-2.01	-1.11	-1.54	-1.96	0.33	-2.61 ~ -1.31	0.05
6	-1.33	-1.83	-1.17	-1.62	-1.67	0.30	-2.26 ~ -1.08	0.16
7	-1.32	-1.83	-1.17	-1.61	-1.66	0.30	-2.25 ~ -1.07	0.17
8	-1.29	-1.78	-1.12	-1.55	-1.74	0.31	-2.35 ~ -1.13	0.04
9	-1.09	-1.50	-1.07	-1.48	-1.35	0.27	-1.88 ~ -0.82	0.15
10	-1.01	-1.39	-1.05	-1.45	-1.35	0.27	-1.88 ~ -0.82	0.04
11	-0.93	-1.29	-0.98	-1.35	-1.36	0.27	-1.89 ~ -0.83	0.07
12	-0.89	-1.23	-0.97	-1.33	-1.29	0.26	-1.80 ~ -0.78	0.06
13	-0.87	-1.21	-0.97	-1.33	-1.07	0.25	-1.56 ~ -0.58	0.14
14	-0.71	-0.98	-0.87	-1.20	-0.91	0.20	-1.30 ~ -0.52	0.07
15	-0.60	-0.83	-0.76	-1.04	-0.84	0.18	-1.19 ~ -0.49	0.01
16	-0.38	-0.53	-0.48	-0.66	-0.44	0.18	-0.79 ~ -0.09	0.09
17	-0.37	-0.51	-0.51	-0.70	-0.47	0.18	-0.82 ~ -0.12	0.04
18	-0.31	-0.42	-0.43	-0.59	-0.47	0.17	-0.80 ~ -0.14	0.05
19	-0.28	-0.38	-0.37	-0.52	-0.40	0.17	-0.73 ~ -0.07	0.02
20	-0.27	-0.37	-0.36	-0.49	-0.36	0.18	-0.71 ~ -0.01	0.01
21	-0.16	-0.22	-0.24	-0.33	-0.27	0.18	-0.62 ~ 0.08	0.05
22	-0.13	-0.18	-0.19	-0.26	-0.20	0.17	-0.53 ~ 0.13	0.02
23	-0.12	-0.16	-0.17	-0.23	-0.15	0.17	-0.48 ~ 0.18	0.01
24	-0.09	-0.12	-0.16	-0.22	-0.18	0.17	-0.51 ~ 0.15	0.06
25	-0.06	-0.09	-0.13	-0.19	-0.13	0.18	-0.48 ~ 0.22	0.04
26	-0.03	-0.04	-0.07	-0.09	-0.12	0.17	-0.45 ~ 0.21	0.08

(continued)

Table 16.2. *(Continued)*

Item #	MDS Estimates				UCON Estimates			
	One-Dimensional		Two-Dimensional					
	Original	Re-Scaled*	Original	Re-Scaled*	Par. Est.	Std. Err.	95% CI	Abs. Diff**
27	0.03	0.04	0.00	0.00	0.03	0.23	−0.42 ∼ 0.48	0.01
28	0.04	0.05	0.02	0.02	−0.02	0.17	−0.35 ∼ 0.31	0.07
29	0.06	0.09	0.03	0.04	−0.09	0.18	−0.44 ∼ 0.26	0.18
30	0.16	0.22	0.16	0.22	0.18	0.23	−0.27 ∼ 0.63	0.04
31	0.29	0.40	0.34	0.46	0.31	0.21	−0.10 ∼ 0.72	0.09
32	0.31	0.43	0.38	0.52	0.40	0.20	0.01 ∼ 0.79	0.03
33	0.35	0.48	0.40	0.56	0.42	0.21	0.01 ∼ 0.83	0.06
34	0.51	0.71	0.62	0.85	0.65	0.20	0.26 ∼ 1.04	0.06
35	0.58	0.79	0.68	0.93	0.70	0.20	0.31 ∼ 1.09	0.09
36	0.84	1.16	0.93	1.28	1.10	0.20	0.71 ∼ 1.49	0.06
37	0.86	1.19	0.97	1.34	1.09	0.19	0.72 ∼ 1.46	0.10
38	0.99	1.37	0.96	1.33	1.46	0.19	1.09 ∼ 1.83	0.09
39	1.03	1.42	1.05	1.45	1.41	0.19	1.04 ∼ 1.78	0.01
40	1.08	1.49	1.01	1.40	1.57	0.19	1.20 ∼ 1.94	0.08
41	1.18	1.63	1.05	1.46	1.67	0.19	1.30 ∼ 2.04	0.04
42	1.20	1.65	1.06	1.47	1.66	0.19	1.29 ∼ 2.03	0.01
43	1.23	1.70	1.04	1.43	1.87	0.18	1.52 ∼ 2.22	0.17
44	1.25	1.73	1.05	1.45	1.88	0.18	1.53 ∼ 2.23	0.15
45	1.29	1.79	1.07	1.47	1.87	0.18	1.52 ∼ 2.22	0.08
46	1.32	1.82	1.01	1.39	1.92	0.19	1.55 ∼ 2.29	0.10
47	1.37	1.89	1.10	1.52	1.79	0.18	1.44 ∼ 2.14	0.10
48	1.37	1.90	1.07	1.48	1.85	0.18	1.50 ∼ 2.20	0.05
49	1.58	2.18	1.12	1.54	2.03	0.18	1.68 ∼ 2.38	0.15
50	1.77	2.44	0.97	1.34	2.54	0.19	2.17 ∼ 2.91	0.10
Mean	0.00	0.00	0.00	0.00	0.00	0.22		0.07
SD	1.01	1.40	0.83	1.40	1.40	0.07		0.05

* Re-scaled to adjust for the standard deviation of the UCON estimates.

** Absolute difference between re-scaled one-dimensional MDS estimate and the UCON estimate.

Note. All values are subject to rounding error.

further and standardized the standard deviation of the scale to 1.00. To remove the artifact in parameter estimates caused by the arbitrary units imposed by the various procedures, the MDS parameter estimates were re-scaled to coincide with the unit of the UCON estimates. This was done for both one- and two-dimensional MDS solutions by weighting each original MDS parameter estimate by the ratio between the UCON standard deviation and the corresponding MDS standard deviation. The results are presented in columns 3 and 5 of Table 16.2. The absolute differences between the UCON estimates and the re-scaled one-dimensional MDS estimates are reported in the last column of Table 16.2. The differences ranged from .01 to .18, with a mean of .07 and a standard deviation of .05. The majority of the differences were below one tenth of a logit, indicating a fairly high degree of agreement between the two sets of parameter estimates. Furthermore, there was no observable pattern of relationship between the direction and the magnitude of the differences and the locations of the items along the difficulty continuum. This suggests that the differences were probably due to random errors.

To provide a formal statistical test of the differences between the one-dimensional MDS and UCON parameter estimates, the 95% confidence intervals around the UCON estimates were constructed. Columns 8 and 9 of Table 16.2 present the lower and upper bounds of the confidence bands. As can be seen from Table 16.2, all of the re-scaled one-dimensional MDS item parameter estimates fell within the 95% confidence bands of the UCON estimates, indicating that none of the differences were statistically significant at the $\alpha = .05$ level.

In addition to the significance test of differences between the UCON and the one-dimensional MDS parameter estimates, the Pearson Product Moment Correlation coefficients among the various sets of parameter estimates were computed (see Table 16.3.) The coefficients reveal the degree of consistency among the various procedures in ranking the items in terms of their difficulties. Note that since re-scaling the parameter estimates did not have an effect on the relative standings of the items, the correlation coefficients were the same whether the original or re-scaled MDS parameter estimates were used. As can be seen from Table 16.3, all coefficients were in the high .90s ($p < .001$). The relationship between the one-dimensional MDS solution and the UCON calibration was nearly perfect ($r = .9980$, $p < .001$). There was a slight decrease in the relationship between the two-dimensional MDS and the other two sets of parameter estimates. Nevertheless, the correlation coefficients were still above .95 ($p < .001$).

The re-scaled one-dimensional MDS parameter estimates were plotted against the UCON estimates in Figure 16.1. Visual inspection of

TABLE 16.3.   Inter-Correlations Among Item Parameter
Estimates for Real Data Through Various Procedures

	One-Dim. MDS	Two-Dim. MDS	UCON
One-Dim. MDS	—	.9618	.9980
Two-Dim. MDS		—	.9550

the scatter plot suggests that all points fell closely along the 45° identity line, with minor fluctuations. A simple regression analysis was
performed, regressing the UCON scale values onto the re-scaled one-
dimensional MDS parameter estimates. Consistent with the result
from visual inspection of the scatter plot, nearly all of the variance (r^2
> .99) in the UCON estimates was accounted for by the variation in
the one-dimensional MDS estimates. When the artifact of the arbi-

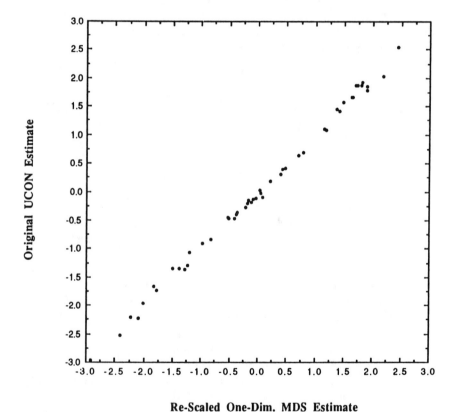

Re-Scaled One-Dim. MDS Estimate

Figure 16.1.   Scatter Plot of Original UCON Versus Re-Scaled One-Dim. MDS
Estimates for Real Data

trary units was removed, the regression slope (which equals the Pearson Correlation coefficient) was close to unity (b = .9980), indicating a point-to-point correspondence of the two sets of parameter estimates.

The results of the significance tests and the strong relationship between the one-dimensional MDS solution and the UCON calibration supported the earlier prediction that the MDS scale values are estimates of the Rasch model item parameters.

Figure 16.2 illustrates the plot of the 50 items in two dimensions yielded in the two-dimensional MDS solution. As predicted by the theory, the configuration plot shows a distinctive U shape, confirming the assumption of unidimensionality. Inspection of Figure 16.2 and Table 16.2 indicates a close correspondence between the ordering of the items along the U-shaped curve and the arrangement of the same items in the one-dimensional configuration.

To better understand the nature of the relationship between the structure of the one-dimensional configuration and the form of the monotone function mapping distance estimates onto the original dissimilarity data, the Shepard diagram was investigated. Figure 16.3

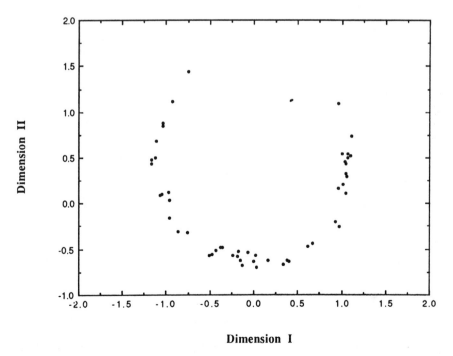

Dimension I

Figure 16.2.   Configuration of Dimension I Versus Dimension II for Real Data

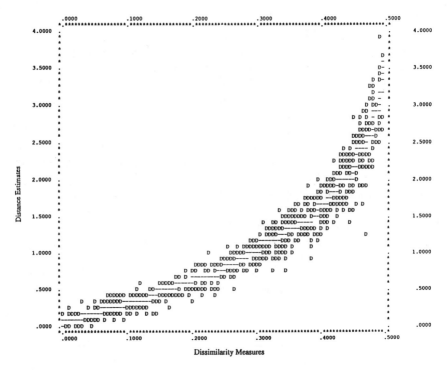

Figure 16.3.   Shepard Diagram Generated from the One-Dimensional MDS Solution for Real Data

presents the Shepard diagram generated from the one-dimensional MDS solution. The diagram, which depicts the scatter plot of the 1225 (i.e., 50*49/2) pairwise dissimilarity measures (X-axis) against their respective distance estimates (Y-axis), shows a clear trend of positive acceleration. Since the Shepard diagram is the inverse of the monotone function relating the observed and estimated distances discussed by Davison and Hearn (1989), the functional relationship between the distance estimates and the similarity measures was in fact negatively accelerating as expected.

The Simulation Study

The simulation data used for the present investigation came from a large-scale Monte Carlo study by Chen (1991). The Chen study reported results of a logistic regression analysis on PC statistics derived from 100 replications of data sets conforming to the Rasch model, which varied in the number of subjects and the number of items. To keep the present presentation simple, only the first replication of data sets containing item responses of 500 *subjects* to 11 *items* was used. The item parameters were set at -1.70, -1.36, -1.02, $-.68$, $-.34$, .00, .34, .68, 1.02, 1.36 and 1.70. The person parameters were simulated to have a standard normal distribution with a mean of .00 and standard deviation of 1.00.

The same MDS procedure described previously was applied to the simulation data. A maximum of two dimensions was specified. The value of STRESS Formula 1 for the one-dimensional solution was .026 and decreased to .010 for the two dimensional solution, indicating that both sets of MDS parameter estimates successfully reproduced the rank order of the true item parameters. Table 16.4 shows the results of the MDS calibrations. Again, the Rasch UCON parameter estimates are presented for reference.

As in the case of real data study, the true and estimated item difficulties were all centered at the zero point, while the units of the scale varied from one set to another. To remove the artifact of arbitrary units, all three sets of parameter estimates were re-scaled to adjust for the differences in the standard deviations between each set of parameter estimates and the true item parameters (see columns labeled "Re-Scaled" in Table 16.4.) The absolute differences between the true item parameters and the re-scaled one-dimensional MDS and UCON estimates are shown in the last two columns of Table 16.4.

It can be seen from Table 16.4 that the one-dimensional MDS and UCON procedures (with re-scaling) were equally efficient in recovering the individual item parameters. The means and standard deviations of the estimation bias in absolute value for both procedures were virtually identical, although there was a slight difference in the range of the absolute bias (.00 to .17 for MDS and .00 to .14 for UCON.) Further, there appeared to be a tendency for larger discrepancies between true and estimated item parameters to occur in the middle of the scale (i.e., Items 5 and 6), while the extreme item difficulties were more likely to be estimated accurately by both techniques.

To test the differences between the MDS and UCON parameter estimates, the 95% confidence intervals for the re-scaled UCON estimates were constructed. None of the re-scaled one-dimensional MDS scale values fell out of the confidence bands, suggesting that the observed differences between the two sets of parameter estimates could be attributed to tolerable random errors at the $\alpha = .05$ level.

Table 16.5 shows the inter-correlations among the true and estimated item parameters obtained from the various procedures. Consis-

Table 16.4. Item Parameter Estimates for Simulation Data

Item #	True Item Par	MDS Estimates				UCON Estimates				Absolute Differences**	
		One-Dimensional		Two-Dimensional						True—One Dim	True—UCON
		Original	Re-Scaled*	Original	Re-Scaled*	Original	Re-Scaled*	Std. Err	95% CI		
1	-1.70	-1.62	-1.74	-1.13	-1.40	-1.94	-1.70	0.13	-1.96 ~ -1.45	0.04	0.00
2	-1.36	-1.17	-1.26	-1.07	-1.34	-1.46	-1.28	0.12	-1.52 ~ -1.05	0.10	0.08
3	-1.02	-0.95	-1.02	-0.98	-1.23	-1.19	-1.04	0.12	-1.28 ~ -0.81	0.00	0.02
4	-0.68	-0.56	-0.60	-0.66	-0.83	-0.70	-0.61	0.12	-0.85 ~ -0.38	0.08	0.07
5	-0.34	-0.47	-0.51	-0.55	-0.69	-0.55	-0.48	0.12	-0.72 ~ -0.25	0.17	0.14
6	0.00	0.10	0.11	0.16	0.20	0.14	0.12	0.12	-0.11 ~ 0.36	0.11	0.12
7	0.34	0.28	0.30	0.34	0.43	0.31	0.27	0.12	0.04 ~ 0.51	0.04	0.07
8	0.68	0.57	0.61	0.69	0.86	0.68	0.60	0.12	0.36 ~ 0.83	0.07	0.08
9	1.02	0.90	0.96	0.95	1.19	1.12	0.98	0.12	0.75 ~ 1.22	0.06	0.04
10	1.36	1.30	1.40	1.12	1.40	1.60	1.40	0.13	1.15 ~ 1.66	0.04	0.04
11	1.70	1.63	1.75	1.12	1.40	2.00	1.76	0.14	1.48 ~ 2.03	0.05	0.06
Mean	0.00	0.00	0.00	0.00	0.00	0.00	0.00	0.12		0.07	0.07
SD	1.13	1.05	1.13	0.90	1.13	1.28	1.13	0.01		0.04	0.04

* Re-scaled to adjust for the standard deviation of the true item parameters.
** Absolute difference between true and estimated item parameters.
Note. All values are subject to rounding error.

Table 16.5.   Inter-Correlations Among Item Parameter Estimates for Simulation Data Through Various Procedures

	True	One-Dim. MDS	Two-Dim. MDS	UCON
True	—	.9972	.9812	.9975
One-Dim. MDS		—	.9798	.9998
Two-Dim. MDS			—	.9809

tent with the results from the real data analysis, all coefficients were extremely high ($r \geq .9798$, $p < .001$). Most notable among them was the nearly perfect relationship between the one-dimensional MDS and UCON estimates ($r = .9998$, $p < .001$). The correlations between the true item parameters and the UCON and one-dimensional MDS estimates were almost identical, and were both very close to unity ($r \geq .9972$). There was a slight decrease in the correlations between the two-dimensional MDS parameter estimates and the true and estimated item parameters from the other two procedures. However, the differ-

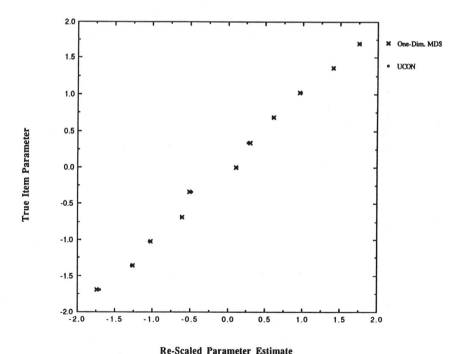

Figure 16.4a.   Scatter Plot of True Versus Estimated (Re-Scaled) Item Parameters for Simulation Data

ences in the correlation coefficients were practically negligible (in the second decimal place or lower).

Regressing the true item parameters onto either one-dimensional MDS or UCON estimates (with re-scaling) indicated that both sets of estimates were excellent predictors of the true item parameters. That is, nearly all of the variance in the true item parameters (>99%) was attributable to the variance in either one-dimensional MDS or UCON scale values. The regression slopes were close to unity (b = r ≥ .9972). Figure 16.4a illustrates the superimposed scatter plots of the true and estimated item parameters. Two pieces of information were evident from Figure 16.4a. First, the two scatter plots (one for the one-dimensional MDS and one for the UCON) were virtually identical, suggesting a high degree of correspondence between the two sets of

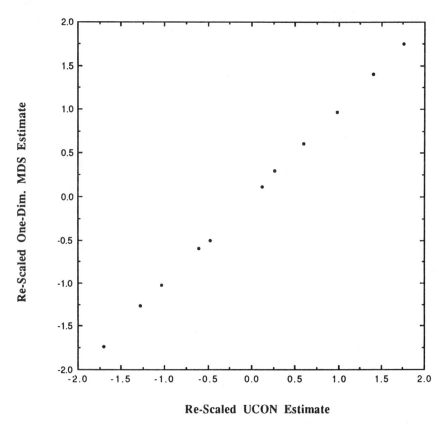

Figure 16.4b.   Scatter Plot of Re-Scaled One-Dim. MDS Versus UCON Estimates for Sim. Data

parameter estimates. Second, all but one point (Item 5) fell closely along the 45° identity line, indicating the adequacy of the two estimation procedures in reproducing the true item parameters. The slight aberration in the scatter plots reflects the fact that the difficulty of Item 5 was consistently under-estimated by both one-dimensional MDS and UCON procedures (by −.17 and −.14 respectively).

Figure 16.4b plots the re-scaled one-dimensional MDS parameter estimates against re-scaled UCON values. The plot clearly shows a nearly perfect relationship, with all points falling right on the 45° identity line. The strong relationships among the various sets of parameter estimates paralleled the findings from the real data analysis and provided sufficient empirical support for the conjecture that the MDS scale values were indeed sound estimates of the Rasch model item parameters.

Figure 16.5 shows the two dimensional configuration plot of the 11 items. As predicted by the theory, a very distinctive U shape was observed when the items were plotted in two dimensions. Inspection of Figure 16.5 shows that the ordering of the items along the U-shaped

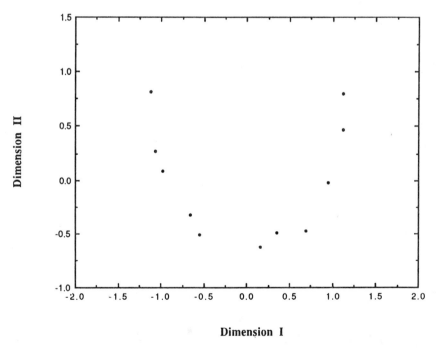

Figure 16.5.   Configuration of Dimension I Versus Dimension II for Simulation Data

curve was exactly that of the one-dimensional item scale values in Table 16.4. This suggests that the latent trait structure underlying the set of items is unidimensional. The Shepard diagram (Figure 16.6), which depicts a prominent upward trend of acceleration, provides further support to the unidimensionality hypothesis.

Since the data were simulated to fit the one-dimensional Rasch model, the findings serve to confirm the theory that a set of stimuli forms a U (or C) shape in two dimensions when its underlying latent space is unidimensional, and when the monotone function relating distance estimates to dissimilarity measures is negatively accelerating (i.e., when the Shepard diagram is positively accelerating). Another implication is that the Rasch PC statistic is a member of the general choice models described in Davison and Wood (1983) that, after a non-monotone transformation, can be fit to the nonmetric MDS model to test the hypothesis of unidimensionality and estimate stimulus scale values.

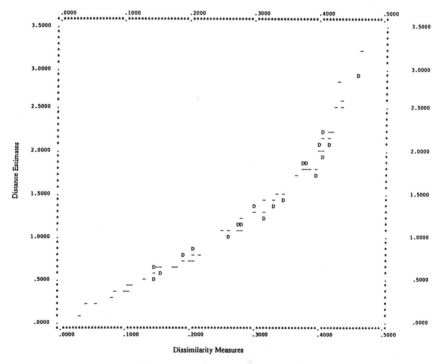

Figure 16.6. Shepard Diagram Generated from the One-Dimensional MDS Solution for the Simulation Data

DISCUSSION

Findings from both real data sets and the simulation studies provided empirical support to the proposed methodology as a viable approach to assessing unidimensionality in the Rasch model. The results demonstrated that when the Rasch model holds, the items are scalable in one dimension via a MDS analysis of the transformed PC statistic. When scaled in two dimensions, the resulting configuration formed a very distinctive U (C) shape with the ordering of the items along the U- (C-) shaped curve closely corresponding to the ordering of the items along the difficulty continuum yielded in the one-dimensional MDS solution. Furthermore, the Shepard diagram revealed a consistent trend of positive acceleration, indicating that the monotone function relating distances to the dissimilarity measures was actually negatively accelerating. All these findings confirmed the predictions of the theory behind the proposed method.

There are several limitations to the proposed method. First, the property of specific objectivity discussed by Rasch (1961, cited in Wright & Stone, 1979) only holds when data fit the one-parameter Rasch model in which the response probabilities are a function of the unweighted differences between person and item parameters. Elimination of person parameters in Equation 4 only occurs when no item characteristic other than difficulty is assumed to influence the behavior of the item, and no person characteristic other than the person's ability tapped by the items is assumed to underlie performance. This prevents application of the proposed technique to situations where the items forming the instrument have varying discriminations and/or where the lower asymptote of the item characteristic curve is greater than zero, as in the two- or three-parameter IRT models.

Second, although the decision criteria for detecting unidimensionality in the present method have strong theoretical and empirical bases, they are qualitative in nature. When the evidence of unidimensionality is not clear-cut, the conclusions reached may largely depend on subjective judgment.

Third, because examining the MDS patterns (e.g., the two-dimensional configuration, the Shepard diagram, etc.) only suggests whether or not the item set forms a single dimension, it does not provide adequate information as to the actual dimensionality when the assumption of unidimensionality is violated.

Finally, the number of PC statistics increases geometrically with the number of stimuli. For instance, a complete PC design with L items will result in $L(L - 1)/2$ unique proximity measures for analysis. With a large number of items the task may go beyond the limits of MDS programs. However, with increasingly more powerful computer technology, the procedure should become feasible for increasingly larger item sets.

Using PC statistics in conjunction with nonmetric MDS to address the issue of dimensionality also possesses several advantages. Most notable is the exclusion of person parameters from the paired comparisons model. As demonstrated in Equation 4, when two items with different response patterns (i.e., the subject responds correctly to one item and incorrectly to another) are compared, the subject parameter, which accounts for individual idiosyncrasies with regard to the latent trait will drop out of the PC model. As a result, the conditional probability π_{jk} is strictly a function of the difference between the parameters of the two items being compared. This not only eliminates the need for the distributional assumptions usually made about person parameters by many popular existing methods (e.g. factor analytic procedures), but also builds on the idea of specific objectivity proposed by Rasch to allow estimation of item difficulty parameters independent of person parameters. Calibration of items is truly population-free.

Factor analysis has been one of the most widely used methods for detecting dimensionality. It has been extensively studied and, because it is included in most statistical computer software available, is most convenient to use. However, several authors (e.g. McDonald, 1965; McDonald & Ahlawat, 1974; Spearman, 1927, cited in Hattie, 1985) have clearly demonstrated that when factor analysis is used on binary variables, the factor loadings tend to change as a linear function of item difficulty. The phenomenon, usually referred to as *difficulty factors,* has often been cited as a reason against application of factor analysis to binary data. One possible cause of the problem is the choice of association measure (Guilford, 1941; Wherry & Gaylord, 1944, both cited in Hattie, 1985). In particular, Wherry and Gaylord argued that difficulty factors result because phi coefficients, whose size tends to be contingent upon item difficulties, were used for factoring. They suggested that, in the case of dichotomous data, tetrachorics rather than phis, should be used for factoring. However, it is well-known (Hattie, 1985) that the matrix of tetrachorics is often not positive definite (i.e., non-Gramian). This may cause problems in using a maximum likelihood approach as opposed to least squares methods to implement the analysis. Further, Lord and Novick (1968) argued that tetrachorics would lead to the emergence of certain spurious factors unless the assumption of normality is satisfied. These problems, however, are not present when the transformed Rasch PC statistic is used as a measure of proximity, because its value is independent of the person parameter and, hence, independent of the distribution of abilities.

Although its primary focus is not on parameter estimation, the procedure proposed here yields scale values that compared favorably with those obtained from the traditional unconditional maximum likelihood method. The low absolute discrepancies and extremely high correlations between the scale values obtained from the one-dimensional MDS solution, the traditional UCON Rasch calibration, and the true parameters suggest that, in addition to being a technique for assessing unidimensionality, the present method can be used as a scaling method in its own right.

A limitation of most indices of unidimensionality reviewed by Hattie, including those based on factor analysis, is the lack of a rational decision criterion for determining the existence of one dominant underlying latent attribute among the set of stimuli. For instance, one commonly used index of unidimensionality based on factor analysis is the percentage of total variance accounted for by the first factor. Nevertheless, there is no established rule of thumb as to how high the percentage should be before the assumption of unidimensionality can be deemed realistic. Furthermore, it is sometimes possible to find a multidimensional set of items which has a higher variance on the first factor than does a unidimensional set. Given the difficulty of finding criteria for such indices, it seems time to try approaches that do not rely on cut-offs for single indices. Rather than relying on any single index, the present approach relies on a search for patterns that follow from the unidimensional, psychometric theory on which it is based: (1) a good fit to the proximity data in one dimension, (2) a U- or C-shaped pattern in two dimensions, (3) a smoothly accelerating Shepard diagram for the one-dimensional solution, and (4) a close correspondence between one-dimensional scale values and item difficulty estimates obtained from a standard calibration program.

The results of the analyses in the present study appear to be very encouraging, with the conjectures made from the various theories behind the proposed methodology borne out empirically. The road to a fully developed, new theoretical perspective, such as the present one, may be long and not without some obstacles. With more analyses of actual test data, theoretical explorations, and Monte Carlo simulations, the new model for analyzing pseudo-choice data may be improved and made more accurate. Research in this area should focus on identifying the universe of situations to which the present findings may (or may not) be validly generalized.

REFERENCES

Andrich, D. (1978). Relationships between the Thurstone and Rasch approaches to item scaling. *Applied Psychological Measurement, 2,* 449–460.

Bock, R.D., & Lieberman, M. (1970). Fitting a response model for *n* dichotomously scored items. *Psychometrika, 35,* 179–197.

Bradley, R.A., & Terry, M.E. (1952). Rank analysis of incomplete block designs. I. The method of paired comparisons. *Biometrika, 39,* 324–345.

Chen, T.H. (1991). *A logistic regression, paired comparisons method for testing Rasch model parameter invariance: A simulation study.* Unpublished doctoral dissertation, Department of Educational Psychology, University of Minnesota.

Choppin, B.H. (1968). An item bank using sample-free calibration. *Nature, 219,* 870–872.

Davison, M.L. (1983). *Multidimensional Scaling.* New York: John Wiley.

Davison, M.L., & Chen, T.H. (1991). *Parameter invariance in the Rasch model.* Paper presented at the annual meeting of the American Educational Research Association, Chicago, April, 1991.

Davison, M.L., & Hearn, M. (1989). Two-dimensional configurations of unidimensional stimulus sets in nonmetric multidimensional scaling. *Applied Psychological Measurement, 13,* 329–334.

Davison, M.L., & Wood, P.K. (1983). Fitting unidimensional choice models with nonmetric multidimensional scaling. *Applied Psychological Measurement, 7,* 333–340.

Guilford, J.P. (1941). The difficulty of a test and its factor composition. *Psychometrika, 6,* 67–77.

Gustafsson, J.-E. (1980). Testing and obtaining fit of data to the Rasch model. *British Journal of Mathematical and Statistical Psychology, 33,* 205–233.

Hambleton, R.K., Swaminathan, H., Cook, L.L., Eignor, D.R., & Gifford, J.A. (1978). Developments in latent trait theory: Models, technical issues, and applications. *Review of Educational Research, 48,* 467–510.

Hattie, J. (1985). Methodology review: Assessing unidimensionality of tests and items. *Applied Psychological Measurement, 9,* 139–164.

Hulin, C.L., Drasgow, F., & Parsons, C. (1983). *Item Response Theory: Applications to Psychological Measurement.* Homewood, IL: Dow & Jones Irwin.

Kruskal, J.B., Young, F.W., & Seery, J.B. (1973). *How to use KYST, a very flexible program to do multidimensional scaling and unfolding.* Murray Hill, NJ: Unpublished manuscript, Bell Laboratories.

Linacre, J.M., & Wright, B.D. (1993). *A User's Guide to BIGSTEPS.* (Version 2.4). Chicago, IL: MESA Press.

Lord, F.M. (1980). *Applications of Item Response Theory to Practical Testing Problems.* New York: Erlbaum Associates.

Lord, F.M., & Novick, M.R. (1968). *Statistical Theories of Mental Test Scores.* Reading MA: Addison-Wesley.

Luce, R.D. (1959). *Individual Choice Behavior.* N.Y.: Wiley.

Martin-Löf, P. (1973). Statistika modeller. Anteckningar från seminarier läs-
året 1969–70 utarbetade av Rolf Sundberg. 2: a uppl. (Statistical models.
Notes from seminars 1969–70 by Rolf Sundberg, 2nd ed.) Institutet för
Försäkringsmatematik och Mathematisk Statistik vid Stockholms Uni-
versitet.

McDonald, R.P. (1965). Difficulty factors and nonlinear factor analysis. *British
Journal of Mathematical and Statistical Psychology, 18,* 11–23.

McDonald, R.P. & Ahlawat, K.S. (1974). Difficulty factors in binary data.
British Journal of Mathematical and Statistical Psychology, 27, 82–99.

Mead, R. (1976a). *Assessing the fit of data to the Rasch model.* Paper presented
at the annual meeting of the American Educational Research Association, San Francisco, April 19–23, 1976.

Mead, R. (1967b). *Assessment of fit of data to the Rasch model through analysis
of residuals.* Unpublished doctoral dissertation, University of Chicago.

Rasch, G. (1960). *Probabilistic Models for Some Intelligence and Attainment
Tests.* Copenhagen: The Danish Institute for Educational Research.

Rasch, G. (1961). On general laws and the meaning of measurement in psychology. In *Proceedings of the Fourth Berkeley Symposium on Mathematical Statistics.* Berkeley: University of California Press, IV, 321–334.

Spearman, C. (1927). *The Abilities of Man: Their Nature and Measurement.*
London: Macmillan.

Stout, W. (1987). A nonparametric approach for assessing latent trait unidimensionality. *Psychometrika, 52,* 589–617.

Tucker, L.R., & Lewis, C. (1973). A reliability coefficient for maximum likelihood factor analysis. *Psychometrika, 38,* 1–10.

Wherry, R.J., & Gaylord, R.H. (1944). Factor pattern of test items and tests as a
function of the correlation coefficient: Content, difficulty, and constant
error factors. *Psychometrika, 9,* 237–244.

Wilkinson, L. (1989). *SYSTAT: The System for Statistics.* Evanston, IL: SYS-
TAT, Inc.

Wollenberg, A.L. van den (1982). Two new test statistics for the Rasch model.
Psychometrika, 47, 123–140.

Wright, B.D., & Master, G.N. (1982). *Rating Scale Analysis.* Chicago: MESA
Press.

Wright, B.D., Mead, R.J., & Draba, R. (1976). Detecting and correcting test
item bias with a logistic response model. *Research Memorandum No. 22,*
Statistical Laboratory, Department of Education, University of Chicago,
1976.

Wright, B.D., & Panchapakesan, N. (1969). A procedure for sample-free item
analysis. *Educational and Psychological Measurement, 29,* 23–48.

Wright, B.D., & Stone, M.H. (1979). *Best Test Design.* Chicago: MESA Press.

Young, F.W., & Lewyckyj, R. (1979). *ALSCAL 4 User's Guide.* (2nd ed.). Chapel
Hill, NC: Data Analysis and Theory Associates.

chapter **17**

A Comparison of Item Selection Strategies Used in a Computer Adaptive Test of Mathematics Ability

Randal D. Carlson and Hoi K. Suen
The Pennsylvania State University

Computerized adaptive testing procedures take advantage of the computer's ability to individualize procedures at low cost. The one-to-one interaction necessary for individualized testing no longer requires the provision of a specially trained human being, which can often be quite costly. Thissen (1990) and Hulin, Drasgow, and Parsons (1983) characterized the adaptive testing procedure as consisting of the following seven components: an item response model, an item pool, an entry level, an item selection strategy, a method for computing the provisional estimate of ability, termination criteria, and a method for final estimation of ability, which may be different from the provisional estimation method. This chapter reports the results of a study that investigated the effects of one of these components, choice of item selection strategy, when used with a specific ability estimation method and termination criteria.

ITEM SELECTION STRATEGIES

An item selection strategy (ISS) is a procedure for selecting the next item or set of items to be administered. At least four ISS have been specifically applied to CAT programs. *Match b_i to $\hat{\Theta}$ (BI)*. With this ISS, the test item with the closest b_i (item difficulty) to $\hat{\Theta}$ is selected as the next item to be administered. This method or some variant was used in the early studies of adaptive testing (Reckase, 1973, Urry, 1970; 1974; Weiss, 1974), and is computationally simple and inexpensive to implement (Hulin, Drasgow, & Parsons, 1983). *Match m_i to $\hat{\Theta}$ (MI)*. For the three-parameter model, the previous method tends to select items that are slightly too difficult. This is because the maximum of the item information function for each item occurs at a value of $\hat{\Theta}$ slightly below b_i. This maximum is defined by Birnbaum (1968) as

$$\mathbf{m_i} = \mathbf{b_i} + \frac{1}{\mathbf{Da_i}} \ln \frac{1 + \sqrt{1 + 8c_i}}{2}, \tag{1}$$

where a_i = item discrimination and c_i = the guessing parameter. Therefore, m_i corresponds to the ability level at which the item is most useful for maximum likelihood ability estimation. This method requires that m_i be computed for each item. But this extra calculation is rewarded by choosing a more informative item. *Quasi-Match m_i to $\hat{\Theta}$ (QM)*. This ISS involves a simplification of the match m_i to $\hat{\Theta}$ strategy above. Quasi-match m_i averages the item parameters (a and c) throughout the entire test and uses these averages ($\bar{a}$ and $\bar{c}$) to compute a single adjustment for every b_i, (Xiao, 1989),

$$\mathbf{m_i'} = \mathbf{b_i} + \frac{1}{\mathbf{D\bar{a}}} \ln \frac{1 + \sqrt{1 + 8\bar{c}}}{2}. \tag{2}$$

This ISS provides a correction toward the maximum information item, while at the same time simplifying computational procedures. Note that when $c_i = 0$ (guessing is absent), $m_i = b_i$. This implies that the preceeding three models are equivalent for Rasch and two-parameter models. *Maximum Information (MI)*. For this strategy, the information for each item not administered is computed at the current value of $\hat{\Theta}$,

$$\mathbf{I}(\hat{\Theta}) = \sum \frac{(\mathbf{P_i'}(\hat{\Theta}))^2}{\mathbf{P_i}(\hat{\Theta})\mathbf{Q_i}(\hat{\Theta})}. \tag{3}$$

The item with the maximum information at $\hat{\Theta}$ is selected. Lord (1980) reports on an adaptive test that uses this ISS. This strategy has been used in a number of applied CATs including the commercially available MicroCAT (1989).

Estimation of Ability

The Golden Section Search Strategy (GSSS) was selected for use in this investigation. It was proposed by Xiao (1989) as a method to provide more robust solutions than maximum likelihood (MLE) estimations when the number of items is relatively small. Results of a Monte Carlo study (Xiao, 1989) showed that GSSS is less subject to guessing effects when compared to MLE for small numbers of items. It provided relatively rapid convergence of ability estimates over all ability levels, obtained almost unbiased and relatively accurate ability estimates, was inexpensive to use, and provided a convenient frame within which to use various item selection methods.

TERMINATION CRITERIA

Two common rules were applied for deciding when to stop the CAT. One was to stop when the standard error of measurement, estimated by the square root of the inverse of the information function, reached a set value. This rule has the advantage of being uniformly precise for all test takers. However it takes more test items for the extreme examinees to reach that precision than it does for the mid-ability examinees. In certain cases, the test item pool would be depleted before the desired precision was met (Thissen & Mislevy, 1990).

Alternatively, the CAT was stopped after a fixed number of items were administered. This method is attractive because of its simplicity and ability to make direct comparisons during simulation studies (Hulin et al., 1983). Because this method measures each test taker to various levels of precision, this rule is chosen less frequently than the former.

This study focused on the four ISS described above when they were used with the GSSS method (Xiao, 1989). Two criteria were used for comparison: efficiency of the CAT, defined as the number of items required to be administered to reach the final estimate of ability when the standard error is fixed, and accuracy of the CAT defined as the standard error of the final estimate of ability when the number of items administered is fixed. Specifically, the following questions were investigated: on tests of equal length, do different item selection strategies produce different ability estimates, or different accuracies? Also, on tests of fixed standard error, do different item selection strategies lead to different ability estimates, or different numbers of items administered?

RESEARCH DESIGN

Instrument

The instrument used in this study was the mathematics subsection of a freshman testing, counseling, and advising program (FTCAP) exam. The mathematics subsection of the exam consisted of 72 questions that assessed basic skills such as manipulation of numbers, reading graphs and tables, simple calculations, elementary algebra, advanced algebra, analytic geometry, and trigonometry. These 72 questions were used as the item bank from which the CAT items were drawn.

Administration

Data derived from the results of the 72-item exam taken by all freshmen entering the university during 1991 were used in the item calibration. The exam allowed enough time for all students to complete the test, approximately 70 seconds per question (Examiner's Manual, 1992). A total of 14,914 students took the exam in 1991. However, students who did not finish or omitted one or more items were not included in the calibration sample. This produced a fully crossed data matrix of 1921 (subjects) by 72 (items).

Choice of Model

The computer program BILOG 3.04 (Mislevy & Bock, 1990) was chosen for the item calibration. It used the calibration method of marginal maximum likelihood (MML), which has been suggested as the best method for item parameterization (Wainer & Mislevy, 1990; Mislevy & Stocking, 1989). Since the sample included nearly 2,000 students who answered all questions from which 1,000 were randomly selected for calibration, this sample should have approximated an MML estimation. Rasch, 2-, 3-parameter models were investigated. All items converged appropriately for all models.

Based on likelihood-ratio chi-squared statistics, the three-parameter model appeared to fit better than the other two models for both individual item fits and total test fit. In addition, based on the differences in the -2 log likelihoods at convergence (Misley & Bock, 1990), the three-parameter model appeared to fit better than the other two models. Thus, the three-parameter logistic model was chosen.

Unidimensionality

The extent to which the test item bank departs from unidimensionality may compromise the validity of the inferences derived from the CAT (Steinberg, Thissen, and Wainer, 1990). To investigate dimensionality, a principal component analysis was conducted on the matrix of tetrachoric correlations (cf. Lord, 1980; Lord & Novick, 1968; Wherry and Gaylord, 1944). The first eigenvalue was 26.81 as compared to the second value of 3.78. The 7.09 ratio of the first to the second factors and the relative consistency of the second (1.96), third (1.22) and fourth (1.08) ratios provided evidence for unidimensionality. Additionally, the first factor accounted for 37.2% of the variation compared to 5.3% or less for the following factors. Bejar's (1980) procedure for investigating the unidimensionality of achievement tests based on item parameter estimates provided further supporting evidence of unidimensionality. Item difficulties were estimated for four content areas and then compared with the item difficulties estimated on the total test. Slopes of the regression lines were close to the theoretical 1.0 (range: 0.91 to 1.15) Intercepts were also close to the theoretical 0 (range: 0.04 to $-.12$). While neither the factor analytic nor Bejar's methods provided indisputable evidence that the exam was unidimensional, the weight of the evidence appeared to substantiate an assumption of unidimensionality.

CAT Simulation

Once the item calibration was complete and the item parameters were determined, they were then input into a FORTRAN computer program written and compiled specifically for this study to simulate CAT. This program allowed the researcher to match various item selection strategies with the other components of the testing algorithm. In the simulation, eight different CAT versions were administered to each of the 1,000 subjects. Those versions differed in the specification of the four-item selection strategies and the two termination criteria.

The test item pool was the 72-item FTCAP mathematics exam. The three-parameter logistic item response model was used. All students had an initial estimate of ability of 0 on the $-\_$ to $+\_$ scale. The four different item selection strategies previously described were used. The method for computing provisional and final ability was Xiao's GSSS (1989).

Two termination criteria were used: termination when the standard error of estimate was less than 0.40 and termination after 20 items had been administered. The item response data from the students were supplied to each version of the program when called for. For instance, if the CAT were to present question number 10 first, the response that the subject had made to question number 10 would be supplied to the CAT. That item would be scored, a new ability estimated, the termination criterion checked, and a new item selected based on the new estimated ability and the test version item selection strategy. If the second item were number 22, then the student response to question number 22 would be supplied to the CAT. A new ability was then estimated. This cycle proceeded until the test termination criterion was met.

Subjects

A subset of the 13,130 entering freshmen who took the same mathematics exam during 1992 served as the subjects for this research. One-thousand subjects were randomly selected from the 4,859 subjects who had answered every question. Responses were recorded in a 1,000 (subject) by 72 (item) matrix and were available to the CAT as subject responses.

CAT Items

The items in the 1992 test were identical to the 1991 test. Because the item parameters are theoretically invariant across sample populations, the item calibration accomplished on the 1991 sample was used to characterize the 1992 exam.

RESULTS AND ANALYSIS

One factor repeated measures ANOVA was used to compare the mean standard error of estimate of examinee ability for each item selection strategy when the termination criteria of test length was met. The average ability estimate for the four-item selection strategies were similar in their descriptive statistics (see Table 17.1) and did not exhibit any statistically significant difference ($p = .21$).

The descriptive statistics for the standard error of the estimated ability (Table 17.2) revealed that the average standard error for three item selection strategies (match b_i to $\hat{\Theta}$, match m_i to $\hat{\Theta}$, and quasi-match m_i to $\hat{\Theta}$) were similar, but the maximum information ISS (MX) was different from the other three. Repeated measures ANOVA showed these differences to be statistically significant ($p = .0001$). Tukey's HSD *post hoc* comparison confirmed that the MX ISS was different from the other 3 ISS.

**Table 17.1. Descriptive Statistics for Final Estimate of Ability
of Item Selection Strategy when Termination Criterion
Is Administration of 20 Items (N = 1000)**

Strategy	Mean	S.D.	Median	Extremes	
				Low	High
b_i to $\hat{\Theta}$ match	−0.21	1.29	−0.22	−4.45	3.21
m_i to $\hat{\Theta}$ match	−0.23	1.30	−0.25	−4.06	3.21
m_i to $\hat{\Theta}$ quasi-match	−0.23	1.29	−0.26	−4.06	3.21
maximum information	−0.23	1.29	−0.23	−4.04	3.21

Figure 17.1 depicts standard error plotted versus estimated ability for each of the four ISS using a third-order polynomial regression line (R^2 range 0.87 to 0.94)). The MX ISS appears to have equivalent or lower standard errors than the other three in the region $\hat{\Theta} \in [-3.0, 2.0]$. In the region $\hat{\Theta} \in [-1.0, 2.0]$, which has approximately 81% of the population, the MX ISS reduces the standard errors by an average of 11% when compared to the next most effective strategy (QM).

One factor repeated measures ANOVA was used to compare the mean number of items administered per student for each ISS when the termination criteria of standard error of estimate was met. The average ability estimate for the four ISS were, again, similar in their descriptive statistics (Table 17.3) and did not exhibit any statistically significant difference (p = .07).

The descriptive statistics for the number of test items administered (Table 17.4) revealed that the mean number of test items administered was similar for three ISS (BI, MI, and QM), but the MX ISS appeared different from the other three.

**Table 17.2. Descriptive Statistics for Standard Error of Estimate
of Ability by Item Selection Strategy when Termination Criterion
Is Administration of 20 Items (N = 1000)**

Strategy	Mean	S.D.	Median	Extremes	
				Low	High
b_i to $\hat{\Theta}$ match	0.38	0.21	0.33	0.23	3.07
m_i to $\hat{\Theta}$ match	0.37	0.19	0.33	0.22	1.99
m_i to $\hat{\Theta}$ quasi-match	0.37	0.19	0.33	0.22	2.32
maximum information	0.35	0.19	0.30	0.21	1.96

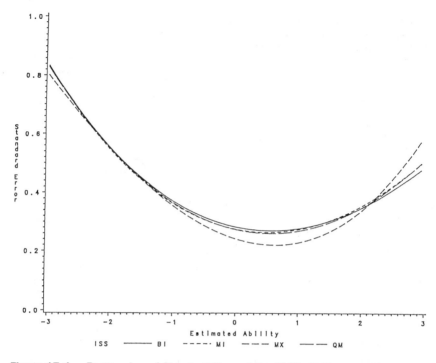

Figure 17.1.   Regression of Standard Error of the Ability Estimate on Estimated Ability using a Third Order Polynomial, CAT Terminated at 20 Items Administered

Repeated measures ANOVA analysis of these differences among the means was statistically significant (p = .0001). Tukey's HSD *post hoc* comparison showed that three distinct ISS groups existed—BI and MI; QM; and MX.

One should also note the large spread between the mean and medi-

Table 17.3.   Descriptive Statistics for Final Estimate of Ability by Item Selection Strategy when Termination Criterion Is Standard Error of the Ability Estimate Is 0.40 (N = 1000)

				Extremes	
Strategy	Mean	S.D.	Median	Low	High
b_i to Θ match	−0.18	1.31	−0.17	−4.27	3.33
m_i to Θ match	−0.19	1.30	−0.17	−4.27	3.33
m_i to Θ quasi-match	−0.18	1.29	−0.13	−4.27	3.33
maximum information	−0.15	1.26	−0.01	−4.27	3.33

Table 17.4. Descriptive Statistics for Number of Items Presented by Item Selection Strategy when Termination Criterion Is Standard Error of Ability Estimate of 0.40 (N = 1000)

Strategy	Mean	S.D.	Median	Extremes Low	Extremes High
b_i to $\hat{\Theta}$ match	20.77	19.42	14	7	72
m_i to $\hat{\Theta}$ match	20.62	19.63	14	7	72
m_i to $\hat{\Theta}$ quasi-match	19.89	20.03	13	6	72
maximum information	16.21	20.48	8	4	72

an value for each ISS. This was caused by a few extreme ability values requiring the administration of all 72 items. In these cases, the test item pool did not contain sufficient information to reach the required precision for the particular ability.

In Figure 17.2, the average number of test items administered was

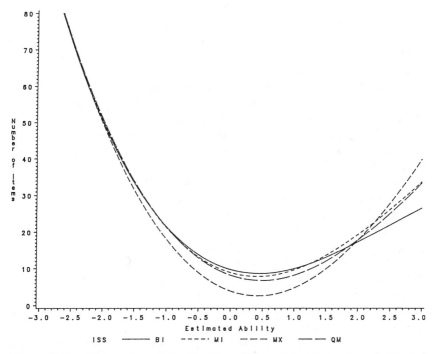

Figure 17.2. Regression of the Number of Items Administered on Estimated Ability using a Third Order Polynomial, CAT Terminated at a Standard Error for the Estimated Ability of 0.40

plotted versus estimated ability for each of the four ISS using a third order polynomial regression line (R^2 range: 0.75 to 0.80).

The BI and the MI ISS appeared quite similar and had the highest number of items administered throughout most of the region of interest. The QM ISS was different from the rest of the ISS, producing moderate numbers of items administered. The MX ISS required fewer average numbers of items administered than the other ISS throughout all of the prediction region except the region $\hat{\Theta} > 2.0$ with reductions in number of items administered up to 70%. In the region $\hat{\Theta} \in [-1.0, 2.0]$, the MX ISS reduces the standard errors by an average of 11% when compared to the next most effective strategy (QM).

DISCUSSION

When combined with the Golden Section Search Strategy for estimation of ability and for this test and model, the maximum information ISS seemed to be superior to the other three ISS tested. Maximum information averaged significantly lower standard errors of estimation and fewer number of items required to be presented to meet the termination criterion throughout most of the region where most of the abilities are expected.

The region where the maximum information ISS showed the greatest advantage over the other ISS is the mid-ability range. As ability moved toward the extreme, the advantage for the maximum information ISS decreased to insignificance. Further toward the extremes, other ISSs appeared to be better, but in those extreme regions less than 20% of the population is expected to lie.

The test item pool used for the CAT was an item pool in current use. It was not designed specifically for a CAT. As such, the number of items and the coverage of items across the difficulty spectrum was not optimal. Because of this fact, the results and recommendations of this study may apply only to cases where the item pool is similar in structure to the research test item pool. Item pools that are larger and more evenly distributed across the difficulty spectrum should be able to apply the results and recommendations of this research, but the size of the advantage of the maximum information ISS over the other ISS may not be the same.

In addition, this research was designed to address only maximum likelihood based strategies. As such, it makes no claims as to the relative accuracy and efficiency of the study strategies compared to Bayesian strategies.

RECOMMENDATIONS

Based on the results of this research, when a CAT is used to test subjects, the following recommendations for practice and future research are offered.

1. If the objective of the CAT is to reduce the number of items administered but still have each subject take the same length test, one can use any of the ISS with a termination criterion of number of items administered.
1a. If accuracy of the ability estimate is also a factor, then the maximum information ISS should be chosen.
2. If the objective of the CAT is to administer as few items as possible to the subject while maintaining a constant standard error for the estimated ability, then choose the maximum information ISS with a termination criterion based on standard error.
2a. If the maximum information ISS cannot be used due to its computational complexity, then the quasi-match m_i to $\hat{\Theta}$ ISS should be used to administer as few items as possible, while still maintaining a constant standard error for the estimated ability.
3. The current study has determined that in most of the region of interest, the maximum information ISS is maximally accurate and efficient. Further research would now be indicated to determine if there is an ability estimation procedure that is superior to others. For example, should a hybrid selection strategy be developed, which uses MI within a center range and another ISS outside that range?
4. This line of research should be broadened to include changes in the test item pool and Bayesian methods.
5. It was found that by requiring a standard error termination criterion in excess of the information available in the test item pool, it was possible to exhaust the number of test items without reaching the desired standard error. This suggests that a termination criterion should be investigated based on the marginal information available from each remaining item in the test item pool. This termination strategy should be investigated beginning with a Monte Carlo study to determine if there are any generalized rules that can be applied to determine at what value of marginal information the CAT should be terminated.

CONCLUSION

This research investigated four item selection strategies with respect to their accuracy and efficiency. All of the ISSs were used in combination with the same item pool (the FTCAP math test), IRT model (the three-parameter logistic model), initial estimate of ability ($\hat{\Theta}$), termination criterion (the number of items administered or the standard error), and provisional and final estimate of ability (GSSS). Throughout virtually the entire ability region of interest, the maximum information ISS proved superior to the other ISS investigated. Therefore, it was determined that the maximum information ISS provided the most accurate and efficient strategy for choosing the next item in a computer adaptive test when used within the limitations of this research.

REFERENCES

Bejar, I.I. (1980). A procedure for investigating the unidimensionality of achievement tests based on item parameter estimates. *Journal of Educational Measurement, 17,* 4, 283–296.

Birnbaum, A. (1968). Some latent trait models and their use in influencing an examinee's ability. In Lord, F.M. & Novick, M.R. (Eds.). *Statistical theories of mental test scores* (pp. 397–479). Reading, MA: Addison-Wesley.

Hulin, C.L., Drasgow, F., & Parsons, C.K. (1983). *Item response theory: Application to psychological measurement.* Homewood, IL: Dow Jones-Irwin.

Lord, F.M. (1980). *Application of item response theory to practical testing problems.* Hillsdale, N.J.: Erlbaum.

Lord, F.M. & Novick, M.R. (1968). *Statistical theories of mental test scores.* Reading, MA: Addison-Wesley.

Assessment Systems Corporation (1989). *MicroCAT testing system users manual (3rd. ed.).* St. Paul, MN: Assessment Systems Corporation.

Mislevy, R.J. & Bock, R.D. (1990). *BILOG 3 Item analysis and test scoring with binary logistic models.* Mooresville, In.: Scientific Software.

Mislevy, R.J. & Stocking, M.L. (1989). A consumers Guide to LOGIST and BILOG. *Applied Psychological Measurement, 13,* 57–75.

Reckase, M.D. (1973). *An interactive computer program for tailored testing based on the one-parameter logistic model.* Paper presented to the National Conference on the Use of On-Line Computers in Psychology, St. Louis, MO.

Reckase, M.D. (1974). *An application of the Rasch simple logistic model to tailored testing.* Paper presented at the Annual Meeting of the American Educational Research Association.

Steinberg, L., Thissen, D., & Wainer, H. (1990). Validity. In H. Wainer (ed.), *Computerized Adaptive Testing: A Primer* (pp. 187–230). Hillsdale, NJ: Erlbaum.

Thissen, D. (1990). Reliability and measurement precision. In H. Wainer (Ed.), *Computerized Adaptive Testing: A Primer* (pp. 161–185). Hillsdale, NJ: Erlbaum.

Thissen, D. & Mislevy, R.J. (1990). Testing algorithms. In H. Wainer (Ed.), *Computerized Adaptive Testing: A Primer* (pp. 103–134). (Hillsdale, NJ: Erlbaum.

Urry, V.W.A. (1970). *Monte Carlo investigation of logistic test models.* West Lafayette, IN: Unpublished doctoral dissertation, Purdue University.

Wainer, H. and Mislevy, R.J. (1990). Item response theory, item calibration, and proficiency estimation. In H. Wainer (Ed.), *Computerized Adaptive Testing: A Primer* (pp. 65–101). Hillsdale, NJ: Erlbaum.

Weiss, D.J. (1974). *Strategies of adaptive ability measurement* (Research Report 74–5). University of Minnesota, Department of Psychology, Psychometric Methods Program.

Wherry, R.J. & Gaylord, R.H. (1944). Factor pattern of test items and tests as a function of the correlation coefficient: Content, difficulty, and constant error factors. *Psychometrika, 9,* 237–244.

Xiao, B. (1989, April). *Golden section search strategies for computerized adaptive testing.* Paper presented at the Fifth International Objective Measurement Workshop, Berkeley, CA.

chapter **18**

Constructing Questionnaires: An Application of Facet Design and Item Response Theory to the Study of Lonesomeness*

Edw. E. Roskam, Nick Broers
Nijmegen Institute of Cognition and Information (NICI),
University of Nijmegen

This chapter reports the design and analysis of a questionnaire on feelings of loneliness. Part 1 describes the general methodological framework. Part 2 describes the design of the questionnaire (facet design) within that framework, and the hypotheses to be tested. In Part 3 we present the psychometric model (Linear Logistic Tests Model, LLTM) to analyze the data, and some preliminary analyses, leading to a specification of the LLTM using orthogonal contrasts. Finally, in part 4 we present some of the results and a conclusion.

---

* This research was made possible by a grant from the University of Nijmegen.

The authors wish to express their gratitude to George Engelhard and Mark Wilson for their critical comments to an earlier draft of this chapter.

The computer program for the LLTM and logistic regression analyses were developed by Koos Zwinderman.

349

This study was part of larger study reported in detail in Broers (1994), following the same design and analyses, including also feelings of uncertainty, indifference, and angriness, and establishing relations with other variables. The results reported here concern the exploratory analysis of "loneliness" in one sample of data only. Subsequent analysis of a second sample of data is reported in Broers (1994), and corroborates many of the results presented here.

PART ONE

Questionnaires and the Definition and Analyses of Behavior

The principal motivation for the work reported in this chapter is to improve questionnaire research methodology. The approach presented in this paper differs from the traditional one in that the questionnaire is treated as a research instrument per se, rather than as a measurement instrument. As a research instrument it will, however, permit measurement conditional upon the presence of a theoretically hypothesized pattern in the responses. This is achieved by taking item response theory (IRT) as the prototypical model for questionnaire responses. This model combines theory development and data analysis and permits the testing of specific hypotheses about the factors which affect a subject's responses.

In particular, this approach is applied to the study of appraisive responses, such as judgments and feelings of lonesomeness. Relating the feeling of lonesomeness to its situational antecedents and to traits or properties of the individual person, leads to what can be called *the anatomy of lonesomeness:* What is it that makes people feel lonesome constitutes what lonesomeness *is* as a socio-psychological condition. In doing so, we will also identify and measure a personality dimension that we call proneness to lonesomeness.

We define behavior as the choice response of a person to a stimulus or situation. Completely analogous to the experimental method, a questionnaire can be conceived of as a set of stimuli that can be varied systematically. Each item in a questionnaire thus acts as the symbolic presentation of a situation. Questionnaires are used whenever a realistic presentation of a situation is technically or ethically not possible. We ask a subject, for example, if he would continue working if he won a million dollars in a lottery. Of course, such questions ask for a response *as if* the depicted situation were true, and we know that the response might not be what the subject would do in a realistic situation, but it is often the best we can do to study preferences and attitudes.

To design a questionnaire systematically, a meta-theory is needed for its design; this meta-theory is taken from Guttman's notion of *facet design*. It starts off with a systematic inventory of relevant facets of situations (as well as of subjects), and constructs the questionnaire accordingly. This inventory is both based on considerations of logic and definition, and on substantive hypotheses. Neither is formally different from experimental design as known in other contexts. The analysis of the data can take on various forms, depending on the hypotheses concerning the pertinent domain of behavior. Stated quite generally, responses are assumed to be some function of *traits* of the subjects and of facets of the situations. Item response theory provides a method to model this approach and to analyze the data accordingly, measuring the pertinent personal and situational determinants of the responses.

The Conceptualization of *lonesomeness*

The term *conceptualization* is often used in a round-about way, roughly indicating one's general ideas about a class of phenomena. Sometimes, conceptual analysis is used to arrive at a description of the content and connotation of a concept. For the purpose of studying loneliness or lonesomeness, it will be useful to distinguish between various possible denotations of the term. First, *loneliness* is meant to refer to a more or less enduring state of absence of (particular) social contacts; in that sense, it appears to be a sociological term, rather than a psychological term. Secondly, the term can refer to feelings of a certain quality, associated with the appraisal of one's (social) life; such feelings may occur incidentally, or more or less permanently as a consequence of the permanent conditions of one's social life, and people may also differ by the degree to which they are prone to such feelings. Thirdly, the term can refer to a condition or disposition of one's psychological make-up, which determines one's perceptions, behavioral choices, and so forth. In the latter sense, it is comparable to dispositions like intelligence, pessimism, or femininity. The second and third meanings seem related to *state* and *trait*. With respect to *lonely* or *lonesome*, language does not seem to offer the possibility to distinguish between these three meanings using different terms. We will use the terms *loneliness* and *lonesomeness* more or less interchangeably, but we prefer *lonesomeness*. Whether or not each of these three conceptualizations of lonesomeness is scientifically meaningful is an open question as far as the present chapter is concerned. From a psychological point of view, it appears relevant first to take the feeling of lonesomeness as a domain for research.

The Use of Facet Design in General

Guttman (1977b; cf. Shye, 1978; Canter, 1983) has introduced *facet theory* as a meta-theory to define domains, to collect data, and to represent the multivariate structure of that domain, mostly by means of *smallest space analysis*. The format of defining the empirical domain is called *facet design*. It is a valuable tool in formulating and testing hypotheses with direct reference to aspects of a domain of observations.

A facet design is formulated by way of a so-called *mapping sentence* (both terms are virtually synonymous). Consider Figure 18.3 as an example, and imagine Figure 18.4 substituted for "{a social exchange situation, S}" in Figure 18.3. Figure 18.3 then contains the definition of a domain that has several aspects, called facets. Basically, there are three facets, *persons* (P), *stimuli* (S), and *responses* (R). Each facet is a set of elements. The Cartesian product P × S × R is the set of all possible observations in the pertinent domain. The term *mapping sentence* refers to the fact that it describes the observations as a mapping of P × S onto R: P × S → R. The set of stimuli (or items, in the case of tests or questionnaires), will itself usually be the Cartesian product of a number of stimulus facets. In Figure 18.4, six facets of situations are listed, A, B, C, D, E, and L called *partner, direction, mode, focus, locus,* and *area of life,* respectively. An element of a facet is called a *struct*. So, *doing* is one of the two structs in facet D. An element from the Cartesian product of stimulus facets is called a *structuple*. (With one or more of the facets left out, we would call it a substructuple). From the numbers of structs in the facets in Figure 18.4 (but ignoring facet L, as will be explained later), we find that the Cartesian product A × B × C × D × E contains 3 × 3 × 4 × 2 × 2 = 144 structuples. In addition, Figure 18.3 contains a frequency facet and a desirability facet. So, Figures 18.3 and 18.4 together define 576 structuples. Each of these structuples can be phrased as an item in a questionnaire. For example: It rarely occurs that a friend asks me about a nice movie I have seen (A_2, B_3, C_3, D_1, E_1, F_1, G_2) → I (would) feel lonesome, where I ε P, and → indicates the response to the situation presented. The actual presentation and phrasing of the items is not a trivial matter. Each structuple might be phrased in a variety of ways, which we will briefly discuss in part 2. Also, some facets may partially be specified, although, in principle, facets should be exhaustively specified and mutually independent in the sense that all structuples are logically possible. Moreover, the mapping sentence should be semantically consistent, and the response facet should semantically fit to all structuples.

As Guttman (1977b) has emphasized, there is an obvious correspondence between facet design and experimental design. Facets in facet design (except the R facet) correspond to factors or independent variables in experimental design.

For psychology as an empirical science, facet design—rather than Guttman's broader system of facet theory—is a tool that serves three purposes:

1. to define the domain of a theory,
2. to define a set of observations, and
3. to define a research design.

In as far as facet design defines the domain of a theory by means of specifying the set of observations that the theory is about, it is also the specification of the *content* of a concept, such as aggression, lonesomeness, risk-taking, or well-being. We will use the term *conceptualization* to indicate the faceted definition of an *empirical* concept. As argued by the present author in earlier papers (Roskam, 1989, 1990), it appears necessary for theory development in general to distinguish between theoretical concepts and empirical concepts. *Theoretical concepts* are concepts that derive their meaning and definition from a theory. A theory states the lawful structure of observations in a particular domain. A theory, also, is *about* a domain (e.g. people's responses to particular stimuli). *Empirical concepts* refers to a domain of observations without implying its particular lawful structure or properties. To illustrate this, consider a set of questions concerning so-called social distance: would you accept such-and-such people in your country, your town, your neighborhood, your house, your family, and so on. With, for example, six such binary questions, there are $2^n = 2^6 = 64$ logically possible response patterns. If a unidimensional latent trait underlies the responses in a deterministic way, one will find empirically at most $(n + 1) = 7$ different response patterns exhibiting a scalogram structure, and subjects and situations can be jointly weakly ordered, that is, actual behavior exhibits a unidimensional structure, and the underlying variable can be called social tolerance toward the people concerned. The existence of this unidimensional structure is a testable hypothesis. *Social tolerance* as a unidimensional trait is a theoretical variable having explanatory power for the variety of the responses actually observed. By contrast, the denotation of the set of (potential) observations to questions of acceptance of various kinds of sociological relations constitutes the content of an empirical concept. (Often, confusingly, the same term is used for both the behavioral domain and the underlying theoretical variable.)

The example just given is simple and primitive, but the reader can imagine that for more complicated sets of observations, much more sophisticated theories (and hence theoretical variables) can be formulated and tested. Signal detection theory (Green & Swets, 1966) is a good example; it specifies two (experimental) facets: stimulus intensity and pay-off. The theory then predicts a particular relation between *hits* and *false alarms,* which is governed by two theoretical quantities: *discriminability* and *bias.*

For the study of behavior, we propose that the basic observational primitive is a subject's *choice* among alternatives. The philosophical implications of this are complex, and beyond the scope of this paper. We assume that a subject responds to a situation by entering into a overt or covert activity where he could or might have chosen a different activity. Behavioral science is interested in the system of regulation and steering that determines this choice as a function of characteristics of the subject and of the situation. This will lead to the introduction of theoretical concepts that have explanatory potential to describe what people actually do or not do. We assume that there are lawful patterns such that, out of a myriad of logically possible choices, only certain choices will actually be observed. (A probabilistic theory will state the probability distribution of what is actually observed.)

A facet design of observations is never in itself true or false. Since the design *defines* and thereby delineates a domain of observations, it is free but not, of course, arbitrary. It systematizes, and it should do so in anticipation of formulating hypotheses, but it should not presuppose the validity of the hypotheses to be tested. A facet design, therefore, is not a theory (Guttman, 1977b), but it specifies the empirical domain about which a theory has something to say, or hypotheses are to be tested. (cf. Roskam, 1989, 1990, for a more detailed discussion).

Mental tests and questionnaires on the one hand, and experimental methods on the other hand, can both be formulated in the basic framework of {stimulus, person, response}. In particular, for questionnaire research where subjects respond by binary judgements, items can be systematically designed and structured as combinations of independent variables (like in experimental design). A typical example of a questionnaire item, asking for an appraisive judgement, is: "Would you feel lonesome if it rarely occurs that a good friend of yours talks to you about his problems?" The (uni)dimensionality of the pertinent judgements may be the first question to be dealt with. A latent trait model serves to analyze these judgements. Specific aspects or facets of the task or stimulus, as well as individual properties, will affect the responses in a particular way, as predicted by theoretical hypotheses, and are represented as parameters in the model. The model is both a representation of the hypothetical theoretical structure involved, and a model for the analysis of the data. Individual differences can be treated as subjects factors, which are also independent variables. Details will be discussed later.

Facet Design for Psychological Research

Any behavioral instance is a {situation, person, response} triplet. It is essential that a set of items (or stimuli) is linked to a specific common response range. We distinguish three broad classes of behavior, as illustrated in Figure 18.1. Three main classes are distinguished by the response facet: inferential behavior (R_{A_1}), preferential behavior (R_{A_2}), and appraisive behavior (R_{A_3}). To each, a second response facet can be observed, namely its speed. The emphasis in this chapter is on appraisive behavior, but for the sake of completeness and clarification, we will briefly discuss inferential and preferential behavior. We will ignore response speed. A specific example illustrating each of the three classes of responses with respect to risk is given in Figure 18.2.

Inferential behavior (A_1)

Behavior is called *inferential* behavior if it can be objectively categorized as correct versus incorrect with respect to some rule. The rule is in general implicit in the situation presented to the subject, for instance if the subject is to recall a friend's telephone number. In inferential behavior there is a rule and it is the observer who decides about the correctness or incorrectness of a response. Typical examples are intelligence and aptitude test items, but also memory and learning

A {S,P,R} triple belongs to the universe of psychological data if and only if a person (P) responds by choosing from a set of alternatives with respect to a

situation (S) according to a $A \begin{cases} 1. \text{ rule} \\ 2. \text{ goal} \\ 3. \text{ category} \end{cases}$ and the response is ordered

as $R_{(A_1)} \begin{cases} \text{correct} \\ \text{incorrect} \end{cases}$ and/or $R_{(A_2)} \begin{cases} \text{approach} \\ \text{avoidance} \end{cases}$ and/or $R_{(A_3)} \begin{cases} \text{affirmative} \\ \text{negative} \end{cases}$

with respect to facet A, and as $R_{\text{speed}} \begin{cases} \text{fast} \\ \text{slow} \end{cases}$.

Figure 18.1. General facet design for psychological data

A {S,P,R} triple belongs to the domain of 'risk' iff a person (P) responds to a gamble

with a $P\begin{Bmatrix}1.\ 30\%\\2.\ 50\%\\3.\ 80\%\end{Bmatrix}$ chance of winning $W\begin{Bmatrix}1.\ \$200\\2.\ \$30\end{Bmatrix}$ or else loosing $L\begin{Bmatrix}1.\ \$100\\2.\ \$10\end{Bmatrix}$, and the

response is (1) that the expected value (EV) of the gamble is $R_{(A1)}\begin{Bmatrix}EV > \$80\\\$80 > EV > \$50\\EV < \$50\end{Bmatrix}$

and/or (2) the gamble is $R_{(A2)}\begin{Bmatrix}attractive\\not\ attractive\end{Bmatrix}$ and/or (3) it is $R_{(A3)}\begin{Bmatrix}fairly\ risky\\fairly\ safe\end{Bmatrix}$.

Figure 18.2. Example of a mapping sentence with inferential (A₁), preferential (A₂), and appraisive (A₃) responses

tasks, attention and vigilance tasks, identification and discrimination, and so forth. The way such data are reported is typically in the form of percentages of correct and incorrect responses, split by stimulus conditions. With response speed added as a second response facet, we have, for example, the domain of time-limit achievement tests.

Preferential behavior (A₂)

The second category is preferential behavior, which is categorized as approach versus avoidance, or as acceptance versus rejection with respect to some goal or objective. Here also, the objective may be implicit in the situation. I may prefer a newspaper over the broadcast to get informed. Preferential responses are typically identified by observing the subject's acceptance or rejection of an object or stimulus. This can take the form of simply asking which alternative the subject prefers, which action he or she would like to engage in, or of observing his or her actual behavioral choices in natural situations. Motivation, attitudes, and valuation are typical instances of preferential behavior. For example, achievement behavior can be defined as a subject's preference for (more) difficult tasks. With response speed added, we are concerned with decision time for preferential choice.

Appraisive behavior (A₃)

This third class is more difficult to characterize: it concerns affirmative/negative judgements with respect to some semantic category like (perceived) risk, seriousness, violence, beauty, fairness, and the like, which cannot be incorrect or correct, and need not imply a preference (e.g. some people like risk, others avoid it); we call this category *appraisive* responses. The fact that most people prefer peacefulness over violence is an empirical fact, but not a logical necessity. Appraisive behavior is subjective in the sense that it is the subject who decides about the meaning of a given situation and the content of the pertinent term, such as risk, beauty, freedom, fairness. This implies that no a priori or objective definition of these terms can be given. "Risk like beauty is in the eyes of the beholder" (Coombs and Huang, 1970). Here the category must be explicitly presented to the subject, or he may pick one from a set of alternative categories.

We assume that various objective properties of stimuli or situations determine to what extent these are experienced as, for example, risky. It is a matter of research to find out what it is, for instance, that makes people feel lonesome, free, secure, etc., or appraise a situation as violent, risky, criminal, etc. Some situations will elicit strong feelings of, for instance, risk, others will elicit the opposite feelings. Whether or not the elicitation of such feelings can be represented unidimensionally is also a matter of empirical research: Is, for example lonesomeness, unidimensional, or is it multidimensional? If it is multidimensional, we should be able to identify these dimensions, and distinguish them as various kinds of lonesomeness, just as we distinguish between various kinds of intelligence (verbal, spatial, etc.). If an appraisal is unidimensional, situations can be simply ordered by the degree to which they elicit the pertinent appraisal, and subjects can be simply ordered by the degree to which they experience the pertinent feeling.

Even though an appraisive category may be unidimensional, the extent to which it is experienced may depend on several situational determinants, which can vary independently in the world. In other words, determinants may be multidimensional, but the experience may be unidimensional.

We will furthermore assume individual differences of sensitivity or proneness to experience a given situation in a particular way. For instance, some people may be easily given to feelings of depression, while others will not. Here, too, the determinants of these individual differences may be manifold, while the proneness may be unidimensional.

Appraisive responses are distinct from inferential responses in that the former are never correct or incorrect by some objective rule. Appraisive responses are also distinct from preferential responses in that there need not be a monotone relation with good or bad feelings, that is, with approach–acceptance versus avoidance–rejection tendencies.

For some appraisive dimensions, a single peaked preference function (Coombs, 1987, Coombs & Avrunin, 1988) seems plausible (e.g. risk: no risk is dull, a little of it is a thrill, too much of it is avoided).

Appraisive responses are related to emotions; sometimes we will use the term *appraisal* and *feeling* interchangeably. Emotions are complex structures consisting of an emotional antecedent, its appraisal, an action tendency, and subsequent expressions and overt activity (Frijda, 1988). The study of feelings and emotions requires the study of the appraisal of antecedent situations. It appears plausible that people are differently sensitive to situational facets or antecedents, and that a given situation may be appraised differently by different people, both qualitatively and quantitatively. Qualitative differences call for a polytomous response format, incorporating several latent traits corresponding to a subject's proneness to appraise a given situation in a particular way.

There is no reason to believe that what it is that makes people feel an emotion like lonesomeness is universal. It is partly inherent in human biological nature, partly inherent in our culture, and therefore the same situational facets may have different effects on people in different cultures. Such interaction effects can be incorporated in the design of the questionnaire analysis.

PART TWO

A Facet Design for the Study of Lonesomeness

Semantically, lonesomeness refers to the absence of social exchange. A nominal definition of the domain of lonesomeness experience is, perhaps trivially, given by Figure 18.3.

A { person x situation x response } triple belongs to the domain of lonesomeness experiences if and only if the subject {P} appraises the

$F \begin{Bmatrix} 1.\ \text{infrequent} \\ 2.\ \text{frequent} \end{Bmatrix}$ occurrence of himself in a {social exchange situation S} of

$G \begin{Bmatrix} 1.\ \text{low} \\ 2.\ \text{high} \end{Bmatrix}$ desirability   as → $R \begin{Bmatrix} (\text{very})\ \text{much} \\ (\text{very})\ \text{little} \end{Bmatrix}$ lonesome.

Figure 18.3.   Domain definition of lonesomeness

Next, a faceted definition of a social exchange situation must be given. Although many social-psychological theories are available listing the psychological dimensions of social exchange situations, the kind of definition necessary for the present purpose is one which lists the facets of social exchange situations in terms that are in a sense objective, in a manner similar to the way that conditions in controlled experiments are objective. In addition, these facets should be psychologically relevant by hypothesis.

We define a social exchange situation as an dyadic situation where some interchange occurs that has (cf. Figure 18.4):

1. a *direction,* depending on who is the actor initiating the exchange; and
2. a *content* or *focus,* which is what the exchange is about.

Upon further consideration it seems reasonable to distinguish three foci: a problem, a (nice) experience or activity, and an opinion or attitude. A subsidiary facet is the area of life to which the problem, opinion, or experience belongs (e.g., family, job, health). Furthermore, it appeared reasonable to specify the following:

3. The general *relation to the other* in a dyadic relation: regular partner, relative, or friend.
4. A behavioral *mode:* Overt action or verbal communication.

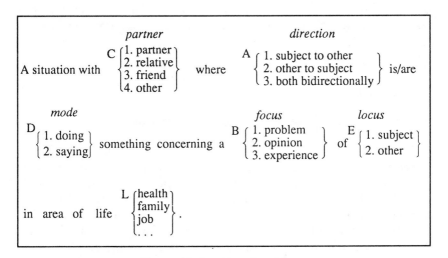

Figure 18.4. Situational facets

Finally, it is necessary to specify the following:

5. The *locus* of the focus: The person whose problem, opinion, or experience is the subject matter of social exchange.

The facet design as presented here does not pretend to cover all relevant situational facets, nor does it pretend to cover them in a way that is most adequate for the purpose of analyzing feelings of lonesomeness. Extension and more detail are also conceivable.

Pilot study and implementation of the questionnaire

The structuples from this design were translated into readable questionnaire items. For various reasons, partly concerned with practical feasibility, facet L ("area of life") was ignored. It is reasonable to assume that there are individual differences as to which area of life is more salient to experiences of lonesomeness than another, creating person $\times$ item interaction and complicating the analysis. Also, facet F ("frequency") was ignored and replaced by "seldom" only. Since "desirability" would appear not to be an objective facet, it was also omitted. Instead, a parallel questionnaire was administered containing the facets A through E, asking for the subjects' evaluation of such situations (see Broers, 1994, for details). Struct C_4 (other partner) was also omitted.

A pilot study indicated, firstly, that questionnaire items phrased as concrete instances of each structuple were often ambiguous and tended to elicit idiosyncratic responses. Therefore, a more generic way of phrasing the questionnaires items appeared more appropriate, such as:

$(A_1, B_1, C_1, D_1, E_2)$:
If you seldom did something for your partner whenever he/she has a problem, would you feel. . . .
$(A_2, B_2, C_2, D_2, E_1)$:
If your relatives seldom said something to you about your opinions, would you feel. . . .

Secondly, the pilot study indicated that A_3 (bidirectional exchange) was usually interpreted as if it was unidirectional (A_1 or A_2). So, all A_3 items were dropped. Furthermore, certain combinations of facets turned out extremely difficult to phrase linguistically in a form that would be easily understood. So, the combination $A_1D_1E_1$ was omitted (the subject doing something to the other concerning {a problem, opinion or experience} of the subject himself), as well as the combination $A_2D_1E_2$ (the other doing something to the subject concerning something of the other). Thirdly, a pilot study indicated that all interactive situations also elicited other judgements or feelings, and so the questionnaire was casted in polytomous response format. To all items the subject could choose a response out of four categories: lonesome, angry, indifferent, insecure. For data analytic purposes these were dichotomously coded as lonesome versus not lonesome. Our attention is on the appraisal of our subjects of situations as either lonesome or not.

The total number of items to be constructed from the five facets A through E, dropping A_3 and C_4 is $2 \times 3 \times 3 \times 2 \times 2 = 72$ items. Omitting also all structuples containing $A_1D_1E_1$ and $A_2D_1E_2$ left 72–$2(3 \times 3) = 54$ items.

Each structuple was represented by one item, for example, if you seldom did something for your partner whenever he/she has a problem, you would feel {lonesome | angry | indifferent | insecure}?

Hypotheses

A review of the literature on lonesomeness research suggests a number of relevant personal and situational determinants of lonesomeness. The facet design (Figure 18.5) represents only an outline of the situational determinants that appear potentially relevant. For those, a number of hypotheses can be formulated regarding the relationship between these determinants and the probability that one feels lonesome.

In the following we use the notation $x > y$, where x and y are structs, to indicate the hypothesis that infrequent occurrence of social interaction of the kind as given in struct x will more likely elicit a response of feeling lonesome than y will. In other words: Items containing x will have a larger item parameter than items containing y. For brevity of exposition, we omit the words "if it rarely occurs that [x, . . .]" from the phrasing in this section.

direction	*focus*	*partner*	*mode*	*locus of focus*
A {1 subject to other, 2 other to subject}	B {1 a problem, 2 an opinion, 3 an experience}	C {1 partner, 2 relative, 3 friend}	D {1 doing, 2 saying}	E {1 subject, 2 other}

Figure 18.5.

Direction of interaction

(2:) Other to subject > (1:) subject to other

It is to be expected that the probability of appraising a situation as lonesome will increase as one's freedom to control the situation decreases. Interactions that flow from the subject to the other are under the control of the subject. He may for example decide to help somebody, or leave it. On interactions that flow from the other to the subject, the subject has no control. Therefore, the probability of an appraisal of lonesomeness will be greatest in this situation.

Focus of interaction

(1:) problem > (3:) (nice) experience > (2:) opinion

Absence of effective interactions can be expected to induce an appraisal of lonesomeness with a greater probability than will the absence of cognitive interactions. Therefore, situations that focus on an opinion will less often lead to an appraisal of lonesomeness than situations characterized by either of the other two foci. As for the other two foci, failure to get help is likely to be a more intensely negative experience than failure to share a nice experience, and for that reason the "problem" focus is expected to effect the most strongly an experience of lonesomeness.

Partner

(1:) partner > (2:) relative > (3:) friend

The ordering of the "partner of interaction" elements is motivated by the psychological distance of the subject to the other. The shorter this distance, the more the absence of this type of situations is thought to lead to a sensation of lonesomeness. Hence, the expectation of the ordering as specified.

Mode of interaction

(1:) (physical) doing > (2:) saying something

Our expectation is that to do something involves a greater emotional investment than merely to say something. Therefore, a lack of interactions that we may characterize as physical actions will more likely yield experiences of lonesomeness than the absence of interactions that we may characterize as verbalizations.

Locus of focus

(1:) subject > (2:) other

It seems reasonable to assume that any problem, experience, or opinion of the subject himself will have a greater impact on feelings of lonesomeness than when it concerns the other person.

Hypotheses on the Subjects

We have formulated a second set of hypotheses on the subject parameters, related to the valuation (importance) and the actual frequency of each social interactive situation, and to the satisfaction with the actual occurrence of these situations. We will not discuss these here. Details are given in Broers (1994). The general model of equation (3), below, can be extended to incorporate these hypotheses.

PART THREE

Facet Design and the Linear Logistic Model

In this section we will first discuss the item response model for analyzing the data and testing the hypotheses. Starting from the dichotomous Rasch model, we present the polytomous linear logistic model (LLTM), and finally the Rasch Regression model (RRM), which allows us to test hypotheses both on facets and on subjects. Next, since the facet design is essentially a factorial design, we discuss how to tailor the specification of the LLTM to that design, including also possible interaction effects among the facets. Constructing the specification of the LLTM was done in an exploratory fashion, using analysis of variance techniques and stepwise regression, as will be shown below. The specification of the LLTM was subsequently validated on a second sample (see Broers, 1994).

The dichotomous Rasch model

Assuming that feelings of lonesomeness have a unidimensional structure, we expect that the probability of appraising a situation as lonesome will satisfy the dichotomous Rasch model:

$$P(Y_{vi} = 1 \mid \xi_v) = \frac{\exp(\xi_v - \sigma_i)}{1 + \exp(\xi_v - \sigma_i)},$$ (1)

where the subject parameter, ξ_v, can be labelled "proneness to lonesomeness," and the item parameter, σ_i, can be labelled elicitation of lonesomeness." The Rasch model, although implying rather strong assumptions, is chosen for two reasons: (a) its statistical property of "specific objectivity," which means that by conditional maximum likelihood estimation, item parameters can be obtained whose statistical expectation is independent of the unknown subject parameters, and so are sample free; (b) various extensions of the model exists that permit the incorporation of a facet design in the analysis.

The Linear Logistic Test Model (LLTM)

In the case that a stimulus (or whatever the object is to which the subject responds) is composed of empirically identifiable components, we can assign an effect parameter η_k to each component. Let $\mathbf{Q}$ be a known matrix consisting of (0,1) entries q_{ik} indicating the absence or presence of struct k in item i. Setting:

$$\sigma_i = \sum_k q_{ik}\eta_k$$ (2)

we impose linear constraints on the item parameters and have the *Linear Logistic Test Model*, LLTM (cf. Fischer, 1983). For dichotomous data, the LLTM is:

$$P(Y_{vi} = 1 \mid \xi_v) = \frac{\exp\left(\xi_v - \sum_k q_{ik}\eta_k\right)}{1 + \exp\left(\xi_v - \sum_k q_{ik}\eta_k\right)}$$ (3)

An algorithm called CLR (conditional logistic regression), which maximizes the conditional likelihood of the data with respect to the η parameters, given the number of positive responses per subject (which is a sufficient statistic for ξ_v), has been developed by Zwinderman (not publ.).

The matrix $\mathbf{Q}$ is usually structured as a binary indicator matrix and the parameters η_k represent the effects of the components (structs) of the items. This indicator matrix is comparable to a design matrix in analysis of variance, and subject to similar restrictions, notably that it must be of full column rank. This implies, for example, that for a facet of three levels, we do not estimate the effect of the first level but set its effect at zero and only estimate η parameters for the second and third level. Rather than structuring $\mathbf{Q}$ as a binary indicator matrix, it can also be structured as a matrix of contrasts. Later, the construction of the $\mathbf{Q}$ will be discussed in detail. Considering that:

$$\text{logit}(P_{vi}) = \xi_v - \sum_k q_{ik}\eta_k,$$

we see that the LLTM is formally equivalent to a logistic regression model for dependent variables, with the subject parameters ξ_v as residual terms. Or, stated alternatively, we have a multiple regression model of the item parameters on the columns of $\mathbf{Q}$ matrix as predictors, and the η parameters as regression coefficients. Any substantive hypotheses we might have concerning the effects of the structs and their possible interaction effects can now be investigated by structuring the $\mathbf{Q}$ matrix and estimating the η parameters. This includes, notably, the possibility of interaction effects among the facets.

The Rasch Regression Model

Any hypotheses about the subject parameters ξ can also be incorporated. Let $\mathbf{X}$ be a matrix of known scores x_{jv} of subjects (v) on some subject attributes or variables (j), (e.g., sex, age, marital status). These can be binary or continuous, but preferably orthogonal contrasts if we have a factorial design of subjects' attributes. We can rewrite the subjects vector ξ as follows, where β_j is the regression parameter of ξ on x_j, and ε is the subject residual independent of $\mathbf{x}$:

$$\xi_v = \sum_j \beta_j x_{vj} + \varepsilon_v \tag{4}$$

and estimate the β parameters and the ε parameters. The variances of ε and ξ indicate how much of the variance in ξ can not be predicted from known characteristics of the subjects. An algorithm to do so in conjunction with the binary Rasch model has been developed by Zwinderman (1991a, 1991b).

Now, inserting the regression (eq. (4)) of ξ_v on exogenous variables x_j as well as the linear constraints on the item parameters (eq. (2)), we can write eq. (1) as follows. Let

$$\mathbf{A} = (\mathbf{X} \mid -\mathbf{Q}), \qquad \alpha = \begin{pmatrix} \beta \\ \eta \end{pmatrix}, \qquad \begin{array}{l} \text{with } \boldsymbol{a}_{vi} = (\mathbf{x}_v \mid -\mathbf{q}_i) \text{ a row vector} \\ \text{and } \boldsymbol{a}'_{vi} \text{ its transpose.} \end{array} \tag{5}$$

Then (1) with (2) and (4) is:

$$P(Y_{vi} = 1 \mid a_{vi}, \varepsilon_v) = \frac{\exp(a'_{vi}\, a + \varepsilon_v)}{1 + \exp(a'_{vi}\, a + \varepsilon_v)}, \tag{6}$$

The latter is not a Rasch model, but the parameters can be estimated by marginal maximum likelihood (MML), i.e. by integrating out the ε_v parameters. Alternatively, we treat all subjects as a single "generalized subject," and incorporate sufficient variables in $\mathbf{X}$ to predict each individual's position on the latent trait, for example:

$$\xi_v = \sum_j \beta_j x_{vj} + \varepsilon \tag{7}$$

$$P(Y_{vi} = 1 \mid a_{vi}, \varepsilon) = \frac{\exp(a'_{vi}\, \alpha + \varepsilon)}{1 + \exp(a'_{vi}\, \alpha + \varepsilon)}. \tag{8}$$

which now is a straightforward logistic regression model and can be estimated by an unconditional ML method (Zwinderman, 1991a; an algorithm to do so is part of the CLR program).

Interaction Effects and Dummy Coding for the LLTM

In general one should not have interaction effects among random factors, because that implies that no prediction is possible of the effect of another level of a random factor. However, with fixed factors, as in the present facet design, interaction can be acceptable, and, in hindsight, also plausible. For example, the effect of the direction of social exchange (facet A) may be different when it concerns one theme ("focus," facet B) rather than another, and also when that theme is the subject's rather than the other person's (facet E). Interaction effects can be estimated as η's by adding appropriately coded columns to $\mathbf{Q}$.

Two interwoven issues should be considered in constructing the $\mathbf{Q}$ matrix: (a) the orthogonality of the design of constructing and administering the items, and (b) the correlations among the columns of the $\mathbf{Q}$ matrix.

(Non-)Orthogonality of the design and its implication for data analysis

As can be seen from the structure of the LLTM, the components of the items act as predictors of the item parameters. In earlier applications of the LLTM in aptitude and achievement research (e.g. Spada, 1976; Häussler, 1977; Van Maanen *et al.*, 1989), an item was conceived as requiring a combination of several mental operations, each having their own difficulty (η). Absence or presence of an operation is coded as a 0 or 1 entry in the pertinent column of the $\mathbf{Q}$ matrix. The item's difficulty thus is the sum of the difficulties of the components contained in that item. Unless some logically possible combinations of components are omitted from the set of items, the matrix $\mathbf{Q}$ will be of full column rank, but not, in general, orthogonal. However, if some combinations of components are omitted or logically impossible, some effects may be confounded. Effects will also be confounded if the numbers of subjects to whom the items are administered is not the same for all combinations of components (this may be negligible if a small number of observations is randomly missing.)

In the case of item facets, each consisting of mutually exclusive structs, we have a slightly different situation. As in Anova, what can be identified in the LLTM is not the effect of each struct by itself, but the difference between the effects of two structs (this is due to the fact that one identifiability constraint must be imposed on the item parameters, for example by setting one item parameter equal to zero.) In Anova, these effects are called contrasts, and for each factor or facet, the number of contrasts is equal to the number of levels (structs) in that factor (facet) minus one. There are many ways of coding contrasts. For instance, with p structs in a facet, the structs can be (arbitrarily) ordered, and structs j = 2, . . , p are each contrasted to the first struct, that is, a three-level facet is represented by two contrasts, {0,1,0} and {0,0,1}. There is one η parameter for each contrast. The jth entry in the contrast corresponds to the jth struct. Consequently, for a facet of three structs, two columns in the $\mathbf{Q}$ matrix are formed and a zero or one is entered in the ith row of the matrix, according to the composition of item i. The columns of $\mathbf{Q}$ will be orthogonal between facets (not necessarily within facets) if the design of the item set is orthogonal, that is, if all facets are factorially crossed with each other to construct the items (and if also each item is answered by an equal number of respondents).

If $\mathbf{Q}$ is orthogonal, there is a simple relation between ηs and σs : $\mathbf{Q}\eta$ = σ implies $\eta = \mathbf{D}^{-1}\mathbf{Q}^{T}\sigma$, where $\mathbf{D} = \mathbf{Q}^{T}\mathbf{Q}$, a diagonal matrix. $\mathbf{D}$ depends on the normalization of $\mathbf{Q}$. In effect, if a binary facet, X, is coded as $(-1,1)$, the corresponding η will be equal to the mean difference between X_1 items and X_2 items. The matrix $\mathbf{Q}$ can be called a matrix of (dummy) predictors. An example of a $\mathbf{Q}$ matrix for items based on two facets X and Y with three and two structs, respectively, is given in the right part of Table 18.1. The columns are labelled X1, X2,

Table 18.1. Uncorrelated Contrast Coding Example for Two Facets (3 × 2 structuples)

Item	Structuples		Q: Orthogonal and Uncorrelated Contrasts				
	X	Y	X1	X2	Y	X1 × Y	X2 × Y*
1	1	1	−1	0	−1	1	−1
2	2	1	1	0	−1	−1	−1
3	3	1	0	1	−1	0	2
4	1	2	−1	0	1	−1	1
5	2	2	1	0	1	1	1
6	3	2	0	1	1	0	−2

* obtained by first replacing column X2 by its equivalent $\{1,1,-2,1,1,-2\}$ and then multiplying its elements with column Y.

Y, etc., and these labels indicate the first and second contrast for facet X, and the single contrast for facet Y, resp. In Table 18.1, the X1 contrast is $\{-1,1,0\}$, the X2 contrast is $\{0,0,1\}$, and the Y contrast $\{0,1\}$. Alternatively, X2 can be replaced by its equivalent X2*: $\{-1,-1,2\}$; Using the latter and multiplying it element-wise with Y, yields the interaction contrast X2Y*.

If the design is not orthogonal, possible interaction effects among different facets will be confounded with main effects. This can be readily seen if one performs the following analysis. Construct a **Q** matrix with (0,1) entries for "main effects" only, as indicated above, and estimate the η parameters by the LLTM model, and reproduce the item parameters by calculating **Q**η. Then perform Anova on these reproduced item parameters, taking the facets as Anova factors. If the design is not orthogonal, the sums of squares for interactions will not be zero, even though no interaction effects were coded in the **Q** matrix.

Uncorrelated coding of the facet and interaction effects, and stepwise analysis

Not any set of contrasts is also uncorrelated. Consider a facet X with three structs, X_1, X_2, X_3. Let σ_{X_1}, σ_{X_2}, and σ_{X_3} be the means of the parameters of items containing X_1, X_2, X_3, respectively. The two contrasts: $[-1,1,0]$ representing the difference $\eta_1 = (\sigma_{X_2} - \sigma_{X_1})/2$, and $[-1,0,1]$ representing the difference $\eta_2 = (\sigma_{X_3} - \sigma_{X_1})/2$ are not orthogonal, and should not be used for constructing **Q**. Replacing these contrasts by $[0,1,0]$ and $[0,0,1]$ yields orthogonal, but yet correlated contrasts and should not be used either. Contrasts will be uncorrelated when they are orthogonal and the mean of all but at most one of them is equal to zero. When contrasts are correlated, the magnitudes of the effects represented by these contrasts cannot be independently interpreted. This problem is not unique to LLTM analysis, but is present as well in Anova and in multiple regression analysis. Uncorrelated orthogonal contrasts for a three-level facet X are, for example: $\{[2,-1,-1], [0,-1,+1]\}$ representing $(2\sigma_{X_1} - \sigma_{X_2} - \sigma_{X_3}))/4$ and $(\sigma_{X_3} - \sigma_{X_2})/2$, respectively. Also orthogonal and uncorrelated are $\{[-1,1,0], [0,0,1]\}$.

Interactions can subsequently be coded by element-wise multiplying the contrasts for the corresponding main effects. For instance, the BC interaction is coded by element-wise multiplying each of the two B contrasts with each of the two C contrasts, yielding four interaction contrasts.

Whatever way the contrasts are coded is immaterial if one is not interested in interpreting the numerical value of the estimated η parameters. If a certain number of contrasts yields an acceptable fit of the LLTM, one can reproduce the item parameters $\sigma = \mathbf{Q}\boldsymbol{\eta}$. Alternative coding of contrasts, although yielding different values of ηs, will not effect the reproduced item parameters, provided that the alternative set of codes covers the same main effects and interaction effects. However, if one is interested in reproducing the item parameters from a minimum number of η parameters, then one set of contrasts may be more efficient than another. For instance, if there is no (mean) difference between B_2 and B_3 items, the single contrast $\{-2,1,1\}$ will be as good as the two contrasts $\{-1,1,0\}$ and $\{-1,0,1\}$ to fit the item parameters.

For correlated contrasts there is a serious problem of interpretation of the estimated η parameters. Interaction contrasts are coded by element-wise multiplication of contrast codes of lower order effects. When the means of the main effects contrast are not equal to zero, multiplying them will generate correlated contrasts. As a consequence, the value (η) of an effect will in part depend on the presence of interaction contrast codes in the $\mathbf{Q}$ matrix. Likewise, the value of the interaction effects will in part depend on the presence of the contrasts for main effects. This is similar to multiple regression analysis, where each regression coefficient represents a partial effect, partialling out other predictors. Adding or deleting predictors will affect the values of the regression coefficients of those that are retained. Also, regression coefficients of additional predictors do not represent an independent additional effect of the added predictors. This is particularly inconvenient for interpretation if one wants to study interaction effects in addition to main effects. Recoding may remove correlations among contrasts. Table 18.1 is an example.

Uncorrelated contrasts do not have the disadvantage of confounding effects: The parameter, η, for each additional contrast represents the independent additive contribution of that contrast. Alternatively, one may interpret the means of the unconstrained item parameters for those (combinations of) facets which were entered into the **Q** matrix.

The proper coding of the **Q** matrix may get rather complicated when the item construction design is not orthogonal (and/or the numbers of respondents to each item are not equal). A set of uncorrelated contrasts for two facets, as in Table 18.1, may get correlated if some substructuples are more frequently contained in the set of items than others due to non-orthogonal crossing with other facets. This may obscure the straightforward interpretation of the effects.

Contrast coding for the present questionnaire and exploratory analyses

For the present questionnaire, one level of facet D ("doing") was meaningful only in situations of social exchange about an issue of the "non-actor," which could be either the subject, or the other, depending on who was actor (i.e. initiated the social exchange). As a consequence, the numbers of items for each of the four combinations obtained by crossing facets A ("direction") and E ("locus of focus") were not equal, and the design is not orthogonal. Therefore, facet E was not coded for itself, but separately for A_1 items and for A_2 items. Facet D was only coded for those items were the distinction between "doing" and "saying" was made, that is, it was coded $[-1, +1]$ if relevant, and coded $[0]$ if not relevant.

It should be noted that in doing so, the E effect is not estimated as main effect, but separately for each level of facet A. Also, the effect of "doing" is not estimated in itself, but only as a contrast to "saying" when the distinction between "doing" and "saying" is meaningful. We call these AE factors and D factors "pseudo main factors", but treat them like main factors.

Exploratory Anova of Rasch parameters. Possible interaction effects can be explored after first fitting the unconstrained unidimensional Rasch model in equation (1) and doing an Anova on the estimated item parameters, taking the five facets as independent variables (cf. Tables 18.4, 18.5, and 18.6). No meaning can be attached to the statistical aspects of that analysis, but the relative values of F ratios indicate which main effects and interactions appear large and which appear small and possibly negligible. Results on the sample discussed below indicated that main effects of facets C and D might be negligible, and that interaction effects of AB and of ABE might not be negligible.

More detailed inspection of the means of item parameters for various combinations of structs provides insight into the nature of these inter-action effects.

Exploratory stepwise multiple regression of Rasch parameters on dummy facet and interaction contrasts. The facets can then be coded into a set of dummy variables, including interaction effects. Several ways of orthogonal coding were tried to fit the data (reported below) most efficiently. With a set of codes used as predictors for the item parameters, entered in the matrix Q (cf. eq. 3, above), preliminary estimates of the vector η can be obtained as the regression coefficients in the multiple regression of the unconstrained item parameter esti-mates (σ) on Q. Using stepwise multiple regression, one can then find out which minimal set of codes reproduces the item parameters ade-quately. It turned out that 15 orthogonal codes (main effects of facets and some second order and third order interactions), fit the uncon-strained Rasch parameters with a multiple correlation of .985. With only nine codes, the multiple correlation was .968 for one set of codes (arbitrarily labelled L-contrasts), and .972 for another set (arbitrarily labelled J-contrast). Details of the stepwise regression are given in Table 18.2. Table 18.2 lists the contrasts by their order of entering into

Table 18.2. Stepwise Multiple Regression of Unconstrained Item Parameters on Two Sets of Contrasts (see text)

Step	L Contrasts	Mult. r	J Contrasts	Mult. r
1	A1	.647	A1	.647
2	A1E	.904	A1E	.904
3	B1*	.933	B1**	.939
4	B1A1E	.902	B1A1E	.948
5	B2(L)	.948	B1A2E	.953
6	AB1	.953	AB1	.959
7	B1A2E	.959	A2E	.963
8	A2E	.963	B1C1E	.968
9	B1C1E	.968	B2A2E	.972
10	B2A2E	.972	C2	.975
11	C2	.976	AB2	.978
12	AB2	.978	C1E	.981
13	C1E	.981	D1	.983
14	D1	.983	B1C2E	.984
15	B1C2E	.985	C1D	.985

* B constrasts coded as B1 = {−1, 2, 1} and B2 = {−1, 0, +1}
** B contrasts coded as B1 = {−1, 1, 0} and B2 = {0, 0, 1}

the multiple regression equation $\sigma = \mathbf{Q}\eta$, together with the multiple correlation coefficient as it increases by successively adding more contrasts as predictors. The two sets of contrasts referred to in Table 18.2 differ with respect to the contrasts used for the main effect of facet B. The set of J contrasts are listed in Figure 18.6 and Table 18.7. The results in Table 18.2 using the L contrasts are given merely to show that one set of contrasts can be less efficient then another set. As the mean estimated item parameter of B_3 items in the sample of data was almost equal to the overall mean of item parameters (see Table 18.5), the pair of contrasts B1 = $\{-1,2,-1\}$ and B2 = $\{-1,0,1\}$ for B is less efficient than B1 = $\{-1,1,0\}$ only, omitting B2 = $\{0,0,1\}$.

The regression coefficients obtained by this analysis can be considered as some kind of least squares estimate of the η parameters in the LLTM (they fit the unconstrained Rasch parameters in the sense of least squares, but their statistical properties vis-à-vis the data are not optimal in some specific sense; however, these regression coefficients were virtually equal to the η parameters obtained by conditional logistic regression (CLR)). In order to construct the ABE contrast, and considering the exploratory results discussed below, the B_1 and B_3 versus

	B1	B2	
B_1	-1	0	B1 contrasts B_1 to B2;
B_2	1	0	B2 contrasts B_3 to the mean of B_1, B_2 .
B_3	0	1	
	C1	C2	
C_1	-2	0	C1 contrasts C_1 to the mean of C_2 and C_3
C_2	1	-1	C2 contrasts C_2 to C_3.
C_3	1	1	
	D		
E_2D_1	-1		This contrasts D_1 to D_2 for E_2 items.
E_2D_2	1		
E_1D_2	0		
	A1E	A2E	
A_1E_1	2	0	A1E contrasts E_1 to E2 for A_1 items;
A_1E_2	-1	0	A2E contrasts E1 to E_2 for A_2 items.
A_2E_1	0	1	
A_2E_2	0	-2	

Figure 18.6. Contrast coding (J) of main effects and pseudo main effects

B_2 contrast was taken as $\{-1,2,-1\}$, and the B_1 versus B_2 contrast was taken as $\{-1,0,+1\}$ and these two were multiplied with the two AE contrasts to obtain the ABE contrasts as in Table 18.7. Other interactions were coded by multiplying the contrasts listed in Figure 18.6.

PART FOUR

Results of Rasch and LLTM Analyses

The questionnaire was administered to a sample of 304 students. Apart from the items asking for the appraisive response, the same items were also administered asking for importance, engagement, and satisfaction in real life. The latter data will not be reported in this chapter. Since the total number of items appeared too large for a single questionnaire, a fractional replication design was used (Figure 18.7). Each subject responded to 27 appraisive items. Four overlapping questionnaire forms were used, making four groups of respondents. Each item appeared in two groups. Subjects who had not responded to all 27 items were omitted from the analysis (for technical reasons: conditional maximum likelihood estimation gets extremely complicated and time-consuming when randomly missing data are to be treated as such). Consequently, 269 subjects were retained in the analyses. Each

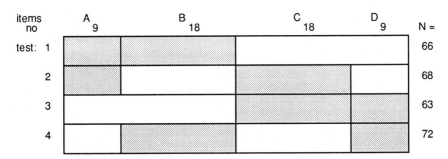

Figure 18.7. Shaded areas: composition of tests (item composition by structuples is listed in the appendix):

Item set A: 2 8 22 24 28 30 46 52 54
Item set B: 6 10 12 14 16 18 20 21 26 31 32 34 36 38 40 42 44 50
Item set C: 4 5 7 9 11 13 15 17 23 33 37 39 41 43 45 47 48 53
Item set D: 1 3 19 25 27 29 35 49 51
By mistake, items #21 in set B and #48 in set C were replaced by #30 and #3, resp. causing duplication of #30 in test 1 and of #3 in test 3.
N = number of respondents.

item was answered by approximately 135 subjects. Due to a mistake in compiling the questionnaire, two items were omitted and two others were duplicated, so effectively only 52 instead of 54 items could be analyzed. A polytomous response format was used, but dichotomized into "lonesome" versus other responses.

Unconstrained Rasch analysis

An adaptation of the computer program RIDA (Rasch analysis of incomplete designs developed by Glas (1989)) was used to obtain estimates of the item parameters (σ) using both Conditional Maximum Likelihood (CML) and Marginal Maximum Likelihood (MML) estimation. These estimates will be referred to as *unconstrained Rasch estimates*.

CML analysis and unconstrained estimation of the item parameters (based on data with no missing responses only) showed a good fit of the Rasch model as evaluated by Glas' (1988, 1989) R_1 and Van den Wollenberg's (1982) Q_1 test statistics ($R_1 = 518.7$, df $= 485$, p $= .14$; $Q_1 = 89.79$, df $= 77$, p $= .16$). The conditional log-likelihood is -2876.8. The parameter estimates, their standard errors, and the facet coding of the items are given in the appendix. The mean of the parameter estimates is set at zero; their standard deviation is 1.03; the range is from -1.858 to 1.771; there is some kurtosis (-1.272) and some skewness (.261).

MML estimation yielded virtually identical item parameter estimates, but the assumption of a normal distribution of the latent trait had to be rejected for this sample ($R_0 = 336.7$, df $= 104$, p $< .0005$). The R_1 test statistic for the MML analysis is 895.73 with 589 df. The difference with the R_0 statistic is only slightly larger than the R_1 statistic from the CML analysis, which corroborates the good fit of the Rasch model. The mean and standard deviation of the subject parameters, as estimated by MML, are $-.962$ and 1.22, respectively.

Unconstrained Rasch analysis: Exploring main effects

A first impression of the relation between the facets and the item parameters is obtained from item parameter means per struct (Table 18.3). Note that a negative item parameter value indicates that the item (i.e. absence of a particular social exchange) "easily" elicits an appraisal of lonesomeness. The means in Table 18.3 show that the hypotheses on A ("direction"), B ("focus"), C ("partner") and E ("focus of focus") are sustained, but the hypothesis concerning D ("doing" vs "saying") is refuted. The difference between D_1 and D_2 appears large

Table 18.3.   Mean Estimated Item Parameter

Facet	Struct		
	1	2	3
A	.661	−.661	—
B	−.284	.333	−.055
C	−.027	−.089	.114
D	.358	−.190	—
D[a]	.358	.201	—
E	−.701	.701	—
A_1E[b]	−.594	1.326	—
A_2E[b]	−.757	−.480	—

[a] Only for items where D_1 and D_2 are distinguished, i.e. excluding A_1E_1 and A_2E_2 items.

[b] E_1 and E_2 means for A_1 and A_2 items separately.

and is contrary to the hypothesis. However, this may be due to the fact that D_1 is confounded with (part of) the AE interaction. Considering only those items where the distinction between D_1 and D_2 is not confounded, the difference appears small. The frequencies and the means of the ADE items are shown in Table 18.4. Evidently, the most pronounced differences are between A_1 and A_2, and between E_1 and E_2, and also notably between A_2E_1 and A_1E_2 as shown in Figure 18.8.

Table 18.4.   Mean Item Parameter Estimates for ADE Substructuple Upper entry in Each Cell: Number of Items; Lower Entry: Mean Item Parameter

	A:	1 Subject to Other		2 Other to Subject			
	E:	1 Subject	2 Other	1 Subject	2 Other	Totals:	Totals[a]
D	1 doing	0 .	9 1.458	9 −.742	0 .	18 .358	18 .358
	2 saying	9 −.594	8 1.178	9 −.775	8 −.48	34 −.19	16 .201
	Totals	9 −.594	17 1.326	17 −.757	9 −.48	52 0	34 .284

[a] excluding A_1E_1 and A_2E_2 items which where all D_2.

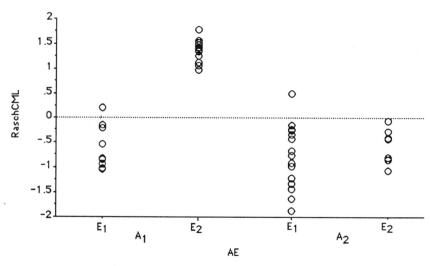

Figure 18.8. Scatterplot of CML parameters estimates grouped by A ("direction") and E ("locus") structs

Unconstrained Rasch analysis: Exploring interaction effects.

There seems a strong interaction between A ("direction") and B ("focus") (see Table 18.5). For A_2 items, the mean item parameter for A_2B_1 items is much smaller (more easily eliciting feelings of lonesomeness) than for A_2B_3 items, and the latter is much smaller than for

Table 18.5. Mean Item Parameter Estimates for AB Substructuple. Upper Entry in Each Cell: Number of Items; Lower Entry: Mean Item Parameter

A:		1 Subject to Other	2 Other to Subject	Totals
B:	1 problem	9 .548	9 −1.116	18 −.284
	2 opinion	9 .867	9 −.20	18 .333
	3 experience	8 .559	8 −.67	16 −.055
	Totals	26 .661	26 −.661	52 0

A_2B_2, items. For A_1 items, the differences between the levels of B are not large, and A_1B_1 items are not different from A_1B_3 items. Table 18.5 suggests coding one B contrast, namely $\{-1,1,0\}$, contrasting B_1 with B_2, since the effect of B_3 is near zero. There is, however a strong interaction effect of B at A_2E_1, as shown in Table 18.6. For A_2 items we find that ($x \gg y$ to be read as: items x elicit much more likely feelings of lonesomeness than items x y):

$A_2B_1E_1 \gg A_2B_1E_2$:
  other rarely {doing | saying} something about a problem of subject $\gg$
  other rarely {saying} something about a problem of other;
$A_2B_3E_1 > A_2B_3E_2$
  other rarely {doing | saying} something about an experience of subject $>$
  other rarely {saying} something about an experience of other;

Table 18.6. Mean Item Parameter Estimates for ABE Substructuple. Upper Entry in Each Cell: Number of Items; Lower Entry: Mean Item Parameter A_1 = "subject to other", A_2 = "other to subject"; B = "focus"; E = "locus"

A_1	E:	1 Subject	2 Other	Totals
	1 problem	3 −.936	6 1.289	9 .548
B:	2 opinion	3 −.045	6 1.323	9 .867
	3 experience	3 −.8	5 1.374	8 .559
	A_1 Totals	9 −.594	17 1.326	26 .661

A_2	E:	1 Subject	2 Other	Totals
	1 problem	6 −1.392	3 −.563	9 −1.116
B:	2 opinion	6 −.148	3 −.302	9 −.20
	3 experience	5 −.727	3 −.575	8 −.67
	A_2 Totals	17 −.757	9 .48	26 −.661

$A_2B_2E_1 < A_2B_2E_2$:

    other rarely {doing | saying} something about opinions of subject <

    other rarely {doing | saying} something about opinions of other.

For A_1 items we observe a different pattern. Within A_1 items, there is a negative effect of B_2 at level E_2, but there is a strong positive effect of B_2 at level E_1: $A_1B_1E_1 \cong A_1B_3E_1 >> A_1B_2E_1$:

$A_1B_1E_1 >> A_1B_1E_2$:

    subject rarely {saying} something about a problem of subject >>

    subject rarely {doing | saying} something about a problem of other;

$A_1B_3E_1 > A_1B_3E_2$:

    subject rarely {saying} something about an experience of subject >

    subject rarely {doing | saying} something about an experience of other;

$A_1B_2E_1 >> A_1B_2E_2$:

    subject rarely {saying} something about opinions of subject >>

    subject rarely {doing | saying} something about opinions of other.

To obtain the ABE contrasts, inspection of the Table 18.6 suggest that the most appropriate way of coding the B effects before multiplying them with the AE contrasts, is by the two contrasts $\{-1,2,-1\}$ and $\{-1,0,1\}$. The resulting contrasts for the ABE interaction are shown in Table 18.7.

LLTM analysis

The LLTM analysis on main effects and pseudo main effects only (cf. Figure 18.6), gave the result shown in Table 18.8. Note that the

Table 18.7. Contrasts for Triple ABE Interaction

Structuples	Contrasts			
	B1A1E	B1A2E	B2A1E	B2A2E
$A_1B_1E_1$	-2	0	-2	0
$A_1B_1E_2$	1	0	1	0
$A_1B_2E_1$	4	0	0	0
$A_1B_2E_2$	-2	0	0	0
$A_1B_3E_1$	-2	0	2	0
$A_1B_3E_2$	1	0	-1	0
$A_2B_1E_1$	0	-1	0	-1
$A_2B_1E_2$	0	2	0	2
$A_2B_2E_1$	0	2	0	0
$A_2B_2E_2$	0	-4	0	0
$A_2B_3E_1$	0	-1	0	1
$A_2B_3E_2$	0	2	0	-2

Table 18.8.   LLTM Estimates of η Parameters (Main and Pseudo-Main Effects Only)

Contrast	Facet Levels[a]				η Estimate
	1	2	3	4	
A (direction)	−1	1	—	—	0.677
B1 (focus)	−1	1	0	—	−0.180
B2 (focus)[b]	0	0	1	—	−0.036
C1 (partner)	−2	1	1	—	−0.001
C2 (partner)	0	−1	1	—	−0.106
D (mode)[c]	−1	1	—	—	0.067
A_1E (locus, A_1)[d]	2	−1	0	0	0.643
A_2E (locus, A_2)[d]	0	0	1	−2	0.101

[a] Columns correspond to the structs of each facet.

[b] A single contrast with non-zero mean does not affect the orthogonality of the contrast.

[c] Only coded where the distinction was made; otherwise coded as zero. See text.

[d] Levels 1 and 2 correspond to A_1E_1 and A_1E_2; Levels 3 and 4 correspond to A_2E_1 and A_2E_2.

main effect of E and its interaction with A are represented by two contrasts to express that a main effect of E in itself cannot be independently estimated. Anova of the reproduced item parameters will show a mean difference between E_1 and E_2 items, as it is a function of the D, A_1E and A_2E contrasts effects. It also apparent from Table 18.8 that the B2 and C1 contrasts are negligible, and that to a lesser extent, the D contrast is also negligible.

This LLTM analysis using main effects and pseudomain effects showed a conditional likelihood of −2929.8. Taking two times the difference between this likelihood and the corresponding one of the unconstrained analysis equals 106, which is approximately χ^2 distributed with $52 - 8 = 44$ degrees of freedom, which is highly significant. However, the standard errors of the η estimates, as well as the stepwise multiple regression analysis of the unconstrained parameters on the contrasts, including interaction contrasts, indicated that some main effects were not significant, and some interaction effects, notably the ABE interaction, might contribute significantly to the values of the item parameters.

Successive analyses, taking these contrasts in the order in which they appeared in stepwise multiple regression of the unconstrained Rasch parameters on these contrasts (Table 18.2), gave the results in Table 18.9. Including only the first nine contrasts yields a fit which

Table 18.9.   Multiple Correlations between Contrasts and Unconstrained
Item Parameter Estimates: Log Likelihood and Likelihood Ratio Tests
(CLR Analysis) for Increasing Numbers of Contrasts Entered into the Design
(Step 1 through 8 Not Listed; Same as in Table 1)

Step	J-Contrast	Unconstr'd Mult r	CLR Analyses				
			$-\ln(L)$	$-2\ln(L/L_u)$	df	p	Mult r
9	B2A2E	.972	2905.40	57.20	42	.059	.971
10	C2	.975	2900.42	47.24	41	.23	.975
11	AB2	.978	2898.74	43.88	40	.39	.977
	unconstr'd		2876.80				

does not deviate significantly from the fitting the unconstrained
Rasch model.

A second look at the ABE interaction

The effects represented by the three ABE interaction contrasts
(omitting main effects, and also omitting the AE and AB interaction)
are as shown in Table 18.10. The absence of the B2A1E contrast (contrasting B_1 with B_3 in addition to the A1E contrast), is shown by the
equality of B_1 and B_3 at A_1. The B1A1E contrast sets off B_2 from B_1
and B_3 at A_1. Similar, but less strong, is the B1A2E offsetting B_2 from
B_1 and B_3 at A_2. Finally, the B2A2E contrast creates a difference
between E_1 and E_2 at A_2. At A_2B_1 this E-difference is larger than at
A_1B_1, and at A_2B_3 the direction of that E-difference is opposite to the
corresponding difference at A_1.

Keeping in mind that (for this sample):

(A) Absence of social exchange initiated by another (A_2) induces
more feelings of lonesomeness than absence of exchange
initiated by the subject (A_1), and

(B) Absence of social exchange about problems (B_1) induces more
feelings of lonesomeness than absence of social exchange
about opinions (B_2), and exchange about experiences is "neu-
tral," but

(AB) The effect of the topic of exchange is smaller, and experiences are like problems, when the exchange is initiated by
the subject, as compared to exchange initiated by the other,
where the effect of the topic is much more pronounced,

(AE) Absence of self-initiated exchange about one's own issues
induces strongly feelings of lonesomeness whereas this is

Table 18.10.   Incidence Table ABE Effect. Numbers of Items and ABE Effects, Ignoring Main Effects and Lower Order Interaction. Upper Entry in Each Cell: Number of Items; Lower Entry: Mean Item Parameter

Direction A:		1 Subject to Other		2 Other to Subject		Totals	
Locus E:		1 Subject	2 Other	1 Subject	2 Other	1 Subject	2 Other
focus B:	1 problem	3 −.166	6 .083	6 −.181	3 .362	9 −.176	9 .176
	2 opinion	3 .332	6 −.166	6 .124	3 −.248	9 .193	9 −.193
	3 experience	3 −.166	6 .083	6 .057	3 −.114	9 −.017	9 .017

not so when it concerns the other's issues, while this difference is much smaller when it concerns absence of exchange initiated by another person, and

(D) Moreover, there is a small (barely significant) difference between "saying" and "doing": rarely saying something induces more lonesomeness than rarely doing something about issues of the person to whom the exchange is directed,

we see from the interaction effect in Table 18.10 the following: Absence of self-initiated exchange on one's own problems or experiences induces more feelings of lonesomeness than when it concerns opinions, but this difference is reversed and smaller when it concerns the other person's issues: Our respondents feel more lonesome when they cannot talk to somebody about the other's opinions than when they can not talk about their own. This pattern is essentially the same when it concerns absence of social exchange initiated by the other, but the effects are definitely more pronounced, and the issue of experiences is appraised like opinions rather than like problems (as it is in self-initiated exchange). One might conclude that when one initiates exchange about experiences, it is like talking about problems, but when the other party initiates exchange about experiences it is like talking about opinions.

DISCUSSION

The motivation for the work reported in this paper was to present a new and hopefully improved methodology for questionnaire research.

The results show that systematic design of a questionnaire in conjunction with LLTM analysis can provide insight in which aspects (facets) of situations as depicted in the items, determine an appraisive emotional response. However, the central question is what is being measured? It is not loneliness as a situational state, or a trait, of the subject. Neither is it lonesomeness as a disposition for behavior. Rather, it is the proneness of the subject to appraise himself in certain situation as lonesome. In that sense it is a trait or disposition to feel lonesome. Whether or not a given person does actually feel lonesome is not measured. A more or less enduring state of lonesomeness would occur if the individual finds himself more or less continuously in situations to which he would respond by feeling lonesome.

Research on lonesomeness has pointed to many variables that are related to feelings of lonesomeness, for example the absence of social support, but also variables like the perception of one's social and material competence may be involved. Correlational studies of operationalized variables do not easily provide insight in causal relations. Quite often, operationalizations of hypothesized causal variables are confounded with the operationalization of the dependent variable. This state of affairs appears to call for an approach that obviates operationalization of hypothetical constructs and introduces theoretical concepts in a more inductive fashion, although guided by hypothetico–deductive reasoning. The introduction of a theoretical variable, which we called "proneness to lonesomeness", and which is empirically justified by the present research, might be further studied by exploring it in relation to other theoretical variables introduced in a similar way by means of facet design and latent trait modeling.

REFERENCES

Broers, N.J. (1994). *Formalized theory of appraisive judgments*. Doct. Diss., Nijmegen Institute for Cognition and Information, University of Nijmegen.

Canter, D. (Ed.) (1985). *Facet theory, approaches to social research*. New York: Springer.

Coombs, C.H. (1987). The structure of conflict. *American Psychologist, 42*(4), 355–363.

Coombs, C.H. & Huang, L. (1970). Polynomial psychophysics of risk. *Journal of Mathematical Psychology, 7*, 317–338.

Coombs, C.H. & Avrunin, G.S. (1988). *The structure of conflict*. Hillsdale, NJ: Lawrence Erlbaum.

Fischer, G.H. (1983). Logistic Latent Trait Models with Linear Constraints. *Psychometrika, 48,* 3–26.

Frijda, N.H. (1988). *De emoties [The emotions]*. Amsterdam: Bert Bakker.

Frijda, N.H., & Mesquita, B. (1992). Emoties: natuur of cultuur [Emotions: nature or culture?]. *Nederlands Tijdschrift voor de Psychologie, 47,* 3–14.

Glas, C.A.W. (1988). The derivation of some tests for the Rasch model from the multinomial distribution. *Psychometrika, 53,* 525–547.

Glas, C.A.W. (1989). *Contributions to estimating and testing Rasch models.* Doct. Diss. University of Twente.

Green, D.M., & Swets, J.A. (1966). *Signal detection theory and psychophysics.* New York: Wiley.

Guttman, L. (1976, 1977a, 1981a). What is not what in Statistics. Paper presented at the Annual Meeting of the Israel Statistical Association, Jerusalem, June 1976. Reprinted in: *The Statistician,* 1977, 26/2, 81–107. Also reprinted in I. Borg (Ed.). *Multidimensional Data Representations, When When and Why,* p. 20–46. Ann Arbor, MI: Mathesis Press, 1981.

Guttman, L. (1977b, 1979, 1981b). What is not what in theory construction. Paper presented at the 8th annual meeting of the Israel Sociological Association, Haifa, 1977. Reprinted in *Quantitative Sociology Newsletter,* 1979, no. 22, 5–36. Also reprinted in I. Borg (Ed.), *Multidimensional Data Representations, When and Why,* p. 47–64. Ann Arbor, MI: Mathesis Press, 1981.

Häussler, P. (1977). Investigation of mathematical reasoning in science problems. In H. Spada, & W.F. Kempf (Eds.) *Structural models of thinking and learning.* p. 263–280. Bern–Stuttgart–Vienna: Huber.

Lord, F.M. (1980). *Application of Item Response Theory to Practical Testing Problems.* Hillsdale, NJ: Erlbaum.

Roskam, E.E. (1989). Operationalization, a superfluous concept. *Quality and Quantity, 23,* 237–275.

Roskam, E.E. (1990). Formalized theory and the explanation of empirical phenomena. In J.J. Hox & J. de Jong-Gierveld (Eds.). *Operationalization and Research Strategy,* pp. 179–198. Amsterdam: Swets & Zeitlinger.

Shye, S. (1978). On the search for laws in the behavioral sciences. In: S. Shye (Ed.), *Theory construction and data analysis in the behavioral sciences.* San Francisco: Jossey–Bass.

Spada, H. (1976). *Modelle des Denkens und Lernens.* Bern–Stuttgart–Wien: Huber.

Van Maanen, L., Been, P., & Sijtsma, K. (1989). The linear logistic model and heterogeneity of cognitive strategies. In Edw. E. Roskam (Ed.) *Mathematical Psychology in Progress,* pp. 267–287. Berlin: Springer.

Van den Wollenberg, A.L. (1982). Two new test statistics for the Rasch model. *Psychometrika, 47,* 123–141.

Zwinderman, A.H. (1991a). A generalized Rasch model for manifest predictors. *Psychometrika, 56,* 589–600.

Zwinderman, A.H. (1991b). A two-stage Rasch model approach to dependent item responses: an application of constrained latent trait models. *Methodika, V,* 33–46.

APPENDIX

Item Structs, Estimated Unconstrained CML Parameters, and Standard Errors.

item	A	B	C	D	E	σ	S.E.
1	1	1	1	1	2	1.2566	.2700
2	1	1	1	2	1	−1.0485	.1982
3	1	1	1	2	2	.9706	.2047
4	1	1	2	1	2	1.7712	.3198
5	1	1	2	2	1	−.8241	.2039
6	1	1	2	2	2	1.0553	.2615
7	1	1	3	1	2	1.4173	.2856
8	1	1	3	2	1	−.9366	.1980
9	1	1	3	2	2	1.2659	.2733
10	1	2	1	1	2	1.5091	.3004
11	1	2	1	2	1	−.1395	.2094
12	1	2	1	2	2	1.1227	.2666
13	1	2	2	1	2	1.4173	.2856
14	1	2	2	2	1	−.206	.2021
15	1	2	2	2	2	1.3399	.2791
16	1	2	3	1	2	1.4239	.2922
17	1	2	3	2	1	.2096	.2181
18	1	2	3	2	2	1.1227	.2666
19	1	3	1	1	2	1.4045	.2824
20	1	3	1	2	1	−.5446	.1958
21	1	3	1	2	2	•	•
22	1	3	2	1	2	1.3552	.2884
23	1	3	2	2	1	−1.0231	.2051
24	1	3	2	2	2	1.0596	.2652
25	1	3	3	1	2	1.5678	.2977
26	1	3	3	2	1	−.8321	.1934
27	1	3	3	2	2	1.4839	.2896
28	2	1	1	1	1	−.8993	.1980
29	2	1	1	2	2	−.8315	.1987
30	2	1	1	2	1	−1.3123	.1621
31	2	1	2	1	1	−1.8583	.2064
32	2	1	2	2	2	−.7965	.1935
33	2	1	2	2	1	−1.4346	.2118
34	2	1	3	1	1	−1.2224	.1943
35	2	1	3	2	2	−.0624	.2063
36	2	1	3	2	1	−1.6252	.2004

37	2	2	1	1	1	−.2228	.2079
38	2	2	1	2	2	−.0467	.2063
39	2	2	1	2	1	−.3456	.2061
40	2	2	2	1	1	−.4341	.1974
41	2	2	2	2	2	−.4265	.2052
42	2	2	2	2	1	−.2448	.2011
43	2	2	3	1	1	−.1395	.2094
44	2	2	3	2	2	−.4341	.1974
45	2	2	3	2	1	.4962	.2285
46	2	3	1	1	1	−.2461	.2058
47	2	3	1	2	2	−1.0633	.2055
48	2	3	1	2	1	•	•
49	2	3	2	1	1	−.982	.1994
50	2	3	2	2	2	−.3968	.1981
51	2	3	2	2	1	−.982	.1994
52	2	3	3	1	1	−.6744	.1991
53	2	3	3	2	2	−.264	.2073
54	2	3	3	2	1	−.7497	.1985

Items #21 and #48 were by mistake omitted from the questionnaire.

chapter **19**

Measuring Quickness and Correctness Concurrently: A Conjunctive IRT Approach*

Robert J. Jannarone
University of South Carolina

Interest in measuring response times has been continuous and intense over the years, among cognitive psychologists (Bejar, 1986; Bejar, Chaffin, and Embretson, 1991; Lohman, 1990; 1991) and psychometricians (Bloxom, 1985; Pashley, 1987; Tatsuoka & Tatsuoka, 1979). Yet, nearly all standardized tests are based on correctness measures alone, because measuring response times in large groups has not been practical in the past. However, rapid and steady computing advances will surely make standardized response time measurement feasible within a decade. As a result, a new focus on models that combine quickness scores and correctness scores may be suitable.

Interest in measuring quickness and correctness concurrently has been lacking, with a few notable exceptions (Thissen, 1983). Also, although Thissen has developed and applied separate models for measuring quickness and correctness responses to the same items, no models have yet appeared for measuring quickness–correctness associations. At first glance, it may seem adequate to treat quickness and correctness as separate but correlated ability measures. However,

* The author thanks Eric Maris for offering useful comments on an earlier draft.

other concerns suggest that this treatment is only adequate up to a point.

In some settings, strong dependencies exist between response speed and accuracy, within persons as well as between persons (Lohman, 1991). In learning a musical instrument, performing an athletic event, or giving a lecture, some persons may make more mistakes when they perform more quickly, because quick and correct performance is demanding for them. Yet, others may make fewer mistakes under the same conditions, because performing more quickly makes them more alert. The former case results in negative correlations between quickness and correctness within persons, and the latter case results in positive correlations. As a result, individual differences in speed–accuracy tradeoffs (in Lohman's terms) are not only possible but also potentially interesting. One motive for this chapter is to supply appropriate models for measuring such speed–accuracy tradeoffs.

A second motive for this chapter is to explain some curious connections between item difficulty, discrimination, and response time that have appeared in psychometric reports (Lord, 1975; 1984; Stocking, 1988a; 1988b; 1989; Yen, 1985) as well as in cognitive reports (Bejar, 1986, Bejar et al., 1991; Lohman, 1991). The psychometric results focus on correlations between item difficulty and discrimination that appear in existing tests. Evidently, highly difficult items tend to be much more discriminating than moderately difficult items, but easy items tend to be slightly more discriminating than moderately difficult items. Lord's early work in this area (Lord, 1975) focused on transforming the latent ability scale to remove offending difficulty–discrimination correlations, when fitting the Birnbaum (two-parameter logistic) model (Lord & Novick, 1968).

On the cognitive side, Bejar (1986) showed that spatial rotation response speed is related to task complexity, difficulty, and item discrimination. Also, Bejar et al. found strong negative correlations between item difficulty and discrimination, for several GRE analogy items. Lohman (1991) reported a variety of relationships between complexity, accuracy, and speed–accuracy tradeoffs as well, based on several studies. In related work (Lord, 1984; see also Kristoff, 1968), Lord considered conjunctive and disjunctive psychometric models that also have interesting cognitive implications. For example, his conjunctive model can be interpreted as requiring that passing an item may require passing each among several latent tasks. If each of these component tasks follows a Rasch model, then the kind of positive difficulty–discriminability associations that have been reported will occur. Also, since performing each of these latent tasks takes time, item response times will reflect the number of required item tasks. Similar observations have been made by researchers examining the application of mixture models to these types of data (Mislevy & Wilson, 1993).

The conjunctive and disjunctive models that were introduced by Lord (1984) and by Kristoff (1968) are distinct from other conjunctive models that have been introduced by Jannarone (1986; 1991; in press). Some of the models to be presented are based on Lord's and Kristoff's models, which require local independence. Others are based on Jannarone's models, which involve local dependencies.

A third motive for this chapter is to supplement existing, nonidentifiable IRT models with identifiable quickness–correctness counterparts. Identifiability problems, which appear in multiple factor analysis models (Steiger, 1979), may also appear in certain item response models (Fischer, 1981; Jannarone, 1994; Swaminathan & Gifford, 1985; Wright, 1977). In the factor analysis case, such problems disappear once a sufficient number of involved latent variables become observable—regression models with observable counterparts to factor scores have no such identifiability problems, for example. Likewise, nonadditive item statistics have been proposed as observable supplements to additive statistics, for achieving item response and learning model identifiability (Jannarone, 1986; 1991; 1994, in press, to appear). Quickness–correctness cross-products will be introduced below as similar supplements for achieving identifiability.

This chapter is organized as follows: an ad hoc model is introduced first that has provisions for individual differences in speed–accuracy tradeoffs but no cognitive process basis. Two cognitive latent task models are introduced next, one requiring all of several component latent tasks to be completed and the other requiring only one of several component tasks to be completed. Technical details are then given that provide a basis for efficient estimation in the ad hoc model case and ad hoc estimation in the latent task model cases.

KEY CONCEPTS

An ad hoc model. To set notation, individuals are labeled by i ($i = 1, \ldots, I$), items are denoted by m ($m = 1, \ldots, M$), persons' binary (correct = 1, incorrect = 0) item responses are denoted by x_{im}, persons' item response times are denoted by t_m, and persons' quickness scores are labeled by q_{im}, where $q_{im} = 1/t_{im}$. Item responses are restricted to $(x_{im}, t_{im}) \in \{0, 1\} \times [t_{min}, \infty)$, where t_{min} is a prespecified positive constant, or equivalently to $(x_{im}, q_{im}) \in \{0, 1\} \times (0, q_{max}]$, where $q_{max} =$

$1/t_{\min}$. Persons' correctness, quickness, and correctness–quickness parameters are denoted by $\theta_i^{(X)}$, $\theta_i^{(Q)}$, and $\theta_i^{(XQ)}$, respectively; and item correctness, quickness and correctness–quickness parameters are labeled by $\beta_m^{(X)}$, $\beta_m^{(Q)}$, and $\beta_m^{(XQ)}$, respectively.

Thus, for $x_i \in \{0, 1\}^M$ and for $\boldsymbol{q}_i \in (0, q_{\max}]^M$, the ad hoc model has the form:

$$p\left(\underset{M\times 1}{x_i}, Q_i \mid \underset{3\times 1}{\theta_i} ; \underset{3\times M}{\beta}\right) = \prod_{m=1}^{M} p_m\left(x_{im}, q_{im} \mid \theta_i ; \underset{3\times 1}{\beta_m}\right)$$

$$\propto \exp\left\{\sum_{m=1}^{M} [(\theta_i^{(X)} - \beta_m^{(X)})x_{im} + (\theta_i^{(Q)} - \beta_m^{(Q)})q_{im}\right.$$

$$\left. + (\theta_i^{(XQ)} - \beta_m^{(XQ)})x_{im}q_{im}]\right\}. \tag{1}$$

Conditional correctness probabilities corresponding to (1) have the form,

$$Pr\left(\underset{M\times 1}{x_i} = x_i \mid \boldsymbol{q}_i, \theta_i ; \beta\right) = \prod_{m=1}^{M} Pr(x_{im} = x_{im} \mid q_{im}, \theta_i ; \beta_m)$$

$$= \prod_{m=1}^{M} \frac{\exp\{[\theta_i^{(X)} + \theta_i^{(XQ)}q_{im} - (\beta_m^{(X)} + \beta_m^{(XQ)}q_{im})]x_{im}\}}{1 + \exp\{\theta_i^{(X)} + \theta_i^{(XQ)}q_{im} - (\beta_m^{(X)} + \beta_m^{(XQ)}q_{im})\}}, x_i \in \{0, 1\}^M,$$

$$\tag{2}$$

$$= 0 \text{ elsewhere.}$$

and corresponding conditional quickness densities have the form:

$$f(\boldsymbol{q}_i \mid x_{im}, \theta_i ; \boldsymbol{\beta}) = \prod_{m=1}^{M} f_m(q_{im} \mid x_{im}, \theta_i ; \beta_m)$$

$$\propto \prod_{m=1}^{M} \exp\{[(\theta_i^{(Q)} + \theta_i^{(XQ)}x_{im} - (\beta_m^{(Q)} + \beta_m^{(XQ)}x_{im})]q_{im}\}, q_i \in (0, q_{\max})^M, \tag{3}$$

$$= 0 \text{ elsewhere.}$$

Equation (2) is easy to interpret because it is formally identical to the Rasch (1980) item response model. In particular the $(\theta_i^{(X)} + \theta_i^{(XQ)}q_{im})$ component corresponds to the Rasch model ability parameter and the $(\beta_i^{(X)} + \beta_i^{(XQ)}q_{im})$ component corresponds to the Rasch model difficulty parameter. Also, the overall effect of persons' quickness measures on their correctness probabilities can be easily seen by rearranging the exponents in (2) to obtain,

$$Pr\{X_i = x_i \mid q_i, \theta_i; \beta\} = \prod_{m=1}^{M} \frac{\exp\{[\theta_i^{(X)} - \beta_m^{(X)} + (\theta_i^{(XQ)} - \beta_m^{(XQ)})q_{im}]x_{im}\}}{1 + \exp\{\theta_i^{(X)} - \beta_m^{(X)} + (\theta_i^{(XQ)} - \beta_m^{(XQ)})q_{im}\}} . \quad (4)$$

Each factor of (4) has a standard logistic regression form that involves a single binary variable, x_{im}, along with its real-valued parameter appearing in the exponent of the denominator (Cox, 1970). Thus, an item quickness score has an increasing, decreasing, or zero effect on successful task completion if the corresponding $(\theta_i^{(XQ)} - \beta_m^{(XQ)})$ values are positive, negative, or zero, respectively. Also, magnitudes of the $(\theta_i^{(XQ)} - \beta_m^{(XQ)})$ values are directly related to the magnitudes of corresponding within person quickness–correctness correlations.

It should be noted that if the $\beta_m^{(X)}$ and the $\theta_i^{(X)}$ are all set to zero in (1) and the q_{im} are replaced by their average $q_m = (q_{1m} + \ldots + q_{Im})/I$ values, then (2) becomes identical to the Birnbaum model, except the discrimination parameters become replaced by the q_m values. This suggests that (2) can be viewed as an alternative to the Birnbaum model that replaces unobservable discrimination parameters with observable quickness measures.

The interpretation of the conditional quickness density (3) is similar to that of the conditional correctness probability function (2). Just as item conditional correctness probabilities depend on x_{im} coefficients in (2), item conditional quickness probabilities depend on q_{im} coefficients in (3), which are given by

$$\pi_{im} = \theta_i^{(Q)} + \theta_i^{(XQ)}x_{im} - (\beta_m^{(Q)} + \beta_m^{(XQ)}x_m) = \theta_i^{(Q)} - \beta_m^{(Q)} + \\ (\theta_i^{(XQ)} - \beta_m^{(XQ)})x_{im}. \quad (5)$$

Figure 19.1 shows conditional quickness densities for selected π values. (As has been discussed elsewhere (Pashley, 1987), one-parameter densities such as these are too simplistic to have general utility—more general versions of (5) are clearly needed for some applications.)

Two Rasch Latent Task Models

The models to be introduced next are closely related to locally independent conjunctive and disjunctive models (Lord, 1984). The first, so-called conjunctive latent task (CLT) model requires that: (a) passing item m by person i involves passing all among ξ_m latent, locally inde-

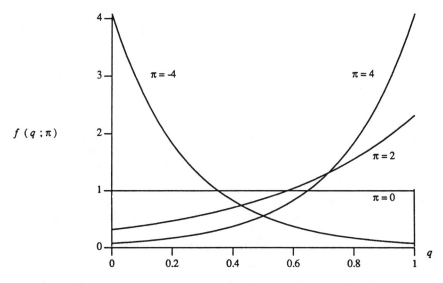

Figure 19.1. Some *ad hoc* quickness densities (q_{max} = 1).

pendent binary tasks, C_{i1} through $C_{i\xi_m}$; and (b) each such task has a Rasch model response function with the same difficulty. Thus, setting each Rasch response function difficulty parameter to 0 without loss of generality results in:

$$Pr\{X_{im} = 1 \mid \theta_i, \xi_m\} = Pr\left\{ \bigcap_{m=1}^{M} C_{ic} = 1 \mid \theta_i \right\}$$

$$= \prod_{c=1}^{\xi_m} Pr\{C_{ic} = 1 \mid \theta_i\}$$

$$= \prod_{c=1}^{\xi_m} \frac{\exp\{\theta_i\}}{1 + \exp\{\theta_i\}}$$

$$= \left[\frac{\exp\{\theta_i\}}{1 + \exp\{\theta_i\}} \right]^{\xi_{mi}}. \qquad (6)$$

For example, if three such items require one, two, and five latent tasks, their item response functions are:

$$Pr\{X_{im} = 1 \mid \theta_i; 1\} = \frac{\exp\{\theta_i\}}{1 + \exp\{\theta_i\}}, \qquad (7)$$

$$Pr\{X_{im} = 1 \mid \theta_i : 2\} = \frac{\exp\{2\theta_i\}}{1 + 2\exp\{\theta_i\} + \exp\{2\theta_i\}}, \tag{8}$$

and

$$Pr\{X_{im} = 1 \mid \theta_i ; 5\} = \frac{\exp\{5\theta_i\}}{1 + 5\exp(\theta_i) + 10\exp\{2\theta_i\} + 10\exp\{3\theta_i\} + 5\exp\{4\theta_i\} + \exp\{5\theta_i\}}, \tag{9}$$

respectively. These response functions are shown in Figure 19.2.

The Rasch CLT model differs from the usual Rasch model in that CLT parameters are not location parameters. As a result, item difficulty cannot be equated with these parameters as in the Rasch model case, but must be defined more broadly. Item "difficulty" will be defined here as the ability level that results in an item passing probability of .5 (Rasch difficulty parameters satisfy this definition as well). Likewise, item discrimination cannot be tied directly to CLT parameters, but must also be defined more broadly. Thus, item "discrimination" will be defined here as the slope of the item response function at the point where ability and difficulty are the same (Rasch model discrimination parameter values also satisfy this definition).

With these extended notions in mind, Figure 19.2 shows that both item difficulty and item discrimination increase with the number of latent tasks. As a result, difficulty and discrimination are positively related in items satisfying the Rasch CLT model, in keeping with results reported by Bejar, Lord, Stocking, and Yen. Also, if data were generated according to (6) but fit to the Birnbaum model, correlation patterns that have been reported between discrimination and difficulty estimates would be expected. In addition, such correlations could account for some major item "drift" calibration problems that occur in test equating and tailored testing settings (Stocking, 1988a). Using (6) as an alternative might avoid such problems.

Kristoff (1968) has shown that alternatives to (6) can be constructed such that all items are equivalent up to changes in scale. For any one-parameter latent conjunct model, Kristoff has shown that latent traits and item parameters can be transformed monotonically so that the transformed item response functions have the form,

$$Pr\{X_{im} = 1 \mid \theta_i', \beta_m\} = \exp\{-e^{-(\theta_i' - \beta_m)}\}, \tag{10}$$

for which the item parameters, β_m, are clearly location parameters. Whether (6) or (10) is used to represent a latent task model is a matter of convenience.

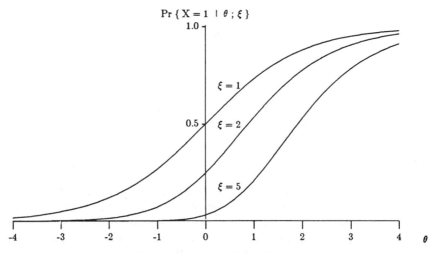

Figure 19.2.   Some Conjunctive Item Response Functions.

The next, so-called disjunctive latent task model requires that passing an item requires passing *any* among several latent, locally independent, and equally difficult binary tasks. If the number of such tasks for item m is denoted by δ_m and the corresponding $(\delta_m \times 1)$ vector of latent binary scores for person i is denoted by D_i, the Rasch disjunctive latent task model has the form,

$$Pr\{X_{im} = 1 \mid \theta_i ; \delta_m\} = 1 - Pr\{X_{im} = 0 \mid \theta_i ; \delta_m\}$$

$$= 1 - Pr\left\{ \bigcap_{d=1}^{\delta_m} D_{id} = 0 \mid \theta_i \right\} \qquad (11)$$

$$= 1 - (1 + \exp\{\theta_i\})^{-\delta_m}$$

Figure 19.3 shows special cases of (11) having δ_m values of one, two, and five. As Figure 19.3 shows, item discrimination increases with the number of latent tasks for the disjunctive case, just as for the conjunctive case.

Some Latent Task, Response Time Connections

The models to be introduced next are based on those in the last section, in that solving an item is assumed to involve solving latent component subtasks. In addition, these models require that: (a) individual differ-

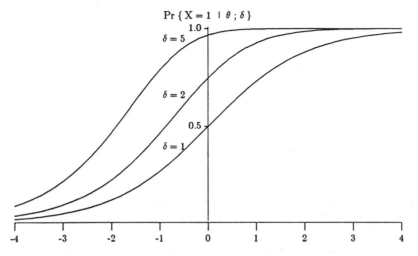

Figure 19.3.   Some Disjunctive Item Response Functions.

ences exist in the number of involved latent tasks; and (b) the number of latent tasks is related to item response time. The first time-related conjunctive latent task (TCLT) model requires that all subtasks for all items have equal difficulties, resulting in:

$$Pr\{X_{im} = 1 \mid \theta_i, t_m\} = \left[\frac{\exp\{\theta_i\}}{1 + \exp\{\theta_i\}} \right]^{t_m}. \tag{12}$$

The disjunctive counterpart to (12) requires that item response times are inversely related to corresponding numbers of latent tasks, resulting in:

$$Pr\{X_{im} = 1 \mid \theta_i, t_m\{ = 1 - (1 + \exp\{\theta_i\})^{-t_{im}}, \tag{13}$$

where t_{im} is the number of conjunctive latent tasks that are performed overtly by person i in answering item m. A hybrid conjunctive–disjunctive version that combines (12) and (13) has the form,

$$Pr\{X_{im} = 1 \mid \theta_i, t_{im}\} = \left[\frac{\exp\{\theta_i\}}{1 + \exp\{\theta_i\}} \right]^{t_{im}}, \quad t_{im} \geq t^*$$

$$= 1 - (1 + \exp\{\theta_i\})^{-t_{im}}, \quad t_{im} \leq t^*, \tag{14}$$

where t^* is a cutoff point separating the use of conjunctive and disjunctive processes. A conjunctive version that includes item difficulty parameters has the form,

$$Pr\{X_{im} = 1 \mid \theta_i, t_m ; \beta_m\} = \left[\frac{\exp\{\theta_i - \beta_m\}}{1 + \exp\{\theta_i - \beta_m\}} \right]^{t_{im}}, \qquad (15)$$

and a conjunctive version that includes response time parameters has the form,

$$Pr\{X_{im} = 1, T_{im} = t_{im} \mid \theta_i^{(X)}, \theta_i^{(T)}, \beta_m^{(X)}, \beta_m^{(T)}\}$$

$$\propto \left[\frac{\exp\{\theta_i^{(X)} - \beta_m^{(X)}}{1 + \exp\{(\theta_i^{(X)} - \beta_i^{(X)})\}} \right]^{t_{im}} \exp\{\theta_i^{(T)} - \beta_m^{(T)})t_{im}\}. \qquad (16)$$

Unfortunately, with the increased explanatory potential of (14) through (16) comes the potential for increased statistical estimation problems. For example, the only clearly useful statistical properties of (15) are the existence of unique maximum likelihood item parameters if person parameters are known and vice versa. Even so, models (14) through (16) have potential advantages over the Birnbaum model, because they include extra response time measures.

TECHNICAL DETAILS

The ad hoc model. Equation (1) does not include a description of the proportionality constant for the ad hoc model. The full version has the form,

$$p(x_i, \mathbf{q}_i \mid \boldsymbol{\theta}_i ; \boldsymbol{\beta}) = \prod_{m=1}^{M} v_m(\boldsymbol{\theta}_i, \boldsymbol{\beta}_m) \exp \left\{ \sum_{m=1}^{M} [(\theta_i^{(X)} - \beta_m^{(X)})x_{im} \right.$$

$$\left. + (\theta_i^{(Q)} - \beta_m^{(Q)})q_{im} + (\theta_i^{(XQ)} - \beta_m^{(XQ)})x_{im}q_{im}] \right\}, \qquad (17)$$

where

$$[v_m(\boldsymbol{\theta}_i, \boldsymbol{\beta}_m)]^{-1} = \int_0^{q_{max}} \sum_{u=0}^{1} \exp\{(\theta_i^{(X)} - \beta_m^{(X)})u + (\theta_i^{(Q)} - \beta_m^{(Q)})v$$

$$+ (\theta_i^{(XQ)} - \beta_m^{(XQ)})uv\}dv$$

$$= \int_0^{q_{max}} \exp\{(\theta_i^{(Q)} - \beta_m^{(Q)})v\}[1 + \exp\{\theta_i^{(X)} - \beta_m^{(X)}$$

$$+ (\theta_i^{(Q)} - \beta_m^{(Q)} + \theta_i^{(XQ)} - \beta_m^{(XQ)})v\}]dv$$

$$
= \frac{\exp\{(\theta_i^{(Q)} - \beta_m^{(Q)})q_{max}\} - 1}{\theta_i^{(Q)} - \beta_m^{(Q)}}
$$

$$
+ \frac{\exp\{\theta_i^{(Q)} - \beta_m^{(XQ)}\}}{\theta_i^{(Q)} - \beta_m^{(Q)} + \theta_i^{(XQ)} - \beta_m^{(XQ)}} \exp\{(\theta_i^{(Q)} - \beta_m^{(Q)} + \theta_i^{(XQ)})q_{max}\}
$$

$$
\begin{cases}
= A_{im}(q_{max}) + B_{im}(q_{max}), & \\
\quad \text{for} \quad \theta_i^{(Q)} - \beta_m^{(Q)}, \theta_i^{(Q)} - \beta_m^{(Q)} + \theta_i^{(XQ)} - \beta_m^{(XQ)} \neq 0, & (18) \\
\\
= q_{max} + B_{im}(q_{max}), \quad \text{for} & \\
\quad \theta_i^{(Q)} - \beta_m^{(Q)} = 0 \neq \theta_i^{(XQ)} - \beta_m^{(XQ)}, & (19) \\
\\
= A_{im}(q_{max})\exp\{\theta_i^{(X)} - \beta_m^{(X)}\}, & \\
\quad \text{for} \quad \theta_i^{(Q)} - \beta_m^{(Q)} \neq 0 = \theta_i^{(Q)} - \beta_m^{(Q)} + \theta_i^{(XQ)} - \beta_m^{(XQ)}, & (20) \\
\\
= q_{max}(1 + \exp\{\theta_i^{(X)} - \beta_m^{(X)}\}), & \\
\quad \text{for} \quad \theta_i^{(Q)} - \beta_m^{(Q)} = 0 = \theta_i^{(XQ)} - \beta_m^{(XQ)}, & (21)
\end{cases}
$$

where

$$
A_{im}(q_{max}) = \frac{\exp\{(\theta_i^{(Q)} - \beta_m^{(Q)})q_{max}\} - 1}{\theta_i^{(Q)} - \beta_m^{(Q)}}
$$

and

$$
B_{im}(q_{max}) = \frac{\exp\{\theta_i^{(Q)} - \beta_m^{(XQ)}\}}{\theta_i^{(Q)} - \beta_m^{(Q)} + \theta_i^{(XQ)} - \beta_m^{(XQ)}} \exp\{(\theta_i^{(Q)} - \beta_m^{(Q)} + \theta_i^{(XQ)})q_{max}\}.
$$

The corresponding likelihood is given by,

$$
\prod_{\substack{i=1}} p(\underset{M \times 1}{x_i}, \underset{1 \times M}{q_i} \mid \underset{3 \times 1}{\theta_i}; \underset{M \times 3}{\beta}) \propto \exp\left\{ \sum_{i=1}^{I} \left[\theta_i^{(X)} \sum_{m=1}^{M} x_{im} + \theta_i^{(Q)} \sum_{m=1}^{M} q_{im} \right. \right.
$$

$$
\left. + \theta_i^{(XQ)} \sum_{m=1}^{M} x_{im}q_{im} \right] + \sum_{m=1}^{M} \left[\beta_m^{(X)} \sum_{i=1}^{I} x_{im} \right.
$$

$$
\left. \left. + \beta_m^{(Q)} \sum_{i=1}^{I} q_{im} + \beta_m^{(XQ)} \sum_{i=1}^{I} x_{im}q_{im} \right] \right\}. \tag{22}
$$

Quickness densities corresponding to (3) and (5) (with person and item subscripts deleted for simplicity) have the form,

$$f(q_i \mid \pi) \begin{cases} = 1 \, / \, q_{max}, & \text{for } \pi = 0, \\[2mm] = \dfrac{\pi e^{\pi q}}{e^{\pi q_{max}} - 1}, & \text{for } \pi \neq 0, \end{cases} \tag{23}$$

with mean values given by,

$$E(Q) = \frac{q_{max}}{1 - e^{\pi q_{max}}} - \frac{1}{\pi}. \tag{24}$$

Since (1) belongs in the exponential family, joint maximum likelihood estimates and posterior modal parameter estimates can be obtained as in similar cases that have been described elsewhere (Jannarone, 1987; Jannarone, Yu, & Laughlin, 1990).

Conjunctive and Disjunctive Latent Task Models

For the Rasch conjunctive latent task model given by (6), it follows that

$$Pr\{X_{im} = 0 \mid \theta_i ; \xi_m\} = 1 - \left[\frac{\exp\{\theta_i\}}{1 + \exp\{\theta_i\}} \right]^{\xi_m}$$

$$= \frac{(1 + \exp\{\theta_i\}^{\xi_m} - \exp\{\xi_m \theta_i\}}{(1 + \exp\{\theta_i\})^{\xi_m}}, \tag{25}$$

When combined with (6) yields likelihoods of the form,

$$\{ \underset{M \times 1}{X_1} = x_1, \cdots, \underset{M \times 1}{X_I} = x_I \mid \underset{I \times 1}{\theta} ; \underset{M \times 1}{\xi} \}$$

$$= \prod_{i=1}^{I} \prod_{m=1}^{M} Pr\{X_{im} = x_{im} \mid \theta_i ; \xi_{im}\}$$

$$= \prod_{i=1}^{I} \prod_{m=1}^{M} \left[\frac{(1 + \exp\{\theta_i\})^{\xi_m} - \exp\{\xi_m \theta_i\}}{(1 + \exp\{\theta_i\})^{\xi_m}} \right]$$

$$\times \left[\frac{\exp\{\xi_m \theta_i\}}{(1 + \exp\{\theta_i\})^{\xi_m} - \exp\{\xi_m \theta_i\}} \right]^{x_m}. \tag{26}$$

The Rasch conjunctive latent trait model (6) is related to Kristoff's one parameter latent conjunct model (10) through monotone transformations of latent traits and item parameters. The required transformations are,

$$\theta' = \log \left[\log \left(\frac{e^{\theta}}{1 + e^{\theta}} \right) \right] \tag{27}$$

and $\beta = log(\xi)$. Kristoff's (1967) one-parameter model is a special case of Lord's (1984) two-parameter model, the parameters of which can be estimated using the LOGIST joint maximum likelihood algorithm (Wingersky, 1983). It follows from the monotone relation that connects (6) and (10) that LOGIST can be used to obtain estimates for the parameters of the Rasch CLT model as well. Perhaps the LOGIST convergence problems that were reported by Lord (1984) for his two-parameter CLT models would not occur in this simpler one-parameter case. Similar results and considerations hold for the disjunctive latent task model given by (11).

Time-related Latent Task Models

For the simple TCLT model given by (12), the likelihood is

$$Pr\{ \underset{M \times 1}{X_1} = x_1, \ldots , \underset{M \times 1}{X_I} = x_I \mid \underset{I \times 1}{\theta} ; \underset{I \times M}{t} \} = \prod_{i=1}^{I} \prod_{m=1}^{M} Pr\{ X_{im} = x_{im} \mid \theta_i, \underset{M \times 1}{t_i} \}$$

$$= \prod_{i=1}^{I} \prod_{m=1}^{M} A(\theta_i, t_{im}) B(\theta_i, t_{im})^{x_m}, \tag{28}$$

where

$$A(\theta_i, t_m) = \frac{1 + \exp\{\theta_i\}^{t_m} - \exp\{\theta_i t_{im}\}}{(1 + \exp\{\theta_i\})^{t_m}}, \tag{29}$$

and

$$B(\theta_i, t_{im}) = \frac{\exp\{t_{im}\theta_i\}}{(1 + \exp\{\theta_i\})^{t_{im}} - \exp\{t_{im}\}}. \tag{30}$$

Thus, the log-likelihood is

$$L\left(x_1, \ldots , x_I ; \underset{I \times 1}{\theta} ; \underset{I \times M}{t} \right) = \sum_{i=1}^{I} \sum_{m=1}^{M} \log[A(\theta_i, t_{im})] + x_{im}\log[B(\theta_i, t_{im})], \tag{31}$$

and

$$\frac{\partial L}{\partial \theta_i} = \sum_{m=1}^{M} \left[\frac{t_{im}(1 + \exp\{\theta_i\})^{t_{im}-1}}{(1 + \exp\{\theta_i\})^{t_{im}} - \exp\{t_{im}\theta_i\}} \right] \left[x_{im} - \frac{\exp\{\theta_i t_{im}\}}{(1 + \exp\{\theta_i\})^{t_{im}}} \right]. \quad (32)$$

It can be shown that (32) is positive in θ_i when $x_{i1} = x_{i2} = \cdots = x_{iM} = 0$, (32) is negative in θ_i when $x_{i1} = x_{i2} = \cdots = x_{iM} = 1$, and $\partial^2 L/\partial\theta_i^2 < 0$. It thus follows that unique maximum likelihood estimates exist for each θ_i unless either $x_i = 0$ or $x_i = 1$. Unique posterior modal estimates can also be obtained for any values of x_i including boundary values (Jannarone, Yu, & Laughlin, 1990).

Turning finally to the TCLT model with an item correctness parameter given by (15), similar results to (28) through (32) can be used to show that unique maximum likelihood/posterior modal Bayes estimates exist for item parameters if person parameters are fixed, and vice versa. Whether or not these estimates will converge jointly to global optimal estimates has not yet been shown, however.

SUMMARY

Some models for measuring quickness and correctness concurrently have been presented, which are based on two distinct conjunctive IRT developments in recent years. The first development, based on conjunctive latent traits underlying observable latent trait scores, has been used to connect item response times to item difficulty and discrimination. The second development, based on locally dependent item response measures, has been used to provide for individual and item differences in speed–accuracy tradeoffs. The models in this chapter have also been presented with a view toward replacing the Birnbaum model unobservable item discrimination parameters with observable item response time measures. The main practical conclusion is that measuring quickness and correctness conjunctively can offer interesting and potentially useful explanations for individual differences in cognitive processing.

REFERENCES

Bejar, I.I. (1986). A psychometric analysis of a three-dimensional spatial task. Research Report (RR-86–19-ONR). Princeton, NJ: Educational Testing Service.

Bejar, I.I., Chaffin, R., & Embretson, S.E. (1991). *A Cognitive and psychometric analysis of analogical problem solving*. New York: Springer Verlag.

Bloxom, B. (1985). Considerations in psychometric modeling of response time. *Psychometrika, 50,* 383–398.

Cox, D.R. (1970). *The analysis of binary data*. London: Methuen.

Fischer, G.H. (1981). On the existence and uniqueness of maximum likelihood estimates in the Rasch model. *Psychometrika, 46,* 59–77.

Jannarone, R.J. (1986). Conjunctive item response theory kernels. *Psychometrika, 51,* 357–373.

Jannarone, R.J. (1987). Locally dependent models for reflecting learning abilities. Center for Machine Intelligence Report #87–67, University of South Carolina.

Jannarone, R.J. (1991). Conjunctive measurement theory: Cognitive research prospects. In M. Wilson (ed.), *Objective measurement: theory into practice.* Norwood, NJ: Ablex, 210–235.

Jannarone, R.J. (1994). Locally dependent measurement: objectively measurable or objectionally abominable? In M. Wilson (ed.), *Objective measurement: theory into practice, Vol. 2.* Norwood, NJ: Ablex, 211–236.

Jannarone, R.J. (in press). Models for locally dependent responses: conjunctive item response theory. In W.J. van der Linden and R.K. Hambleton (eds.) *Handbook of modern item response theory*. New York: Springer–Verlag.

Jannarone, R.J. (to appear). *Concurrent information processing: a psycho-statistical model for real-time neurocomputing*. New York: Van Nostrand Reinhold.

Jannarone, R.J., & Roberts. J.S. (1984). Reflecting item interactions in scale construction: Meehl's paradox revisited. *Journal of Personality and Social Psychology, 47,* 631–637.

Jannarone, R.J., Yu, K.F., & Laughlin, J.E. (1990). Easy Bayes estimates for Rasch-type models. *Psychometrika, 55,* 449–460.

Kristoff, W. (1968). On the parallelization of trace lines for a certain test model. Research Report (RR-68–56). Princeton, NJ: Educational Testing Service.

Lehmann, E.L. (1983). *Theory of Point Estimation*. New York: Wiley.

Lohman, D.F. (1990). Estimating individual differences in information processing using speed-accuracy models. In R. Kanfer, P.L. Ackerman, & R. Cudeck (Eds.). *Abilities, motivation, and methodology: the Minnesota Symposium on Learning and Individual Differences.* Hillsdale, NJ: Erlbaum.

Lohman, D.F. (1991). Estimating individual differences in information processing using speed-accuracy models. In R. Kanfer, P.L. Ackerman, & R. Cudeck (Eds.). *Abilities, motivation, and methodology: the Minnesota Symposium on Learning and Individual Differences.* Hillsdale, NJ: Erlbaum.

Lord, F.M. (1975). The "ability" scale in item characteristic curve theory. *Psychometrika, 40,* 205–217.

Lord, F.M. (1984). Conjunctive and disjunctive item response functions. Research Report (RR-84-45-ONR). Princeton, NJ: Educational Testing Service.

Lord, F.M., & Novick, M.R. (1968). *Statistical theories of mental test scores.* Reading, MA: Addison-Wesley.

Mislevy, R.J., & Wilson, M.R. (1993). Marginal maximum likelihood estimation for a psychometric model of discontinuous development. Princeton, NJ: Educational Testing Service.

Pashley, P. (1987). *The analysis of latency data using the inverse Gaussian distribution.* Montreal, Quebec: Unpublished doctoral dissertation, McGill University.

Rasch, G. (1980). *Probabilistic Models for Some Intelligence and Attainment Tests.* Chicago: University of Chicago Press.

Steiger, J.H. (1979). Factor indeterminacy in the 1930's and the 1970's: some interesting parallels. *Psychometrika, 44,* 157–167.

Stocking, M.L. (1988a). Scale drift in on-line calibration. Research Report (RR-88–28-ONR). Princeton, NJ: Educational Testing Service.

Stocking, M.L. (1988b). Some considerations in maintaining adaptive test item pools. Research Report (RR-88–33-ONR). Princeton, NJ: Educational Testing Service.

Stocking, M.L. (1989). Empirical estimation errors in item response theory as a function of test properties. Research Report (RR-89–05). Princeton, NJ: Educational Testing Service.

Swaminathan, H. and Gifford, J.A. (1985). Bayesian estimation in the two-parameter logistic model. *Psychometrika, 50,* 349–364.

Tatsuoka, K. & Tatsuoka, M. (1979). *A model for incorporating response-time data in scoring achievement tests* (CERL Report No. E-7). Urbana, IL: University of Illinois Computer-based Education Research Laboratory.

Thissen, D. (1983). Timed testing: an approach using item response theory. In D.J. Weiss (Ed.), *New horizons in testing: latent trait test theory and computerized adaptive testing.* New York: Academic Press.

Wingersky, M. (1983). LOGIST: A program for computing maximum likelihood procedures for logistic test models. In R.K. Hambleton, (Ed.), *Applications of item response theory.* Vancouver: Educational Research Institute of British Columbia.

Wright, B.D. (1977). Solving measurement problems with the Rasch model. *Journal of Educational Measurement, 14,* 97–116.

Yen, W.M. (1985). Increasing item complexity: a possible cause of scale shrinkage for unidimensional item response theory. *Psychometrika, 50,* 399–410.

part   five

Mathematical and Statistical Applications to Measurement

chapter 20

An Optimization Model for Test Assembly to Match Observed-Score Distributions*

Wim J. van der Linden
University of Twente
Enschede, The Netherlands

Richard M. Luecht
National Board of Medical Examiners

A traditional objective in test assembly is to maximize the reliability of the test. From a classical test theory point of view, maximum reliability is an attractive feature of a test because tests with a high reliability are sensitive to the differences in true scores between the examinees in the population and have a low standard error of measurement. With the advent of item response theory (IRT), however, the objective of test assembly changed and it became possible to assemble tests to meet a targeted information function. It was Birnbaum (1968) who paved the way for this new objective, proposing an attractive two-

* The authors are indebted to Peter Yang for his computational assistance in preparing the empirical example in this paper.

stage test procedure based on item and test information functions. The first step in Birnbaum's procedure is to establish a target for the information function of the test. This requirement forces test assemblers to think about the intended use of the test scores and their translation into an optimal distribution of the information in the test scores along the ability scale. Once a target for the test information function is established, the test is assembled such that the sum of the item information functions matches the target for the test information function.

The objective addressed in this paper is new in that a model for test assembly from a calibrated item pool is presented to match a target for the *observed-score distribution* for a given population of examinees. This objective may seem unusual because it the shares the assumption of an IRT-calibrated item pool with an explicit interest in observed-score distributions—something usually associated with classical test theory. However, this new test assembly model perfectly reflects much of modern testing practice, where IRT is increasingly used to produce high-quality tests (i.e., using IRT item parameters estimates to assemble the test or to pre-equate test forms) but test scores are still reported on an observed-score scale. This practice can be found, for example, in testing programs with observed-score scales established before IRT was introduced and where it is impossible to change reporting practices without upsetting the consumers.

In such testing programs, it is important to have control of the observed-score distribution. If changes in the testing program are introduced, the practical consequences of these changes could be minimized if test assembly would offer the possibility to explicitly control their effects on the observed-score distribution. Examples of changes in testing programs that may affect observed-score distributions are: (a) the introduction of new specifications for the item pool; (b) a change of item calibration procedures; and (c) item parameter drift. It should be noted that the intent here is not to control individual scores but only their distribution. This approach is applicable, for example, if some items with new specifications are added to the pool leading to minor changes in the relative abilities of examinees, whereas the same observed-score distribution represents the order between the abilities as adequately as the old pool.

ALTERNATIVE SOLUTIONS

An attempt to control the observed-score distribution is also present in some procedures already in use in educational measurement. A few examples of such procedures are: equipercentile equating, item matching, and test assembly using target information functions.

In equipercentile equating, the cumulative distribution function of the observed scores on a new test form is equated to the same function of an old test form. However, equipercentile equating can only take place after the new test form is administered. In addition, this method of equating obtains its results by distorting the observed-score scale of the new test form. A better solution would be to assemble all new test forms to automatically produce the required distribution of observed scores. Attempting to achieve the latter solution is a fundamental rationale for the procedure described here. It is, however, correct to view this new procedure as a variant of equipercentile *pre*-equating.

With item matching, a new test form can be matched item-by-item to an old test form. One method introduced to realize this objective is Gulliksen's (1950) Matched Random Subsets Method. Linear Programming (LP) models that implement Gulliksen's method are given in Armstrong and Jones (1992) and van der Linden and Boekkooi-Timminga (1988). If items are matched on the basis of estimates of parameters describing their marginal and joint distributions—for example, item p-values and covariances—then two test forms with perfect match are bound to produce identical observed-score distributions for the same population of examinees. However, methods of item matching may involve new and stringent constraints on a test assembly process in addition to all other constraints that are typically needed (e.g., the test content, the format of the items, the length of the item-related text, and the distribution of the keys across response alternatives). As a result, in practice, perfect matches may not be approached closely enough to produce satisfactory observed-score distributions. The model proposed in this paper is not restricted by any new constraints on the assembly process.

Finally, it is possible to assemble a test using target information functions. A popular definition of parallel tests in IRT is Samejima's (1977), which considers tests to be parallel if they have the same information function. However, unlike classical definitions of parallel tests, Samejima's definition does not guarantee identical observed-score distributions. One reason is that in test assembly two different sets of item response functions may approach the same target information function. A more fundamental reason, however, is that a test information function only governs the (asymptotic) distribution of error in the ability estimates on the θ-scale but not the distribution of the true scores for the test.

AN OPTIMIZATION MODEL

The approach in this chapter is to assemble a test using a target for the characteristic function rather than the information function of the test. This characteristic function is the transformation needed to transform the θ-scale in the IRT model into the true-score scale underlying the test. The true-score scale is identical to the observed-score scale of the test. The transformation is amply demonstrated in Lord and Novick's (1968, sect. 16.14) well-known graphs of "typical distortions in mental measurement." Tests with identical characteristic functions produce the same true-score distributions if the ability distribution of the examinees is the same. For the professional tests of sufficient length, with items produced by trained item writers, the reliability coefficients typically are in the upper .80s or lower .90s. Therefore, differences between the shapes of the observed-score and true-score distributions are usually minor compared to the differences between the observed-score distribution and the ability distribution on the θ-scale. Also, a target for the characteristic function of the test implicitly constrains the information function of the test to have its larger values in the region where the characteristic function has its steepest slope. Typically, the ability distribution is centered in this region, and therefore the impact of random error on the true-score distribution for the test is automatically reduced for the majority of the examinees. However, it is a straightforward extension to provide the model with explicit constraints for the information function of a test.

An attractive feature of the test characteristic function is that, like the test information function, it is *additive* across the items. This facts allows us to design Linear Programming (LP) models for test assembly that minimize the differences between a test characteristic function and its target. LP models for test assembly have been introduced earlier for a variety of other test assembly problems (Adema, 1990a, 1990b, 1992; Adema & van der Linden, 1989; Armstrong & Jones, 1992; Armstrong, Jones & Wu, 1992; Boekkooi-Timminga, 1987, 1989, 1990a, 1990b; Theunissen, 1985; van der Linden, 1994; van der Linden & Boekkooi-Timminga, 1988, 1989).

Model

The following notation is needed to present the model. Let $i = 1, \ldots, I$ denote the items in the pool and let $x_i = \{0,1\}$ be decision variables to denote whether or not the item will be assigned to the test. Suppose that the test characteristic function, which is defined as the sum of the item response functions $P_i(\theta)$ in the test, has to be controlled for a grid of fixed ability values θ_k, $k = 1, \ldots, K$. The target values for the test characteristic function are denoted by $T_C(\theta)_k$. Finally, the positive and negative deviations of the test characteristic function from its target values are defined as (non-negative) variables u_k and v_k, respectively. Then the following model minimizes the sum of the deviations of the test characteristic function form its target values:

$$minimize \sum_{k=1}^{K} (u_k + v_k) \tag{1}$$

subject to

$$\sum_{i=1}^{I} P_i(\theta_k)x_i - u_k + v_k = T_C(\theta_k), \qquad k = 1, \ldots, K; \tag{2}$$

$$\sum_{i=1}^{I} x_i = n; \tag{3}$$

$$\sum_{i \in V_j} x_i \geq n_j^{(1)}, \qquad j = 1, \ldots, J; \tag{4}$$

$$\sum_{i \in V_j} x_i \leq n_j^{(2)}, \qquad j = 1, \ldots, J; \tag{5}$$

$$x_i = 0, 1, \qquad i = 1, \ldots, J; \tag{6}$$

$$u_k, v_k \geq 0. \tag{7}$$

In (2) the variables u_k and v_k are defined. The constraint in (3) puts the length of the test equal to n items. The constraints in (4) and (5) impose lower and upper bounds to the numbers of items to be selected from subsets V_j, $j = 1, \ldots, J$, in the item pool, where each subset V_j is supposed to cover a content area represented in the pool. These constraints will be used in the example below to guarantee that existing content specifications for the test are met.

The constraints in the model are a small sample of the possibilities available to realize test specifications when assembling tests through the use of LP models. Any specification that can be represented as a linear (in)equality in the decision variables can be inserted in the model. A review of other possibilities is given in van der Linden and

Boekkooi-Timminga (1989). Algorithms and heuristics for solving LP models for test assembly are described in Adema, Boekkooi-Timminga and van der Linden (1991), Armstrong, Jones and Wu (1992) and Luecht and Hirsch (1992).

AN EMPIRICAL EXAMPLE

To illustrate the practical use of the model in this paper, a test was assembled from an item pool previously in use for the Mathematics Test in the ACT Assessment Program (AAP). The pool consisted of 520 items all calibrated under the 3-parameter logistic model using an MML method with Θ distributed as N(0,1).

Method

The following steps were taken in this study:

First, a 40-item test, assembled by hand to meet the specifications in the AAP at an earlier occasion, was selected from the pool to generate a target for the distribution of the observed scores. The target was generated assuming the abilities in the population of examinees to be distributed N(0,1) and using the generalized binomial as the conditional probability function of the observed score given the ability level of the examinee (Lord, 1980, sect. 4.1).

Second, the relative true-score distribution associated with the observed-score distribution was assumed to follow a four-parameter beta density with function:

$$g(\tau) = n^{-1}(-l + \tau)^{a-1} (u - \tau)^{b-1}/(u - l)^{a+b-1}B(a,b), \qquad (8)$$

where τ is the relative true score, B(a,b) is the Beta function with parameters a and b, and the density is defined on the interval [l,u] with $0 \le l \le u \le 1$. All four unknown parameters were estimated from the first four factorial moments of the target for the observed-score distribution using a program by Hanson (1991).

Three, because the test characteristic function transforms the θ-scale into the true-score scale, it can be calculated from the distribution functions of the abilities and the true scores. Let $G(\tau)$ be the distribution function associated with the beta density in (8) and $F(\theta)$ the N(0,1) distribution function. Then the test characteristic function is given by:

$$T_C(\theta) = 40G^{-1}(F(\theta)). \qquad (9)$$

Four, target values for the test characteristic function were calculated from (9) and inserted into the constraint in (2). The model was solved to assemble a 40-item test from the pool with a test characteristic function meeting the target values in (2). The model was solved using an adapted version of the heuristic in Luecht and Hirsch (1992).

Five, two different versions of the model were solved. One model was the full model with the content constraints in (4)-(5). The following six content areas were represented in the pool: Arithmetic and Algebraic Reasoning (14); Arithmetic and Algebraic Operations (4); Geometry (8); Intermediate Algebra (8); Number and Numeration Concepts (4); and Advanced Topics (2). The numbers between parenthe-

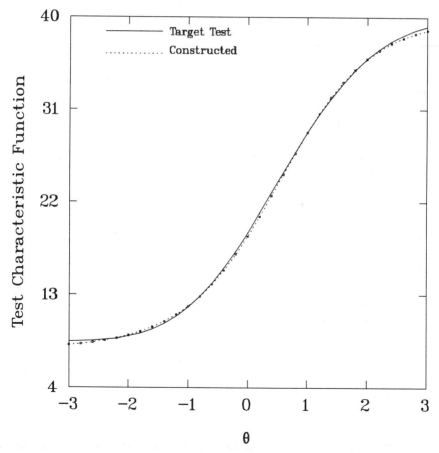

Figure 20.1. Comparison between the characteristic function of the assembled test and its target (model without content constraints)

ses are the required numbers of items in the test for each of the content areas. The second model ignored all content constraints.

Six, for both solutions the observed-score distributions were generated using the same procedure as in Step 1.

Results

The characteristic functions of the tests assembled without and with the content constraints are presented in Figures 20.1 and 20.2, respectively. Each functions appears to closely approximate its respective

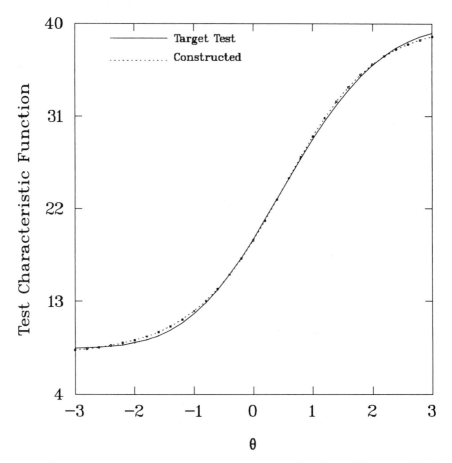

Figure 20.2. Comparison between the characteristic function of the assembled test and its target (model with content constraints)

target characteristic function. The effects of imposing content constraints on the assembly process seem to be negligible. Figure 20.3 plots the difference between the test characteristic functions in Figures 20.1 and 20.2 as a function of θ. The difference is never larger than .26 on the true-score scale, which runs from 0-40, whereas the mean difference is equal to .18.

In Figures 20.4 and 20.5, the observed-score distributions generated for the two solutions are plotted. Both for the model with and the model without the content constraints the distributions fit the distribution of the original target test tightly over the whole score range, except for a small bump just to the left of the middle of the scale. It is unclear to the authors whether these bumps, which were a systematic phenomenon in runs with other problems by the authors, are caused by

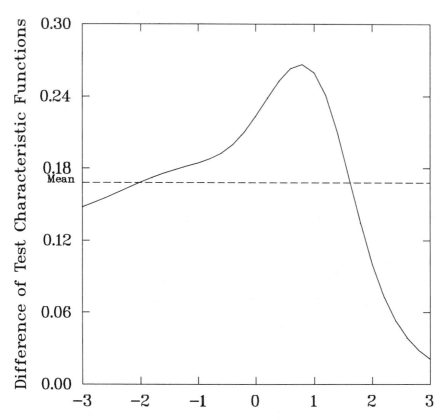

Figure 20.3.   Differences between the characteristic functions of the assembled tests in Figures 20.1 and 20.2 as a function of Θ.

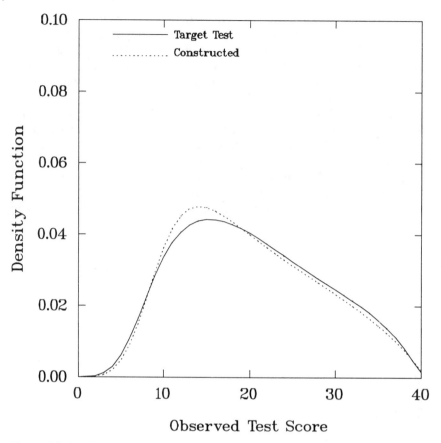

Figure 20.4. Comparison between the density function of the observed-score distribution on the assembled test and its target (model without content constraints)

the actual composition of the item pool and/or features of the heuristic used to solve the model. As displayed in Figure 20.6, the mean difference between the two distributions is equal to zero and is never larger in absolute value than .0008 across the observed-score scale.

DISCUSSION

The empirical study should be repeated for other item pools and test assembly problems to provide further support for the practical feasibility of the model presented in this chapter. Also, it might be worth-

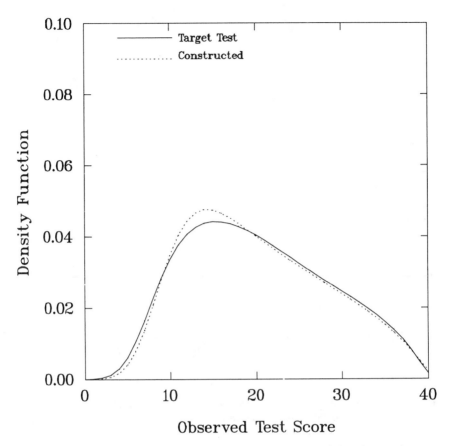

Figure 20.5.   Comparison between the density function of the observed-score distribution on the assembled test and its target (model with content constraints)

while to study the effect of introducing a target for the test information function as an additional contraint in the model. Such a target could be used for fine tuning the observed-score distribution in certain regions, for instance, at its right-hand tail if the test is used to award scholarships to the best students.

The remarkable thing about the method followed in the empirical example is that no distribution of *actual* observed scores is required to set a target for the test; the only information needed is the density of this distribution. In principle, all a test assembler has to do is to draw a curve on paper that represents the density of the observed-score distribution he or she has in mind. The method of moments, commonly in use as a method for estimating the parameters in the beta-binomial

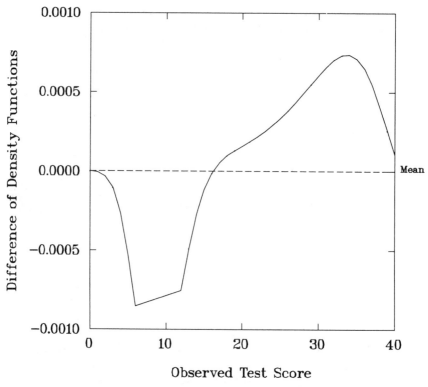

Figure 20.6. Differences between the density functions of the assembled tests in Figures 20.4 and 20.5 as a function of Θ.

model and implemented in the program by Hanson used in the empirical example in this paper, allows us to estimate the target for the true-score distribution directly from this curve, and from there on it is only one step to derive a target for the characteristic function of the test. However, in addition to this approach, it is always possible to administer a real test to a random sample of examinees for the population for which the test program is designed, and use its scores as a target for the observed-score distribution in the program.

REFERENCES

Adema, J.J. (1990a). The construction of customized two-staged tests. *Journal of Educational Measurement, 27,* 241–253.

Adema, J.J. (1990b). *Models and algorithms for the construction of achievement tests*. Ph.D. thesis, University of Twente, Enschede, The Netherlands.

Adema, J.J. (1992). Methods and models for the construction of weakly parallel tests. *Applied Psychological Measurement, 16,* 53–63.

Adema, J.J., Boekkooi-Timminga, E., & van der Linden, W.J. (1991). Achievement test construction using 0–1 linear programming. *European Journal of Operations Research, 55,* 103–111.

Adema, J.J. & van der Linden, W.J. (1989). Algorithms for computerized test construction using classical item parameters. *Journal of Educational Statistics, 14,* 279–290.

Amstrong, R.D. & Jones, D.H. (1992). Polynomial algorithms for item matching. *Applied Psychological Measurement, 16,* 365–373.

Amstrong, R.D., Jones, D.H., & Wu, I-L. (1992). An automated test development of parallel tests. *Psychometrika, 57,* 271–288.

Birnbaum, A. Some latent trait models and their use in inferring an examinee's ability. In F.M. Lord and M.R. Novick (1968), *Statistical theories of mental test scores*. Reading, MA: Addison-Wesley.

Boekkooi-Timminga, E. (1987). Simultaneous test construction by zero-one programming. *Methodika, 1,* 1101–112.

Boekkooi-Timminga, E. (1989). *Models for computerized test construction*. Ph.D. thesis, University of Twente, Enschede, The Netherlands.

Boekkooi-Timminga, E. (1990a). The construction of parallel tests from IRT-based item banks. *Journal of Educational Statistics, 15,* 129–145.

Boekkooi-Timminga, E. (1990b). A cluster-based method for test construction. *Applied Psychological Measurement, 15,* 129–145.

Gulliksen, H. (1950). *Theory of mental tests*. New York: Wiley.

Hanson, B.A. (1991). *Method of moments estimates for the four-parameter compound binomial model and the calculation of classification consistency indices* (ACT Research Report Series 91-5). Iowa City, IA: American College Testing.

Lord, F.M. (1965). A strong true-score theory, with applications. *Psychometrika, 30,* 239–270.

Lord, F.M. (1980). *Applications of item response theory to practical testing problems*. Hillsdale, NJ: Lawrence Erlbaum.

Lord, F.M. & Novick, M.R. (1868). *Statistical theories of mental test scores*. Reading, MA: Addison-Wesley.

Luecht, R.M. & Hirsch, T.M. (1992). Computerized test construction using average growth approximation of target information functions. *Applied Psychological Measurement, 16,* 41–52.

Samejima, F. (1977). Weakly parallel tests in latent trait theory with some criticism of classical test theory. *Psychometrika, 42,* 193–198.

Theunissen, T.J.J.M. (1985). Binary programming and test design. *Psychometrika, 50,* 411–420.

van der Linden, W.J. (1994). Optimum design in item response theory: Applications to test assembly and item calibration. In G.H. Fischer & D. Laming (Eds.), *Contributions to mathematical psychology, psychometrics, and methodology* (pp. 303–316). New York: Springer-Verlag.

van der Linden, W.J. & Boekkooi-Timminga, E. (1988). A zero-one programming approach to Gulliksen's matched random subsets method. *Applied Psychological Measurement, 12,* 201–209.

van der Linden, W.J. & Boekkooi-Timminga, E. (1989). A maximin model for test design with practical constraints. *Psychometrika, 53,* 237–247.

chapter 21

An Interactive Approach to Modifying Infeasible 0–1 Linear Programming Models for Test Construction*

Ellen Timminga
University of Groningen

Jos J. Adema
PPT-Research, The Research and Development Department
of PTT Nederland N.V.

A large amount of research on test construction from item banks has been carried out since the mid-1980s. Mathematical programming models for a series of specific test construction applications have been developed, and simulations were carried out (e.g. Adema, 1990, 1992a; Adema & van der Linden, 1989; Armstrong, Jones, & Wu, 1992; Baker, Cohen, & Barmish, 1988; Boekkooi-Timminga, 1987, 1990a, 1990b; de Gruijter, 1990; Theunissen, 1985, 1986; van der Linden & Boekkooi-Timminga, 1989). One of the problems met in these studies was the computational complexity associated with the application of 0–1 inte-

---

* We would like to thank Prof. Dr. Wim J. van der Linden, University of Twente for his comments on a previous version of this paper.

ger linear programming techniques. Heuristic procedures are needed to find fairly optimal solutions to the integer linear programming problems in a reasonable amount of time. In the publications mentioned above, one or more heuristic procedures are applied to determine nearly optimal solutions that fit the total set of constraints.

Another problem that can be met by applying integer linear programming techniques has only been briefly mentioned in the above publications. This is the problem of not finding any feasible solution fitting the total set of constraints due to the inconsistent specifications formulated by the test constructor. In practice, this problem is likely to occur occasionally. In this case, most computer programs respond with the message that no test can be found fitting the total set of constraints. No indications whatsoever are given as to the cause. However, it may be expected that a test constructor tries to formulate consistent test requirements, which implies that modifying a test specification can be far from obvious.

In this chapter, the infeasibility problem is considered. Basically two types of infeasible solutions can be distinguished. In the next section, descriptions of both are given. Next, a series of possible ways to modify test specifications that yield infeasibility is discussed. Then, a procedure is described that, first, checks whether a solution fitting all requirements can be found. If not, it guides the test constructor in modifying his or her test specifications such that a feasible solution can be obtained. This procedure can be applied to all test construction models proposed in the literature. Two examples and a discussion conclude the chapter.

TWO TYPES OF INFEASIBLE SOLUTIONS

Mathematical programming models for test construction consist of an objective function, and a set of constraints that have to be fulfilled. The decision variables x_i used in the models are usually of the 0–1 type, and denote whether an item is ($x_i = 1$) or is not ($x_i = 0$) selected for the test. As an example, a basic version of the Maximin Model (van der Linden & Boekkooi-Timminga, 1989) is presented:

$$\text{Maximize } y \tag{1}$$

subject to

$$\sum_{i=1}^{I} I_i(\theta_k)x_i - r_k y \geq 0, \qquad k = 1, \ldots, K, \tag{2}$$

$$\sum_{i=1}^{I} x_i = N, \qquad (3)$$

$$x_i \in \{0, 1\}, \qquad i = 1, \ldots, I, \qquad (4)$$

where $I_i(\theta_k)$ is the information of item i ($i = 1, \ldots, I$) at ability level θ_k, and N is the required number of items in the test. The model does not expect the test constructor to specify exact target information values. Instead it assumes that he or she is able to specify the relative shape of the target information function at a number of ability levels θ_k ($k = 1, \ldots, K$). The constants r_k in the model represent this relative shape. In (1) and (2) the total test information is maximized. In fact, the decision variable y is maximized, such that the obtained information values at the ability levels θ_k are at least y times r_k.

To solve complex test construction problems like (1) − (4), heuristic procedures have to be used. Most heuristic procedures start by solving the relaxed problem, defined by taking $0 \le x_i \le 1$ instead of $x_i \in \{0,1\}$ and using the simplex method. Next, a 0–1 solution is obtained, for instance, by rounding (e.g., Theunissen, 1985), optimal rounding (van der Linden & Boekkooi-Timminga, 1989; Boekkooi-Timminga, 1990b), or the Adema-heuristic (e.g., Adema, 1992a, 1992b; Adema, Boekkooi-Timminga, & van der Linden, 1991; Boekkooi-Timminga, 1990a, 1990b).

In solving test construction problems, two types of infeasibility can occur (which are not inherent to the use of heuristic procedures). The first is the infeasibility of the relaxed 0–1 model. Some of the results given by Boekkooi-Timminga (1987) and (1990a), respectively, illustrate this case. The second type of infeasibility is more uncommon; it yields a feasible solution to the relaxed 0–1 model, but not to the 0–1 model (e.g., Boekkooi-Timminga, 1990a).

The second type of infeasibility can only be detected by solving the original test construction problem. The first type of infeasibility, however, can be detected easily by applying the simplex method to the relaxed test construction problem.

MODIFYING TEST SPECIFICATIONS

In this section an overview is given of possible ways to modify test specifications. It is assumed that the test specifications are formulated as syntactically correct Linear Programming (LP) models. Thus, the constraints and objective functions are linear expressions of the decision variables, and the model includes exactly one objective function.

The basic cause of infeasibility is that the set of test requirements is in contradiction with the characteristics of the item bank. For example, the test specification states that the test should consist of 20 items and that the test information has to be at least 10 at a certain ability level, while the maximum amount of test information that can be obtained at this ability level for 20 items is 9. On the other hand, it is possible that a nonattentive test constructor formulates requirements that are obviously contradictory. For example, it is required that a test contains 20 items, while it is also required that the test contains 10 multiple choice and 15 essay items.

It can be assumed that the latter cause of infeasibility is detected relatively easily by the test constructor and that it will occur infrequently if the test constructor is an experienced user. The first, however, is expected to be the cause of infeasibility more often. In this case it will be much more difficult to detect the problematic requirements, because infeasibility may be caused by a set of interacting requirements.

There are several ways to modify a test specification. The following test specification is used for illustration:

$$\text{Maximize } y \tag{5}$$

subject to

$$\sum_{i=1}^{I} I_i(\theta_k) x_i - y \geq 0, \qquad k = 1, \ldots, K, \tag{6}$$

$$\sum_{i=1}^{I} x_i = N, \tag{7}$$

$$\sum_{i \in V_1} x_i = N_1, \tag{8}$$

$$\sum_{i \in V_2} x_i = N_2, \tag{9}$$

$$b_i x_i \leq \text{maxb} \qquad i = 1, \ldots, I, \tag{10}$$

$$x_i \in \{0, 1\}, \qquad i = 1, \ldots, I. \tag{11}$$

Objective function (5) and the set of constraints in (6) state that the minimum amount of test information obtained at the ability levels k should be maximal. Constraint (7) requires that the test consists of N items. Furthermore, the test should contain N_1 items from subset V_1, and N_2 items from subset V_2 (Constraints [8] and [9]). The set of constraints in (10) requires that the item difficulty values b_i of the items in the test should be less than maxb.

In the remainder of this section the possible ways of changing a test specification are discussed. The basic idea is to increase the feasible region, that is, to increase the set of feasible solutions. In case there is no feasible solution, the feasible region is empty.

Right-Hand-Side Coefficients

The right-hand-side coefficient of a constraint is the constant part of the expression that is not multiplied by any decision variable. In the above model they are, respectively: 0 for all constraints in (6), N in (7), N_1 in (8), N_2 in (9), and maxb for all constraints in (10). Changing the right-hand-sides in (6) will not increase the feasible region, because these constraints do not restrict this region in any way. A modification of N, N_1, and/or N_2 might help, however, it is not obvious how to change them (increase or decrease). On the other hand, increasing maxb may create a feasible region, if the infeasibility is due to this constraint.

Equalities versus Inequalities

Another option is to replace equalities with inequalities. For example, replacing the equality signs in constraints (7), (8), and/or (9) with inequality signs will increase the feasible region if the infeasibility is caused by the constraint considered. However, it is generally not obvious whether to replace them with a greater than or equal or less than or equal sign. In this case the test constructor might also prefer to add an extra constraint to limit the range of the number of items, for example, the test should include at least N items and at most N + 3 items.

Replacing inequality with equality signs is not recommended, because this may reduce the size of the feasible region. Carefulness is recommended if equality signs are used. For example, there is an extremely large chance that no solution can be found if it is required to construct a test with a mean item difficulty of exactly 0.5. Therefore, equality signs should only be used in constraints that involve integer-valued variables and constants.

Item Sets

It is also possible to change the set of items that is considered in a certain constraint. For example, in (8) and (9) items can be added to or deleted from the item sets V_1 or V_2. In practice, this type of modification is not acceptable most of the time because the sets are formed by items with certain specific characteristics. For example, it is not acceptable to add essay items to the set of multiple choice items. Note that only an increase in the number of items in a set may enlarge the feasible region; a decrease may reduce the size of the feasible region. Whether it actually enlarges or reduces the size of the feasible region, and to what extent, depends on the other constraints in the test construction model.

Delete Constraints

It is possible that deleting a constraint causes an increase of the feasible region. The test constructor might consider deleting a constraint if it is not that important to him or her.

Combine Constraints

Combining constraints may also enlarge the feasible region. For example, taking (8) and (9) together as

$$\sum_{i \in v_1 + v_2} x_i = N_1 + N_2. \tag{12}$$

However, here the acceptability problem occurs again.

Objective Function versus Constraints

If the same item characteristics are considered in the objective function and in one or more constraints, it is possible that they are in conflict with each other. If this is the case the constraint(s) or objective function has to be changed.

A PROCEDURE FOR DETECTING AND HANDLING INFEASIBILITY

In this section a method is presented that can detect whether infeasibilities occur. If so, it advises the test constructor on modifying the test requirements, such that there is a greater chance that a feasible solution is found.

Without loss of generality the procedure is described for the general 0–1 LP test construction model:

$$\text{Maximize } c'x, \tag{13}$$

subject to

$$Ax \le b, \tag{14}$$

$$x \in \{0, 1\}, \tag{15}$$

where c and x are n-vectors, A is an mxn-matrix, and b is an n-vector. The procedure consists of five steps summarized in Figure 21.1.

Step 1: Check Constraints

Check whether the specifications formulated by the test constructor are consistent with the items available in the bank by checking each constraint separately. For example, if 20 grammar items are required for a test and the bank contains only 15 grammar items, this can be reported immediately after the demands have been formulated.

Step 2: Solve Relaxed LP Problem

It is checked whether a feasible solution to the relaxed LP problem exists. The following relaxed LP problem in matrix-notation is solved:

$$\text{Minimize } z, \tag{16}$$

subject to

$$Ax + z = b, \tag{17}$$

$$0 \le x \le 1, z \ge 0. \tag{18}$$

The solution $x = 0$ and $z = b$ is used as a feasible starting solution for this problem. In this model the decision variables z are called artificial variables; they represent the deviations between the required coefficients b, and their actual values represented by Ax. Note that in case of the Maximin Model, the constraints in (2) are always satisfied, and can be left out of the LP model.

If the problem has an optimal solution with an objective function

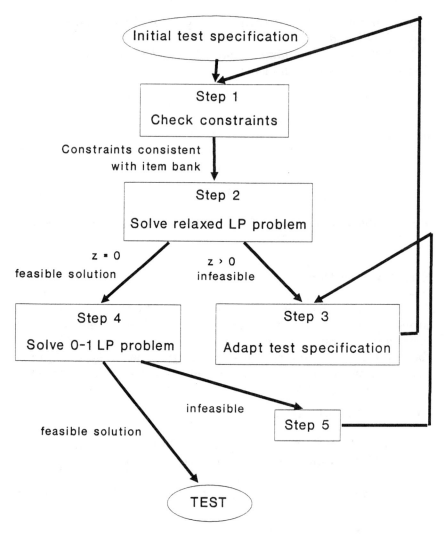

Figure 21.1. Overview of the procedure for handling infeasibility.

value of zero, this implies that a feasible solution can be found for the relaxed problem. In this case, go to Step 4. Otherwise, the first type of infeasibility is met, and Step 3 should be carried out.

The procedure applied in Step 2 is described in most textbooks on mathematical programming (e.g., Daellenbach, George & McNickle, 1978, pp. 100–102; Papadimitriou & Steiglitz, 1982, pp. 55–58; Rao, 1985, pp. 121–127). In fact, it is Phase 1 of the so-called Two-Phase method. In these textbooks, it is indicated how to check whether there is a feasible solution, but no discussion is given to what to do if no feasible solution can be obtained.

Step 3: Modify Test Specification

In this step the test specification is modified by the test constructor, such that there is a larger chance that a test can be selected. The values of the artificial variables z, and the reduced costs of the non-basic artificial variables that were obtained in Step 2, are used for advising the test constructor. For a maximization problem, the reduced cost of such a variable is defined to be the decrease of the objective function value that is obtained if the value of this variable is increased by one unit and fixed at this value, solving the remaining problem to optimality. In case of a minimization problem the reduced costs represent an increase of the objective function value.

Two lists are generated. In List 1 the constraints with artificial variable values $z_i > 0$ are listed in decreasing order of the z_i's. In List 2 the constraints with reduced costs > 0 are listed in decreasing order of the reduced costs. Next, the procedure formulates an initial change proposal that will always result in a model with a feasible solution. This proposal is to subtract a number equal to z_j from the right-hand-sides of the corresponding constraints. However, it is very likely that the test constructor will not accept this proposal.

In this case, the test constructor can think of other ways to modify the test specification (see previous section). He or she is advised to first review the individual constraints carefully. Next, combinations of constraints have to be checked for consistency, and finally the relationships between the objective function and the constraints have to be examined. Special attention should be given to the constraints at the top of the lists because they are most responsible for the infeasibility. It is not necessary to change all constraints included in the lists; most of the time it suffices to modify one or a few constraints at the top of the lists.

On basis of Lists 1 and 2, it is possible to guide the test constructor in changing the right-hand-sides of the constraints. The right-hand-sides of the constraints at the top of List 1 should be decreased, and the right-hand-sides of the constraints at the top of List 2 should be increased. The actual amount of change should be decided by the test constructor; the values of the z_j's can be used as a guideline for the amount of change necessary. Lists 1 and 2 are also used to advise the test constructor on replacing equality signs by inequality signs.

The test constructor should examine the possibility of enlarging the item sets for the constraints at the top of the lists, and/or the possibility of replacing equality signs in constraints at the top of the lists. The equality signs in constraints at the top of List 1 should be replaced by less than or equal signs, and those in constraints at the top of List 2 by greater than or equal signs.

Unfortunately, it is not possible to indicate in more detail than was done above and in the previous section what changes will result in a feasible test specification. However, if the test constructor focuses on the constraints at the top of Lists 1 and 2, it is expected that he or she will succeed in reformulating the test specification successfully.

After the test specification has been modified, Step 1 and 2 have to be repeated. It is advised to modify only one or a few constraints at a time, and check the new results in Steps 1 and 2. Most of the time the modification of one or a few constraints suffices to obtain a feasible solution. It is no problem to consider several modifications in a row, because solving LP problems takes only small amounts of time.

Step 4: Solve 0–1 LP Problem

Solve the original 0–1 LP problem in (13)–(15), with adjustments if made. The final optimal solution of Step 2 is used as the initial solution. This problem belongs to the set of so-called NP-hard problems (e.g., Papadimitriou & Steiglitz, 1982, pp. 342–371) and should be solved by a heuristic procedure. If a feasible 0–1 solution is found then STOP. Otherwise, the second type of infeasibility is met, and in this case go to Step 5.

Step 5: Solve (16)–(18) as 0–1 LP Problem

To handle the second type of infeasibility, model (16)–(18) with $x_i \in \{0, 1\}$ instead of $0 \leq x_i \leq 1$ is solved. As the problem in Step 4, this problem is NP-hard and should be solved using a heuristic procedure. After the problem has been solved, the values of the artificial variables z are used to advise the test constructor in changing his or her test specifications in Step 3.

In theory it is possible that no feasible solution is found in Step 4, although a feasible solution exists, because a heuristic procedure is used. In that case there are two options: (1) try another heuristic procedure, and (2) change the test requirements, if an accurate heuristic procedure was used, because in this case it can be assumed that the demands are very hard to be satisfied.

EXAMPLES

An example is given for each type of infeasibility to illustrate the above procedure. Two simple examples are given to show clearly how the method works. It was considered important that the reader could observe the infeasibility directly from the data used. Thus, the examples may look a little far-fetched. However, note that if the extra information on the item characteristics had not been given, the causes of infeasibility would not have been obvious.

For both examples the same item bank was used. It consisted of 100 items that fitted the Rasch model. The difficulty parameter values were drawn from a normal distribution with mean 0 and variance 2. Item information values were considered at $\theta = -1$, 0, and 1 logits.

Example 1

This example illustrates the way the first type of infeasibility—no feasible solution exists for the relaxed test construction model—is handled by the method.

The test to be constructed was required to measure as accurately as possible at the ability levels -1, 0, and 1. To maximize the total test information, while the information at each ability point should be about equal, the Maximin Model was applied with the r_k's set equal to 1. In addition to these constraints, some practical constraints with respect to the item formats and contents were formulated. Items 1–50 were multiple-choice items, and items 51–100 were not, and we chose to select multiple-choice items only. Assume items 1–40 concern content A, and items 41–100 content B. We chose to select 15 items on content A, and 15 items on content B for the test. The corresponding test construction model was:

$$\text{Maximize } y \qquad\qquad (19)$$

subject to

$$\sum_{i=1}^{100} I_i(\theta_k)x_i - y \geq 0, \qquad k = 1, 2, 3, \qquad (20)$$

$$\sum_{i=51}^{100} x_i = 0, \qquad\qquad (21)$$

$$\sum_{i=1}^{40} x_i = 15, \tag{22}$$

$$\sum_{i=41}^{100} x_i = 15, \tag{23}$$

$$x_i \in \{0, 1\}, \quad i = 1, \ldots, 100. \tag{24}$$

Note that it is not possible to find a solution to the above model, because it is required to select 15 items from the 10 items numbered 41 to 50. Next, each step of the method was followed.

In Step 1 it was checked whether each individual constraint was feasible; this was the case. In Step 2 the following relaxed model was solved:

$$\text{Minimize} \sum_{j=1}^{3} z_j \tag{25}$$

subject to

$$\sum_{i=51}^{100} x_i + z_1 = 0, \tag{26}$$

$$\sum_{i=1}^{40} x_i + z_2 = 15, \tag{27}$$

$$\sum_{i=41}^{100} x_i + z_3 = 15, \tag{28}$$

$$0 \le x_i \le 1, \quad i = 1, \ldots, 100, \tag{29}$$

$$z_j \ge 0, \quad j = 1, 2, 3. \tag{30}$$

The obtained values of the artificial variables and their reduced costs are summarized in Table 21.1. The objective function value was equal to 5.

In Step 3 the two lists of constraints were obtained. List 1 consisted of constraint (28) only. The order in List 2 was: constraints (26), (27). The initial change proposal was to have 5 items less on content B (see

Table 21.1. Results of Step 2 for Example 1

j	Expression		z_j	Reduced Costs
1	(26)	only multiple-choice items	0	2
2	(27)	items on content A	0	1
3	(28)	items on content B	5	0

Note: Objective function value = 5

Modification 1 in Table 21.2). It was assumed that the test constructor did not like this. From Lists 1 and 2, it is clear that the objective function value can be decreased by decreasing the right-hand-side of (28), and by increasing the right-hand-sides of (26) and (27). Some possibilities that were tried are summarized in Table 21.2. For Modification 2 the right-hand-side of (26) was increased to 5, while the others stayed the same. In this case the objective function value became 0 for Modification 1. On the other hand, an increase of 5 for (27) did not show any improvement of the objective function value (Modification 3). If both the right-hand-sides of (26) and (27) were increased by 5, the objective function value became 0. However, the increase for (27) was not needed to obtain this result (compare Modifications 2 and 4). Both increasing and decreasing the right-hand-sides of (26) and (28), respectively, also gave an improvement (see Modifications 5–7). Again, an increase of the value for (27) did not result in any improvement (compare Modification 6 and 7). These results confirm the order of the constraints in List 2. The table shows that several possible modifications result in feasible test specifications (Modifications 1, 2, 4, and 5). It depends on the desires of the test constructor which one is to be preferred.

Table 21.2. Possible Modifications for Example 1

Case	Right-Hand-Sides			Objective Function
	(26)	(27)	(28)	
original	0	15	15	5
Modification 1	0	15	10	0
Modification 2	5	15	15	0
Modification 3	0	20	15	5
Modification 4	5	20	15	0
Modification 5	3	15	12	0
Modification 6	2	15	13	1
Modification 7	2	20	13	1

Replacing equalities by inequalities was also viewed to be of interest. From Table 21.2 it is clear that replacing the equality sign in (28) by a less than or equal sign, or replacing the equality sign in (26) by a greater than or equal sign would also have resulted in a feasible test specification. Other possible changes in the test specification were not considered, because they were not viewed as acceptable.

Suppose the test constructor preferred Modification 5. Next, Step 4 was carried out. The relaxed solution was obtained having an objective function value of 4.7002. There were two fractional decision variable values: $x_{59} = 0.01663$, and $x_{82} = 0.98337$. The optimum 0–1 solution had an objective function value of 4.69967. It turned out that the optimum solution was the same as the rounded solution (rounding the above decision variables to the nearest integer). Thus, a feasible 0–1 solution was obtained to the modified test construction problem.

Example 2

This example will illustrate the second type of infeasibility: there is a relaxed solution, but no 0–1 solution. As for Example 1, the test to be constructed was required to measure as accurately as possible at the ability levels −1, 0, and 1. Furthermore, it was required that the test includes 20 items, and that the test administration time was exactly 116 minutes. The test construction model used was:

$$\text{Maximize } y \tag{31}$$

subject to

$$\sum_{i=1}^{100} I_i(\theta_k)x_i - y \geq 0, \qquad k = 1, 2, 3, \tag{32}$$

$$\sum_{i=1}^{100} x_i = 20, \tag{33}$$

$$\sum_{i=1}^{100} t_i x_i = 116, \tag{34}$$

$$x_i \in \{0, 1\}, \qquad i = 1, \ldots, 100, \tag{35}$$

$$y \geq 0, \tag{36}$$

$$\text{where } t_i = 5 \quad \text{for } i \leq 50,$$
$$t_i = 10 \quad \text{for } i \geq 51.$$

In the model, t_i is the item administration time of item i. Observe that a 0–1 solution with a test administration time of 116 minutes can never be obtained because the t_i's only take the values 5 and 10.

The objective function value obtained in Step 2 was zero, thus a relaxed solution could be found. Next, Step 4 was carried out. The relaxed solution had an objective function value of 3.87. It included 3 fractional decision variables: $x_{41} = 0.800$, $x_{66} = 0.80975$, and $x_{67} = 0.39025$. Furthermore, 16 items were selected from item numbers 1–50, and 2 from item numbers 51–100. Given the fractional decision variable values, the test administration time was exactly 116. An attempt was made to obtain a 0–1 solution using several heuristic procedures, but no feasible solution could be obtained.

Next, Step 5 was carried out. The objective function value obtained was 2, and $z_1 = z_2 = 1$. Thus, in Step 3 List 1 consisted of (33) and (34), and List 2 was empty. The initial change proposal was to decrease the right-hand-sides of both (33) and (34) by 1, which would result in an objective function value of 0. Next, after checking the constraints in Step 1, for each individual constraint a decrease of 1 was examined in Step 2. In case of (33) Step 2 resulted in an objective function value of 0. However, again no feasible solution could be obtained in Step 4. Step 5 showed an increase of the objective function value to 7, with $z_1 = 1$ and $z_2 = 6$. The decrease of 1 for (34) also resulted in an objective function value of 0 in Step 2. Next, Step 4 was carried out for this case. The relaxed solution had an objective function value of 3.868 with two fractional decision variables $x_{66} = 0.10166$, and $x_{67} = 0.89834$. Rounding these values to 0 and 1, respectively, resulted in a feasible 0–1 solution, with objective function value 3.86587. The optimum solution was also obtained; it had an objective function value of 3.86634. In case the initial change proposal was followed, the objective function value of the optimum solution was 3.69048. The former modification was preferred, because the test specification had to be modified less and the objective function value was higher.

Replacing the equality signs in (33) and/or (34) by less than or equal signs was also acceptable for the test constructor. Observe that again a change of (34) is required.

It is not recommended to add constraints like (34) to a test construction model. Such constraints should always be formulated as (a series of) inequalities instead of equality constraints. This constraint has been included here for the sake of illustration.

DISCUSSION

Infeasibility is a problem not explicitly dealt with in the literature on test construction using 0–1 integer linear programming techniques.

However, it is an important problem, since to apply these new test construction methods successfully in practice, it has to be taken care of. In this chapter a procedure is proposed that if no feasible solution can be found, guides the test constructor in adjusting his or her test requirements such that a feasible solution can be found. The test constructor who applies this procedure will always be able to construct a test, in contrast to the current practice in which only the message "no test found suiting your specifications" will be obtained if the problem is infeasible.

Two types of infeasibility exist. The proposed method consists of five steps that are taken into account depending on whether infeasibility occurs, and what type of infeasibility is met. If no feasible solution can be found, the procedure helps modify the test construction model, such that the test requirements will become suitable for the item bank.

Here, test construction is viewed as an interactive process, during which the test constructor may modify his or her requirements several times, even if a feasible solution is obtained. Although the proposed procedure can be carried out without consulting the test constructor, the ideal is to have the computer present an initial change proposal. If the test constructor follows this proposal, a feasible solution will definitely exist. However, the test constructor has the opportunity to (partially) follow the advice of the computer, and/or change other aspects of the test specification.

REFERENCES

Adema, J.J. (1990). The construction of customized two-stage tests. *Journal of Educational Measurement, 27,* 241–253.

Adema, J.J. (1992a). Methods and models for the construction of weakly parallel tests. *Applied Psychological Measurement, 16,* 53–63.

Adema, J.J. (1992b). Implementation of the branch-and-bound method for test construction problems. *Methodika, 6,* 99–117.

Adema, J.J., Boekkooi-Timminga, E., & van der Linden, W.J. (1991). Achievement test construction using 0–1 linear programming. *European Journal of Operational Research, 55,* 103–111.

Adema, J.J., & van der Linden, W.J. (1989). Algorithms for computerized test construction using classical item parameters. *Journal of Educational Statistics, 14,* 279–290.

Armstrong, R.D., Jones, D.H., & Wu, I.L. (1992). An automated test development of parallel tests from a seed test. *Psychometrika, 57,* 271–288.

Baker, F.B., Cohen, A.S., & Barmish, B.R. (1988). Item characteristics of tests constructed by linear programming. *Applied Psychological Measurement, 12,* 189–199.

Boekkooi-Timminga, E. (1987). Simultaneous test construction by zero-one programming. *Methodika, 1,* 101–112.

Boekkooi-Timminga, E. (1990a). The construction of parallel tests from IRT-based item banks. *Journal of Educational Statistics, 15,* 129–145.

Boekkooi-Timminga, E. (1990b). A cluster-based method for test construction. *Applied Psychological Measurement, 14,* 341–354.

Daellenbach, H.G., George, J.A., & McNickle, D.C. (1978). *Introduction to operations research techniques* (2nd ed.). Boston: Allyn and Bacon.

de Gruijter, D.N.M. (1990). Test construction by means of linear programming. *Applied Psychological Measurement, 14,* 175–181.

Papadimitriou, C.H., & Steiglitz, K. (1982). *Combinatorial optimization: Algorithms and complexity.* Englewood Cliffs, NJ: Prentice Hall.

Rao, S.S. (1985). *Optimization theory and applications* (2nd ed.). New Delhi: Wiley Eastern Limited.

Theunissen, T.J.J.M. (1985). Binary programming and test design. *Psychometrika, 50,* 411–420.

Theunissen, T.J.J.M. (1986). Some applications of optimization algorithms in test design and adaptive testing. *Applied Psychological Measurement, 10,* 381–389.

van der Linden, W.J. & Boekkooi-Timminga, E. (1989). A maximin model for test design with practical constraints. *Psychometrika, 54,* 237–247.

chapter **22**

A Review of Selection Methods for Optimal Test Design

Martijn P.F. Berger
University of Limburg, The Netherlands

Wim J.J. Veerkamp
University of Twente, The Netherlands

Since World War I, the construction of tests in education and psychology has gone through a number of different stages, and tests have been administered in various different forms. Although at first the construction of tests was done by hand, the recognition that the construction of tests could be improved by taking into account the psychometric characteristics of the items has led to alternative and more structured methods of test construction. Perhaps one of the most promising directions in the construction of tests is the use of the idea of so-called item banks. An item bank is a very large set of items. These items are grouped into certain content areas and it is assumed that the psychometric characteristics of these items have been estimated. When such an item bank is available, the construction of a test is done by selecting items from the bank according to certain specifications. A lot of research has been done on optimal item selection methods. Many of these methods are based on mathematical programming procedures. (See Adema (1990), Boekkooi-Timminga (1989), and Theunissen (1986) for a review of these methods.) Although the mathematical programming methods were mainly proposed for the construction of fixed-form tests, other forms like two-stage and parallel tests (Adema, 1990) can also be handled by these methods. Recently two computer programs based on mathematical programming algorithms have been developed; namely the CONTEST program (Boekkooi-Timminga and Sun, 1991), and the OTD program (Verschoor, 1991).

The fact that fixed-form tests do not have equal reliability or equal validity over the whole range of abilities in the population has motivated Lord (1971, 1980) and Weiss (1976, 1978), among others, to propose adaptive test forms. The central idea was that if each examinee in a sample is given an individually designed test, this would lead to more efficient estimation of the abilities of these examinees. The availability of fast computers and item response theory (IRT) models has made the development of computerized versions of adaptive testing (CAT) possible. (See Wainer (1990) for a review of various aspects of CAT.)

With the development of item banks and computerized adaptive tests, the special skills of the test developer were replaced by statistical characteristics. This development was criticized by Wainer and Kiely (1987). They argued that the test developer's skills are still needed in the construction process. Because several practical problems with the existing CAT procedures were not solved satisfactory, Wainer and Kiely (1987) and Wainer and Lewis (1990) proposed the application of so-called testlets. Testlets are actually small bundles of items, where examinees follow a fixed number of paths. A test may consist of a number of different testlets, and an examinee does not have to take every testlet in the test nor does an examinee have to take all items within the testlet. The many advantages and disadvantages of fixed-tests and adaptive tests are combined in a testlet design.

The above-described construction of different test forms can be regarded as an optimal design problem. Optimal design methods have been applied in various fields of research. Although most of the developments have been reported and applied in bioassay research, optimal design methods can also be applied in educational measurement. Berger (1991) and Berger and van der Linden (1992), for example, have recently described the application of optimal design methods for the designing of optimal samples for item parameter estimation in IRT models.

The objective of this paper is to give a review of the different optimal design methods and criteria for item selection for the construction of different test forms. This review places these methods within the general framework of optimal design theory. Silvey (1980) and Ford,

Kitsos and Titterington (1989) give a review of optimal design research for nonlinear models. The present paper also indicates that the optimal design methods all have the same characteristics and can be applied to any IRT model. This review not only includes the already known methods but also introduces some alternative selection methods that may prove useful in the future.

First a description of a test design will be given. Then the two most frequently applied information measures will be described, and finally the different criteria for the selection of items for different situations will be reviewed.

TEST DESIGN

A test design is characterized by the pattern of the examinee–item combinations. Actually, a test design is connected with a particular test form. For example, a fixed-form test where examinees all take the same items in the test may be designed in such a way that the items are ordered from very easy to extremely hard. If examinees take the items in the test starting with the most easy item, and stop whenever they give a wrong answer to an item, then the most able examinees will have to answer more items than the examinees with a low ability level. When examinees are also ordered according to their ability level, then the scores of a test design will approximately have a Guttman scale pattern. In Figure 22.1 an example of such an approximate Guttman test design is given. The crosses in Figure 22.1 indicate the examinee–item combinations. The 16 examinees take a test consisting of 20 items. The examinee with the lowest ability level only takes two out of 20 items and the most able examinee takes 19 out of 20 items. It should be emphasized that the empty cells in the score matrix of the approximate Guttman Test design are empty by design, (i.e., the design will determine whether a response is available or not).

Adaptive tests also have special designs. Most adaptive tests are administered in such a way that each examinee takes a different set of items. The full $N \times n$ matrix of responses of N examinees on a total of n different items will therefore contain a lot of empty cells. In an adaptive test design, the pattern of the cells in the $N \times n$ response matrix is determined by the adaptation process. The design pattern connected with an adaptive test form is certainly not fixed, and may be completely different for examinees having the same ability levels. An example of an adaptive test design is also given in Figure 22.1. Note that for this particular design an equal number of 10 out of 20 items is administered to each of the 16 examinees.

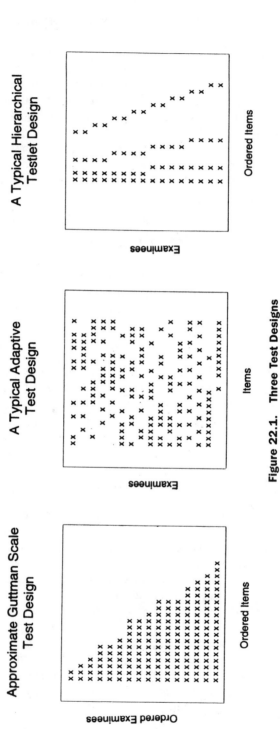

Figure 22.1.   Three Test Designs

The designs connected with testlets are more fixed than adaptive test designs. A test containing several testlets will usually have a limited number of paths for an examinee to run though. Depending on their responses to previous items, examinees may take different items in the testlet and may even take only some of the testlets in the test. The response pattern in a testlet design often follows a kind of branching scheme. Actually, two different types of branching in a testlet design may be distinguished. Examinees may not have to take every testlet in the test. Such a branching may be referred to as *between testlet branching*. When a testlet is structured in such a way that a fixed number of branches of the items within that testlet is made possible, this will be referred to as *within testlet branching*. The third diagram in Figure 22.1 displays a typical within testlet design connected with a hierarchical testlet (Wainer & Kiely, 1987). In this example, the 16 examinees all take the first item. Then, depending on their response to the first item, they take the second or the third item, and so on. Testlet designs are not as flexible as adaptive test designs, but more flexible than the designs for fixed-form tests.

For the description of a test design some notation is needed. Suppose that we wish to construct an optimal test design for a sample of N examinees ($j = 1, \ldots, N$) and n distinct items ($i = 1, \ldots, n$). Let the matrix $U = \{u_{ij}\}$ represent the response pattern. If the θ-scale with all possible abilities is divided into c distinct categories θ_j, such that $1 \leq c \leq N$, then these categories can be gathered in $\theta' = (\theta_1, \theta_2, \theta_3, \ldots, \theta_c)$, where $\theta \in \mathbb{R}^c$, and $\mathbb{R}^c$ is a c-dimensional set of real numbers. Corresponding with the vector θ is a vector of weights, $W' = (w_1, w_2, w_3, \ldots, w_c)$. These weights can be used in different ways.

The weights in W may be used to characterize the distribution of the sample for which the optimal test is constructed. If, for example, all weights in W are equal, then the sample will have a uniform distribution for the abilities. By a suitable selection of weights a normal ability distribution can also be approximated. The weights can also be used to select only a few θ-levels. If we wish to find an optimal test design for only two extreme θ-levels, then all but the corresponding two weights w_j will be equal to zero. The weights can also be used to give more weight to certain θ_j-values than to others. Weights can also be used to emphasize the sizes of the intervals between the different θ_j-levels. Some of the criteria discussed in this chapter will make use of such weights.

The items in the test design can be characterized by the vector of structural parameters $\xi' = (\xi_1, \xi_2, \xi_3, \ldots, \xi_n)$, where each element ξ_i may be a vector representing more than one item parameter. For example, for the Rasch model ξ_i will represent the difficulty or location parameter. For extensions of the Rasch model, ξ_i may contain more than one parameter. Of course, items with the same item parameter values may be represented by the same vector ξ_i.

The probability of obtaining a response can now be given by the function $P(\theta_j; \xi_i)$. The mean and variance of the parametric family are $P(\theta_j; \xi_i)$ and $\{P(\theta; \xi_i) [1 - P(\theta_j; \xi_i)]\}$, respectively, and the likelihood function for the data matrix U and θ is:

$$L[u;\theta;\xi] = \prod_{j=1}^{c} \prod_{i=1}^{n} P_i(\theta_j;\xi_i)^{w_j p_{ij}}[1 - P_i(\theta_j;\xi_i)]^{w_j(1-p_{ij})}, \tag{1}$$

where p_{ij} is the proportion of correct responses on item i in category j of θ, and estimation of the parameters $\{\theta_j; \xi_i\}$ can take place by means of the usual maximum likelihood (ML) estimation procedures.

After a model $P(\theta_j; \xi_i)$ is chosen, the test design can be selected. The selection of a test design must be done in such a way that it will lead to the most accurate estimation of the parameters. The problem, however, is to find such test designs. More specifically, the problem is to find the set of parameters ξ connected with a certain test form that will enable the most efficient estimation of the parameters in the sample characterized by $\{\theta, W\}$.

The problem of finding optimal test designs cannot be answered in any general sense and will depend on a number of factors. First, the assumed response model will determine the final outcome. An optimal test design for the Rasch model will generally not be optimal for the two-parameter logistic model. Fortunately, however, the methods for finding optimal test designs can be applied to practically any parametric IRT model.

A second problem is connected with the test form. An optimal test design will differ per test form. For example, an optimal design for a fixed-form test may not be optimal at all for an adaptive test, and vice versa.

Another problem is connected with the parameters themselves. The accuracy of the parameter estimates will depend on the amount of information in the data, and test designs may differ in their amount of information. The variance of the estimators is usually inversely related to the amount of information in the data, and some suitable information measure must be chosen before one can find an optimal test design.

Finally, a selection criterion for the items must be chosen. Since the optimality of a test design will depend on the optimality criterion that was used, the choice of criterion may be crucial. In fact, two alternatives can be distinguished. The first kind of criterion is based on all parameters in $\{\theta, W\}$. This enables a simultaneous optimization procedure for all the parameters in θ. The second kind is formulated on a subset of parameters, or even for single parameters, and allows for a stepwise optimization, (i.e. for each of the θ_j-values separately). Although the latter group of criteria has been frequently applied in adaptive testing, these criteria can also be used for the designing of fixed-form tests.

INFORMATION MEASURES

Many different types of information measures for the estimation of parameters have been proposed. Two of the most frequently applied information measures are Fisher's information measure and the Bayesian measure, which is based on the inverse variance of the posterior distribution.

Let the information measure be symbolized by $J(\theta_j)$. Then Fisher's information function connected with the parameter θ_j is defined as:

$$J(\theta_j) \equiv E \left\{ \frac{\partial}{\partial \theta_j} Log\ L[u;\theta;\xi] \right\}^2 , \qquad (2)$$

where $L[u;\theta;\xi]$ is the likelihood function. Higher values for $J(\theta_j)$ indicate that more information on the parameter θ_j is available in the sample. Fisher's information has been the most often used measure in test construction. Not only the mathematical programming methods for the construction of fixed-form tests make use of this measure, this measure is also very popular for the construction of adaptive tests.

The second measure is the Bayesian measure. The Bayesian approach to test construction was first proposed by Owen (1975). Instead of using Fisher's information on the ability parameters, Owen (1975) proposed to use the posterior variance. To our knowledge, no mathematical programming procedure based on the maximization of the inverse posterior variance criterion has yet been proposed. To do this, one must first formulate a suitable prior distribution on the abilities being measured. Then, after the selection of response data, the posterior distribution has to be developed by combining the prior distribution with the response data. This means that the use of a Bayesian selection criterion to select items for inclusion in a fixed-form test would not be very practical. On the other hand, the implementation of such a Bayesian procedure in the mathematical programming models for two-stage or multi-stage testing procedures proposed by Adema

(1990) would be feasible, and it would probably increase the efficiency of the selection procedure, at least when a suitable prior is selected.

When the expected posterior variance is used for item selection, then:

$$J(\theta_j) \equiv E\ \{Var^{-1}(\theta_j \mid M(\theta_j))\}, \tag{3}$$

where $M(\theta_j)$ is the prior information on θ_j.

For all the parameters in $\{\theta, W\}$, the information measures $J(\theta_j)$ can be grouped into the following vector:

$$J(\theta \mid \xi)' = [J(\theta_1), J(\theta_2), J(\theta_3), \ldots, J(\theta_c)]. \tag{4}$$

This vector $J(\theta \mid \xi)$ contains all available information on the parameters θ in the data and optimality of a test design is usually represented by a function of the two vectors $J(\theta \mid \xi)$ and W. It should be noted, that for multidimensional IRT models the vector θ will become a matrix and $J(\theta \mid \xi)$ will also be a matrix, but the optimality procedures will generally remain the same.

A CLASS OF OPTIMAL DESIGN CRITERIA

The above given information measures are related to the amount of uncertainty of the estimators of the elements in θ. Optimality of a test design can be defined simultaneously for all the parameters in $\{\theta, W\}$ by considering a function $\Phi(.)$ of $J(\theta \mid \xi)$ and W. Such a simultaneous optimization has the advantage that it will lead to an optimal design for the whole sample of examinees characterized by $\{\theta, W\}$, and also takes into account the shape of its ability distribution.

An optimal test design is a design for which the function $\Phi\ \{J(\theta \mid \xi), W\}$ has the largest possible value, and the problem of finding an optimal test design is actually the problem of maximizing a real-valued concave objective function, i.e.:

$$\text{maximize } \Phi\ \{J(\theta \mid \xi), W\} \tag{5}$$

subject to

$$\sum w_j = N_{\text{max}}, \tag{6}$$

where N_{max} is some prior specified maximum sample size. In most cases this maximization problem is not easy to solve, and the solution

**Table 22.1.   Different Item Selection Criteria
for Simultaneous and Stepwise Optimization**

Simultaneous Optimization	Stepwise Optimization
Product Criterion	Maximum Information Criterion
Sum Criterion	Interval Information Criterion
Min. Value Criterion	Weighted Interval Criterion

will generally depend on the function $\Phi(.)$ and the information measure being used.

Kiefer (1974) considered a general class of optimality criteria $\Phi(.)$ and discussed their properties within an approximate equivalence theory. Members of this class are the so-called product criterion, the sum criterion, and the minimum value criterion. Conceptually, the product criterion can be regarded to correspond with the well-known geometric mean and the sum criterion may be regarded to correspond to the arithmetic mean. This class not only includes these simultaneous optimality criteria, but also includes criteria that are suitable for stepwise optimization. In Table 22.1 different optimality criteria are displayed, and each of these criteria will be discussed in the following sections.

OPTIMALITY CRITERIA FOR SIMULTANEOUS OPTIMIZATION

Product Criterion

The first criterion is a product criterion. The most frequently applied form is the determinant criterion. Usually this criterion is defined as the determinant of an inverse variance-covariance matrix of the estimators, and is often referred to as the D-optimality criterion. This measure was first proposed by Wald (1943), and it is also known as the generalized variance criterion (Anderson, 1984). It can be shown that this criterion is related to Shannon's (1948) information measure of uncertainty about the parameters (Berger, 1991). If the vector $J(\theta \mid \xi)$ represents the main diagonal of a diagonal matrix, then the determinant of that matrix is the product of the main diagonal elements. For an optimal test design the product criterion will become:

$$\Phi \{J(\theta \mid \xi), W\} = \prod_{j=1}^{c} J(\theta_j)^{w_j}. \tag{7}$$

This criterion has many advantages. Perhaps one of the main reasons for using this criterion is that it has a natural interpretation. It can be shown that it is related to the volume of a confidence region in the parameter space. This means that it can be used to formulate a confidence interval around the parameter estimates. A second feature is that it does not depend on the scale of the independent variable. For the well-known one-, two-, and three-parameter IRT models, this means that the D-optimality criterion is invariant under linear transformation of the logit scale. Finally, it must be mentioned that its upper bounds for the two-parameter logistic model have been derived by Khan & Yazdi (1988). This means that the actual optimality function value can be compared to the maximal achievable value of the criterion. Such a comparison, for example, was done by Berger (1992b) for two-stage sampling designs.

The D-optimality criterion has also been appealing because of its equivalence with other criteria. The general Equivalence Theorem of Kiefer and Wolfowitz (1960) shows that the D-optimality criterion is equivalent to the G-optimality criterion, which minimizes the maximum variance of the predicted response over the design space. This result indicates that a design is D-optimal if and only if it is G-optimal.

The D-optimality criterion also has some disadvantages. The first disadvantage is that it is generally not sensitive to misspecifications of the model. For example, Abdelbasit & Plankett (1983) showed that for the two-parameter logistic model a D-optimal sampling design for the estimation of the two parameters of a single item consists of only two distinct ability levels. Berger (1992a,b) presents figures of these sampling designs. Because such D-optimal designs are only based on two distinct design points or ability levels, they may not be sensitive to changes in the model specification. Not only minor, but also large deviations in the item characteristic curve may not be detected with data collected according to these designs. Although these problems have been encountered for sampling designs, it can be inferred that these problem will also occur when the D-optimality criterion is applied to test designs.

Another disadvantage of this criterion is that models with a different number of parameters cannot be compared with each other, because the function depends on the number of parameters being used. It should be noted, however, that this problem also occurs with the other functions.

Sum Criterion

A second criterion is the trace or A-optimality criterion. For the test design this function is defined as a weighted sum of information measures connected with the c θ_j-parameters in the sample:

$$\Phi \{J(\theta \mid \xi), W\} = \sum_{j=1}^{c} w_j J(\theta_j). \qquad (8)$$

This criterion has also often been applied in optimal design research. Although there are cases in which A-optimality is more easily demonstrated than D-optimality, the A-optimality criterion does not have the same advantages as the D-optimality criterion. It is not invariant under linear transformation of the parameter scale and its upper bounds depend on the actual values of the parameters themselves. Although this criterion may seem more appealing to practitioners than the D-optimality criterion, it has hardly been applied in IRT modelling. An example of such a sum criterion for mathematical programming methods has been given by van der Linden and Boekkooi-Timminga (1989).

Minimum Value Criterion

This criterion may have different forms. Either the minimum value of the information on the parameters is maximized, or the maximum value of the inverse information or asymptotic variance is minimized. An alternative formulation is based on the smallest eigenvalue of the information matrix, and is referred to as the E-optimality criterion. For IRT models and test designs the smallest value of the vector $J(\theta \mid \xi)$ is maximized:

$$\Phi \{J(\theta \mid \xi), W\} = \min_{j=1}^{c} \{J(\theta_j)\}. \qquad (9)$$

This criterion is often called a MAXIMIN criterion. An example of a MAXIMIN criterion used as objective function in mathematical programming is given by van der Linden & Boekkooi-Timminga (1989).

OPTIMALITY CRITERIA FOR STEPWISE OPTIMIZATION

The function $\Phi(.)$ is defined for the whole set of parameters $\{\theta, W\}$. In some cases, however, optimality for some subset of parameters or for each single parameter may be of interest. For example, a test constructor may want to find a test design that is optimal for the estimation of only the lower ability levels in a sample. Such a selection of the parameters in θ can be established by setting the weights corresponding to the higher θ_j-values equal to zero. The problem is then to find an optimal test design for the subset $\{\theta_s, W_s\}$, where $1 \leq s \leq c$ is the number of parameters in the subset. In many cases, the estimators of the parameters in the subset will not be independent of the estimators of the remaining parameters. In these cases, this dependency should be taken into account when items are selected. The solution to the maximization problem for a reduced set of parameters is often referred to in the optimal design literature as Φ_s-optimality.

In this section, criteria which are formulated for a single parameter θ_j, (i.e. for a single examinee), will be given. These criteria are special cases of the above given criteria for a whole sample of examinees. Instead of a simultaneous maximization, these methods allow for a stepwise optimalization for each single parameter separately. These criteria have been mainly used for the construction of adaptive tests.

In adaptive testing, the construction of a test is individualized for each examinee, and the item selection criterion is formulated for each examinee separately, that is for a single parameter. A distinction between construction methods for fixed-form tests and adaptive tests is that item selection in adaptive testing is based on previous responses. If an examinee x has an ability θ_x $(x \in N)$, then the selection criterion is based on an estimate of the parameter θ_x instead of on the parameter itself. Given such a provisional point estimate, items are selected with the largest information on the ability estimate, i.e.:

$$\Phi \{J(\theta \mid \xi), W\} = J(\hat{\theta}_x). \tag{10}$$

This criterion was first suggested by Lord (1977) and has been referred to as the maximum information selection criterion (Thissen & Mislevy, 1990). An adaptive test is composed sequentially after successive administration of the selected items. Compared to the fixed-form test, the adaptive test form may lead to more efficient estimates of the ability, but the stepwise search, for each examinee separately, through a relatively large number of items will, of course, be more time-consuming than for the construction of a fixed-form test.

There is, however, a disadvantage. Criterion (10) is based on a provisional point estimate of θ_x. Especially when the information measure is based on relatively few items, the uncertainty of the estimator may be very high. In these cases the selection of items may be improved by applying a criterion that will take into account the uncertainty of the estimators. Some objective functions that do take into account the uncertainty of the estimators have been proposed by Veerkamp & Berger (1994).

A $100(1-\alpha)\%$ confidence interval for θ_x with lower limit θ_L and upper limit θ_R can be formulated by means of the well-known property that its estimator is asymptotically normally distributed with mean θ_x and variance $J(\theta_x \mid \xi)^{-1}$, which may be replaced by (10). If the pair of vectors $\{\theta_s, W_s\}$ contain all discrete values of the abilities lying within the confidence interval for θ_x, so that the first (lowest) θ_j-value is θ_L and the highest (last) θ_j-value is θ_R, then the area under the information function with limits θ_L and θ_R may be roughly approximated by:

$$\Phi \{J(\theta \mid \xi), W\} = \sum_{j=L}^{R} \omega_j J(\theta_j), \tag{11}$$

where $\omega_j = |\theta_{j-1} - \theta_j|$. These weights are used to include the size of the intervals between the distinct θ_j-levels, and as such enables approximation of the area under the information function. Item selection in adaptive testing may be improved by applying this interval criterion instead of the maximum (point) information criterion.

An extension of the interval selection criterion is also possible by including additional weights. If, for example, more weight is given to the information measure $J(\theta \mid \xi)$ when the likelihood is high and less weight is given when the likelihood is low, then a likelihood weighted selection criterion may be formulated as:

$$\Phi \{J(\theta \mid \xi), W\} = \sum_{j=2}^{c} L[u^{(n)};\theta_j;\xi^{(n)}] \, \omega_j J(\theta_j), \tag{12}$$

where $L[u^{(n)}; \theta_j; \xi^{(n)}]$ is the likelihood for the responses of the n already administered items. It should be noted that equations (11) and (12) are equivalent to the weighted sum criterion given in equation (8). Only the weights differ. Some advantages of these criteria are given by Veerkamp & Berger (1994). Because of the additional use of the amount of uncertainty of the estimators, these criteria are expected to perform at least as good as the maximum information criterion. Simulated results given by Veerkamp and Berger (1994) seem to support this conjecture.

AN ILLUSTRATION

One of the main features of simultaneous optimization criteria is that the shape of the ability distribution can be taken into account. An illustration of this feature is presented in Figures 22.2 and 22.3. Sup-

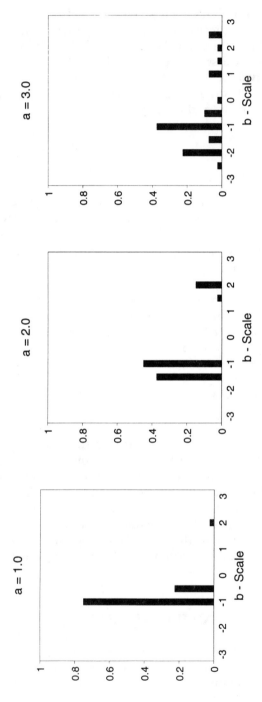

Figure 22.2. Simultaneously Designed Optimal Test Design for a Positively Skewed Ability Distribution

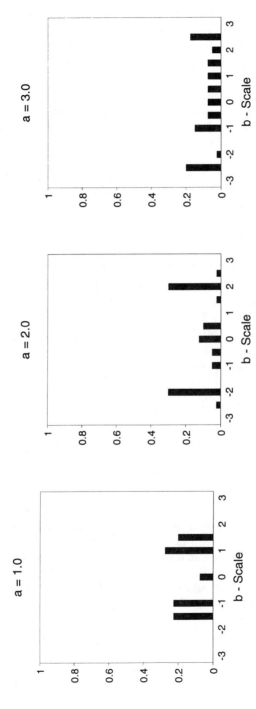

Figure 22.3. Simultaneously Designed Optimal Test Design for a Uniform Ability Distribution

pose that we have an item bank with an infinite number of items. These items have been calibrated by means of the two-parameter IRT model, and cover the full range of combinations of $b_i \in \langle -3,+3 \rangle$ and $a_i \in \langle 0.5,3.0 \rangle$. The product criterion in (7) was used to select the items from the item bank.

In Figure 22.2 the probability mass functions of the resulting optimal test designs for a positively skewed ability distribution are given for items having three different values of the discrimination parameter a_i = 1.0, 2.0, and 3.0, respectively. These functions indicate that if the items have a discrimination parameter a_i = 1.0, the optimal test would consist of about 80% of the items having difficulty parameter value b_i = −1 and about 20% of the items with difficulty b_i = −0.5. A very small proportion of items would have a difficulty parameter value b_i = 2.0. When the items have a higher value for a_i, the shape of the probability mass function on the difficulty scale will resemble the positively skewed ability distribution for which the test was designed.

In Figure 22.3 the optimal test designs are given for a uniform ability distribution. The results in Figure 22.3 show that for a uniform ability distribution the probability mass functions will also approximately have a uniform shape on the difficulty scale. It should be noted that the selection of items from the item bank is rather artificially structured, (i.e. the items are assumed to have a constant discrimination parameter in each test and exhaustion of the item bank does not play a role), because of the infinite number of items. In this case, the most optimal combination of parameter values can be selected as often as required. For small item banks, the results will be expected to be quite different.

DISCUSSION AND CONCLUSION

An important aspect of objective measurement in education is the construction of test forms that are not only valid and reliable, but also will produce efficient estimates for the latent trait distribution for which the particular test is designed. In this chapter the designing of different test forms is placed within the general theory of optimal designs. Different methods for optimal design are reviewed in this paper and their properties are discussed. The main conclusion of this paper is that the different test forms, such as fixed-form tests, adaptive tests and testlets, can be constructed by means of comparable methods, and that these methods are actually the same as the procedures that have been used in optimal design theory.

The construction of an optimal test design can be viewed as an optimization problem, and several algorithms for finding optimal designs have been proposed in the literature. Among those optimization procedures are the mathematical programming procedures, which have been used for the construction of fixed-form tests by Adema (1990) and Boekkooi (1989), among others. Apart from these procedures, several other optimal design algorithms have been applied in other fields of research. See Cook and Nachtsheim (1980) for a review. Perhaps the most promising algorithms for test construction are the sequential design algorithms. These procedures have been studied extensively by Ford, Titterington and Wu (1985), Wu (1985), Wu and Wynn (1978) and Wynn (1970), and were applied to IRT modelling by Berger (1992ab, 1994). The sequential construction of optimal test designs by means of the methods discussed in this paper is straightforward.

REFERENCES

Abdelbasit, K.M. & Plankett, R.L. (1983). Experimental design for binary data. *Journal of the American Statistical Association, 78*, 90–98.

Adema, J.J. (1990). *Models and algorithms for the construction of achievement tests*. Ph.D. thesis, University of Twente.

Anderson, T.W. (1984). *An introduction to multivariate statistical analysis (2nd ed.)* New York: Wiley.

Berger, M.P.F. (1991). On the efficiency of IRT models when applied to different sampling designs. *Applied Psychological Measurement, 15*, 293–306.

Berger, M.P.F. (1992a). Generation of optimal designs for nonlinear models when the design points are incidental parameters. In: Y. Dodge and J. Whittaker (Eds.) *Computational Statistics*. Volume 2 (pp. 200–208), New York: Springer Verlag.

Berger, M.P.F. (1992b). Sequential sampling designs for the two-parameters item response theory model. *Psychometrika, 57*, 521–538.

Berger, M.P.F. (1994). D-optimal sequential sampling designs for item response theory models. *Journal of Educational Statistics*.

Berger, M.P.F. & van der Linden, W.J. (1992). Optimality of sampling designs in item response theory models. In: M. Wilson (Ed.), *Objective measurement: Theory into practice* (pp. 274–288). Norwood, NJ: Ablex Publishing Company.

Boekkooi-Timminga, E. (1989). *Models for computerized test construction*, Ph.D. Thesis, University of Twente.

Boekkooi-Timminga, E. & Sun, L. (1991). Contest: A computerized test construction system. In: Hoogstraten, J. & van der Linden, W.J. (Eds.), *Methodologie: Onderwijsresearchdagen 91* (pp. 69–77). Amsterdam: SCO.

Cook, R.D. & Nachtsheim, C.J. (1980). A comparison of algorithms for constructing exact D-optimal designs. *Technometrics, 22*, 315–324.

Ford, I., Titterington, D.M. and Wu, C.F.J. (1985). Inference and sequential design. *Biometrika, 72,* 545–551.

Ford, I., Kitsos, C.P. and Titterington, D.M. (1989). Recent advances in nonlinear experimental design. *Technometrics, 31,* 49–60.

Khan, M.K. & Yazdi, A.A. (1988). On D-optimal designs. *Journal of Statistical Planning and Inference, 18,* 83–91.

Kiefer, J. (1974). General equivalence theory for optimum designs (Approximate theory). *The Annals of Statistics, 2,* 849–879.

Kiefer, J. & Wolfowitz, J. (1960). The equivalence of two extremum problems. *Canadian Journal of Mathematics, 30,* 271–319.

Lord, F.M. (1971). Robbins-Monro procedures for tailored testing. *Educational and Psychological Measurement, 31,* 3–31.

Lord, F.M. (1980). *Applications of item response theory to practical testing problems,* Hillsdale, NJ: Erlbaum.

Mislevy, R.J., & Wu, P.K. (1988). *Inferring examinee ability when some item responses are missing* (Research Report 88–48-ONR). Princeton, NJ: Educational Testing service.

Owen, R.J. (1975). A Bayesian sequential procedure for quantal response in the context of adaptive mental testing. *Journal of the American Statistical Association, 70,* 351–356.

Shannon, C.E. (1948). A mathematical theory of communication. *Bell System Technical Journal, 27,* 379–423, 623–656.

Silvey, S.D. (1980). *Optimal design.* London: Chapman & Hall.

Theunissen, T.J.J.M. (1986). Binary programming and test design. *Psychometrika, 50,* 411–420.

Thissen, D. and Mislevy, R.J. (1990). Testing algorithms. In: Wainer, H. (Ed.) *Computerized adaptive testing: A primer* (pp. 103–135). Hillsdale, NJ: Lawrence Erlbaum Ass.

Van der Linden, W.J. & Boekkooi-Timminga, E. (1989). A maximin model for test design with practical constraints. *Psychometrika, 53,* 237–247.

Veerkamp, W.J.J. & Berger, M.P.F. (1994). *A comparison of different item selection criteria for adaptive testing.* Research Report, Enschede: University of Twente, Faculty of educational Science and Technology.

Verschoor, A. (1991). OTD: *Optimal Test Design,* (Computerprogram). Arnhem: CITO.

Wainer, H. (1990). *Computerized adaptive testing: A primer.* Hillsdale, NJ: Lawrence Erlbaum Ass.

Wainer, H. & Kiely, G.L. (1987). Item clusters and computerized adaptive testing: A case for testlets. *Journal of Educational Measurement, 24,* 185–202.

Wainer, H. & Lewis, C. (1990). Towards a psychometrics for testlets. *Journal of Educational Measurement, 27,* 1–14.

Wald, A. (1943). On the efficient design of statistical investigations. *Annals of Mathematical Statistics, 14,* 134–140.

Weiss, D.J. (1976). Adaptive testing research in Minnesota: Overview, recent results, and future directions. In C.L. Clark (Ed.), *Proceedings of the First*

Conference on Computerized Adaptive Testing (pp. 24–35). Washington, DC: United States Civil Service Commission.

Weiss, D.J. (1978). *Proceedings of the 1977 Computerized Adaptive Testing Conference.* Minneapolis: University of Minnesota.

Wu, C.F.J. (1985). Asymptotic inference from sequential design in nonlinear situation, *Biometrika, 72,* 533–558.

Wu, C.F.J. and Wynn, H.P. (1978). The convergence of general step-length algorithms for regular optimum design criteria. *The Annals of Statistics, 6,* 1273–1285.

Wynn, H.P. (1970). The sequential generation of D-optimum experimental designs. *Annals of Mathematical Statistics, 41,* 1655–1664.

Appendix

Measuring change in functional performance
Larry H. Ludlow and Stephen M. Haley, Boston College

Rasch model applications to determine the equivalence of a
readiness test in two languages
W. Steve Lang, University of South Florida

SESSION 2: Saturday, April 10, 1993, 11:00–12:00

LINEAR PROGRAMMING AND TEST EQUATING
Chair: Ben Wright, The University of Chicago

A 0-1 linear programming model for observed-score equating
Wim J. van der Linden, American College Testing

The design of an intelligent human-computer interface for
linear programming based test construction systems
Ellen Boekooi-Timminga, University of Groningen,
The Netherlands

Item component equating
Richard M. Smith, University of South Florida

SESSION 3: Saturday, April 10, 1993, 1:00–2:30

COMPUTER ADAPTIVE TESTS
Chair: Wim van der Linden, American College Testing

Comparability of performance results for written and
computer adaptive tests
Gregory E. Stone and Mary E. Lunz,
American Society of Clinical Pathologists

Some design issues for adaptive tests and testlets
Martijn P.F. Berger, University of Twente, The Netherlands

A comparison of item selection strategies used in a computer
adaptive test of math ability
Randal D. Carlson and Hoi K. Suen, Penn State University

Using Rasch analysis to create parallel Raven items
Mario Sanchez and WIlliam Koch, University of Texas at Austin

SESSION 4: Saturday, April 10, 1993, 3:00–5:00

SYMPOSIUM: THE RCML FAMILY

The RCML Family
Mark Wilson, University of California, Berkeley;
Raymond Adams, Australian Council for Educational Research

Applying RCML to item bias detection
Steve Moore, University of California, Berkeley

Comparing multiple-choice and performance-based items
Wen-chung Wang and Mark Wilson,
University of California, Berkeley

Using the RCML to investigate linear logistic test models
in a complex domain
Karen Draney, Peter Pirolli and Mark Wilson,
University of California, Berkeley

The Multilevel RCML Model
Raymond Adams, Australian Council for Educational Research;
Mark Wilson, University of California, Berkeley

Parameter Recovery and the Two Level RCML
Margaret Wu and Raymond Adams,
Australian Council for Educational Research

SESSION 5: Sunday, April 11, 1993, 8:30–10:30

MEASUREMENT THEORY
Chair: David Andrich, Murdoch University, Australia

Facet design and the linear logistic test model
Constructing a questionnaire on 'what makes
people feel lonely'
Edw. E. Roskam, University of Nijmegen, The Netherlands

Evaluation, assessment and measurement in education
F.B. Shaw, Ministry of Culture and Education,
Republic of South Africa

Real time cognitive process measurement:
A "neurocomputing" approach
Robert J. Jannarone, Universitiy of South Carolina

A compensatory model for setting simultaneously cutting
scores for selection-placement-mastery decisions
Hans J. Vos, University of Twente, The Netherlands

Analyzing unfolding data with BIGSTEPS
Mike Linacre and Ben Wright, The University of Chicago

Rasch Composition Analysis
Ben Wright, The University of Chicago

SESSION 6: Sunday, April 11, 1993, 11:00–12:00

ANALYSIS OF RATING SCALES
Chair: Mark Wilson, University of California, Berkeley

Theoretical and empirical evidence on the dichotomization
of graded responses
David Andrich, Murdoch University, Australia

Threshold location and multiple category items
Barry Sheridan, Edith Cowan University, Australia

Item and scale information functions for the successive
intervals Rasch Model
Barbara G. Dodd and Willian Koch, University of Texas at Austin

SESSION 7: Sunday, April 11, 1993, 1:00–2:30

UNIDIMENSIONALITY AND
DIFFERENTIAL ITEM FUNCTIONING
Chair: Richard Smith, Universitiy of South Florida

A multidimensional scaling, paired comparison approach to
assessing unidimensionality in the Rasch Model
Tsuey-Hwa Chen, American Guidance Service;
Mark L. Davison, University of Minnesota

Assessing unidimensionality in the Rasch Model:
The development and evaluation of a logistic-regression,
paired-comparisons method
Ronald O. Anderson, University of Minnesota

Comparison of item bias detection methods when data
do not fit the Rasch Model
Stuart Luppescu, University of Chicago

The W and B Indexes as extensions of the Sato Caution Index
Ayres D'Costa, Ohio State University

Sex bias in science achievement and the Hierarchical Linear Model: An analysis of the Australian Second International Science Study
Deidra J. Young, Curtin University of Technology, Australia

SESSION 8: Sunday, April 11, 1993, 3:00–5:00

MEASUREMENT APPLICATION
Chair: Judy Monsaas, West Georgia College

Measuring and modeling voting and electoral behavior
Filemon S. Cerda, The University of Chicago

What is the effect of demographic variables on measures of students' evaluations of instruction?
Roger Wilk, University of South Florida

Item Response Theory Models applied to student outcomes assessment in institutions of higher education
L. Rose Bruce, Sonoma State University

Predicting academic performance in college: An investigation of the utility of the Partial Credit Model for scaling first year course grades
Carol A. Morrison, National Board of Medical Examiners

Quality of life
Pedro Alvarez, University of Extremadura, Spain

The Partial Credit Rasch Model revisited: An analysis of a school leaving mathematics examination
Fred B. Shaw, Ministry of Culture and Education, Republic of South Africa

Author Index

Subject Index

469